CIVIL SOCIETY, INTERNATIONAL COURTS AND COMPLIANCE BODIES

CIVIL SOCIETY, INTERNATIONAL COURTS AND COMPLIANCE BODIES

Editors

Tullio Treves, Marco Frigessi di Rattalma, Attila Tanzi,
Alessandro Fodella, Cesare Pitea, Chiara Ragni

A project of the Universities of Milano, Brescia and Verona
with the co-operation of
PICT – the Project on International Courts and Tribunals

T·M·C·ASSER PRESS
The Hague

Published by T.M.C.ASSER PRESS
P.O.Box 16163, 2500 BD The Hague, The Netherlands

www.asserpress.nl

T.M.C.ASSER PRESS' English language books are distributed exclusively by:

Cambridge University Press, The Edinburgh Building, Shaftesbury Road,
Cambridge CB2 2RU, UK,
or
for customers in the USA, Canada and Mexico:
Cambridge University Press, 40 West 20th Street, New York, NY 10011-4211, USA

www.cambridge.org

ISBN 90-6704-186-6

Table of Contents

Contributors and Editors

Jessica Maria ALMQVIST

Research Associate, Project on International Courts and Tribunals, the Center on International Cooperation, New York University (USA)

Laurence BOISSON DE CHAZOURNES

Professor and Head of Department, Department of Public International Law and International Organization, Law Faculty, University of Geneva (Switzerland)

Mariacarmen COLITTI

Legal Adviser, No Peace Without Justice, Rome (Italy)

Duncan E.J. CURRIE

LL.B. (Hons.) LL.M. Legal Adviser, Greenpeace International Amsterdam (The Netherlands)

Patrizia DE CESARI

Professor of International Law, University of Trento (Italy)

Marcella DISTEFANO

Researcher in International Law, University of Verona (Italy)

Alessandro FODELLA

Lecturer of International Law and International Protection of Human Rights, University of Trento (Italy)

Marco FRIGESSI DI RATTALMA

Professor of International Law, University of Brescia (Italy)

Philippe GAUTIER

Registrar, International Tribunal for the Law of the Sea; Visiting Professor, Catholic University of Louvain, Louvain-la-Neuve (Belgium)

Catharina HARBY

Legal consultant, the AIRE Centre, London (United Kingdom)

Lise JOHNSON

Graduate of the University of Arizona Law School (USA). BA Yale University. She worked on chapter 18 as an intern of the Center for International Environmental Law (CIEL), Geneva, Switzerland

Ruth MACKENZIE

Centre for International Courts and Tribunals Faculty of Laws, University College London (United Kingdom).

Mónica PINTO	Vice-Dean, Professor, University of Buenos Aires Law School (Argentina)
Cesare PITEA	Ph.D in International Law, University of Milan (Italy); LL.M. University of London – SOAS (United Kingdom)
Mauro POLITI	Professor of International Law, University of Trento (Italy); Judge at the International Criminal Court
Chiara RAGNI	Ph.D. in International Law, University of Milan (Italy)
Gianluca RUBAGOTTI	Ph.D. Candidate in International Economic Law, Bocconi University, Milan (Italy)
Attila TANZI	Professor of International Law, University of Verona (Italy)
Tullio TREVES	Professor of International Law, University of Milan (Italy); Judge at the International Tribunal for the Law of the Sea
Francesca TROMBETTA-PANIGADI	Reseacher in International Law, University of Milan (Italy); Lecturer of Private International Law, University of Parma (Italy)
Elisabeth TUERK	Graduate of MILE (Masters of International Law and Economics), Bern (Switzerland); staff attorney of the Center for International Environmental Law (CIEL), Geneva (Switzerland)
Nina VAJIC	Judge at the ECHR (European Court of Human Rights), formerly Professor of Public International Law at the Faculty of Law at Zagreb University (Croatia)
Eduardo VALENCIA-OSPINA	Eversheds, Consultant; Former Registrar of the International Court of Justice
Jeremy WATES	Secretary to the Aarhus Convention, United Nations Economic Commission for Europe, Geneva (Switzerland)
Dean ZAGORAC	Bachelor of political science (international relations), post-graduate student of criminal law at University of Ljubljana, Slovenia, and member of Amnesty International's Working Group on Impunity and Universal Jurisdiction

Abbreviations

ADP	Asian Development Bank
AIRE	Advice on Individual Rights in Europe
AsDB	Asian Development Bank
ASP	Assembly of States Parties
AU	African Union
AUSAID	Australian Agency of International Development
BPEAR	Bureau for the Placement and Education of African Refugees
CAJ	Committee on the Administration of Justice
CAO	Compliance Officer/Ombudsman
CAT	Convention Against Torture
CCAMLR	Convention on the Conservation of Antarctic Marine Living Resources
CCBE	Council of the Bars and Law Societies of the European Union
CCO	Chief Compliance Officer
CDDH	Council of Europe Steering Committee for Human Rights
CEDAW	Convention on the Elimination of Discrimination Against Women
CEFIC	European Chemical Industry Federation
CEJIL	Centre for Justice and International Law
CELS	Centre for Legal and Social Studies
CERD	Convention on the Elimination of Racial Discrimination
CESCR	Convention on Economic, Social and Cultural Rights
CFI	Court of First Instance
CICC	NGO Coalition for an ICC
CIEL	Center for International Environmental Law
CITAC	Consuming Industries Trade Action Coalition
CITES	Convention on International Trade in Endangered Species of Wild Fauna and Flora
COFI	FAO Committee on Fisheries
COP	Conference of the Parties
CRAE	Children's Rights Alliance for England
CRC	Convention of the Rights of the Child
CRP	Compliance Review Panel
DSB	WTO Dispute Settlement Body
DSU	WTO Dispute Settlement Understanding
ECB	European Central Bank
EBRD	European Bank for Reconstruction and Development
ECE	United Nations Economic Commission for Europe
ECJ	European Court of Justice
ECHR	European Court of Human Rights

ECLA	European Company Lawyers Association
ECO	Environmental Citizens Organization
ECOSOC	United Nations Economic and Social Council
ECSC	European Coal and Steel Community
EEA	European Economic Area
EEB	European Environmental Bureau
EEC	European Economic Community
EEZ	Economic Exclusive Zone
EFTA	European Free Trade Agreement
ETAN	East Timor Action Network
FAO	Food and Agriculture Organization
FICSA	Federation of International Civil Servant's Associations
FIDH	Fédération Internationale des Ligues des Droits de l'Homme
FIELD	Foundation for International Environmental Law
GATT	General Agreement on Tariffs and Trade
GM	Genetically modified
GMO	genetically modified organism
HRC	Human Rights Committee
IALANA	International Association of Lawyers against Nuclear Arms
IBAMA	Instituto Brasileiro do Meio Ambiente e dos Recursos Naturais Renováveis
IBAN	International Ban Asbestos Network
IBRD	International Bank for Reconstruction and Development
ICC	International Criminal Court
ICCPR	International Covenant on Civil and Political Rights
ICJ	International Court of Justice
ICJ	International Commission of Jurists
ICSID	International Centre for the Settlement of Investment Disputes
ICTR	International Criminal Tribunal for Rwanda
ICTY	International Criminal Tribunal for the former Yugoslavia
IDA	International Development Association
IDB	Inter-American Development Bank
IFC	International Finance Corporation
IFET	International Federation for East Timor
IGC	Intergovernmental Conference
ILC	International Law Commission
ILO	International Labour Organization
IMO	International Maritime Organization
IPS	International Press Service
IRM	Independent Recourse Mechanism
ITLOS	International Tribunal for the Law of the Sea
IUCN	International Union for the Conservation of Nature and Natural Resources
IUU	Illegal, unregulated and unreported
IWC	International Whaling Commission
JSMP	Judicial System Monitoring Programme (East Timor)
MEA	multilateral environmental agreement

MIGA	Multilateral Investment Guarantee Agency
MOP	Meeting of the Parties
NAFTA	North American Free Trade Agreement
NCM	Non-compliance mechanism
NGO	Non-governmental organization
NPWJ	No Peace Without Justice
OAS	Organization of American States
OAU	Organization of African Unity
OCHA	Office for the Coordination of Humanitarian Affairs
ODIHR	Office for Democratic Institutions and Human Rights
OECD	Organization for Economic Co-operation and Development
OTP	Office of the Prosecutor
PCIJ	Permanent Court of International Justice
PIC	Public Information Centre
PIC	Prior Informed Consent Convention
PICT	Project on International Courts and Tribunals
POP	Persistent Organic Pollutant
PRTR	Pollutant release and transfer registers
RSPB	Royal Society for the Protection of Birds
SPF	Special Project Facilitator
SPS Agreement	Agreement on Sanitary and Phytosanitary Measures
TBW	Technologien Bau- und Wirtschaftsberatung
UN	United Nations
UNAMET	United Nations Mission in East Timor
UNAT	United Nations Administrative Tribunal
UNCITRAL	United Nations Commission on International Trade Law
UNCLOS	United Nations Convention for the Law of the Sea
UNDP	United Nations Development Programme
UNECE	United Nations Economic Commission for Europe
UNEP	United Nations Environment Programme
UNESCO	United Nations Educational, Scientific and Cultural Organization
UNFCCC	United Nations Framework Convention on Climate Change
UNMIK	United Nations Interim Administration Mission in Kosovo
UPA	Unión de Pequeños Agricultores
UNRIAA	United Nations Reports of International Arbitral Awards
UNTAET	United Nations Transitional Administration for East Timor
USAID	United States Agency for International Development
WILPF	Women's International League for Peace and Freedom
WSSD	World Summit on Sustainable Development
WTO	World Trade Organization
WWF	World Wildlife Fund

Law Reports

Journals

ILR	International Law Reports
Am. J. Int'l L.	American Journal of International Law
Am. U. J. Int'l L.& Pol'y	American University Journal of International Law and Policy
Ariz. J. Int'l & Comp. L.	Arizona Journal of International and Comparative Law
Baltic YB Int'l L.	Baltic Yearbook of International Law
Boston College Int'l & Comp. L. Rev.	Boston College International and Comparative Law Review
Buff. Hum. Rts. L. Rev.	Buffalo Human Rights Law Review
Chicago J. Int'l L.	Chicago Journal of International Law
Colo. J. Envt'l L. & Pol'y	Colorado Journal of Environmental Law and Policy
Colu. Hum. Rts L. Rev.	Columbia Human Rights Law Review
Cornell Int'l L.J.	Cornell International Law Journal
Crim. L. Forum	Criminal Law Forum
Dir. Com. Sc. Int.	Diritto Comunitario e degli Scambi Internazionali
Envt'l Pol'y & L.	Environmental Policy and Law
Eur. J. Int'l L.	European Journal of International Law
Eur. Rev. Pr. L.	European Review of Private Law
Fordham Int'l L. J.	Fordham International Law Journal
Ger. YB Int'l L.	German Yearbook of International Law
Ham L. Rev.	Hamline Law Review
Harvard Hum. Rts. J.	Harvard Human Rights Journal
Hum. Rts Q.	Human Rights Quarterly
Int'l & Comp. L. Q.	International & Comparative Law Quarterly
Int'l L. Forum	International Law Forum
Int'l J. Minority & Group Rts	International Journal on Minority and Group Rights
Int'l Rev. Red Cross	International Review of the Red Cross
Iowa L. Rev.	Iowa Law Review
J. Int'l Econ. L.	Journal of International Economic Law
J. W. T.	Journal of World Trade
Max Planck YB UN L.	Max Planck Year Book of United Nations Law
McGill L. J.	McGill Law Journal
Melbourne J. Int'l L.	Melbourne Journal of International Law
Melbourne U. L. Rev.	Melbourne University Law Review
Mich. J. Int'l L.	Michigan Journal of International Law
Netherlands Int'l L. Rev.	Netherlands International Law Review
Non-State Actors & Int'l L.	Non-state Actors and International Law
NYU J. Int'l L. & Pol.	New York University Journal of International Law and Politics

RdC	Recueil des Cours de l'Académie de Droit International de La Haye
Rev. Bel. Dr. Int.	Revue Belge de Droit International
Rev. Gén. Dr. Int. Pub.	Revue Générale de Droit International Public
Riv. Dir. Int.	Rivista di Diritto Internazionale
Riv. Dir. Proc.	Rivista di Diritto Processuale
Riv. Dir. Proc. Civ.	Rivista di Diritto Processuale Civile
Riv. Trim. Dir. Proc. Civ.	Rivista Trimestrale di Diritto e Procedura Civile
Syracuse J. Int'l L. & Commerce	Syracuse Journal of International Law and Commerce
Tul. J. Int'l & Comp. L.	Tulane Journal of International and Comparative Law
U. New South Wales L. J.	University of New South Wales Law Journal
U. Pa. J. Int'l Econ. L.	University of Pennsylvania Journal of International Economic Law
YB Int'l Envt'l L.	Yearbook of International Environmental Law
WP	World Politics
ZaöRV	Zeitschrift für ausländisches öffentliches Recht und Völkerrecht

Introduction

Tullio Treves

This book focuses on a particular but challenging and indeed central aspect of a broader subject. It is the task of this brief introduction to locate the study of the role of civil society in its relationship with international courts, tribunals and compliance mechanisms, on the map of the broader study of the role of civil society in international law. This broader subject has been the starting point of the investigation of three teams of researchers at the Universities of Milano, Brescia and Verona. It soon appeared clear to us that questions concerning civil society and international courts and tribunals (to which we soon realized that compliance mechanisms had to be added) were at the crossroads of all or most other aspects of the broader topic. This is why a conference on 'Civil Society, International Tribunals and Compliance Mechanisms' was convened in Milan, Italy, on 24–25 October 2003 to consider what could appear, but certainly is not, only a minor aspect of a broader set of issues.[1]

It seems useful, at the outset, to say something about terminology. International law literature mentions especially 'civil society', 'non-state actors', 'international non-governmental organizations'. Each of these expressions contains a grain of truth but none, as is true of labels, fully describes the content of the notion we are tackling. Looking at international practice and at the reasons that make this study topical and timely, we have to recognize that the phenomenon these expressions try to cover is the result of the increased weakness of the dogma that the state is the only actor in international relations, and of the devel-

---

[1] The research has been carried out within the joint project on 'Civil Society and the Development of International Law' of the Universities of Milano (Prof. Tullio Treves), Brescia (Prof. Marco Frigessi di Rattalma) and Verona (Prof. Attila Tanzi). The project has been coordinated by Prof. Tullio Treves and co-financed by the Italian Ministry of University and Scientific and Technological Research (MURST). This book is mainly the result of the works of the Milan Conference: the support of PICT (Project on International Courts and Tribunals, London–New York) and the participation of a number of the members of its Steering Committee and staff at the Conference is acknowledged with gratitude; in particular, although some of the contributions to the Conference such as the enlightening introduction by Pierre Marie Dupuy and concluding remarks by Philippe Sands are not reproduced here, they had an extremely significant impact on the results of the project and on the present publication.

T. Treves et al., eds., Civil Society, International Courts and Compliance Bodies
© 2005, T·M·C·ASSER PRESS, *The Hague, The Netherlands, and the Authors*

opment of the means of communication, in one word of 'globalization'. State sovereignty, of course, still exists, the sovereign state is still the main centre of power, the main concentrator of military might, the main organizer of human societies. However, today it is almost commonplace to observe that states' sovereignty has undergone a process of erosion, that in international society other actors, apart from the state, are exercising an influence or some degree of power, which has recently been labelled as 'soft' – 'soft power', in analogy with that other recent notion of post-modern international law, 'soft law'.

When we look at these other actors we immediately observe that they constitute a rather heterogeneous crowd: they range from certain individuals (e.g., ultra-rich press, television and finance 'moguls'), to a variety of groups including trade unions, business and industrial associations, non-governmental organizations supporting causes of general interest (humanitarian, environmental, developmental, etc.), to more or less covert political or religious groups (such as the Opus Dei), even to terrorist organizations. All these have in common that they are not states, that they try, *inter alia*, to influence the decisions and activities of states, acting not only through the channels accepted (or even set up) by states, but also outside of them.

Even though they have common features, the different individuals and groups that compose this crowd (which can be described by the broad but negative term 'non-state actors') are separated by many elements, the most important of which is subjective and ideological. This element consists in the values and interests that they defend and propagate. For instance, even though the condemnation of terrorism has become generalized, especially after September 11, it remains true that in many cases he who is a terrorist for one, is a hero for another. Professional associations of workers or of industrialists are commonly seen as pursuing valuable economic and social purposes, but they are also undoubtedly working for the interest of one side of social or economic conflict. Finally, non-governmental organizations supporting causes of general interest, which will be briefly designated 'NGOs', may be seen by some (i.e., industrialists, but sometimes also governments of developed and developing states) as obstacles to development or to the maintenance of public order.

While recognizing that 'non-state actors' is a broad and heterogeneous group whose impact on international law is interesting to explore, it has seemed preferable to focus on one subgroup – international non-governmental organizations supporting causes of general interest, or NGOs. We have chosen, in other words, the group of the 'good' non-state actors, even though, for the reasons mentioned above, we are aware that this qualifier, although widely accepted, is still subjective and far from being universally shared. What are the 'causes of general interest' may vary depending on the viewpoint: political, economic, cultural, social, geographical, etc.

The presence of, and the need for, NGOs may be seen as a symptom of the fact that states are in some cases insufficient as mechanisms in which certain interests can be represented and also of the need for these interests to obtain more recognition than they would receive through the mediation of states. Is this a factor of 'democratization' of the international environment or a channel for particular interests to prevail over general ones? It depends on the NGOs and their objectives, but also on the level of 'democracy' of states. Certain 'general interest causes' – that of human rights in particular – which in developed Western societies may appear as simply 'politically correct', may be considered as revolutionary in other contexts and entail great risks for those who support them.

Coming now to the role of NGOs in international law, they have been referred to as 'actors'. This expedient term, originating in American literature on international relations, raises some problems, as Pierre-Marie Dupuy has shown in a well-known study.[2] Because of its being borrowed from a discipline different from international law, this term permits us to avoid the question whether NGOs (and perhaps other non-state 'actors') are subjects of international law. This is not a useful question as the answer depends on the very notion of 'subject' of international law. To draw an analogy, we may recall that studies on the role of the individual in international law show that there are rules of international law establishing rights and obligations for individuals, but that the assessment whether this is sufficient in order to consider individuals as 'subjects' of international law is highly subjective, and in the end irrelevant. The same can be said of NGOs.

Much more interesting seems to be a study on the basis of practice, and not of theoretical concepts, of what NGOs do in the international environment (again a term we can use to avoid expressions such as 'international community', 'international society', 'international system', etc., all of which, more or less, traditionally refer to states). In order to conduct such a study, three sectors seem to be particularly significant, and were retained as the main field of investigation. These are the sectors of international law in which collective interests of individuals are the subject matter of international law rules: human rights, environmental law, international criminal law.

The study conducted in these sectors (as well as in some others, such as international trade law) immediately shows that the activities of NGOs in the international environment concern two aspects that are directly relevant for international law: the creation and development of rules, on the one hand, and their implementation, on the other. NGOs conduct these activities within states or national societies, and also (and perhaps more interestingly) within the very international environment in which states act.

As regards the function of NGOs in *international rule-making*, they influence the elaboration of written rules established by the will or consent of states, in other words treaties and rules of soft law. NGOs often propose new issues for treaty-making, they convince states to take the initiative in international negotia-

---

[2] P.M. Dupuy, 'Le concept de société civile internationale, identification et genèse' in H. Gherari and S. Szurek (eds.), *L'émergence de la société civile internationale vers la privatisation du droit international?* (Paris, 2003), pp. 5–18.

tions on these topics and influence the agendas of intergovernmental organizations, in order to include such topics (one may recall, for example, the successful campaigns waged by NGOs for the adoption of the Convention against Torture,[3] or for the adoption of the Convention for the banning of landmines).[4]

When negotiations, especially multilateral negotiations, are underway and perhaps a diplomatic conference has been convened, NGOs endeavour to exercise an influence on negotiators and negotiations. They do so by lobbying, by exercising pressure through the media and also by providing, especially to negotiators from 'weak' countries, scientific expertise, documentary materials and sometimes even personnel to conduct, or help conduct, the negotiations. The case of the drafting of the Rome Statute of the International Criminal Court, and of the work that followed, and continues to follow within the Assembly of the States Parties, is a recent and remarkable example.[5]

Once negotiations are concluded and states have adopted, or are on the verge of adopting, new rules, NGOs are often relevant and sometimes decisive as regards the success of these rules. They may, for instance, actively lobby governments and members of national parliaments in order to set in motion or hasten the process leading to the ratification and to the adoption of the necessary implementing legislation as regards a treaty they consider as particularly important (again the case of the Rome Statute must be quoted among others). NGOs may also exercise pressure, through media campaigns and lobbying of governments and parliaments, against the adoption or ratification of a treaty, when the result of the relevant international negotiations is contrary to some of their deeply felt views. The decision of Australia and France, followed by all other states of the 'Antarctic system', not to ratify the Wellington Convention on Antarctic Mineral Resources of 1988,[6] is due to the action of environmental NGOs. Similarly, the failure of the negotiations for a Multilateral Treaty on Investment within the framework of the OECD, was due to the campaign against it conducted by NGOs.

It is more difficult to assess the influence of NGOs in the formation of customary rules, the unwritten (and at least in part involuntary) rules of international law. It may nonetheless be held that the perception of the public (and of NGOs seen as organized groups thereof) of what is permitted and of what is prohibited to states in their relationship with other states influences the perception of governments and ultimately their *opinio juris*.

---

[3] Convention against Torture and Other Cruel, Inhuman or Degrading Treatment or Punishment (adopted and opened for signature, ratification and accession by General Assembly Res. 39/46, 10 December 1984, entered into force on 26 June 1987).

[4] Convention on the Prohibition of the Use, Stockpiling, Production and Transfer of Anti-Personnel Mines and on their Destruction (Ottawa, 3 December 1997, entered into force on 1 March 1999).

[5] See F. Trombetta-Panigadi, Chapter 9 below.

[6] Convention on the Regulation of Antarctic Mineral Resource Activities (Wellington, 2 June 1988).

As far as the role of NGOs in the *implementation* of international law rules is concerned, NGOs may act, through the usual means of lobbying and public opinion campaigns, as 'guardians' of compliance by states with certain international obligations. They may also help states, for instance, in fields such as human rights and environmental law, by providing materials for complying with reporting obligations that are often quite onerous for governmental authorities. They also exercise pressures on, and (perhaps more often) provide help to, intergovernmental organizations which may have to comply with substantive obligations, or that, more often, may be entrusted with tasks concerning compliance by states in which assistance by NGOs can be important.

There is a further question that arises when we consider the role of NGOs in international law: how do states, that remain the main subjects of international law and actors of international relations, react to the role and action of NGOs?

The reactions of states are diverse and ambivalent. They range from appreciation and acknowledgement of positive contributions to suspicion and hostility. So, on the one hand, we see that often states and intergovernmental organizations recognize NGOs and sometimes grant them specific functions in international processes. On the other hand, suspicion and sometimes open or latent hostility have brought states to conduct even an internationally illegal action against NGOs (as in the case of the sinking by French agents in a New Zealand harbour of the Greenpeace ship *Rainbow Warrior* which gave rise to complex arbitration proceedings).[7] More often they have brought states to attempt to influence and manipulate NGOs.

The ambiguous or ambivalent attitude of states and intergovernmental organizations as regards NGOs and their activities appears in a clear light when states regulate, for instance through rules of procedure of conferences, organizations or courts and tribunals, the role that NGOs can play in these fora, and even more so, when they make the recognition of NGOs, or their right to perform certain functions in international fora, subject to the existence of certain requirements concerning their internal structure and functioning. The legitimate need of establishing some order, and of distinguishing those NGOs that are, for instance, representative, competent and democratic, from those that are not so, may hide the less commendable purpose of privileging the 'good' or 'tame' ones.

Indeed, a recurrent theme that emerges in the study of NGOs in international law is the tension between the ambition of NGOs to be recognized as legitimate participants and the concern for maintaining their spontaneous character, which runs parallel to the tension between the desire of states to integrate NGOs in their legal environment in order to take advantage of their expertise, and at the same time to keep them away, in order to avoid disruption of the normal processes states are accustomed to.

This book focuses on a very relevant aspect of the action of NGOs in international law. Such aspect concerns what NGOs do as regards international tribunals

---

[7] Decision of 2 October 1987, *New Zealand v France*, UNRIAA, vol. 20, p. 3.

and compliance mechanisms. Such endeavour requires contributions from a variety of points of view and experiences. In the present book scholars join forces with experts from NGOs and judges and registrars from international courts to meet this requirement.

The interest of studying these aspects of the role of NGOs is witnessed by the growing number of courts and tribunals, and of verification and compliance mechanisms or inspection panels. It may be noted that in courts and tribunals which directly involve individuals (such as human rights and criminal courts and tribunals), as well as in compliance mechanisms and inspection panels, the role of NGOs is more accepted than in traditional courts dealing with inter-state disputes. However, recent developments witness strong pressure by civil society for NGOs also to play a role before the latter courts and tribunals.

Human rights, international criminal law and international environmental law are the fields in which it is particularly interesting to consider the role of NGOs in law-making, especially as far as the establishment of international courts and tribunals is concerned, in the implementation of the law, especially as regards the functioning of international courts, tribunals and compliance mechanisms and, finally, as far as the reactions of states are concerned.

First, NGOs contribute to the establishment and functioning of judicial and compliance institutions. As emerges from the contributions set out in this book, a major example is their role as regards the International Criminal Court. NGOs were decisive in putting the establishment of such a court on the international agenda, in helping the drafting of the Rome Statute and connected international instruments, and in convincing states to sign and ratify the Statute.[8] Similarly, NGOs played an essential role in the establishment of Special Panels for serious crimes in East Timor.[9]

Secondly, NGOs influence and facilitate the work of judicial and quasi-judicial institutions. They sometimes appear before international human rights courts and bodies or help individuals in presenting their cases before them. Though relevant, such a role encounters many limitations. As contributions to this book show, these do not depend only on legal constraints imposed by applicable provisions. They depend especially on the fact that the financial and human resources of NGOs are limited. This has entailed that NGOs develop criteria for choosing the cases in which to become involved. A trend seems to be emerging, especially for major NGOs, to choose cases which may have the greatest relevance for the development or implementation of principles and rules in general. The interest of the individual involved in the decision on the specific case may thus be given a low priority.[10]

---

[8] See M. Colitti, Chapter 7 below, F. Trombetta-Panigadi, Chapter 9 below and the comments by Judge M. Politi, Chapter 11 below.

[9] See C. Ragni, Chapter 10 below.

[10] See D. Zagorac, Chapter 1 below.

Thirdly, sometimes states recognize the role of NGOs before courts and tribunals or compliance mechanisms. For example, as illustrated in this book, their role is recognized formally in the proceedings before the UN Human Rights Committee[11] and the European Court of Human Rights,[12] as well as, among others, in the compliance mechanism recently set up by the Aarhus Convention on Access to Information, Public Participation in Decision-Making and Access to Justice in Environmental Matters of 1998.[13] In other cases, however, states show suspicion towards the involvement of NGOs and try to limit their role. The position taken by the member states of the WTO as regards participation of NGOs as *amici curiae* in proceedings before the Panels and the Appellate Body is a clear example.[14]

The practice of NGOs as regards international courts, tribunals and compliance mechanisms varies depending on the body it refers to. However, as emerges from contributions set out in this book,[15] there is substantial cross-fertilization between the different experiences. Especially as regards the participation of NGOs as *amici curiae*, the rules applicable and practical experience gathered before certain bodies have had an influence in proceedings before other bodies. One may wonder whether common rules are emerging. Perhaps the main conclusion of this book is that the role of NGOs is becoming an important chapter of the growing field of the law of international courts and tribunals.

---

[11] See D. Zagorac, Chapter 1 below and G. Rubagotti, Chapter 5 below.

[12] See M. Frigessi di Rattalma, Chapter 4 below and the comments by Judge N. Vajic, Chapter 6 below.

[13] See J. Wates, Chapter 13 below.

[14] See M. Distefano, Chapter 19 below.

[15] See R. Mackenzie, Chapter 21 below.

Part I

NGOs and Human Rights Courts and Compliance Bodies

Chapter 1

International Courts and Compliance Bodies:
The Experience of Amnesty International

Dean Zagorac

1. INTRODUCTION

The protection of an individual human being transcends the boundaries of any individual state. It is a matter of international responsibility and concern. This is the
principle on which Amnesty International is founded and the concept that lies behind the creation of international human rights standards and mechanisms to
monitor and enforce those standards. With regard to these standards and mechanisms, Amnesty International has played from its very beginnings an important
role on two levels. First, by promoting international standards and advocating for
strengthening them and for providing effective means of enforcing them, the organization actively contributes to the standard-setting process in international human rights protection. A call for effective international human rights mechanisms
was part of the initial 1961 appeal by the organization's founder, Peter Benenson,
from which Amnesty International came into being. Secondly, by overseeing the
implementation of standards agreed at the international level, the organization
provides a link between these standards and individual human beings.

Although it is difficult to draw a clear line between these two levels and although one naturally leads to the other, it is the experience of Amnesty International at the second level that will be the topic of this chapter. It will consider the
main aspects of Amnesty International's experience with international courts and
other compliance mechanisms, such as treaty bodies established to monitor
implementation of a particular international treaty's provisions, at both levels:
universal and regional. At the universal level, Amnesty International's experience
with mechanisms and bodies under the auspices of the United Nations (UN) will
be presented and at the regional level the organization's experience with mechanisms and bodies within the framework of the three main regional organizations –
Council of Europe, Organization of American States and Organization of African
Unity / African Union – will be considered.

Amnesty International's experience and relationships with these mechanisms
is multifaceted and complex. This chapter will consider only those aspects of
these relationships that concern the making of the organization's submissions to

T. Treves et al., eds., Civil Society, International Courts and Compliance Bodies
© 2005, T·M·C·ASSER PRESS, *The Hague, The Netherlands, and the Authors*

the mechanisms. Equally important are the organization's efforts, supplemented by its proposals, for reform of these mechanisms or for the setting up of new ones at various periods, but due to the complexity of this issue a separate survey would be needed.

In more than four decades of its existence, Amnesty International has had experience with different forms of participation in proceedings before various kinds of international bodies, from legal representation and third party intervention to supplying the respective body with relevant information on human rights violations, from participating in international court proceedings and commenting on court decisions when such participation was not possible to cooperating with various international treaty-monitoring bodies. The aim of this chapter is to present such participation and to evaluate the level of success. The reader, however, should bear in mind that Amnesty International's participation in proceedings with various international bodies is just a fraction of the organization's activities and is almost invariably accompanied by various forms of campaigning and lobbying efforts and different degrees of membership involvement.

2.   UNIVERSAL LEVEL

Since its beginnings, when no major international human rights treaty had even been adopted let alone entered into force, Amnesty International has been in contact with various human rights offices within the United Nations. Consultative status with the UN's Economic and Social Council was granted to Amnesty International in 1964, i.e., three years after the organization was founded. At the time, Amnesty International's representatives were in contact with UN's Human Rights Division. It is these beginnings that enabled the organization to develop elaborate relationships with various organs and agencies within the UN, which in turn provided avenues for the organization's participation in processes of standard setting and providing information on compliance with those standards.

At the universal level, i.e., under the auspices of the UN, Amnesty International has experience with the UN treaty-monitoring bodies and some indirect limited experience with the International Court of Justice, the UN's principal judicial organ. The organization also has elaborate experience with the UN's main human rights body, the Commission on Human Rights, but because the Commission is not a treaty-monitoring body in the strict sense it falls outside the scope of this chapter. For the same reason, Amnesty International's submissions to other international organizations or agencies which are not treaty-monitoring bodies in the strict sense, such as UNESCO, will not be considered here.

2.1   Treaty-monitoring bodies

International human rights standards are elaborated in a number of international treaties adopted under the auspices of the UN. The vast majority of these treaties established special bodies for the purpose of monitoring the implementation of the treaty's provisions by its states parties. The international human rights treaties which established bodies for oversight of their implementation are as follows:

- International Covenant on Civil and Political Rights – Human Rights Committee (HRC);
- International Covenant on Economic, Social and Cultural Rights – Committee on Economic, Social and Cultural Rights (CESCR);
- International Convention on the Elimination of Racial Discrimination – Committee on the Elimination of Racial Discrimination (CERD);
- Convention on the Elimination of Discrimination Against Women – Committee on the Elimination of Discrimination Against Women (CEDAW);
- Convention Against Torture and Other Cruel, Inhuman or Degrading Treatment or Punishment – Committee Against Torture (CAT);
- Convention on the Rights of the Child – Committee on the Rights of the Child (CRC); and
- International Convention on the Protection of the Rights of All Migrant Workers and Members of Their Families – Committee on the Protection of the Rights of All Migrant Workers and Members of Their Families.

Apart from receiving and considering periodic reports by the states parties on implementation of the treaty's provisions, some monitoring bodies also provide for receiving complaints from individuals whose human rights have been violated. Treaty bodies also elaborate general comments on the respective treaty's provisions and two of the treaty bodies undertake investigations (CAT and CEDAW).

Amnesty International has developed work mainly around the CAT and the HRC; it has had some limited experience with the remaining four (not including the newly established Committee on Protection of Migrant Workers) and has only a limited relationship with their Secretariats and with some members, and limited knowledge of how they function.

In various degrees Amnesty International carries out all crucial tasks of NGOs in relation to the treaty bodies identified by Michael O'Flaherty:[1]

- the channeling of independent information to members of treaty bodies;
- the promotion of knowledge and understanding of the reporting process; and
- the unofficial oversight of the ongoing effectiveness of the reporting process following the examination of states parties reports by the treaty bodies.

One of the most important aspects of Amnesty International's work with the treaty monitoring bodies is providing them with information on human rights vio-

---

[1] M. O'Flaherty, *Human Rights and the UN Practice before the Treaty Bodies* (2nd edn., Martinus Nijhoff Publishers, Leiden / Boston, 2002), pp. 3–4.

lations in a particular country, especially after the country submits its periodic report and before it is considered. The organization's submissions to the treaty-
monitoring bodies are usually presented as a survey of the organization's
concerns in a particular country, with individual cases used as an illustration of
patterns or trends. The information submitted is based on the organization's own
research and usually on the information that the organization has already made
public. Amnesty International, however, does not submit its reports to the treaty
bodies on every single state party. Out of over 100 periodic reports submitted by
states parties in 2003, the organization provided its reports on 15 states. It is expected that the number of Amnesty International's submissions will increase in
the years to come.

Amnesty International also recognizes the importance of a second crucial task.
The organization, sometimes through its national sections and coordinating structures,[2] endeavours to raise awareness among the general public and, in particular,
among the local NGO community of the importance of the work of treaty-monitoring bodies. Through its website,[3] the organization seeks to inform national
NGOs of the various possibilities of their participation in the treaty-monitoring
bodies' work. The organization's national sections can either participate (with the
coordination and approval of the International Secretariat) or encourage the
preparation and publication of reports issued by local NGOs on the levels of
compliance with and implementation of a particular treaty by their government, at
the time when the state submits its own report to the treaty-monitoring body. Amnesty International's sections are discouraged from signing reports on the initiatives of other NGOs, because such reports are usually not based on Amnesty
International's research.

Conducting an oversight of implementation of recommendations issued by a
particular monitoring body to the state after consideration of its report is a natural
follow-up to making submissions to the body. Amnesty International, either
through the International Secretariat or through its national sections or both, over-
sees the implementation of the monitoring body's recommendations and reminds
governments of the need to do so if they ignore them. However, this is done only
in the minority of countries, almost exclusively in those cases when Amnesty International submits its briefing to the relevant treaty monitoring body and is
therefore in a stronger position to evaluate the concluding observations of the
treaty body (if the organization agrees with the concluding observations, which is
not always the case).

Besides these crucial tasks, Amnesty International has also provided input on
the treaty bodies' general comments of their respective treaties' provisions and
(potential) work on investigations. The organization has also worked for ratification of the human rights treaties and has provided input on the broader function-

---

[2] Where there is no national section recognized, but there is in fact a strong local presence of the
organization's membership, it is called a 'coordinating structure'.

[3] <www.amnesty.org/treatybodies>.

ing of the treaty-monitoring bodies, such as reform, appointments and resources available to them, but further elaboration of these aspects falls outside the scope of this chapter.

To systematize its work with the treaty-monitoring bodies and further contribute to development of international human rights law, Amnesty International has established a 'treaty body team'. It is comprised of two Assistant Legal Advisers based at the organization's headquarters in London who are supported by Amnesty International's UN office in Geneva.

2.2 International Court of Justice

The Statute of the International Court of Justice (ICJ), the principal judicial organ of the UN for adjudicating disputes between states and providing advisory opinions, does not expressly provide for participation of NGOs in its proceedings. Article 66(2) of its Statute provides that with regard to advisory opinions:

> [t]he Registrar shall also, by means of special and direct communication, notify any state entitled to appear before the Court or international organization considered by the Court, or, should it not be sitting, by the President, as likely to be able to furnish information on the question, that the Court will be prepared to receive ... written statements, or to hear, at a public sitting to be held for the purpose, oral statements relating to the question.

Although the ICJ has in the past interpreted this provision so as to allow submissions from international NGOs, it appears in fact to have done so on only one occasion where the NGO made a submission and the ICJ is not known to have permitted an NGO submission since.[4] Indeed, it regrettably refused to permit the International Committee of the Red Cross to make such a submission in an advisory opinion. Amnesty International also has not had an opportunity to participate as a third party as yet.

However, recently the organization published a report that served the function of an *amicus curiae* (friend of the court) brief. It issued a 750-page memorandum on universal jurisdiction that was submitted in the form of a CD-ROM by the Belgian government in the ICJ case of *Democratic Republic of Congo v Belgium*.[5] Unfortunately, the judges reportedly did not have facilities to read CD-ROMs, and although the memorandum was referred to by some judges, it is not clear whether all the judges saw the entire memorandum or only excerpts cited by Belgium.

On the eve of oral arguments before the Belgian Court of Cassation in February 2003, Amnesty International reiterated that Belgian prosecutors have jurisdiction under international law to investigate on behalf of the entire international

---

[4] See pleadings in *International Status of South-West Africa*, advisory opinion of 11 July 1950.

[5] Amnesty International, *Universal Jurisdiction* (AI Index: IOR 53/002-018/2001, September 2001).

community crimes under international law such as war crimes, crimes against humanity and genocide committed abroad even when the suspect is not present in the state where the prosecutors are located.[6]

The case involved the killing of at least 900 Palestinian civilians in the Sabra and Chatila refugee camps in the suburbs of Beirut, Lebanon in September 1982. Amnesty International declared that the then recent judgment by the Court stating that certain serving high government officials enjoyed immunity from arrest by foreign courts for war crimes and crimes against humanity could not deprive the Belgian prosecutor of jurisdiction to conduct a criminal investigation of the incident. Amnesty International also stated that the contention by the Chief Prosecutor of the Court of Cassation that international law prohibited national prosecutors from acting on behalf of the international community to investigate crimes under international law committed abroad by suspects not found in the territory where the prosecutors are located, is an assertion that has no basis whatsoever under international law.

Amnesty International has used this approach in other courts as well (see 2.3 below).

2.3   International criminal courts and tribunals

Although Amnesty International's International Justice Project never had sufficient resources to develop and implement a programme of submission of *amicus curiae* briefs to the International Criminal Tribunals for the former Yugoslavia and for Rwanda, it has been developing a list of issues that it hopes to be able to address in such submissions to the International Criminal Court over the coming decade, depending on the cases in which these issues are present. It has identified a range of issues that are likely to arise in early cases, such as the scope of definitions of crimes of sexual violence, and areas where there is room for a teleological interpretation of the Rome Statute, such as the burdens of proof on questions of admissibility. Rule 103 of the Rules of Procedure and Evidence of the International Criminal Court permits the submission of such briefs, but it is currently limited to submissions in connection with a particular case.[7] Amnesty International intends to recommend modification of the rule to permit the submission of such briefs on particular issues that are not necessarily connected to a particular case pending before the International Criminal Court. However, pending that modification, it intends to continue to make informal submissions to the judges on a range of issues that they may face, both in the establishment of the institution and in litigation.

---

[6] Amnesty International, *Universal Jurisdiction: Belgian Prosecutors Can Investigate Crimes under International Law Committed Abroad* (AI Index: IOR 53/001/2003, February 2003).

[7] Rules of Procedure and Evidence of the International Criminal Court, Rule 103, U.N. Doc. ICC-ASP/1/3 (2002).

In addition, the International Justice Project plans to issue documents on issues related to impunity, reparations and fair trial that are pending or likely to be considered by internationalized courts in particular cases or to make *amicus curiae* submissions in those courts, where permissible and time permits. For example, in the summer of 2003, the International Justice Project learned shortly before a hearing by the Appeals Chamber of the Special Court for Sierra Leone, under a rule that permitted it to decide the issues without a prior determination by the Trial Chamber, that the accused were challenging the hearing itself as a denial of the right to an appeal and that they were arguing that their trials were barred by an amnesty. There was insufficient time to seek leave to file an *amicus curiae* brief, so it was decided to address these issues in a public document that was then provided as a courtesy to the Special Court and all parties before the hearing.[8] The document was cited during argument and in the decision on the first issue; the second issue was still pending at the time of writing.[9]

3.   REGIONAL LEVEL

3.1   Council of Europe

The first procedure for lodging individual human rights violations' complaints and the first international court of human rights were established under the auspices of a European regional organization – the Council of Europe. The cornerstone of the European human rights system is the Convention for the Protection of Human Rights and Fundamental Freedoms of 1950 ('the European Convention') which established a two-tier complaints system, where a case first had to be brought before the European Commission of Human Rights which then decided whether to bring it to the European Court of Human Rights (ECHR) or the Committee of Ministers, the Council of Europe's governing body. If the case was brought to the ECHR, the latter rendered the judgment and, according to Article 41 of the European Convention, could have 'afforded just satisfaction to the injured party'. If the case was not brought before the ECHR, the Committee of Ministers rendered decision on the case based upon the Commission's recommendation. In both cases, the Committee of Ministers was and still is responsible for the enforcement of the judgments and decisions. After entry into force of Protocol No. 11 to the European Convention on 1 November 1998, the Commission ceased to exist.

---

[8] Amnesty International, *Sierra Leone: Special Court for Sierra Leone: Denial of Right to Appeal and Prohibition of Amnesties for Crimes under International Law* (AI Index: AFR 51/012/2003, October 2003).

[9] Special Court for Sierra Leone, *Prosecutor v Norman* (Case No. SCSL-2003-08-PT), *Prosecutor v Kallon* (Case No. SCSL-2003-07-PT) and *Prosecutor v Gbao* (Case No. SCSL-2003-09-PT), Decision on the s for a Stay of Proceedings and Denial of Right to Appeal, 4 November 2003, para. 2.

(a)   Participation in the European Convention's mechanisms

One of the first experiences with the ECHR, though indirect, stemmed from the mid-1960s. At the time, the founder of Amnesty International, British lawyer Peter Benenson, established the Human Rights Advisory Service designed to give assistance to persons wishing to bring cases before the ECHR. However, Amnesty International first gained some experience with the Commission.

The series of events which prompted Amnesty International to become fully involved in the Commission's proceedings were initiated by a military coup in Greece in April 1967. Soon after the coup, the organization sent a mission to the country in response to reports of widespread use of torture. The allegations were confirmed and a detailed report was published which was circulated to foreign ministries of the Council of Europe's member states.[10] The report prompted the governments of Denmark, the Netherlands, Norway and Sweden to widen their initial charges against Greece's violations of the European Convention to include torture.[11] In response to international pressure, the Greek government invited Amnesty International in March 1968 to return to Greece. During the second visit, the Minister of Interior Stylianos Pattakos gave Amnesty International every facility to inspect any prison and talk to any prisoner it wanted. The second mission to Greece confirmed the widespread and systematic use of torture. The violations were so widespread and of such magnitude that, when concluding the mission, the organization's representative, Anthony Marreco, pointed out to the Minister of Interior that unless the allegations were disproved Greece must inevitably face expulsion from the Council of Europe.[12]

After the applications of Denmark, Norway, Sweden and the Netherlands had been declared admissible in January 1968, the Commission proceeded with the case. During the proceedings in 1968, Amnesty International presented evidence on torture, alleging violation of Article 3 (prohibition of torture) of the European Convention. The organization's representatives, Anthony Marreco and James Becket, a British and an American lawyer, respectively, who a year earlier conducted a mission to Greece, appeared as witnesses before the Commission. Apparently, no issue arose concerning the identity of any confidential sources. The series of events which had been undoubtedly set in motion by the reports of Amnesty International's mission led to withdrawal of Greece from the Council of Europe in December 1969 under the threat of expulsion. 'It was Amnesty which provided the first evidence of torture, thus enabling the governments of Denmark, Norway and Sweden to amend their pleadings at Strasbourg', the organization wrote in its Annual Report.[13] Concurrently, Greece also denounced the European

---

[10] Amnesty International, *Situation in Greece*, 27 January 1968.

[11] See *Denmark, Norway and Sweden v Greece* (Nos. 3321-23/67) and *Netherlands v Greece* (No. 3344/67).

[12] Amnesty International, *Torture of Political Prisoners in Greece, Second Report by Amnesty International*, 6 April 1968.

[13] Amnesty International, *Annual Report 1969-70*, p. 20.

Convention. The Commission's report was published almost half a year later – in April 1970 – when the Committee of Ministers to which the report was referred decided to make it public. On the question of torture, the Commission 'found it established beyond doubt that torture or ill-treatment contrary to Article 3 has been inflicted in a number of cases'.[14] On the basis of the report the Committee of Ministers, *inter alia,* urged the Government of Greece 'to restore, without delay, human rights and fundamental freedoms in Greece'[15] and 'to abolish immediately torture and other ill-treatment of prisoners and to release immediately persons detained under administrative order'.[16] The Committee of Ministers also resolved to follow developments in Greece in this respect.[17] The latter process was discontinued in November 1974 in light of the fall of the military regime five months earlier.[18]

For Amnesty International, this first formal participation in the Commission's proceedings was undoubtedly very successful and encouraging. However, at the same time the organization learned from the first such experiment that it was very resource-demanding. At the time when the whole of Amnesty International's International Secretariat was formed of 19 people (including the Secretary General and administrative and technical staff), two of them were assigned to Greece alone. It is true that preparing a report and testifying in front of the Commission were not the only tasks of the two researchers. Nevertheless, the additional strain prompted the organization to write in its Annual Report 1969-70:

> In addition to the extra work involved, such a concentration of effort beyond the normal function of adopting prisoners of conscience also drains the financial reserves and gives an additional reason for seeking new sources of income to supplement the contribution from [Amnesty International's] groups.[19]

In spite of such concerns Amnesty International continued to provide the Commission with its information on human rights abuses in Council of Europe member states. Just a year after the Commission's decision on the case of Greece in 1970, the organization's report on ill-treatment of prisoners in Northern Ireland was distributed to members of the Commission.

In appearing before the European Court of Human Rights, Amnesty International now limits its role to presenting third party interventions. However, the organization's first attempt at appearance before the ECHR was not in the role of a third party but in the form of legal representation.

The case concerned Pat Arrowsmith, a British pacifist and a member of Amnesty International's International Secretariat staff. She was arrested in 1973 at an

---

[14] Ibid., p. 21.
[15] Committee of Ministers Resolution No. DH (70)1, 15 April 1970, para. 23.
[16] Ibid., para. 24.
[17] Ibid., para. 25.
[18] Committee of Ministers Resolution No. DH (74)2, 26 November 1974.
[19] Amnesty International, *Annual Report 1969-70,* p. 20.

army base in Warminster as she distributed leaflets describing how British soldiers who did not want to serve in Northern Ireland could receive help in leaving the armed forces and becoming conscientious objectors. After the conviction in May 1974 by a court in London and confirmation of the conviction by the Court of Appeal for inciting disaffection of the troops, Amnesty International decided to take the case jointly with then National Council for Civil Liberties (today Liberty) to the European Commission of Human Rights.[20] Ms Arrowsmith was represented by (now Sir) Nigel Rodley, the Legal Adviser of Amnesty International, and Howard Levenson, a solicitor and legal officer of the National Council for Civil Liberties.

The Commission considered the case raised important issues under Article 9 (freedom of thought, conscience and religion) and Article 10 (freedom of expression) of the European Convention and in May 1977 declared the application admissible but rejected it on the merits.[21] In accordance with Article 31 of the European Convention at the time, the Commission drew up a report on the facts and stated its opinion and transmitted it to the Committee of Ministers. Since no party that had a legal standing referred the case to the ECHR within three months, it was taken by the Committee of Ministers, which decided in 1979 that in this case there had been no violation of the European Convention.

Almost a decade passed before Amnesty International decided to become involved again in the European Convention's mechanisms. The organization limited its participation to submissions analogous to *amicus curiae* submissions. The series of cases in which Amnesty International became involved started with *Soering v United Kingdom*[22] which was referred to the ECHR by the Commission in January 1989. The applicant had been facing extradition to the USA from the United Kingdom on a capital murder charge. Upon request, Amnesty International was granted leave to submit written comments in this case.

In April 1989, the organization submitted a written comment (in effect, an *amicus curiae* brief) asking the ECHR to rule that, in the light of evolving European standards, the death penalty itself should be considered as an inhuman and degrading punishment within the meaning of Article 3 (prohibition of torture) of the European Convention. It also provided information about the 'death row phenomenon' as a form of inhuman or degrading treatment and in support attached copies from relevant chapters of its own reports.[23] In the judgment, which was delivered unanimously, the ECHR held that if the United Kingdom were to extradite Soering it would violate its obligations under Article 3 of the European Conven-

---

[20] *Arrowsmith v United Kingdom.*

[21] *Arrowsmith v United Kingdom,* No. 7050/75, decision of 16 May 1977 (admissibility), 19 DR 19.

[22] Case No. 1/1989/161/217.

[23] The attached chapters were taken from Amnesty International, *United States of America: The Death Penalty* (Amnesty International Publications, London, 1987), pp. 108–119; and Amnesty International, *When the State Kills ... The Death Penalty v. Human Rights* (Amnesty International Publications, London, 1989), pp. 54–61.

tion. Although the ECHR did not find that the application of the death penalty was in itself a violation of the European Convention, it held that the circumstances in which it is imposed can give rise to issues under Article 3, especially a combination of factors relating to the 'death row phenomenon'.

In the 1990s Amnesty International submitted written comments in nine other cases. In the majority of them, the ECHR ruled along the lines of the organization's submissions. These are as follows.

(i) Chahal v United Kingdom[24]

In August 1990 the applicant, a Sikh separatist who had lived in the United Kingdom for 20 years, was arrested and detained pending deportation to India. Although he sought asylum in the United Kingdom, claiming that he would face torture if forcibly returned, his asylum application was rejected on 'national security' grounds. The case went all the way to the ECHR. In November 1995, Amnesty International was one five NGOs which were granted leave to submit interventions. The organization was allowed to intervene both on questions of law and on facts. The legal issues concerned procedural rights in relation to persons who are at possible risk of torture or other serious human rights violations in the country to which return is being considered. The factual issues were related to the organization's research and experience concerning the risk faced by prominent Sikh separatists suspected of being linked to armed groups in the Punjab of extrajudicial execution, 'disappearance', torture, and arbitrary detention. In accordance with the organization's request to the ECHR and the indication given in the letter from the ECHR, the brief did not address the specific facts of the case before the ECHR. In November 1996, the ECHR ruled that the prohibition of torture was paramount and that allegations of national security risk were immaterial to determination of whether a person faced a 'real risk' of torture if returned.[25]

(ii) McCann, Farrell and Savage v United Kingdom[26]

In its written comments, Amnesty International urged the ECHR to declare that the intentional lethal use of firearms could only be compatible with the European Convention when its use was strictly unavoidable in order to protect life. To illustrate the extent of the incidence of excessive use of lethal force in the world, the organization attached two of its reports.[27] In September 1995, the ECHR ruled that the UK government had violated the right to life of three unarmed IRA mem-

---

[24] Case No. 70/1995/576/662.

[25] Chahal v United Kingdom, No. 22414/93, judgment of 15 November 1996, para. 150, (1996-V) ECHR Reports.

[26] Case No. 17/1994/464/545.

[27] The reports were Amnesty International, Report 1994 (Amnesty International Publications, London, 1994) and Amnesty International, 'Disappearances' and Political Killings: Human Rights Crisis of the 1990s (Amnesty International Publications, London, 1994).

bers shot dead by undercover SAS soldiers in Gibraltar in 1988. The ECHR stated that it was 'not persuaded' that the killings 'constituted the use of force which was no more than absolutely necessary'[28] and that there had been a 'lack of appropriate care in the control and organization of the arrest operation'.[29]

(iii) Akdivar v Turkey

In March 1996, Amnesty International was granted leave to intervene both on questions of law and on facts. The former question concerned admissibility of a case with particular reference to the exhaustion of local remedies and the latter question, based on the organization's research and experience, concerned its evaluation of the effectiveness of domestic remedies for government action in Turkey. The ECHR found that the national remedies available to the applicants were so ineffective that they were not obliged to exhaust them before lodging a complaint with the European Commission.[30]

(iv) Aydin v Turkey[31]

Amnesty International submitted that the rape of a woman prisoner by a state official constitutes torture under Article 3 (prohibition of torture) of the European Convention. Furthermore, the organization argued that under the same article, together with Article 13 (right to an effective remedy), states parties must conduct prompt, impartial and effective investigations of torture and ill-treatment. In a judgment in September 1997, the ECHR found that Turkish security forces had tortured the applicant, Sükran Aydin, who was 17 years old at the time, while she was detained. The ECHR found that she had been raped, paraded naked in humiliating circumstances and beaten, and that the Turkish authorities had failed to conduct an adequate investigation into her complaint.[32]

(v) Assenov and others v Bulgaria[33]

The case arose in the context of the failure of the Bulgarian authorities to conduct prompt and impartial investigations of reports and complaints of torture. It concerned the content and scope of the obligation of a state party under Articles 3 (prohibition of torture) and 13 (right to an effective remedy) to investigate reports

---

[28] *McCann, Farrell and Savage v United Kingdom* [GC], No. 18984/91, judgment of 27 September 1995, para. 213, ECHR A324.

[29] Ibid., para. 212.

[30] *Akdivar and others v Turkey* [GC], No. 21893/93, judgment of 16 September 1996, (1996-IV) ECHR Reports.

[31] Case No. 57/1996/676/866.

[32] *Aydin v Turkey* [GC], No. 23178/94, judgment of 25 September 1997, (1997-VI) ECHR Reports.

[33] Case No. 90/1997/874/1086.

and allegations of torture, prohibited by Article 3 of the Convention. In its intervention of 13 February 1998, Amnesty International maintained that Article 3 itself is violated when a state party has failed to provide for prompt, impartial, independent, thorough and effective investigation of complaints or reports of torture or ill-treatment. Such a state should not escape responsibility for a violation of Article 3 as a result of its failure to investigate. In a judgment delivered on 28 October 1998, the ECHR held that there had been a violation of Article 3 of the Convention based on the absence of an effective official investigation into the applicant's allegations of ill-treatment by the police (unanimously) but that there had been no violation of Article 3 arising from the alleged ill-treatment itself or from the conditions in which the applicant had been held in pre-trial detention (eight votes to one). The ECHR also found, unanimously, violations of Article 13.[34]

(vi) Kurt v Turkey[35]

Amnesty International addressed the question of which articles of the European Convention are violated by a 'disappearance' and what is a 'disappearance'. In its submission, the organization first identified the elements of the crime of 'disappearance', based on the analyses of relevant international instruments. The organization maintained further that a 'disappearance' is to be seen as constituting a violation not only of the liberty and security of the individual but also of other fundamental rights. It referred to the decision of the Inter-American Court of Human Rights in *Velásquez Rodríguez v Honduras*.[36] The ECHR ruled that Turkey had violated Articles 3 (prohibition of torture), 5 (right to liberty and security of the person), 13 (right to an effective remedy) of the European Convention. The ECHR also found that Articles 14 (prohibition of discrimination) and 18 (limitation on use of restrictions on rights) had not been violated.[37]

(vii) Tashin Acar v Turkey[38]

In its submission, Amnesty International addressed the scope of the power of the ECHR to strike out a case (this one involving an unresolved 'disappearance') under Article 37(1) of the European Convention on the unilateral undertaking of a state which fails to address many of the issues raised in the application. The organization maintained that striking an application out under Article 37(1) on the sole basis of an undertaking by a respondent state to improve procedures in future

---

[34] *Assenov and others v Bulgaria*, No. 24760/94, judgment of 28 October 1998, (1998-VIII) ECHR Reports.

[35] Case No. 15/1997/799/1002.

[36] Since Amnesty International acted as *amicus curiae* in that case, as well, it is discussed below in section 3 on Inter-American regional human rights mechanisms.

[37] *Kurt v Turkey*, No. 24276/94, judgment of 25 May 1998, (1998-III) ECHR Reports.

[38] Case No. 26307/95.

without an acknowledgement of liability and without providing an effective remedy within the meaning of Article 13 (right to an effective remedy) in the particular case concerned would fundamentally undermine respect for human rights and be perceived, in cases concerning disappeared persons, as condoning a continuing violation of the individual applicant's human rights. In May 2003, in the judgment on this preliminary issue, the ECHR rejected the Turkish government's request to strike the application out of the list and decided to pursue the examination of the merits of the case.[39]

(viii) Murray v United Kingdom[40]

In one other case, *Murray v United Kingdom*, the ECHR agreed with Amnesty International's positions only partially. The organization, in its written submission, argued that the right to silence is an essential safeguard of the internationally recognized presumption of innocence and the right not to testify against oneself. Amnesty International also argued that the right of suspects to have legal assistance in criminal pre-trial detention procedures is crucial to ensure that statements taken in evidence from the detainee are given freely and not as a result of coercion. Under the emergency legislation in Northern Ireland the applicant had been denied both rights. In February 1996, the ECHR ruled that the denial to the applicant of legal assistance while being interrogated violated his right to a fair trial. However, the ECHR also found that, in this particular case, his right to silence had not been violated.[41]

(ix) Brannigan and McBride v United Kingdom[42]

In another case, the ECHR ruled contrary to Amnesty International's submissions. This case concerned prompt access to a judge by individuals who were deprived of their liberty in times of emergency. In May 1993, the ECHR upheld the United Kingdom's derogation from Article 5(3) of the European Convention which requires that detainees are brought promptly before a judicial authority. Amnesty International maintained that strict scrutiny was required by the ECHR when examining derogation from fundamental procedural guarantees which were essential for the protection of detainees at all times and that it is precisely when states take exceptional measures that the need for safeguards is the greatest. The organization attached copies of its reports in which this need was demonstrated in numerous cases.[43] Although the ECHR quoted and addressed Amnesty Interna-

---

[39] *Tashin Acar v Turkey* (preliminary objections), No. 26307/95, judgment of 6 May 2003.

[40] Case No. 41/1994/488/570.

[41] *Murray v United Kingdom* [GC], No. 18731/91, judgment of 8 February 1996, (*1996-I*) ECHR *Reports.*

[42] Case Nos. 5/1992/350/423 – 424.

[43] The attached reports were: Amnesty International, *Report 1992* (Amnesty International Publications, London, 1992); Amnesty International, *Torture in the Eighties* (Amnesty International Pub-

tional's arguments in its judgment in more extensive manner than in other judgments, one of the judges in his separate (concurring!) opinion expressed his view that the organization's argument was not adequately addressed:

> For my part, I found Amnesty International's arguments against so deciding persuasive, especially where Amnesty emphasized developments in international standards and practice in answer to world-wide human rights abuses under cover of derogation and underlined the importance of the present ruling in other parts of the world. Consequently, I regret that the Court's only refutation of those arguments is its reference to a precedent which is fifteen years old.[44]

The common denominator of almost a dozen cases described above in which Amnesty International became involved was that on questions of law, the ECHR was expected to rule on important legal principles. The pronouncements of the ECHR in those cases were not expected to be significant just for the interpretation of the legal principles as enshrined in the European Convention, but also for use by other international courts and treaty-monitoring bodies outside Europe and in national courts throughout the world, thus contributing to the development of international human rights law. This was the guiding principle which Amnesty International followed when deciding in which cases to become involved. Very careful consideration was given, because the organization was fully aware that proper preparation and participation would put significant additional strain on its researchers and legal advisers.

In fact, participation by Amnesty International in cases brought in the late 1980s and 1990s was made possible mainly due to the personal commitment and voluntary work of certain individuals outside the International Secretariat. The organization's participation was encouraged by Peter Duffy, late British barrister of Essex Court Chambers and formerly a member and chairperson of Amnesty International's International Executive Committee (1989–1991). He not only monitored the cases brought to the ECHR and suggested those in which the organization should become involved, but he also drafted or assisted in drafting almost all of Amnesty International's interventions. In preparing these interventions, Amnesty International was also assisted, among others, by barristers Laura Cox (*Aydın v Turkey*), Tim Eicke (*Akdivar v Turkey*), Ben Emmerson (*Assenov v Bulgaria*), Christopher Greenwood (*Akdivar v Turkey*), Barbara Hewson (*Aydın v Turkey*), Richard Plender (*Chahal v United Kingdom*), Nigel Rodley (*Brannigan and McBride v United Kingdom*), Jessica Simor (*Assenov v Bulgaria*) and Rabinder Singh (*Kurt v Turkey*).

Amnesty International has never had any difficulties in approaching the ECHR. Whenever requested, the organization was granted leave to submit writ-

---

lications, London, 1984); and Amnesty International, United Kingdom, *Allegations of Ill-Treatment in Northern Ireland* (AI Index: EUR 45/19/91, 1991).
[44] *Brannigan and McBride v United Kingdom*, Nos. 14553/89 and 14554/89, judgment of 26 May 1993, concurring opinion of Judge Martens, para. 3, ECHR A258-B.

ten comments on a certain issue. This was usually done after the Chamber to which the case had been assigned was consulted by either its President or Vice-President. Furthermore, Amnesty International's reports have been quoted by applicants, the Commission and the ECHR itself in their decisions on admissibility and judgments even when the organization did not submit or participate in the proceedings.[45]

The organization's participation in the European Convention's mechanisms ceased at the end of 1990s due to lack of resources and a temporary shift of priorities. Between 1998 and 2000, Amnesty International played a major role as one of a group of third parties in the case of the former Chilean dictator Augusto Pinochet whose extradition from the United Kingdom was sought by four European states on grounds of his alleged responsibility for widespread and systematic use of torture while in power. Being perhaps one of the organization's most high profile and laborious cases ever, it demanded significant amount of resources which had to be redirected from some other similar efforts.

(b)   Other treaty-monitoring bodies

The European Convention for the Prevention of Torture and Inhuman or Degrading Treatment or Punishment of 1987 established a committee to monitor compliance of the states parties with the Convention. The European Committee for the Prevention of Torture and Inhuman or Degrading Treatment or Punishment conducts visits to places of detention in the states parties and examines treatment of persons deprived of their liberty with a view to strengthening, if necessary, the protection of such persons from torture and from inhuman or degrading treatment or punishment.

Since the Committee started its work back in 1990, Amnesty International has been following its work and submitting information to it that falls within the scope of its mandate.

3.2   Organization of American States

A system for promotion and protection of human rights in the Western hemisphere was established under the auspices of the Organization of American States (OAS). The Inter-American system consists of two bodies: the Inter-American Commission on Human Rights and the Inter-American Court of Human Rights. The two bodies oversee implementation of the major human rights treaty in the

---

[45] See, e.g., the ECHR's judgments in the following cases: *Cruz Varas et al. v Sweden*, No. 15576/89, judgment of 20 March 1991, ECHR A201; *Ulku Ekinci v Turkey*, No. 27602/95, judgment of 16 July 2002; and *Hilal v United Kingdom*, No. 45276/99, judgment of 6 March 2001, (2001-II) ECHR Reports; and the Commission's admissibility decisions and reports in the following cases: *Donnelly et al. v United Kingdom*, Nos. 5577-83/72; *Vilvarajah et al. v United Kingdom*, Nos. 13163-65/87, 13447-48/87; *Kiliç v Turkey*, No. 22492/93; *Nsangu v Austria*, No. 25661/94; *Mbemba v Austria*, No. 25664/94; and *Bahaddar v Netherlands*, No. 25894/94.

hemisphere, the American Convention of Human Rights, ('the American Convention') which was adopted in 1969 and entered into force in 1978. In addition, victims of human rights violations committed by OAS member states that have not ratified the Convention can file petitions to the Commission on the basis of the American Declaration of the Rights and Duties of Man adopted in 1948.

The Inter-American Commission was created in 1959 at a meeting of OAS foreign ministers and it was reconstituted by the American Convention of Human Rights. It is an autonomous and permanent body of the OAS mandated by the OAS Charter and the American Convention of Human Rights. The Commission has some of the most flexible procedures for dealing with human rights abuses of any of the international human rights bodies. The Inter-American Court was established by the American Convention in 1978. It has both contentious jurisdiction and jurisdiction to render advisory opinions interpreting the American Convention and certain other human rights treaties.

The Inter-American Commission examines petitions and determines the facts based on relevant information from a petitioner. It can also gain information on its own motion by conducting investigations, on-site visits, etc. When the Commission decides it has sufficient information, it prepares a report with a conclusion and, if it finds a violation, recommendations to the state. The report is not public, but the Commission may decide to make it public after expiration of a period of time given to the state to resolve the situation and to comply with the recommendations. After expiration, the Commission must bring the case in accordance with Article 51 of the American Convention to the Inter-American Court (where the states have accepted its jurisdiction) within three months. If it decides not to refer the case to the Inter-American Court, the Commission issues a final public report after the expiration of that period. A state concerned can do the same. The Inter-American Court's judgment is binding, but there is no specific mechanism to oversee enforcement other than informing the OAS General Assembly of cases of non-compliance.

(a)   Providing information to the Commission

Amnesty International has maintained close contact with the Inter-American Commission for more than three decades. A year after entry into force of the Protocol of Buenos Aires in 1970 which transformed the Commission into a formal OAS Charter organ, Amnesty International made one of its first formal submissions to the Commission. It was concerning deaths, 'disappearances' and torture of individuals in Guatemala. In the following years, the organization continued to submit further information on Guatemala. Despite its requests, the Guatemalan government at the time refused to allow the Commission to conduct an on-site investigation.

Throughout the 1970s, Amnesty International has not only brought specific cases and situations to the attention of the Inter-American Commission, but has also sought to provide the Commission with general information and background

documentation pertinent to its work. The organization's Annual Report 1977 fea-
tured the following cases, which are illustrative of the extent and level of quality
of its early relations with the Commission.[46]

(i) Argentina

Ten days after Josefa Martinez was arrested in November 1976, Amnesty International cabled the Inter-American Commission requesting that it seek information on her whereabouts. After another 10 days, the Commission, in turn, cabled
the Argentinian government. Although the authorities had previously denied that
she was in official custody, a week after the Commission's cable they replied that
Josefa Martinez had been released after an investigation into her background.

(ii) Guatemala

The Inter-American Commission informed Amnesty International of the Guatemalan government's response to its allegations of 'disappearances' in their country as submitted in June 1975. The government insisted that it exhaustively
investigated the cases but failed to offer any facts concerning the named individuals. In its response to the Commission of September 1976, Amnesty International
noted this omission.

(iii) Haiti

Following Amnesty International's May 1975 submission to the Inter-American
Commission of a list of prisoners about whom little was known, the President of
the Commission wrote to the Haitian government insisting that it send complete
information relevant to the case. The Commission eventually secured a reply
from the Haitian government that a careful investigation had disclosed that one of
Amnesty International's cases had been used to accuse the government of human
rights violations. In April 1977, Amnesty International drew the Commission's
attention to the unresponsiveness of this position and supplied it with details on
various cases before the Commission, which demonstrated that the Haitian government had frequently denied knowledge of detentions, only to acknowledge
them later by announcing the detainees' releases.

(iv) Paraguay

Two months after Amnesty International's March 1976 submission concerning
55 detainees or 'disappearances', the Inter-American Commission adopted a
resolution presuming the accuracy of the facts and observing that they constitute

---

[46] Amnesty International, *Report 1977* (Amnesty International Publications, London, 1977),
pp. 26–28.

'the gravest violations of the right to freedom, security and integrity of the person; of the rights to protection of the family; of the right to the inviolability of the home; of the right to justice; of the right to protection against arbitrary detention and of the right to a fair trial'. In July 1976, Amnesty International drew the attention of the Commission to a recent wave of repression resulting in the arrest of approximately 1,000 persons. Half a year later, the Commission requested from the Paraguayan government the appropriate information regarding the general situation of human rights in the country.

(v) Uruguay

In October 1976, Amnesty International updated the previous joint report with the International Commission of Jurists of May 1974 on that country by making a general submission to the Inter-American Commission. After the Uruguayan government refused permission to send the Commission's sub-commission to 'complete the information', the Commission decided to issue a report of the case for the June 1977 General Assembly of the OAS. Amnesty International's general submission also led the Commission to request information from the Uruguayan government concerning five named individuals.

Throughout the years that followed, Amnesty International has continued to submit to the Commission relevant information on human rights violations in the Western hemisphere. In some years, the organization formally provided the Commission with information on human rights violations for more than a dozen countries. The information provided to the Commission was based on the organization's own sources and research. The scope of cooperation was such that the organization recommended in October 1979 that formal consultative mechanisms should be created by the OAS to make possible enhanced cooperation with NGOs. This was done at the annual session of the OAS General Assembly. Since 1977, Amnesty International has attended all the Annual Regular Sessions of the OAS General Assembly as a 'special guest'. The organization has also submitted *amicus curiae* briefs to the Commission, such as in the case of Fray Juan Antonio Puigjané, Capuchin friar and a human rights activist, adopted by Amnesty International as a prisoner of conscience.

(b) *Amicus curiae* briefs in contentious cases before the Inter-American Court

Amnesty International submitted its first *amicus curiae* brief in January 1988 in the first three contentious cases before the Inter-American Court: *Velásquez Rodríguez, Godínez Cruz* and *Fairén Garbi and Solís Corrales*. They were involving four unclarified 'disappearances' in Honduras and, as noted by Amnesty International in its brief, were examples of a consistent pattern of 'disappearance' in Honduras during the early 1980s.[47]

---

[47] In the Inter-American Court of Human Rights, brief of Amnesty International as *amicus curiae*, 7 January 1988, p. 8.

The Inter-American Court handed down its first judgment in a contentious case in July 1988. The Court found that Honduras had violated the American Convention in the case of a 'disappeared' prisoner, Angel Manfredo Velásquez Rodríguez. The Court held that Honduras had failed to ensure respect for the rights to personal liberty guaranteed by the American Convention, to humane treatment and to life. As urged by Amnesty International in its brief, the Inter-American Court considered that 'disappearance' violated the prohibition against torture or cruel, inhuman or degrading treatment or punishment and ordered compensation to be paid to the next-of-kin.[48]

In January 1989 the Inter-American Court handed down its second judgment. Again, the Court found the Honduran government responsible for violations of Article 4 (the right to life), Article 5 (right to humane treatment) and Article 7 (right to personal liberty) of the American Convention in the case of Saúl Godínez Cruz. The Court ordered the Honduran government to pay compensation to his family.[49] In the two other outstanding cases, concerning the 'disappearances' of Francisco Fairén Garbi and Yolanda Solís Corrales, a Costa Rican couple, the Inter-American Court concluded that 'numerous and insoluble difficulties' prevented it from establishing whether the 'disappearance' occurred in Honduras and could definitely be attributed to the Honduran government, although it noted that the government had apparently presented obstacles to the case's clarification.[50]

In one case in the early 1990s, Amnesty International also stood as a co-complainant before the Inter-American Court. It was the case of the Cayara massacre in Peru, in which at least 31 people were killed by the army in Cayara region, Ayacucho, in May 1988. In 1990, Amnesty International had joined Americas Watch as co-complainant in the case and had continued to urge the Commission to submit the case to the Inter-American Court. The organization's delegates attended sessions of the Commission in February and October 1991 and argued in support of transmitting the case to the Court. The Commission formally submitted the case against Peru to the Inter-American Court in February 1992. The first hearing by the Court was held in June the same year and dealt with 12 preliminary objections raised by the Peruvian government. Staff members of Amnesty International were appointed advisers to the Commission and attended the hearing in this capacity. The amount of time spent on this case was considerable. In February 1993, the Inter-American Court decided on the Peruvian government's preliminary objections. The Court ruled that the Commission had filed the case after the time limit allowed by the American Convention had expired, and ordered that the case be dismissed. As a result, strong evidence of the government's responsibility for the massacre could not be considered. Subsequently, the Com-

---

[48] *Velásquez Rodríguez v Honduras*, judgment of 29 July 1988, (1988) Ser. C, No. 4.

[49] *Godínez Cruz v Honduras*, judgment of 20 January 1989, (1989) Ser. C, No. 5.

[50] *Fairén Garbi and Solís Corrales v Honduras*, judgment of 15 March 1989(1989) Ser. C, No. 6.

mission submitted a full report on the Cayara case to the General Assembly of the OAS, but the Assembly took no action to secure the government's compliance with the recommendations of the Commission.

(c) *Amicus curiae* briefs with regard to advisory opinions of the Inter-American Court and the Commission

Amnesty International submitted *amicus curiae* briefs also with regard to advisory opinions that the Inter-American Court or the Commission had been asked to deliver.

The first Amnesty International's third party brief in proceedings delivering an advisory opinion was concerning interpretation of Article 27(2) of the American Convention. In September 1986, Uruguay requested the Inter-American Court to give an advisory opinion on the scope of the prohibition of the suspension of the judicial guarantees essential for the protection of the rights mentioned in Article 27(2) of the American Convention. Article 27 first defines the circumstances under which rights set down in the Convention may be suspended and then lists a number of rights from which no derogation is permitted. The main argument of Amnesty International's 40-page brief was that the judicial guarantees essential to protecting basic human rights to which Article 27(2) refers are:

> those which logic and experience have proven to be indispensable for safeguarding rights most often violated during a state of emergency. Rights most vulnerable during a state of emergency and which can be best protected by judicial guarantees are the right to life and the right to humane treatment.[51]

In its opinion, the Inter-American Court listed the following essential judicial guarantees which are not subject to derogation: (1) *habeas corpus, amparo,* and any other effective remedy before judges or competent tribunals; and (2) those judicial procedures that are inherent to representative democracy. The Court also held that those judicial guarantees should be exercised within the framework and the principles of due process of law, expressed in Article 8 (right to a fair trial) of the American Convention.[52]

In December 1997, Mexico requested an advisory opinion on the issue of minimum judicial guarantees and the requirements of due process when a court sentences to death foreign nationals whom the host state has not informed of their right to communicate with and seek assistance from the consular authorities of the state of which they are nationals. In June 1998, Amnesty International, among other NGOs and individuals, addressed the Inter-American Court on the issues. It argued that the right to access to consular authorities for foreign citizens facing a possible death penalty was part of the internationally recognized right to a fair

---

[51] In the Inter-American Court of Human Rights, brief of Amnesty International as *amicus curiae,* 16 June 1987, p. 4.

[52] Advisory Opinion OC-9/87 of 6 October 1987.

trial, as enshrined in Article 36(1)(b) of the Vienna Convention on Consular Relations 1963, to which both Mexico and the USA were states parties. In 1999, the organization filed a follow-up *amicus curiae* brief with the Inter-American Court providing an analysis of the law on the right to information on consular assistance. Both briefs were prepared with assistance to Amnesty International by Evangeline de Gracia, Wayne Clarke, Beth Lyon, Richard Wilson and Hugo Relva. The latter two also acted as representatives of the organization at the public hearing. In October 1999, the Inter-American Court delivered its advisory opinion in which it stated, in line with Amnesty International's arguments, that the failure to provide information on consular assistance has an impact on due process and, in the case of the imposition of the death penalty, constitutes a violation of the right not to be arbitrarily deprived of life.[53]

In 1999, Amnesty International submitted an *amicus curiae* brief to the Commission on conscientious objection to military service in the case of Luis Gabriel Caldas Leon, a conscientious objector who was adopted by Amnesty International as a prisoner of conscience. The organization argued that conscientious objection is a universally recognized right and reflection of freedom of expression and freedom of religion and conscience. This right is protected and guaranteed by Article 3 of the American Declaration and Article 12 of the American Convention. At the time of writing, the case was still in process before the Commission and it is not known whether the organization's considerations were taken on board.

3.3   Organization of African Unity / African Union

Within the Organization of African Unity (OAU) which was transformed into the African Union (AU) in 2002, the main human rights mechanism was created under the African Charter on Human and Peoples' Rights ('the African Charter'). Soon after the African Charter entered into force in October 1986 its monitoring body, the African Commission on Human and Peoples' Rights ('the African Commission'), was established, being the youngest regional human rights protection system.

The four areas of mandate of the African Commission are: promotional activities, protective activities (individual complaint), the examination of state party reports and the interpretation of the African Charter. One of the main characteristics of the individual petition system of the African Charter which makes it different from the systems of the European and Inter-American Conventions is that it was not designed to deal with individual cases of violations of human or people's rights. Article 58(1) of the African Charter requires that a communication addressed to the African Commission reveals 'the existence of a series of serious or massive violations of human and peoples' rights'. Another important feature of the African human rights system is enshrined in Article 55(1) which states that

---

[53] Advisory Opinion OC-16/99 of 1 October 1999.

before each session, the Secretary of the African Commission makes 'a list of the communications other than those of States Parties ... and transmit[s] them to the members of the Commission, who shall indicate which communications should be considered by the Commission'. The language of this provision suggests that, besides states parties, the complaints can also be filed by other entities, such as individuals or NGOs.

In May 2003, when the OAU was replaced by the African Union, the African system underwent some significant changes. Unlike the Charter of the OAU, which contained limited provisions on human rights, the Constitutive Act of the African Union attaches a particular significance to human rights in a more comprehensive manner. Further changes are envisaged in January 2004 when the Protocol to the African Charter on Human and Peoples' Rights Establishing an African Court on Human and Peoples' Rights enters into force and the African Court on Human and Peoples' Rights is established. The African Court will consider cases referred to it by the African Commission and states parties to the Protocol and, where a state party accepts such a jurisdiction, by individuals and NGOs. Establishment of the African Court is expected to reinforce the African Commission and contribute to effective protection of human rights on the continent. The Court will rule not just on alleged violations of the African Charter but also on any other relevant human rights instrument ratified by the state concerned, for which the victim seeks redress.

One serious limitation of the Protocol establishing the African Court is that it allows individuals and NGOs with observer status before the Commission to institute cases directly before the Court only if the state against which they want to proceed has made a declaration accepting such individual and NGO submission of cases. Without such declaration, the African Court will not directly receive any petition from an individual or NGO.[54] Amnesty International has repeatedly called upon states parties to make such declarations, but, as of yet, without much success.

(a) First contacts

Amnesty International's contacts with the OAU (AU) were first formalized before the African Charter entered into force. In April 1972, the organization was granted observer status on the OAU's Coordinating Committee on Refugees, a branch of the OAU Secretariat which was later transformed to OAU's Bureau for the Placement and Education of African Refugees (BPEAR). Although no Amnesty International permanent representative was appointed, the observer status fostered development of the organization's relationship with the OAU. At the time, Amnesty International even financially assisted the BPEAR with legal aid

---

[54] For summarized analyses of the African Court's features and complete text of the Protocol see Amnesty International, *African Court on Human and People's Rights: An Opportunity to Strengthen Human Rights in Africa* (AI Index: IOR 63/001/2002, July 2002).

to refugees detained in their countries of refuge or faced with repatriation to their countries of origin.

Relations with the OAU gained more substance in December 1975 when it was agreed with representatives of the OAU that Amnesty International would set up a system whereby the OAU would be kept informed, through the production of country dossiers, of the organization's evaluation of the human rights situation in various African states. This was an important development since the OAU at the time did not have a body specifically constituted to deal with human rights issues.

(b)   Communications to African Commission on Human and Peoples' Rights

Relations with the OAU were further strengthened at the end of the 1980s and beginning of the 1990s when the African Charter entered into force and Amnesty International began submitting communications to the African Commission.

In April 1988, i.e., soon after the African Charter entered into force and its monitoring body was constituted in October 1986 and July 1987, respectively, Amnesty International was granted observer status with the African Commission. Under the Rules of Procedure adopted at the African Commission's 2nd Session in February 1988, Amnesty International was permitted to participate in public sessions and to cooperate with the African Commission in its activities. The Rules of Procedure, however, provided that, in general, the African Commission would meet in private session.

Soon after constitution of the African Commission, Amnesty International decided to file several communications about situations involving human rights violations in particular contexts. Besides efforts to address effectively widespread human rights violations in the respective countries, the organization's goals were also to assist the African Commission to develop its own jurisprudence and to promote and test the newly established mechanism. For the same purpose, in 1987 Amnesty International also produced a paper on the OAU and the African Charter as part of its series explaining various international procedures which address allegations of human rights violations.

Amnesty International submitted its first communication under Article 55 of the African Charter before the October 1990 Session of the African Commission.[55] The communication, which was declared admissible, dealt with human rights violations in Sudan since the June 1989 military coup. In the two-page communication, with annexes, the organization summarized its main concerns and connected them to respective provisions of the African Charter which had been violated. The organization also attached its own documents describing the concerns in detail.[56] Attaching its own documents which had been produced

---

[55] *Amnesty International v Sudan*, Communication No. 48/90.

[56] The attached documents were *Sudan: The Military Government's First Year in Power – A Permanent Human Rights Crisis* (AI Index: AFR 54/10/90, 1990) and *Sudan: Human Rights Violations in the Context of Civil War* (AI Index: AFR 54/17/89, 1989).

largely from the organization's own sources was important because one of the admissibility criteria as set forth in Article 56 of the African Charter requires that the submitted communication not be based 'exclusively on news disseminated through the mass media'. Soon after receipt, the African Commission transmitted the communication to the Sudanese government, because Article 57 of the African Charter requires that all communications, prior to any substantive consideration, have to be brought to the knowledge of the state concerned. In reply to Amnesty International's allegations, the Sudanese government in January 1991 sent a memorandum it had prepared as response to the similar criticism by the UN Human Rights Commission's Special Rapporteur on Summary or Arbitrary Executions. In the memorandum, the draconian measures taken by the Sudanese government with which it suppressed the most basic rights of many of its people were justified by various provisions of Sudanese legislation. On its understanding of international human rights standards the Sudanese government wrote:

> The Sudan endorses the universally accepted point of view that fundamental rights guaranteed by Universal Declarations and the Constitution are subject to the right of the State to restrict those rights by law for maintaining public order, security and safety. These rights are also subject to suspension at times of emergency provided for under the Constitution.[57]

In March and October 1992, Amnesty International sent further information relating to the first communication. The African Commission repeatedly postponed the decision on the communication until its 26th Session when it joined several communications concerning Sudan. In the decision, which was taken on 15 November 1999, more than nine years after Amnesty International's initial communication, the African Commission found violations of a number of the African Charter's articles.

Before the October 1991 Session of the African Commission, Amnesty International submitted a second communication under Article 55 of the African Charter. It concerned extrajudicial executions, routine torture of political detainees, unfair trials and other human rights violations in Mauritania.[58] Again, the communication was based on the organization's own documents which were enclosed.[59] Amnesty International was informed by the African Commission that the communication had been declared admissible at its 17th Ordinary Session in March 1995. That means it took the African Commission three years and a half

---

[57] Permanent Representative of the Republic of the Sudan to the United Nations Office at Geneva, *Preparation for the 47th Session of the Commission on Human Rights, Geneva, February 1991*, 1 January 1991, p. 4.

[58] *Amnesty International v Mauritania*, Communication No. 61/91.

[59] The enclosed documents were: *Mauritania: 1986-1989: Background to a Crisis – Three Years of Political Imprisonment, Torture and Unfair Trials* (AI Index: AFR 38/13/89, November 1989), *Mauritania: Human Rights Violations in the Senegal River Valley* (AI Index: AFR 38/10/90, October 1990) and *Mauritania: Personal Details on 339 Political Prisoners Reported to have been Killed Between November 1990 and March 1991* (AI Index: AFR 38/07/91, August 1991).

just to declare the organization's communication admissible. It took another five years for the African Commission to take a decision in which it found violation of a number of the African Charter's articles.

Although the African Commission had not reached a decision on the merits of any of the 74 communications submitted during its first five years, Amnesty International decided in 1992 to submit new communications concerning human rights violations in Burundi, Malawi[60] and Tunisia.[61] At the same time the organization urged the African Commission to act on the backlog of communications promptly and to make public as much information as possible concerning the procedure. These urgings were repeated the following year when the African Commission's backlog of admitted communications had become well over 100 and a decision on the merits had not been taken on even a single case. Furthermore, Amnesty International called for a thorough public discussion of the Article 55 procedure, with a view to making it effective. The outcome of each of the three cases that Amnesty International filed in 1992 was different. With regard to Burundi, the African Commission did not consider the information submitted as a communication; on Malawi, it found violations of a number of the African Charter's articles, and the communication on Tunisia was declared inadmissible because it had also been filed under the UN's 1503 procedure.

In one case, Amnesty International requested the African Commission to adopt provisional measures under Rule 111 of its Rules of Procedure. According to that Rule, prior to forwarding its final decisions (recommendations) on a communication to the state party concerned, the African Commission may inform that state whether it considers interim measures desirable to prevent irreparable damage to the victim. In April 1998, Amnesty International together with Interights, sent a communication to the African Commission informing its members of imminent execution of 23 people by the Rwandese authorities. They had been found guilty of participation in genocide in 1994. The organizations had difficulty in obtaining their names as the Rwandese Ministry of Justice indicated that the names were confidential. The organizations were concerned that those who were to be executed might have included several individuals whose trials had been grossly unfair and they believed that if persons who had been denied the right to a fair trial were to be executed, this would have amounted to arbitrary deprivation of the right to life and thus violation of Article 4 (right to life) of the African Charter. The African Commission responded to the organizations' request by sending urgent messages appealing for a stay of execution as the intended executions would have been in violation of the African Charter. Upon confirmation that the executions were carried out in public, the African Commission authorised the Chairperson to write to the Rwandese government and express the outrage of the African Commission at this blatant disregard of the provisions of the African

---

[60] *Amnesty International v Malawi*, Communication Nos. 68/92 and 78/92.
[61] *Amnesty International v Tunisia*, Communication Nos. 69/92 and 79/92.

Charter.[62] The African Commission also issued a press release with the same message.

Amnesty International's communication under Article 55 of the African Charter was submitted on behalf of individuals to the African Commission in October 1997 and soon thereafter declared admissible.[63] The communication concerned William Steven Banda and John Lyson Chinula, political opposition figures who were forcibly deported by the Zambian government to neighbouring Malawi. In April 1999, the African Commission found that the forcible deportation of the two men violated various provisions of the African Charter, including the right to freedom of expression and the right to free association. The African Commission also stated that their deportation was politically motivated. Despite this ruling by the African Commission, the Zambian government continued to deny William Banda the right to return to Zambia. Mr Chinula did not live to see the ruling. After the ruling, the Zambian government continued to use deportation or threat of deportation as a method of suppressing dissent.

(c) Cooperation with other monitoring bodies and the African Commission's special mechanisms

Amnesty International has also been observing sessions of the African Committee of Experts on the Rights and Welfare of the Child. This monitoring body was created by the African Charter on the Rights and Welfare of the Child adopted in 1990 which entered into force on 29 November 1999. The constitutive session of the Committee was held in April and May 2002. Furthermore, Amnesty International has been engaged with the special mechanisms of the African Commission, including the Special Rapporteur on the Rights of Women in Africa and the Special Rapporteur on Prison Conditions.

4. CONCLUSION

In four decades of its existence, Amnesty International has developed elaborate relationships with many of the international courts and compliance bodies. It maintains relationship with mechanisms under the auspices of the United Nations and three major regional organizations, the Council of Europe, Organization of American States and African Union. Amnesty International notes the potential within a fourth regional organization, the League of Arab States, for development of a similar relationship and, regrettably, the lack of such regional mechanisms in Asia.

---

[62] Final Communiqué of the 23rd Ordinary Session of the African Commission on Human and Peoples' Rights, Banjul, Gambia, 20–29 April 1998, para. 9.

[63] *Amnesty International v Zambia*, Communication No. 212/98.

When Amnesty International is granted permission to submit its comments on questions of facts, especially on general situations in respective countries, the organization submits as enclosures some of its most important reports relating to the issue. Also, in cases when its comments are on questions of law, the organization frequently refers to its factual findings in similar situations. Undoubtedly, Amnesty International's worldwide and decades-long experience and research on human rights violations gives it the expertise and additional credibility when presenting legal arguments.

Third party interventions and *amicus curiae* submissions are filed on behalf of the entire movement and are approved by the International Secretariat, the organization's headquarters. Interventions in international court proceedings are not filed by individual Amnesty International groups, structures or sections because they could raise questions in the minds of the judges about whether the view presented in the intervention was really the considered view of the movement. The same rules apply with regard to third party interventions and *amicus curiae* submissions before national courts.

Amnesty International's policy on the scope of participation in the proceedings of international tribunals and courts, regional courts and treaty-monitoring bodies is currently undergoing a process of review. However, it is likely that the organization will continue to limit its litigation role in courts to third party interventions and *amicus curiae* submissions designed to develop international law and standards and its involvement in treaty body complaint mechanisms to asking treaty bodies to address general situations.

There are a number of reasons for continuing to maintain a limited role. First, are the resource constraints. Depending on the profile and complexity of the case and the strategy Amnesty International follows, active participation in a single case of an international tribunal or court may require significant investment in terms of staff time and priorities' reallocation. Litigating even a single case can be extremely costly and can risk in certain jurisdictions having court costs and legal fees of the other parties awarded against the organization. Monitoring which cases represent significant opportunities to develop law and standards is ambitious enough, let alone drafting expert third party interventions and *amicus curiae* submissions within tight deadlines. This is especially the case with those mechanisms with a higher caseload, such as the ECHR. Secondly, the organization does not want to put its researchers on the stand where they might be compelled to reveal confidential sources and working methods. Current international law on the protection of journalists' confidential sources is unsatisfactory and the extent to which international or national courts would protect such information has yet to be tested.

There are other concerns which also have to be taken into account when deciding to take a more proactive role *vis-à-vis* international tribunals and courts, such as increasing the risks to the organization's researchers in the field where they might be seen by perpetrators as a danger to them, the need for completely different working methods and the need to hire new lawyers with extensive litigation experience in civil and common law jurisdictions.

Until these concerns are addressed, Amnesty International is likely to continue to focus on third party or *amicus curiae* submissions on the definition, interpretation and implementation of international law and standards in the proceedings of international tribunals and courts and treaty-monitoring bodies, which are likely to have a far greater impact on the development of international law than the representation of individual victims in a handful of cases.

Chapter 2

The Experience of the AIRE Centre in Litigating before the European Court of Human Rights

Catharina Harby

1. INTRODUCTION

The AIRE Centre is a small non-governmental organization based in London, United Kingdom. The Centre was set up 10 years ago, and we were celebrating our 10-year anniversary in November last year with a two-day seminar.[1] At this seminar we discussed various topics that the AIRE Centre has been involved in over the last 10 years, including 'The free movement of persons into and within the EU' and 'Human rights in Central and Eastern Europe'. A substantial amount of time, however, was allocated to the subject 'Litigation before the European Court of Human Rights: past, present and future'. It is our involvement in taking cases to the European Court of Human Rights (ECHR) in Strasbourg that I will be focusing on in this chapter. I will be looking particularly at the *practical* rather than theoretical problems a small NGO such as the AIRE Centre might encounter in its work.

2. RESOURCES

The AIRE Centre was set up specifically to assist individuals to obtain the rights they are guaranteed by international agreements but that they have not been accorded by their national authorities. Our greatest expertise lies in our knowledge of the European Convention on Human Rights and Fundamental Freedoms 1950 ('the European Convention') and litigation before the ECHR. Up until today we have been involved in taking over 60 cases, either as the representative on the record with full conduct of all aspects of the case, or as part of a legal team, against 11 different jurisdictions within the Council of Europe. Sometimes we have simply advised on some point of procedure and practice before the ECHR, and other times helped counsel to draft the speech for an oral hearing. We have accumulated a vast experience in litigating before the Strasbourg Court, and

---

[1] For more information on the AIRE Centre, see <www.airecentre.org>.

T. Treves et al., eds., Civil Society, International Courts and Compliance Bodies
© *2005, T·M·C·ASSER PRESS, The Hague, The Netherlands, and the Authors*

members of the AIRE Centre, especially our Director Nuala Mole, have written a
number of books on the subject.[2] We are also often called upon by the Council of
Europe and other international organizations to provide training on the subject all
throughout Europe but especially in the Russian Federation and the former Yugoslavia.

When the AIRE Centre was set up in 1993 our assets consisted of one chair,
one desk and a laptop computer in a room in our Director's house. We were
kindly given access to a library by an academic institute in London, the British
Institute of International and Comparative Law. If we had not been allowed this,
it would have been impossible for the Centre to function. One of the biggest
problems at this time was definitely the lack of resources. It took time to obtain
up-to-date material on new case law and other developments at the ECHR.

Today, the situation is very different thanks to the Internet. Press releases and
judgments are posted on the ECHR's website[3] the same day as they are handed
down. You can access new information immediately. The Internet has become
such an integral part of our daily working life and is one of our most important
resources – it is almost difficult to remember what it was like to work without it!

However, even if we can now access new case law from the ECHR immediately one problem remains – language. The official languages of the Court are
French and English. Many judgments only exist in one of these languages. In our
office we have staff members who speak both these languages, but this is not the
case everywhere. In the regions where we organize seminars there are many very
talented and bright lawyers with a keen interest in human rights law, and who
would like to represent clients before the ECHR, who speak neither English nor
French.

The Council of Europe has produced a number of publications, e.g., in Russian and Bosnian containing translation of key judgments. It is still, however, difficult to find up-to-date information on the newest developments at the ECHR in
any other languages than English and French. With this in mind, the AIRE Centre
started producing our own monthly Legal Bulletin over four years ago. This Bulletin contains summaries with explanatory comments of the most recent decisions
of the ECHR. We focus our reporting on cases which we consider are the most
relevant to the countries where it is distributed. The Bulletin is currently produced in Serbian, Albanian, Polish and Romanian and we are looking to expand
the publication. The Bulletin is sent to judges, lawyers and NGOs, many of
whom have also attended AIRE Centre seminars.

3. TAKING CASES TO STRASBOURG

Most of the cases which the AIRE Centre has been involved in have been suc-

---

[2] See, e.g., N. Mole, L. Clements and A. Simmons, *European Human Rights: Taking a Case
Under the Convention* (2nd edn., London, 1999).

[3] See the ECHR's website <www.echr.coe.int>.

cessful – the ECHR has declared at least part of the application admissible and found one or more violations of the European Convention. This is not only due to skilled litigation – it is important to be sure whether to take on a case in the first place. We are often asked how we choose the cases which we litigate. You could say that the answer is: we do not. The AIRE Centre takes up *any* case which is brought to us if we are satisfied:

- that the person's rights under the European Convention have been violated;
- that the case meets the admissibility criteria;
- that the documentation is in a language that we speak or we have access to competent free translation or the national lawyer that we work with is a reliable partner and speaks a language we speak.

Identifying arguable cases is not an easy task. Sometimes we can see that what happened was unfair but cannot quite see how to shape this into an argument that the European Convention has been violated. Sometimes, sadly, cases with clear violations of human rights have to be rejected: as mentioned above, the admissibility criteria such as the six months' time limit have not been met.

If we are satisfied that these conditions have been met we will start the often long process of litigating the case before the European Court of Human Rights. This consists of mainly two stages – admissibility and merits. If the case is declared admissible and a judgment on the merits is obtained, this is a process that takes many years. I will briefly discuss the problem of the caseload facing the ECHR towards the end of this chapter.

All through this process, the representative of the applicant will never actually be in direct contact with the judges of the Court but with the Registry. The Registry is staffed by highly skilled lawyers from throughout the Council of Europe. We have during the past 10 years become extremely impressed with their knowledge of substantive and procedural aspects of the European Convention and the work of the ECHR, and their dedicated commitment to justice and human rights.

When we speak at seminars training lawyers how to take cases to Strasbourg, we always stress how important it is to maintain a good relationship with the lawyers at the Registry. Although the Registry lawyers are naturally not there to act as your legal advisers, they will be able to help you by e.g. clarifying Court procedures and updating you on the latest developments in your case.

4. Costs of Litigating

I would like to refer back to section 2 on resources before I move on to discuss the proposals to reform the ECHR.

Just as it is problematic for a small organization like the AIRE Centre that represents individuals before the Court to find money for resources such as books, another problem is of course costs directly related to the litigation.

Even though the AIRE Centre does not actually 'means test' clients who would like us to represent them, they do not generally have any financial assets. It is our policy not to ask the client to pay for our services whilst the case is ongoing. If we win the case and the ECHR finds a violation, we will ask the Court to order the government to pay for our costs and expenses.[4]

Legal aid is available from the Council of Europe, but not in the initial stage of the complaint process. Legal aid can be applied for after a case has been 'communicated' to the respondent government and their observations have been received.[5] This means that the case has not been declared immediately inadmissible and has been sent to the government for their comments, and these have been returned to the ECHR.

Even if legal aid is granted, it is highly unlikely to cover the actual costs of litigation, at least in Western Europe. For example, the average legal aid for the preparation of a case is € 330. It is not unusual for this to take approximately 70 lawyer hours. By comparison, the legal aid rate in the United Kingdom (which is often criticised for being too low) varies between £35/hours and £80/hour depending on the case.

The costs and expenses you might receive if you win the case also rarely cover the real costs of litigating. On a few occasions we have divided the amount awarded to us at the end of a case with the number of hours we have spent working on it. It has then become clear that we were paid significantly less than the minimum wage in the United Kingdom!

5.   PROPOSALS TO REFORM THE EUROPEAN COURT OF HUMAN RIGHTS

I will now briefly outline some of the problems facing the ECHR and therefore the individuals who apply to the Court and the lawyers who represent them.

This year it is 50 years since the European Convention entered into force. At that time, 10 countries had signed and ratified the Convention. Today the number is 45, with Serbia and Montenegro as the most recent member of the Council of Europe.[6] It is mainly in the last 10 years that the number of member states has expanded so rapidly, as many Central and Eastern European countries are now members. This has, of course, had a major impact on the work load of the ECHR.

Initially, cases were processed by the European Commission of Human Rights, through first an admissibility stage and then a merits stage. Only then could cases proceed to the ECHR for a decision. In the 1980s, various proposals were discussed to simplify the procedure.

In November 1998, the 11th Protocol to the European Convention was brought into effect abolishing the two-tier system of a Commission and a Court.

---

[4] In accordance with Article 41 of the European Convention.
[5] Rule 91 of the Rules of the Court.
[6] Serbia and Montenegro ratified the European Convention on 3 March 2004.

Instead a single full-time permanent Court was created. Persons wishing to apply under the European Convention now do so directly to the ECHR. However, it has become apparent that the 11th Protocol is not sufficient for the Court to manage the ever-increasing flow of cases. New proposals to reform the work of the ECHR are therefore discussed at present.

In April last year the Steering Committee for Human Rights (CDDH) presented its final report with proposals for reform of the working procedures of the ECHR.[7] This was divided into three sections: (A) preventing violations at national level and improving domestic remedies, (B) optimising the effectiveness of the filtering and subsequent processing of applications and (C) improving and accelerating execution of judgments of the Court. I will here mention some of the proposals in (B) as I think they are most relevant for our discussions.

Two months after the CDDH had submitted its final report, the Council of Europe Committee of Ministers issued a declaration instructing the Ministers' Deputies to draft a new protocol to the European Convention to implement the CDDH's proposals. Another meeting to consult with (or inform) NGOs was held in February this year. The Committee of Ministers will meet again in May where they plan to take a decision with regard to the proposed amendments.

There are a number of very good proposals in the CDDH report from 2003. For example, a panel of three judges will now be able not only to declare cases inadmissible but also to declare them admissible and give a judgment on the merits. This is only possible in so called 'clone' cases – repetitive cases – other cases will still be decided by a Chamber of seven judges. The proposal that the AIRE Centre and many other NGOs and legal practitioners are concerned about is the suggestion to tighten the admissibility criteria. This would make it more difficult for individuals to take their cases to Strasbourg than it already is. At the time of writing[8] it is still unclear what the exact wording will be that the Committee of Ministers will consider at their meeting in May. Various proposals that have been discussed, including that the ECHR will declare a case inadmissible:

- 'if the applicant has not suffered a significant disadvantage';
- 'if the case raises neither a serious question affecting the interpretation or application of the Convention...nor a serious issue of general importance';
- 'unless respect for human rights ... require an examination on the merits'.

We do recognize the problems that the ECHR is facing at the moment, and one of the most difficult things for us to explain to our clients is why the process of reaching a decision takes so long. However, we do not think that this is the appropriate way to tackle the situation. The ECHR's biggest problem is that over 90 per cent of all cases received are inadmissible already by applying the criteria used today. Making it more difficult to be declared admissible will not solve that

---

[7] CDDH(2003)006 Addendum final.
[8] 15 March 2004.

problem. On the contrary, it will simply mean that approximately 98 per cent of the cases received are inadmissible – but someone at the ECHR will still have to process them.

6. CONCLUSION

Let me point out that the AIRE Centre has in general had very good experiences from litigating before the ECHR. The biggest problems as we see them, as a small NGO, is the long time it takes before the individuals in question can receive a decision in their case, and the 'inequality of arms' in resources between the applicant and the government.

Chapter 3

NGOs and the Inter-American Court of Human Rights

Mónica Pinto

1. INTRODUCTION

This chapter will consider the relationship between non-governmental organizations (NGOs) and the Inter-American Court of Human Rights ('the Inter-American Court'). In so doing, I will deal with the links between NGOs and civil society. For systemic reasons, I will refer to the whole Inter-American System of Human Rights, even when focusing on the effects *vis-à-vis* the Court. In fact, because of history and of legal regulations, the Inter-American Commission of Human Rights is the organ that feeds the docket of the Inter-American Court of Human Rights.

2. CIVIL SOCIETY, NGOS AND HUMAN RIGHTS

Links exist between human rights and civil society. Through the concept of human rights, individuals – i.e., non-state actors – are the addressees of international legal rules and states become responsible for breach of the obligations arising from those international legal rules. Because of the notion of human rights, governments have to pay attention to standards, whether legal or not, in force in civil society. The levels of tolerance of civil (and democratic) society is one of the criteria for permissible restriction of human rights.

Although reference to 'civil society' is frequent in this field, there is no generally accepted definition for this concept. The term 'civil society' has been described so broadly as to encompass all non-state sectors – some would say 'society' as opposed to the formal structure of the state.[1]

In the words of the Commission on Global Governance, civil society covers 'a multitude of institutions, voluntary associations, and networks – women's groups, trade unions, chambers of commerce, farming or housing cooperatives, neighborhood watch associations, religion-based organizations, and so on'.[2]

---

[1] H.J. Steiner and P. Alston, *International Human Rights in Context: Law, Politics, Morals* (Clarendon Press, Oxford, 1996), p. 470.

[2] Commission on Global Governance, *Our Global Neighborhood: The Report of the Commission on Global Governance* (Oxford, 1995), p. 32.

T. Treves et al., eds., Civil Society, International Courts and Compliance Bodies
© 2005, T·M·C·ASSER PRESS, *The Hague, The Netherlands, and the Authors*

Non-governmental organizations are established within civil society; they are composed by its members and are deemed to be concerned with the welfare of civil society.

Those dealing with human rights are supposed to bring with them the views of civil society. Even when there seems to be a trend towards considering them as the whole civil society, because of a sort of inexplicable metonymy, they are the formal organized manifestation of a certain part of it, namely the human rights movement. It is clear that these NGOs reflect some specific perspective of civil society about what human rights are.

As stated by Alston and Steiner, the subsets of NGOs that are involved with human rights issues are 'a category that can have porous boundaries'.[3] They may be located in the group of NGOs of general public interest.

When international society became institutionalized through the United Nations, it defined certain purposes, certain matters of common (international) interest, among them human rights and fundamental freedoms for all without discrimination. In so doing, the scope of international objects was widened and room was made for (certain) NGOs to exercise civil society's representation.

Accordingly, the UN Charter assigns a role to non-governmental organizations concerned with matters within the competence of the Economic and Social Council: they can be bound through suitable arrangements for consultation.[4] This consultative status is, therefore, the recognition of a privileged relationship that allows them to participate in the developments related to human rights[5] and to become a vital strand in the rope that pulls human rights forward.[6]

In 1993, the World Conference on Human Rights recognized the important role of NGOs in the promotion of all human rights and:

> appreciate(d) their contribution to increasing public awareness of human rights issues, to the conduct of education, training and research in this field, and to the promotion and protection of all human rights and fundamental freedoms. While recognizing that the primary responsibility for standard setting lies with States, the conference also appreciates the contribution of non-governmental organizations to this process. In this respect, the World Conference on Human Rights emphasizes the importance of contin-

---

[3] Steiner and Alston, n. 1 above, at p. 459.

[4] Article 71: 'The Economic and Social Council may make suitable arrangements for consultation with non-governmental organizations which are concerned with matters within its competence. Such arrangements may be made with international organizations and, where appropriate, with national organizations after consultation with the Member of the United Nations concerned'. For the action of NGOs in the UN, see S. Guillet, *Nous, Peuples des Nations Unies* (Montchristien, Paris, 1995).

[5] M. Bettati and P.-M. Dupuy, *Les ONG et le Droit International* (Economica, Paris, 1986), p. 16.

[6] D. Cassel, 'Does International Human Rights Law Make a Difference?' (2001) 2 *Chicago J. Int'l L.* 121.

ued dialogue and cooperation between Governments and non-governmental organizations.[7]

3.   HUMAN RIGHTS NGOS AND THE VICTIMS

In the Americas, NGOs are the product of specific civil and political struggle and most of them have emerged as the human rights movement evolved. The authoritarian regimes that periodically used to take office in Latin American countries, especially in the 1970s and 1980s, led to the gathering of the victims and their relatives, and so to the creation and establishment of a full set of NGOs related to them, namely, the *movimiento de familiares* (Relatives Movement), *coordinadora de viudas* (Widows' Coordinating Committee), *madres* (Mothers), *abuelas* (Grandmothers), *hijos* (sons) and others. The idea lying behind them is that the gathering strengthens the legitimacy of the struggle against dictatorship and policies of gross and systematic violation of human rights.

A small group of other NGOs organized with a view to provide certain services, including legal counselling and assistance for presentations to international organizations.

Founded in 1979 to foster and protect human rights and to strengthen the democratic system and the rule of law in Argentina, through the litigation of judicial cases, the Center for Legal and Social Studies (CELS) aims to denounce violations of human rights, to influence the process of expression of public policies based on respect for fundamental rights and to promote the widest practice of these rights for the most vulnerable classes of society.[8]

The Andean Commission of Jurists is an international non-profit organization that develops its activities through six Andean countries, namely Bolivia, Colombia, Chile, Ecuador, Peru and Venezuela. It provides the region with legal services in the public interest. Its mission is to contribute to the strengthening of the rule of law and democratic institutions and respect for human rights. It was founded in 1982 and its headquarters are in Lima, Peru.[9] It is a branch of the International Commission of Jurists, based in Geneva. In 1988, an affiliate was established in Bogotá, Colombia – the Colombian Commission of Jurists.[10]

Other NGOs directed their action to public protest and channelled their efforts into the formation of public opinion through massive campaigns and other means.

The Permanent Assemblies of Human Rights in different countries provide a pluralistic political umbrella for protest and demonstration. The Permanent Assembly for Human Rights founded in Argentina in 1975 defines itself as a civil association with a broad composition that works for the consolidation of

---

[7] Vienna Declaration and Program of Action, World Conference on Human Rights, Vienna, 14-25 June 1993, A/CONF.157/23, para. 38.

[8] <www.cels.org.ar/english>.

[9] <www.cajpe.org.pe/english>.

[10] <www.nd.edu/kellogg/ccj.html>.

democracy through respect for human rights as embodied in the International Charter of Human Rights, through the creation of fields suitable for pluralistic co-operation so as to strengthen respect for and consolidate human rights.[11] In Bolivia, this institution pursues the same goals.[12]

By the end of the 1970s, local action was not enough in the struggle for human rights. Accordingly, NGOs decided to initiate international advocacy in certain areas. Human Rights Watch, which started in 1978 as Helsinki Watch, set up Americas Watch in the 1980s 'to counter the notion that human rights abuses by one side in the war in Central America were somehow more tolerable than abuses by the other side'. The organization grew to cover other regions of the world, until all the 'Watch' committees were united in 1988 to form Human Rights Watch.[13]

In 1991, a group of human rights defenders in Latin America and the Caribbean who had developed a certain practice in the Inter-American System founded the Center for Justice and International Law (CEJIL) as a non-governmental organization with a view to achieve the full implementation of international human rights norms in the member states of the Organization of American States (OAS) through the use of the Inter-American System for the Protection of Human Rights and other international protection mechanisms.[14]

Notwithstanding the number and diversity of NGOs in the region, it should be noted that nearly all of them have been established by victims or because of the victims and focusing on their own interests. Later, they developed a public interest agenda. However, their action expresses a reconciliation of the victim's interest with their public interest.

4.   NGOs' Legal Standing in the Petition and Judicial Contexts

NGOs have been present in the Inter-American System from its very beginning. The great majority of complaints registered with the Inter-American Commission on Human Rights ('the Inter-American Commission') are lodged by NGOs acting as petitioners. Both during proceedings at the headquarters of the Commission and when cases are transferred to the Inter-American Court, local NGOs seek the assistance of international institutions, based in the USA, with well-known expertise in order to manage the hearings with the Commission, and to appear before the Court.

Shortly after its establishment in 1959, because of a decision of the Consultative Meeting of Ministers on Foreign Relations, the Inter-American Commission was given the competence to handle communications containing denunciations or

---

[11] <www.apdh.com.ar>.
[12] <www.entelnet.bo/apdhdb>.
[13] <www.hrw.org/abou/whoweare.html>.
[14] <www.cejil.org/main>.

complaints of violation of human rights in the American states. The Rules of the Commission in force from 2 May 1967 stated in Article 38(2) that associations could lodge communications.

During the time that this formula became written law, was implemented and enforced, Article 44 of the American Convention on Human Rights was being drafted. Both provisions enshrined the same idea, namely that NGOs were allowed to be petitioners before the Inter-American Commission. Accordingly, the American Convention states:

> Any person or group of persons, or any non-governmental entity legally recognized in one or more member states of the Organization, may lodge petitions with the Commission containing denunciations or complaints of violation of this Convention by the State Party.

Urgent situations required rapid and pragmatic responses; this policy reached NGOs.[15] The possibility to lodge a complaint with the Inter-American Commission was given to these institutions as a means of providing assurances and safety guarantees to the victims. Accordingly, the only formal requisite to be satisfied is that the entity be recognized by one or more member states of the OAS. In fact, the Commission's practice considers certain associations as 'groups of persons',[16] so as to avoid any questioning by the state concerned in the complaint.

Such a policy dilutes the features of NGOs and downgrades their profile with a view to preserving their capabilities as petitioners. This policy also explains the silence of the Inter-American Commission on the scope of the concept.

No matter what is the role actually played by NGOs in the proceedings in the Inter-American System, the victim and the petitioner are different actors. Furthermore, the victim does not need to participate in the whole proceedings even when their existence is a *conditio sine qua non*. Notwithstanding the wording of the Rules, over the years, the Inter-American Commission has changed its approach towards this issue.

Early in the 1980s, the Inter-American Commission considered a case known as *Baby Boy*. It accepted a petition filed by an NGO, Catholics for Christian Political Action, seeking a decision outlawing the judicial authorization for an abortion carried out on a 17-year-old, unmarried woman, she and her mother having requested an abortion and consented to the operation. The medical doctor who intervened was accused of manslaughter for his conduct in connection with the operation but on 17 December 1976, the Supreme Judicial Court of Massachusetts acquitted him.

---

[15] I developed this idea in 'Sistema Interamericano de Derechos Humanos: Respuesta Normativa a la Urgencia' in *Compilación de Trabajos Académicos del Curso Interdisciplinario en Derechos Humanos (1983-1987)* (Instituto Interamericano de Derechos Humanos, San José, 1989), pp. 119–156.

[16] E. Vargas Carreño, 'Algunos Problemas que Presentan la Aplicación y la Interpretación de la Convención Americana sobre Derechos Humanos' in *La Convencion Americana sobre Derechos Humanos* (OEA, Washington, 1980), pp. 149–169, at 159.

Even when it was evident that the NGO did not represent the victim and that the mother of 'Baby Boy' and her parents consented to the abortion, the Inter-American Commission accepted the legitimacy of Catholics for Christian Political Action acting in the case[17] and required no link between them.

The decision adopted in *Baby Boy* allowed a reading of the intervention of NGOs according to which they express the views of a certain sector of civil society, with vested interests in a matter of public policy. This practice did not last long.

In the mid-1990s, the Inter-American Commission held that:

> The liberal standing requirement of the inter-American system should not be interpreted, however, to mean that a case can be presented before the Commission *in abstracto*. An individual cannot institute an *actio popularis* and present a complaint against a law without establishing some active legitimation justifying his standing before the Commission. The *applicant must claim to be a victim of a violation of the Convention, or must appear before the Commission as a representative of a putative victim of a violation of the Convention by a state party.* It is not sufficient for an applicant to claim that the mere existence of a law violates her rights under the American Convention, it is necessary that the law have been applied to her detriment. If the applicant fails to establish active legitimation, the Commission must declare its incompetence *ratione personae* to consider the matter.[18]

This ruling means that when acting as petitioners, NGOs are deemed to be representatives of the victims not of a global civil society. In such cases, it has to be assumed that the victim's interest has become a public interest.

In the proceedings before the Inter-American Court, there are some differences. According to Articles 21 to 23 of the Rules of Procedure of the Inter-American Court of Human Rights, only states who have accepted its jurisdiction and the Inter-American Commission have legal standing before the Court; the victims, their next of kin or their duly accredited representative may participate in the proceedings, submitting requests, arguments and evidence autonomously. This means that NGOs' role is to act as the victim's representatives. In the Honduran cases, Juan Mendez and José Miguel Vivanco, on behalf of Americas Watch and CEJIL, gained the first and very valuable experience in this role.[19]

In the framework of legal definitions that the Inter-American Commission has been drafting in the last six or seven years, is included the scope of the term 'non-governmental entity' in the context of Article 44 of the American Convention. The Commission considered 'that private juridical persons [could] be assimilated to the notion of non-governmental entity legally recognized' and, therefore, could

---

[17] Case No. 2141, *Annual Report of the Inter-American Commission of Human Rights 1980-1981* (OEA/Ser.L/V/II.54 Doc 9 rev. 1).

[18] Report No. 48/96, Case No. 11.553, *Annual Report of the Inter-American Commission of Human Rights 1996* (OEA/Ser.L/V/I/II.95 doc.7 rev.), paras. 27–28 (emphasis added).

[19] J. Méndez and J.M. Vivanco, 'Disappearances and the Inter-American Court: Reflections on a Litigation Experience' (1990) 13 *Ham L. Rev.* 507.

act as petitioners.[20] It decided, accordingly, that a corporation had standing to lodge a petition on its own.

Whether this is a legal strategy so as to have a wider field of petitions and whether it means that the concept of NGO in the System is not restricted to the ordinary non-governmental, non-profit institution of general public interest remains open.

By contrast, the Inter-American Commission has taken no position towards complaints lodged by legal persons of a public character such as the Bar of the City of Buenos Aires.[21]

5. NGOs AND STANDARD SETTING

International NGOs have developed a full range of strategies in standard setting. In all of the 18 advisory opinions rendered by the Inter-American Court, the main international non-governmental organizations have influenced the proceedings through *amici curiae* briefs.

International Human Rights Law Group, the Lawyers Committee for International Human Rights, the Washington Office for Latin America, the Americas branch of Human Rights Watch and the Center for Justice and International Law have expressed their views in nearly all the proceedings.

NGOs working in very specific fields or with limited mandates, such as the Inter-American Press Association or Death Penalty Focus of California, as well as the Human Rights Institutes of different universities (e.g., Urban Morgan Institute for Human Rights of the University of Cincinnati College of Law, the Institute for Human Rights of the International Legal Studies Program at the University of Denver College of Law, the International Human Rights Law Institute of Depaul University College of Law, the Harvard Immigration and Refugee Clinic of Greater Boston Legal Services, the Harvard Law School, the Working Group on Human Rights in the Americas of Harvard and Boston College Law Schools, the Facultad de Derecho de la Universidad Nacional Autónoma de México (UNAM), the Clínicas Jurídicas del Colegio de Jurisprudencia de la Universidad San Francisco de Quito) have expressed their views on different occasions.

The issue at stake here is, again, the criteria for participation. The Inter-American System has adopted a very broad standard in defining who can apply as an *amicus curiae*. In fact, the only legal rule on the subject is a provision contained in Article 63.2 of the Rules of the Inter-American Court stating, 'The President

---

[20] Report No. 39/99, Mevopal S.A., *Annual Report of the Inter-American Commission of Human Rights 1998*, vol. I (OEA/Ser.L/V/I/II.102 doc.6 rev.), para. 12.

[21] Report No. 22/00, Case No. 11.709, *Annual Report of the Inter-American Commission of Human Rights 1999*, vol. I (OEA/Ser.L/V/I/II.106 doc.3 rev.), p. 135, para. 23. It should be noted that in its report on Cases Nos. 9777 and 9781, the Inter-American Commission acknowledged the public nature of the legal personality of the Bar of the City of Buenos Aires.

may invite or authorize any interested party to submit a written opinion on the issues covered by the request. If the request is governed by Article 64(2) of the Convention, he may do so after consulting with the Agent'.

Because of this open clause, the Inter-American Court decided to use the broad definition adopted by the Inter-American Commission, i.e., one that included business NGOs and corporations.

This has meant that different mass media have expressed their views and protected their own interests when the Inter-American Court has had to deal with the enforceability of the right to reply or correction, e.g., the *Miami Herald*, *Newsweek*, *USA Today*, the *Wall Street Journal* and the *International Herald Tribune*.[22]

It is hard to believe that these important corporations were in fact 'the friends of the Court' and not the advocates of their own interests. Even when this concept may be useful in order to allow NGOs and other private associations to become petitioners – i.e., one of the parties in the proceedings – it is not suitable to be applied to the *amicus curiae* – essentially, a third and neutral party in the proceedings.

It should be noted that in the context of the OAS, in December 1999, the Permanent Council adopted the Guidelines for the Participation of Civil Society Organizations in OAS Activities.[23] The idea is that after registering with the OAS, a civil society organization has the following responsibilities: (a) to answer inquiries from the organs, agencies and entities of the OAS and provide advisory services to them upon request; (b) to disseminate information on OAS activities to its members; (c) to present to the General Secretariat, before 31 December of each year, a report, containing an executive summary, on its participation in OAS activities during that year, its financial situation and sources of funding, and the activities planned for the coming year; (d) to keep the information on its executive officers up to date.

Standard setting is a field in which the contribution of human rights NGOs has been rich. They have assisted the Inter-American Court with their views about sensitive problems and they have appeared before it. In so doing, they have laid down important precedents. What should be kept in mind and in practice is that these organizations have to be in a position so as to be the Court's friends.

6.   NGOs AND THE IMPLEMENTATION OF THE SYSTEM'S LEGAL RESOURCES

It was because of the requirement set forth by the Committee to Protect Journalists that the Inter-American Commission asked the Inter-American Court to order

---

[22] Inter-American Court, Enforceability of the Right to Reply or Correction (Articles 14(1), 1(1) and 2 of the American Convention on Human Rights), Advisory Opinion OC-7/86, 29 August 1986, Series A No. 7.

[23] CP/RES 759 (1217/99).

provisional measures in the *Bustios-Rojas* case in favour of a journalist and the relatives of another one in Ayacucho, Peru. It was on 8 August 1990 that the Inter-American Court applied for the first time Article 63(2) of the American Convention providing that:

> [I]n cases of extreme gravity and urgency, and when necessary to avoid irreparable damage to persons, the Court shall adopt such provisional measures as it deems pertinent in matters it has under consideration. With respect to a case not yet submitted to the Court, it may act at the request of the Commission.

The whole story of provisional measures has been built on the initiative of petitioner NGOs. The first time the Inter-American Court ordered provisional measures relating to a human right other than the right to life or to integrity was in the case of Haitians and Haitian-origin Dominicans in the Dominican Republic in 2000.

The International Human Rights Law Clinic at American University, founded and headed by Richard Wilson, acted in two cases involving Ecuador. When dealing with *Suarez Rosero*, it was stated that there were three good reasons for the Clinical Program to be involved: that it was the first case against Ecuador, also the first case in which the victim could address the Court and that it was the first case that awarded fees to the victim's counsel. They worked together with CEJIL, which joined the delegation to the Inter-American Commission.

It is evident that personnel in NGOs are well trained and that they have the time and the initiative to explore new avenues. In so doing, they assist in the progressive development of international human rights law.

7. SOME PRELIMINARY CONCLUSIONS

NGOs head the human rights movement and evolve with it. In doing so, they pervade civil society and in certain instances are seen as its representatives. However, they only express a portion of that civil society, the one enrolled in the human rights movement.

NGOs play a large role in the context of international human rights systems. They make facts known, they act on behalf of the victims and they contribute to standard setting as well as to the enforcement of human rights.

In the Inter-American System of Human Rights, NGOs have precise functions to perform. From the beginning, they have acted as petitioners in cases lodged with the Inter-American Commission and have represented the victims in applications filed with the Inter-American Court. The broad scope of their action in the petition system was narrowed in the 1990s when the Inter-American Commission decided that NGOs had to credit their representation. In the proceedings before the Inter-American Court in contentious cases, they have always been the counsels of the victims.

International NGOs have worked hard in standard setting in the System and have assisted the Inter-American Court with their views on different matters. It should be kept in mind that during almost 10 years, the Inter-American Court was dedicated to its advisory competence for no applications were filed with it. In this period and afterwards, these organizations contributed significantly to the interpretation of the norms. Their personnel include academics as well as activists and that is reflected in their rich contribution.

The ambiguity of the Inter-American Court in the interpretation of the rules allowing *amicus curiae* briefs and its borrowing of a very flexible definition of a non-governmental entity adopted by the Inter-American Commission in order to ensure the greatest access to the petition system, has led to corporations with vested interests in the matters to be decided by the Court being able to convey their views to the Court through documents improperly called *amicus curiae* briefs.

NGOs have a good knowledge of the System and they have accordingly made a meaningful contribution to the development of its legal resources. Provisional measures are only one example of the developments initiated with their help.

It follows that NGOs had and still have a large role to play in the Inter-American System of Human Rights. Their participation should be encouraged in a plural arena where they can reinforce the petitioner's position, promote protection and foster the ideals of dignity and freedom for people all over the world.

It is true that every system develops as its own world and that it is not universally possible to transpose experiences, but some lessons are available from the Inter-American System of Human Rights relating to the participation of NGOs that can benefit other mechanisms.

Chapter 4

NGOs before the European Court of Human Rights: Beyond *Amicus Curiae* Participation?

Marco Frigessi di Rattalma

1. NGOs' *AMICUS CURIAE* PARTICIPATION BEFORE THE EUROPEAN COURT OF HUMAN RIGHTS

This chapter examines if the participation of non-governmental organizations (NGOs) in the proceedings before the European Court of Human Rights (ECHR), which at present may only take the form of *amici curiae* participation, should become more prominent through the attribution of a *locus standi* to NGOs who may thus propose an *actio popularis*.

It is well known that an *amicus curiae*[1] is a person or an organization with an interest in or views on the subject matter of a case who, without being a party, petitions the ECHR for permission to file a brief suggesting matters of fact and of law in order to propose a decision consistent with its own views.

The interest of an *amicus* tends to be of a general nature, such as the desire to promote public interests.

---

[1] On *amicus curiae* and on the role of NGOs in international litigation see H. Ascensio, 'L'amicus curiae devant les jurisdictions internationals' (2001) 5 *Rèv. Gèn. Dr. Int. Pub.* 897; Y. Beigbeder, *Le role international des organisations non gouvernementales* (Bruxelles/Paris, 1992); M. Bettati and P.-M. Dupuy, *Les O.N.G. et le droit international* (Paris, 1986); C. Chinkin, *Third Parties in International Law* (Oxford, 1993), p. 120 *et seq.*; A.K. Lindblom, *The Legal Status of NGOs in International Law* (Uppsala University, 2002), p. 280 *et seq.*; P. Mavroidis, *Amicus Curiae Briefs Before the WTO: Much Ado About Nothing* (Harvard, Jean Monnet Working Paper 2/2001); F. Orrego Vicuna, 'Individual and Non-State Entities Before International Courts and Tribunals' (2001) 5 *Max Planck YB UN L.* 53; J. Razzaque, 'Changing Role of Friends of the Court in the International Courts and Tribunals' (2001) 1 *Non-State Actors & Int'l L.* 169; D. Shelton, 'The Participation of Nongovernmental Organizations in International Judicial Proceedings' (1994) 88 *Am. J. Int'l L.* 611; more specifically on the role of NGOs before the European Court of Human Rights, see O. De Schutter, 'Sur l'èmergence de la sociéte civile en droit international: le rôle des associations devant la Cour Européenne des droits de l'homme' (1996) 7 *Eur. J. Int'l L.* 372; A. Lester, 'Amici Curiae: Third Party Intervention before the ECHR' in F. Matscher and H. Petzold (eds.), *Protecting Human Rights: The European Dimension* (Cologne, 1988); E. Bergamini, 'L'intervento amicus curiae: recenti evoluzioni di uno strumento di common law fra Unione europea e Corte europea dei diritti dell'uomo', (2003) 42 *Dir. Com. Sc. Int.*, 181 *et seq.*

T. Treves et al., eds., Civil Society, International Courts and Compliance Bodies
© 2005, T·M·C·ASSER PRESS, *The Hague, The Netherlands, and the Authors*

The European Convention on Human Rights and Fundamental Freedoms of 1950[2] ('the European Convention'), by providing that 'the President of the Court may in the interest of the proper administration of justice invite ... any person concerned who is not a party to the proceedings to submit written comments or take part in hearings'[3] is open to the participation of *amici curiae* in its proceedings.

Amicus curiae intervention by NGOs seeks five main objectives:

- to reinforce the position of individual applicants by giving external and objective support to the arguments invoked;
- to put forward common interests that are not represented by the individual applicant;
- to contribute to the development of international law as far as possible;
- to promote fund-raising;
- to raise the attention of public opinion.

Intervention by NGOs as *amici curiae* has sometimes achieved relevant goals. One notable example is *Soering v United Kingdom*, decided by the ECHR in 1989.[4] In this case, the USA sought extradition of a German national from the United Kingdom. Soering had been charged with murder, and if convicted, faced the death penalty. With the active involvement of Amnesty International in the

---

[2] On the European Convention on Human Rights see S. Bartole, B. Conforti and G. Raimondi, *Commentario alla Convenzione europea per la tutela dei diritti dell'uomo e delle libertà fondamentali* (Padova, 2001); I. Cameron, *An Introduction to the European Convention of Human Rights* (Uppsala, 1999); G. Cohen-Jonathan, *La Convention européenne des droits de l'homme* (2nd edn., Paris, 1989); M. De Salvia, *La Convenzione europea dei diritti dell'uomo – Procedure e contenuti* (3rd edn., Napoli, 2001); K. De Vey Mestdagh, 'Reform of the European Convention on Human Rights in a Changing Europe' in R. Lawson and M. De Blois (eds.), *The Dynamics of the Protection of Human Rights in Europe: Essays in Honour of Henry G. Schermers* (Dordrecht, 1994), pp. 337-360; M. Delmas-Marty (ed.), *The European Convention for the Protection of Human Rights: International Protection Versus National Restrictions* (Dordrecht, 1992); M.A. Eissen, 'Convention Européenne des Droits de l'homme et Pacte des Nations Unies relatif aux droits civils et politiques: problèmes de "coexistence"' (1970) 30 *ZaöRV* 237; J.A. Frowein and W. Peukert, *Europaische Menschenrechtskonvention, Kommentar* (Kehl, 1997); D. Gomien, D. Harris and L. Zwaak, *Law and Practice of the European Convention on Human Rights and the European Social Charter* (Strasbourg, 1996); E. Konstantinov, *The Reform of the Control Mechanism of the European Convention for the Protection of Human Rights and Fundamental Freedoms: The New Permanent European Court of Human Rights* (Sofia, 1997); R. St. J. Macdonald, F. Matscher and H. Petzold (eds.), *The European System for the Protection of Human Rights* (Dordrecht/Boston/London, 1993); L. Pettiti, E. Decaux and P.H. Imbert (eds.), *La Convention européenne des droits de l'homme – Commentaire article par article* (2nd edn., Paris, 1999); P. Van Dijk and G.J.H. Van Hoof, *Theory and Practice of the European Convention on Human Rights* (The Hague, 1998); J. Velu and R. Ergec, *Convention européenne des droits de l'homme* (Bruxelles, 1990); T. Zwart, *The Admissibility of Human Rights Petitions: The Case Law of the European Commission of Human Rights and the Human Rights Committee* (Dordrecht, 1994).

[3] See European Convention, Article 36(2).

[4] *Soering v United Kingdom*, judgment of 7 July 1989, 161 Ser. A.

case, which acted as *amicus curiae*, the ECHR was convinced that the 'death row phenomenon' constituted inhuman treatment in violation of the European Convention.

It is, however, a matter of fact regarding the ECHR that considering the high number of judgments delivered by the Court, *amicus curiae* submission is not frequent at all.

2. THE *LEX LATA*: NGOs HAVE NO GENERAL AUTHORITY TO ACT ON BEHALF OF ALLEGED VICTIMS

It might also be for this reason that the discussion among representatives of NGOs and of the academic world (and this happened also at the workshop of November 2002 in Fiesole)[5] has shifted from '*amicus curiae* participation' to the question 'Is there a need for NGOs' *locus standi* before the European Court of Human Rights?'.

It is interesting to note that, as the report of the Fiesole workshop shows, among NGOs there are different and even conflicting positions on the issue.

In favour of such an attribution, it has been said that some rights often have a collective dimension that individual application may not correctly represent or have the interest to raise. This means taking into serious consideration the possibility of giving NGOs a proper *locus standi* before international jurisdictions as far as general interests are concerned. NGOs would be the best suited to put forward the public interest as such through an *actio popularis*.[6]

Against the attribution of a *locus standi* to NGOs it has been said in the first place that the establishment of an *actio popularis* would reduce the scope of individual applications and would threaten the guarantee system provided for by the European Convention; secondly, there is concern that only those who have access to 'vocal' organizations would fully benefit from the new instrument; finally the workload of the ECHR would be increased and this would contribute to further increasing the length of the proceedings.[7]

In order to evaluate these two conflicting positions, one needs to have a clear picture of some basic features of the European Convention. It must especially be borne in mind that the Convention provides the so-called victim requirement, according to which an individual application will not be accepted if the applicant has not suffered personally from a violation of the Convention, nor if the complaint is brought by a non-state actor about the compatibility *in abstracto* of national legislation with the Convention.[8]

---

[5] See Workshop Report by E. Rebasti, *A Legal Status for NGOs in Contemporary International Law? A Contribution to the Debate on Non-State Actors and Public International Law at the Beginning of the Twenty-First Century, 15-16 November 2002* ('Workshop Report').

[6] O. De Schutter in Workshop Report, n. 5 above, at p. 9.

[7] See C. Harby in Workshop Report, n. 5 above, at p. 9.

[8] *Klass and others v Germany*, No. 5029/71, judgment of 6 September 1978, ECHR A28, pp. 17–18; *Marckx v Belgium*, No. 6833/74, judgment of 13 June 1979, ECHR A31. However, Van Dijk and Van Hoof, *Theory and Practice*, n. 2 above, at p. 47 note that the 'Commission has declared

It follows from the undisputed existence of the so-called victim requirement in order to make a valid claim before the ECHR[9] that there is general agreement among scholars that the European Convention does not allow for an *actio popularis*.[10]

In fact the Commission has held that, if the alleged breach of the Convention does not affect the rights of the applicant NGO, but the rights of a group of individuals, even if it is the group of individuals which the NGO represents and protects according to its own statute: 'The fact alone that the NGO considers itself as guardian of the collective interests of its members does not suffice to make it the victim within the meaning of the Convention'.[11]

It is thus clear that NGOs are not regarded as having any general authority to act on behalf of alleged victims within their field of competence. Accordingly, an NGO has a *locus standi* before the ECHR as claimant only if the organization itself is claiming to be a victim of a violation of the European Convention. Clearly, this means a strict limitation on the possibilities for NGOs to institute cases before the ECHR with the aim of broadening and strengthening international human rights standards.

3.   THE *LEGE FERENDA*: WOULD GRANTING AN *Actio Popularis* TO NGOS BE APPROPRIATE?

It is in the light of this legal background that the question has been raised whether the *lex lata* should be changed and whether the granting of a *locus standi* to NGOs before the ECHR would be appropriate *de lege ferenda*.

I will now discuss three different positions which emerged, even if they were only partial and hinted at, from the Fiesole workshop.

According to the first proposal, NGOs would be granted an unrestricted *locus standi* before the ECHR. This proposal is based on the assumption that NGOs would be the best suited to put forward 'public interest as such', 'collective interest' and 'collective rights' through an *actio popularis*.[12]

---

admissible individual applications which had a *partly* abstract character'. Reference is made to *Donnelly v United Kingdom*, Nos. 5577-5583/72, (1973) XVI Yearbook 212, at 260.

[9] *Ludi v Switzerland*, No. 12433/86, judgment of 15 June 1992, ECHR A238, p. 18; *De Jong, Baljet and Van den Brink v the Netherlands*, Nos. 8805/79; 8806/79 and 9242/81, judgment of 22 May 1984, ECHR A77, p. 20; *Van der Sluys, Zuiderveld and Klappe v the Netherlands*, Nos. 9362/81, 9363/81 and 9387/81, judgment of 22 May 1984, ECHR A78, p. 16; *Groppera Radio AG v Switzerland*, No. 10890/84, judgment of 28 March 1990, ECHR A173, p. 20.

[10] See H.C. Kruger and C.A. Norgaard, 'The Right of Application' in Macdonald, Matscher and Petzold (eds.), n. 2 above, at pp. 657, 663. Van Dijk and Van Hoof, n. 2 above, at p. 48 *et seq*. See, e.g., No. 7045/75, 19 December 1976, 7 DR 87.

[11] *Purcell v Ireland*, No. 15404/89, (1991) 70 DR 262, at 273.

[12] See O. De Schutter in Workshop Report, n. 5 above, at p. 9.

In my opinion this proposal is neither realistic nor appropriate. To explain the reasons for my disagreement, I have to recall another basic feature of the European Convention.

Under the Convention, a state may lodge a complaint (the so-called 'inter-state application') about violations committed against persons who are not its nationals or against persons who are not nationals of any of the contracting states or even about violations against nationals of the respondent state. Moreover, states may equally lodge a complaint about the incompatibility with the European Convention of national legislation or of an administrative practice of another state without having to allege a violation against any specified person: the so-called 'abstract applications'. Thus, the right of complaint for states assumes the character of an *actio popularis*: any contracting state has the right to lodge a complaint about any alleged violation of the Convention, regardless of whether there is a special relation between the rights and interests of the applicant state and the alleged violation.[13]

In the *Pfunders* case between Austria and Italy the European Commission stressed that a state which brings an application under Article 24 'is not to be regarded as exercising a right of action for the purpose of enforcing its own rights, but rather as bringing before the Commission an alleged violation of the public order of Europe'.[14]

It is well known that states have lodged very few of these inter-state applications and that this was one of the reasons leading to the provision of the individual right of complaint in order to ensure a higher degree of effectiveness to the European Convention.[15]

In any case, what is important to stress here is that the attribution of an unrestricted *actio popularis* to states can be defended with the argument that in the European reality, states are democratic entities representing – even if with imperfections and defects – their peoples.

It is thus clear that the discussion on the attribution of a *locus standi* to NGOs before international tribunals in general and human rights courts in particular is strictly connected to the question of the representativity of NGOs and, ultimately, to the debate reflected in international law journals – which has been harsh at times – on the 'legitimacy' of such organizations.

During this debate, it has been stated, on the one hand, that NGOs do not have a democratic legitimacy and that 'the glory of organizations of civil society is not democratic legitimacy, but the ability to be a pressure group'.[16] The NGOs do not represent the popular will or the general will and thus cannot be viewed as

---

[13] See Kruger and Norgaard, n. 10 above, at p. 660; *Ireland v United Kingdom*, judgment of 18 January 1978, 25 Ser. A, p. 91.

[14] Application No. 788/60, 11 January 1961, Yearbook 4, p. 140.

[15] Van Dijk and Van Hoof, n. 2 above, at p. 43.

[16] K. Anderson, 'The Ottawa Convention Banning Landmines: The Role of International Non-Governmental Organisations and the Idea of International Civil Society' (2000) 11 *Eur. J. Int'l L.* 91, at 118.

conveying the 'common good' or the 'general good'. In any case each single NGO represents particular issues and interests.

In a provocative way it has also been stated that:

> Human rights workers sometimes talk of their movement as an emblem of democracy. Yet it is possible to view it as an undemocratic pressure group, accountable to no one but its own members and donors with enormous power and influence.[17]

On the other hand, it has been said that 'to ascribe to national democracies the full virtues of representativity requires ... to ignore the fact that, in many states, democracy is a weak concept'.[18] Moreover, while the lack of democratic legitimacy of NGOs, in the sense of general representativity, is evident, it remains that 'there are other forms of legitimacy, of which the rule of law is one'.

It is not possible to go here into the details of this debate, but I think that it is clear that there is a link between the issue of representativity of NGOs and the role which NGOs may have before international tribunals and human rights courts in particular.

The role of representativity in NGO *amicus curiae* participation is not the same as it is in the case of the proposed NGO attribution of the *actio popularis*. While the lack of general representativity is in no way an obstacle to the participation of NGOs as *amicus curiae*, I think that the same lack should exclude the attribution of an unrestricted *actio popularis* to NGOs.

We come now to the second position that emerged from the Fiesole workshop, which does not approve of the attribution of an *actio popularis* to NGOs at all.

One argument was that the establishment of an *actio popularis* for NGOs would reduce the scope of individual applications and would threaten the guarantee system provided for by the European Convention. Moreover, it has been stated that even the more timid form of participation of NGOs in proceedings, i.e., *amicus curiae* submission, may threaten the individual applicant's position, either by alleging facts that he or she would not have alleged or by proposing new legal arguments.[19]

The danger of similar drawbacks would be even more serious if an *actio popularis* were granted to NGOs.

I agree with many points of this position.

It is submitted that modern international human rights law constitutes a synthesis of various generations, dimensions, concepts and philosophies of human rights. However, the human rights enshrined in the European Convention are modelled on the classical concept of civil and political rights, the most important and lasting achievements of the American and French revolutions. The indi-

---

[17] D. Rieff, 'The Precarious Triumph of Human Rights', *New York Times Magazine*, 8 August 1999, 6, at 41.

[18] H. Cullen and K. Morrow, 'International Civil Society in International Law: The Growth of NGO Participation' (2001) 1 *Non-State Actors & Int'l L.* 7, at 12.

[19] See C. Harby in Workshop Report, n. 5 above, at pp. 9–10.

vidual, enjoying a series of individual freedoms, is the real focus of the European Convention, and consequently collective rights or group rights play a less significant role. The hard core of the Convention is based on the modern liberal concept of achieving individual freedom by creating a private sphere for every human being and thus protecting him or her against undue interference by the state.

The collective dimension is much more evident if we consider economic and social rights, even if it is submitted that according to many scholars and states the fact that they are not 'justiciable' should prevent them form being deemed as proper human rights.

The strong individual nature of the rights enshrined in the European Convention entails the consequence that as a rule, only the victim of the violation of the right should have the procedural right to bring the action.

The most revolutionary aspect of the European Convention is undoubtedly the individual right of complaint. Precisely because states are generally reluctant to submit an application against another state, the individual right of complaint constitutes a fundamental expedient for achieving the aim of the Convention to secure the rights and freedoms of individuals against states. The importance of the individual right of complaint for the functioning of the supervisory system under the European Convention may be seen from the large number of individual applications that are submitted to the European Commission.

Summing up, in my view, interferences by third parties (such as the proposed unrestricted *actio popularis* for NGOs) do not accord with the individual and personal nature of the human rights contained in the European Convention.

4. A LIMITED *LOCUS STANDI* FOR NGOs

However, at the Fiesole workshop a third position was also hinted at. Although it was only sketched out very briefly, its core element is the proposal to grant NGOs what I would call a limited or restricted *actio popularis*. NGOs would be granted the right to bring a complaint through an *actio popularis* if and only if they can show they have an interest in litigation. Clearly, the existence of this interest could be challenged by the respondent state.[20]

It was not explained what the expression 'interest in litigation' should mean. It is thus very difficult to evaluate this proposal. However, I think that we can find some useful elements if we look at the laws of some European states as to NGOs' *locus standi* before national courts. For obvious reasons, I will speak of Italy, but the same can also be said more or less with regard to other European states.

We find that only in a few exceptional cases do NGOs have a *locus standi* before Italian courts and are they granted an *actio popularis* to put forward the public interest.

---

[20] See P. Sands in Workshop Report, n. 5 above, at p. 16.

The main cases are those provided for by Law No. 281 of 1998[21] and Law No. 765 of 1967.[22] The first law implements in the Italian legal order European Community Directive 98/27 of 19 May 1998 on injunctions for the protection of consumers' interests.[23] This law attributes to consumer protection associations (consumer NGOs) the power to seek an injunction in order to bring the contested infringement to an end. The *ratio* of the law is to allow infringements harmful to the collective interests of consumers to be terminated in good time.

The second law provides that 'everyone may challenge before the Italian courts a building-licence which he or she asserts to be illegitimate'.

Italian courts have recognized that Italia Nostra (the main Italian environmental NGO) has a *locus standi* since it has a specific interest in litigation because its statute indicates the protection of the *'bellezze naturali'* ('sites of natural beauty') as the main objective of the organization.[24]

It has to be noted that even if the wording of the law was very broad as to the *locus standi*, the Italian courts have judged it necessary to examine the statute of the NGO in order to decide if it had a 'specific interest' in litigation or not. This seems to me to confirm the restrictive attitude of Italian law with regard to the *locus standi* of NGOs which are not claiming the protection of their own rights but the protection of so called 'common' or 'shared' rights.

Another interesting development on this issue is the recent European Directive on environmental liability with regard to the prevention and remedying of envi-

---

[21] Law of 30 July 1998, No. 281, *Gazzetta Ufficiale*, 14 August 1998, No. 189.

[22] Law of 6 August 1967, No. 765, *Gazzetta Ufficiale*, 31 August 1967, No. 218.

[23] On this law see G. Alpa and A. Levi (eds.), *I diritti dei consumatori e degli utenti* (Milano, 2001); G. Alpa, 'Le legge sui diritti dei consumatori' (1998) *Corr. Giur.* 997; G. De Nova, 'I contratti dei consumatori e la legge sulle associazioni' (1998) *I Contratti* 545; A. Giussani, 'La tutela di interessi collettivi nella nuova disciplina dei diritti dei consumatori' (1998) *Danno e Responsabilità* 1061; S. Mazzamuto and A. Plaia, 'Provvedimenti inibitori a tutela del consumatore: la legge italiana 30 luglio 1998, n. 281 e la direttiva 98/27/C' (1999) *Europa e Diritto Privato* 669; R. Sciaudone, 'I diritti dei consumatori e degli utenti nella l. 30 luglio 1998, n. 281' (1999) *Il Nuovo Diritto* 5; E. Minervini, 'I contratti dei consumatori e la l. 30 luglio 1998, n. 281' (1999) *I Contratti* 938; I. Pagni, 'Tutela individuale e tutela collettiva nella nuova disciplina dei diritti dei consumatori e degli utenti (prime riflessioni sull'art. 3 L. 30 luglio 1998, n. 281)' in A. Barba (ed.), *La disciplina dei diritti dei consumatori e degli utenti* (Napoli, 2000), p. 127 *et seq.*; on the Directive see D.H. Hoffmann, 'Directive Action en cessation en matière de protection des intérets des consommateurs (dir. 98/27/CE du 19/5/98)' (2000) 8 *Eur. Rev. Pr. L.* 149.

[24] See Consiglio di Stato sez. IV, 9 March 1973, No. 253 (1974) III *Foro Italiano* 33, which judgment, though, has been annulled (see Cassazione sezioni unite, 8 May 1978, No. 2207 (1978) I *Foro Italiano* 1090) on the ground that there are no rules on which the *locus standi* of the association may be founded. A further development on this issue may be seen in Law of 8 July 1986, No. 349 (in *Gazzetta Ufficiale*, 15 July 1986, No. 162, supplemento ordinario No. 59), which creates the Ministry of the Environment and grants environmental associations the right to denounce facts that can harm the environment, as well as to intervene in the trial before the civil judge and to act before the administrative courts (Article 18(4)); it should be noted that, from the point of view of the Italian law of civil procedure, the intervention of NGOs in a case of compensation for environmental damages is an *intervento adesivo dipendente*, therefore rather similar to *amicus curiae* participation (see E. Grasso, 'Una tutela giurisdizionale per l'ambiente' (1987) *Riv. Dir. Proc. Civ.* 505).

ronmental damage,[25] which grants rights and powers to 'natural or legal persons' as established in Article 12(a) affected or likely to be affected by environmental damage, or (b) having a sufficient interest in environmental decision-making relating to the damage, or alternatively (c) alleging the impairment of a right, where administrative procedural law of a member state requires this as a precondition.

The role of NGOs is enhanced by the provision according to which 'the interest of any non-governmental organization promoting environmental protection and meeting any requirements under national law shall be deemed sufficient' as regards the purposes of both subparagraph (b) and (c) quoted above.

Article 12 specifies that such NGOs:

> shall be entitled to submit to the competent authority any observations relating to instances of environmental damage or an imminent threat of such damage of which they are aware and shall be entitled to request the competent authority to take action under this Directive.

The provision of Article 13(1) goes further, stating that 'The persons referred to in Article 12 shall have access to a court or other independent and impartial public body competent to review the procedural and substantive legality of the decisions, acts or failure to act of the competent authority under this Directive'.

Coming now to the evaluation of these developments, it should be observed that both Italian laws mentioned above have limited scope and are based on very specific reasons.[26]

The consumer law is based on the well-founded assumption that consumers very often do not resort to courts because of the high legal costs that this would involve compared to the modest sums at stake.

The environmental law is based on the fact that '*valori urbanistici*' ('urbanistic values') are regarded as a sort of supra-individual interest and more prosaically and decisively that we have had, in Italy, especially in the past decades, a wanton destruction of beautiful shores and sites through illegal construction.

As to the recent European Directive, it should be noted that it relates to instances of environmental damage, i.e., a kind of damage which typically cannot

---

[25] Directive 2004/35/CE of the European Parliament and of the Council of 21 April 2004 on environmental liability with regard to the prevention and remedying of environmental damage, [2004] OJ L 143/56–75, 30 April 2004.

[26] On the protection of collective interests in the Italian experience see G. Alpa, 'Interessi Diffusi' in IX *Digesto Discipline Privatistiche, Sezione Civile* (Torino, 1993); M. Cappelletti, 'Formazioni sociali e interessi di gruppo davanti alla giustizia civile' (1975) *Riv. Dir. Proc.* 365; M. Cappelletti, 'Appunti sulla tutela giurisdizionale di interessi collettivi o diffusi' (1975) IV *Giurisprudenza Italiana* 49; B. Capponi, 'Diritto comunitario e azioni d'interesse collettivo dei consumatori' (1994) IV *Foro Italiano* 439; F. Carpi, 'Cenni sulla tutela degli interessi collettivi' (1974) *Riv. Trim. Dir. Proc. Civ.* 544; V. Denti, 'Interessi Diffusi' (1983) IV *Novissimo Digesto Italiano Appendice* 313; E. Grasso, 'Gli interessi della collettività e l'azione collettiva' (1983) *Riv. Dir. Proc.* 242; V. Vigoriti, *Interessi collettivi e processo – La legittimazione ad agire* (Milano, 1979).

be claimed, or at least easily claimed, by private individuals and/or corporations before national tribunals.

Thus, with regard to the human rights contained in the European Convention, the question is: are there specific situations where an exceptional *locus standi* for NGOs to claim before the ECHR is justified by strong reasons?

I have to admit that this is a very difficult question to answer. In any case if such reasons exist, I do not think there should be an aprioristic opposition to admit as an exception a *locus standi* for NGOs which have a specific interest in litigation according to their statutes.

Chapter 5

The Role of NGOs before the United Nations Human Rights Committee

Gianluca Rubagotti

1. INTRODUCTION: MECHANISMS AND PROCEDURES BEFORE THE UNITED NATIONS HUMAN RIGHTS COMMITTEE

The International Covenant on Civil and Political Rights[1] (ICCPR) provided for the creation of a Human Rights Committee (HRC), a non-jurisdictional body whose aim is monitoring the actual respect, by member states, of the rules enshrined in it.[2]

The HRC is composed of 18 members, 'persons of high moral character and recognized competence in the field of human rights' (Article 28), elected in their personal capacity among the citizens of the states parties to the ICCPR.

The ICCPR, together with the First Optional Protocol,[3] provides for three different monitoring systems of the states parties.

The first consists in the submission by states of periodic reports, to be considered by the HRC, as far as effective implementation within the national jurisdiction of the rights enshrined in the ICCPR is concerned.[4]

The second and third monitoring systems are based on a different communications system. On the one hand, the ICCPR provides for the possibility for a state to complain about a supposed breach by another state of one of the rights protected by the Covenant,[5] while on the other hand the First Optional Protocol paves the way for communications submitted by individuals, who claim to be victims of a violation committed by a state against them, as respects the relevant right listed in the ICCPR.[6]

---

[1] For an integral version of the text of the Covenant (open to signature in New York, 19 December 1966), as well as of the First and Second Optional Protocol, see the United Nations website <www.un.org>.

[2] See ICCPR, Part 4, Articles 28–45.

[3] The First Optional Protocol to the ICCPR was adopted on 19 December 1966, and is relevant to this work in that it provides for the possibility of submitting individual communications to the HRC (see below); the Second Optional Protocol (New York, 15 December 1989) relates to the abolition of the death penalty.

[4] See ICCPR, Article 40.

[5] See ICCPR, Article 41.

[6] See First Optional Protocol, Article 1.

T. Treves et al., eds., Civil Society, International Courts and Compliance Bodies
© 2005, T·M·C·ASSER PRESS, *The Hague, The Netherlands, and the Authors*

In both cases, the purpose is to try to protect those who claim to have suffered a violation of their rights, for which no remedy would be available under the local remedies in the state involved.

Nonetheless, the scope of these two mechanisms seems to be significantly narrower than that of periodic reports, and their application dependent on a further act of will of the state than the simple ratification of the ICCPR, which *per se* is sufficient to raise the reporting obligation.

The inter-state communications in fact may be received and considered only if submitted by a state party which has made a declaration recognizing in regard to itself the competence of the Committee. No communication shall be received by the Committee if it concerns a state party which has not made such a declaration.[7]

The possibility of submitting individual communications is instead provided for by the First Optional Protocol, which is a legal instrument separate from the ICCPR, and which therefore requires signing and ratification from each state to enter into force.[8]

2. THE SYSTEM OF PERIODIC REPORTS

2.1 Scope and function of the reporting obligation and sources of information

Article 40 of the ICCPR requires a commitment from member states 'to submit reports on the measures they have adopted which give effect to the rights recognized herein and on the progress made in the enjoyment of those rights'.[9] The basic idea is to create an inter-institutional dialogue between individual states on the one hand and the HRC on the other.

The reports submitted by states are addressed to the Secretary General of the United Nations, and then transmitted to the HRC to be considered. The Secretary General may furthermore decide, after consultation with the HRC, to 'transmit to the specialized agencies concerned copies of such parts of the reports as may fall within their field of competence'[10]

---

[7] See ICCPR, Article 41.

[8] For a complete list of the states parties to the ICCPR (151) and to Optional Protocols (First Optional Protocol: 104, Second Optional Protocol: 50), as well as to other UN treaties on human rights, see <www.unhchr.ch/pdf/report.pdf>. See also P. Sands, R. Mackenzie and Y. Shany, *Manual on International Courts and Tribunals* (London, 1999), p. 170 ('So far, 96 states have accepted the jurisdiction of the HRC to receive individual communications and 47 states have authorised the HRC to receive inter-state complaints').

[9] The work which provides the most in-depth analysis of periodic reports is D. McGoldrick, *The Human Rights Committee: Its Role in the International Covenant on Civil and Political Rights* (Oxford, 1991).

[10] See ICCPR, Article 40(3).

The starting point of the system based on the ICCPR is a first report, submitted by the state 'within one year of the entry into force of the present Covenant',[11] which has the function of providing a first picture of the state of implementation, within the state involved, of the rights enshrined in the Covenant.

The concrete practice highlights the existence of two further types of reports: additional or supplementary ones[12] and reports broadly speaking referred to as 'periodic'.

The need to submit additional reports arises from the lacunose description of many initial reports.[13] Reading Article 40 of the ICCPR, one cannot but notice the difficulties of any attempt to obtain from the legal text precise information on the content of such reports. Manifestly ambiguous words such as 'measures' and 'progress'[14] are used, with the aim of not narrowing excessively the freedom of states in the preparation of the reports. As a consequence, the state may refer to laws of different nature adopted in conformity with the ICCPR, as well as to the practice of law courts and of administrative bodies, and any other relevant fact.

It is clear that granting states an ample degree of discretion on the one hand facilitates the preparation of the report, by not imposing an excessive burden in terms of requisites and details, but on the other hand it has the defect of allowing a sort of heterogeneity in the factual contents, since all the states will frame their report according to their internal situations and peculiarities.

The HRC itself felt the need to intervene directly, elaborating General Guidelines regarding the Form and Content of Reports from States Parties under Article 40 of the Covenant.[15]

According to these guidelines the first report of a state should be divided into two parts as follows.

Part I: General: this part should briefly describe the general framework within which civil and political rights are protected in the reporting state. In particular it should indicate:

(a) whether any of the rights referred to in the ICCPR are protected either in the Constitution or by a separate Bill of Rights, and, if so, what provisions are made in the Constitution or in the Bill of Rights for derogations and in what circumstances;

---

[11] See ICCPR, Article 40(1)(a).

[12] The two adjectives can be used interchangeably, as the HRC itself does.

[13] See, e.g., the statements of some members of the HRC on the two-page report submitted by Kenya, considered either 'inadequate' or 'too brief' to meet the needs of the Committee (UN Press Release HR/2079, 30 March 1981, at 4).

[14] See ICCPR, Article 40(1).

[15] See Doc. CCPR/C/5 and Doc. A/32/44, App. IV, adopted by the HRC during its 44th meeting, 2nd Session, 29 August 1977.

(b) whether the provisions of the ICCPR can be invoked before and directly en-
     forced by the courts, other tribunals or administrative authorities or whether
     they have to be transformed into internal laws or administrative regulations
     to be enforced by the authorities concerned;
(c) what judicial, administrative or other competent authorities have jurisdiction
     affecting human rights;
(d) what remedies are available to an individual who claims that any of his or
     her rights have been violated;
(e) what other measures have been taken to ensure the implementation of the
     provisions of the ICCPR.

Part II: Information relating to each of the articles in Parts I, II and III of the Covenant: this part should describe in relation to the provisions of each article:

(i)   the legislative, administrative, or other measures in force in regard to each
      right;
(ii) any restrictions or limitations even of a temporary nature imposed by law or
      practice or any other manner on the enjoyment of the right;
(iii) any other factors or difficulties affecting the enjoyment of the right by per-
      sons within the jurisdiction of the state;
(iv) any other information on the progress made in the enjoyment of the right.

The guidelines furthermore provide that the state report should include copies of
the main legal texts, particularly those mentioned in it.

The guidelines, however, cannot be construed as legally binding rules, and
in practice they have not prevented states from submitting lacunose or not
completely satisfactory initial reports. The HRC, therefore, had no option but to
intervene directly, asking on a case by case basis for clarifications, further information, which could enable it to obtain the most accurate and objective picture of
the actual level of respect for the human rights enshrined in the ICCPR.

The legal basis for such additional reports, submitted by states as a response to
requests coming from the HRC, can be found either in Article 40(1)(b), which
binds the states to submit reports on the measures adopted, as well as on the
progress made, not only, as seen above, within one year from the entry into force
of the ICCPR but also 'thereafter whenever the Committee so requests';[16] or in
the duty of states to fulfil their reporting obligations pursuant to Article 40(1)(a).

Both these hypotheses seem correct, in that, as underlined in academic opinion,[17] it would not appear reasonable to allow a state first to submit an inadequate
report and afterwards to refuse to give further information and clarifications on
its content.

The analysis, however, would not be consistent if there were no provisions
concerning further reports, referred to as 'periodic' reports, subsequent in time to

---

[16] See ICCPR, Article 40(1)(b).
[17] See McGoldrick, n. 9 above, at p. 65.

this first phase of initial report/additional report, with the aim of keeping a dialec-
tic process going, in which every stage could be an improvement on and a cross-
fertilization from the previous ones (the state elaborates a report, the HRC
considers it, the state prepares the next updated report according to the considerations of the HRC and so on),[18] in a framework of continuous development and
progress.

These further reports imply the same difficulties and problems we have no-
ticed for the initial reports, in considering the breadth of the obligation.

The HRC therefore decided to adopt, in its 13th Session (July 1981) a further
series of guidelines, relating to both the form and the content of the periodic reports pursuant to Article 40(1)(b).

A state's periodic report should therefore be divided into two parts:

Part I: General: this part should contain information concerning the general
framework within which the civil and political rights recognized by the ICCPR
are protected in the reporting state.

Part II: Information in relation to each of the articles in Parts I, II and III of the
Covenant: this part should contain information in relation to each of the provisions of individual articles.

Under these two main headings the contents of reports should concentrate especially on:

(a) the completion of the information before the HRC as to the measures
     adopted to give effect to rights recognized in the ICCPR, taking account of
     the questions raised in the HRC on the examination of any previous report
     and including in particular additional information as to questions not previ-
     ously answered or not fully answered;
(b) information taking into account general comments which the HRC may have
     made under Article 40(4) of the ICCPR;
(c) actions taken as a result of experience gained in cooperation with the HRC;
(d) changes made or proposed to be made in the laws and practices relevant to
     the ICCPR;
(e) factors affecting and difficulties experienced in the implementation of the
     ICCPR;
(f) the progress made since the last report in the enjoyment of rights recognized
     in the ICCPR.

The report should include copies of the main legal texts mentioned in it.

---

[18] For this mechanism to be effective the problem of the periodicity of reports is crucial, though
outside the scope of this work, i.e., how often the state is to submit a report to update the state of
implementation of human rights within the state. As the ICCPR is again silent on this issue, the HRC
itself intervened again, and established in a 'decision on periodicity' (Doc. A/36.40, App. V, adopted
on 22 July 1981) a temporal cycle of five years.

As regards this second set of guidelines, one can consider valid the comments made above as far as their lack of legally binding force is concerned.

But what kind of sources could such a detailed report be based on?

Article 40(2) of the ICCPR prescribes that states 'indicate the factors and difficulties, if any, affecting the implementation of the Covenant', but in practice, as the report is the official version of the state regarding the implementation of human rights within its jurisdiction, it seems quite obvious to expect it to be extremely favourable towards the existing situation.[19]

As a consequence, we cannot but share the views expressed in academic opinion[20] according to which the effectiveness of the HRC as an implementation organ is strictly linked to and dependent on its possibility to resort to other sources than state reports, to verify and complete the information received.

The United Nations Specialized Agencies are the first possible alternative source that could play an important role, especially in consideration of Article 40(3) of the ICCPR, pursuant to which the Secretary General 'may, after consultation with the Committee, transmit to the specialized agencies concerned copies of such parts of the reports as may fall within their field of competence'.[21]

The two specialized agencies to which attention is mainly drawn are the International Labour Organisation (ILO)[22] and the United Nations Educational, Scientific and Cultural Organisation (UNESCO),[23] both of which have more than once expressed their willingness to establish a profitable cooperation with the HRC.

It is in fact necessary to avoid conflicts and contradictions in the definition of standards for the evaluation of rights that are common to other international treaties, and it is furthermore useful to use the studies which have already been prepared by specialized agencies, both to give more coherence to the whole United Nations system of protection of human rights and to enable members of the HRC to ask the national delegates more focused questions.

But there is the problem of how the words 'parts of the reports as may fall within their field of competence' should properly be construed.

---

[19] See F. Jhabvala, 'The Practice of the Covenant's HRC, 1976-82: Review of State Party Reports' (1984) 6 *Hum. Rts Q.* 81.

[20] See F. Capotorti, *Patti Internazionali sui diritti dell'uomo: studio introduttivo* (CEDAM, Padova, 1967), p. 137, and A. Dormenval, *Procédures Onusiennes de mise en œuvre des droits de l'homme: limites ou défauts?* (Presses Universitaires de France, Paris, 1991).

[21] The General Assembly (Third Committee) understood that the Secretary General would not transmit the report of a state which was not a member of the specialised agency involved (see Doc. A/6546).

[22] The International Labour Organisation was established in 1919, with the peace treaties that ended the First World War, in order to promote at the international level domestic working conditions and social justice with a view to contributing thereby to world peace.

[23] The United Nations Educational, Scientific and Cultural Organization was born on 16 November 1945, and according to its Constitution its purpose is 'to contribute to peace and security by promoting collaboration among nations through education, science and culture in order to further universal respect for justice, for the rule of law and for the human rights and fundamental freedoms which are affirmed for the peoples of the world, without distinction of race, sex, language or religion, by the Charter of the United Nations'.

One may argue that transmitting the whole report would amount to an *ultra vires* action considering what is provided for by Article 40(3) of the ICCPR, but nonetheless the points of interest for specialized agencies are to be found throughout the text, and it would be rather difficult to understand them outside the general context.

The compromise solution is to send the whole report, but together with an explanatory note pointing out the parts that are supposed to fall within the scope of the agencies.

A second issue relates more specifically to the value of the comments by the specialized agencies. In 1977 the HRC, while drafting the rules of procedure, had included a rule stating that 'the Committee may invite the specialized agencies to which the Secretary General has transmitted parts of the reports to submit comments on those parts within such time limits as it may specify'.[24]

If some members considered giving value to the comments of specialized agencies to be a positive idea, this view was not unanimously shared. There was a risk of exceeding the scope and limits of Article 40 of the ICCPR, by granting an excessive power to agencies and limiting the main organ according to the ICCPR, which is the HRC. Such a hypothesis would have resulted in the possibility for states not party to the Covenant actively to take part in the process of evaluation of other states' performances, at least within the scope of the specialized agencies to which they were party.

The HRC then adopted a provisional decision, according to which 'the specialized agencies could not submit comments, it being understood that the Committee could revert to the matter at a later stage and in the light of the experience it had gained', seeking ways to 'further strengthen its cooperation with the specialized agencies'.[25]

The concrete result of this compromise is that the idea of cooperation between the HRC and the specialized agencies is formally accepted, but *de facto* the agencies limit their role to providing information or giving interpretations of questions falling within the scope of their competence, leaving to the members of the HRC a broad discretion in how to use such information.

But the United Nations specialized agencies are not the only source from which the HRC could take the information it deems necessary, outside the boundaries of the official member states' reports. International law has recently seen an enhancement of the role of the so-called non-governmental organizations (NGOs), a rather broad definition encompassing heterogeneous entities.[26]

---

[24] See Rule of Procedure 67(2).

[25] Cf., Doc. A/34/40, para. 60 and Doc. A/35/40, para. 414.

[26] On the subject of NGOs, especially within the UN system, see R. Hofmann (ed.), *Non-State Actors as New Subjects of International Law: International Law – From the Traditional State Order Towards the Law of the Global Community* (Duncker & Humblot, Berlin, 1999); S. Charnovitz, 'Two Centuries of Participation: NGOs and International Governance' (1997) 18 *Michigan J. Int'l L.* 183; A. Clark, E. Friedman and K. Hochstetter, 'The Sovereign Limits of Global Civil Society: A Comparison of NGO Participation in UN World Conferences on the Environment, Human Rights,

Unlike the position regarding the United Nations Specialized Agencies, there is no express mention of NGOs either in Article 40 or in any other article of the ICCPR, and one could therefore infer that they do not actually play any role in the implementation procedures.

From this lack of legal references, some members initially drew the conclusion that the HRC was not entitled to found its consideration of the reports upon sources other than the states' reports themselves or official United Nations documents.

Against this absolutely restrictive interpretation, however, a more open one has been presented, backed by the majority of member states and against which nowadays no one seems to be willing to argue any longer, according to which the provisions of the ICCPR do not in fact restrict the HRC as to the choice of what sources of information it deems appropriate to resort to for the evaluation of states' reports.[27]

The concrete practice shows as a rule the cautious tendency not expressly to mention the source of information, where it does not come from either the member states or the United Nations system. The members of the HRC have consequently either used such expressions as 'I have reason to believe', 'it had been reported', 'he had information', or simply referred to vaguely identified 'other sources' or 'reliable sources'.[28]

It may seem difficult, with such a practice, to be able to determine clearly the sources involved, as well as to what actual extent they have been deployed. However, the members of the HRC have sometimes indicated their, so to speak, 'external' sources, and one can say that they encompass very different entities: for instance, reports and documents of the Human Rights Commission, the Interna-

---

and Women' (1988–99) 51 *WP* 1; I.J. Gassama, 'Reaffirming Faith in the Dignity of Each Human Being: The United Nations, NGOs and Apartheid' (1996) 19 *Fordham Int'l L. J.* 1464; J.S. Ovsiovitch, 'Philanthropic Support for Human Rights NGOs' (1998) 4 *Buff. Hum. Rts. L. Rev.* 341; D. Otto, 'Non Governmental Organizations in the United Nations System' (1996) 18 *Hum. Rts Q.* 107; W. Korey, *NGOs and the Universal Declaration of Human Rights: A Curious Grapevine* (New York St. Martin Press, New York, 1998); P. Alston, 'The United Nations Committee on Non Governmental Organizations: Guarding the Entrance to a Political Divided House' (2001) 12 *Eur. J. Int'l L* 943.

[27] For this issue, see McGoldrick, n. 9 above, at pp. 104, 111: 'Mr Movchan and Mr Graefrath have suggested that a "gentleman's agreement" had been reached within the HRC that the Secretariat should not distribute insessional documents emanating from NGOs and that members should in no case refer to documents issued by an NGO or mention the name of an NGO during the exchange with delegations or in their presence. Mr Movchan complained that some members were violating this agreement and thereby damaging the HRC's prestige by not agreeing to the "Rules of Play", SR 572 pr. 11. Mr Tomuschat replied that he wished to "State specifically that the Committee had no clearly defined rules that members had undertaken not to mention their sources". It seemed to him that there had never really been an agreement along those lines and that, consequently, there could be no question of violating established rules. He also considered that all members of the Committee had always been duly discreet in that regard, ibid., pr.13'.

[28] See below on the actual influence of NGOs in the reporting procedure as well as the conclusions.

tional Labour Organisation, the International Red Cross Commission, reports under other UN Committees (Committee on the Elimination of Racial Discrimination, Committee on the Elimination of Discrimination Against Women), parliamentary debates, lawyers' associations, Church organizations, the press, information from communications submitted pursuant to Article 1 of the Optional Protocol and NGOs for the protection of human rights such as Amnesty International, the International Commission of Jurists and the International League for Human Rights.[29]

As one could easily argue, the members have tried to enlarge the number of available sources, in consideration of the fact that the ICCPR does not provide the HRC with an autonomous fact-finding mechanism, which could interact, in the reconstruction of the concrete situations, with the state reports, which will inevitably tend to draw a picture of the situation as favourable to the member states as possible.[30]

For the work of the HRC to be really effective, there is no other feasible solution than enlarging the circle of the available sources, and not limiting it to the information submitted by the parties and obtainable from UN official documents, especially considering that state reports are often abstract, not substantiated, framed in such a way as to give the impression that the issue of human rights is not a top priority, since everyone is doing their best to implement them.

NGOs have been able to find a niche in spite of the lack of any legal provision about their status, and their actions are consequently carried out in a completely informal manner, often relying on the personal intercourse between members of the organizations themselves and of the HRC.

To be able to understand fully how NGOs can fit within this regime, it is necessary to return to the structure of consideration of national reports, which we have already defined as dialectical.[31]

Each member state of the ICCPR submits its report (initial, supplementary or periodic) to the HRC, but at the same time one or more NGOs[32] prepare and deliver one or more *ad hoc* submissions, in the light of all the information that the local networks can collect.

---

[29] For an exhaustive list, see McGoldrick, n. 9 above, at pp. 78–79.

[30] One could cite, for instance, the discussion of the report of the State of El Salvador (see McGoldrick, n. 9 above, at pp. 112, 133), during which a member of the HRC commented as follows: 'The coincidence and precision of the information received from a variety of sources could not but raise questions'.

[31] The information on the concrete actions and activities of NGOs is also based on a series of interviews with the personnel of some London-based NGOs, held in London from April 2002 to December 2003, especially with staff within the International Law and Organizations Program of Amnesty International, International Secretariat.

[32] The largest and most active international NGO for the protection of human rights is definitely Amnesty International, but what we are outlining could of course also refer to any other NGO working in this sector. Clearly, indeed, not every NGO presents *ad hoc* submissions for every report under consideration, and therefore it is obvious that a theoretical description cannot pretend to give a full account of the many shades of concrete situations.

These *ad hoc* submissions are sometimes referred to as 'shadow' reports (even if some NGOs reject this term in that it could convey the idea of counter-information, as part of a contraposition between NGOs and member states) and can be the result both of the action of a single NGO and of the cooperation between more actors.

The limited dimensions of NGOs do not always allow them to have all the necessary information available, since the periodic reports under the ICCPR and other international treaties are rather complex documents, requiring a high degree of specialization and a thoroughly widespread monitoring capacity for concrete situations in possible breach of the obligations provided for by international treaty law.

In these cases, the need for a profitable exchange of data and comments between the various NGOs emerges, especially when their scope is limited to a specific sector, which is merely a part of the whole reporting obligations. Besides, so to speak, the 'universal' NGOs we have organizations for the protection of the rights of infants, of disabled people, of refugees, fighting against racial and ethnic discrimination, aiming at eliminating social inequalities, trying to enhance the role of women in society, and so on.

Each of these organizations knows the problems of the specific sector, within the vast category of human rights, to which it devotes its efforts; on its own it does not have the capacities (both human and financial) to elaborate a complete report, which can require a broad knowledge of all the major issues relating to the protection of human rights, but it nonetheless can be of invaluable help, especially in relation to the concrete cases they are familiar with, for larger and more organised NGOs, acting, in these cases of cooperation, as the coordinating focal point.

From a practical point of view, the cooperation among all the actors involved is made easier by some circumstances, such as location in the same city (many NGOs have their headquarter or main operating branch in London, New York or Geneva), the personal intercourse between members of staff (cases of activists working first for one NGO and then for another are quite common, and in this way you create and keep contacts between the organizations) and more generally the possibility of communicating through the Internet, and therefore of constant updating.

This kind of cooperation happens for all the periodic reporting systems provided for by international treaties, and is not limited to the preparation of reports regarding the ICCPR.[33] The United Nations Secretariat therefore receives two or

---

[33] One could mention, e.g., the *Joint NGO Shadow Report to the United Nations Committee on Economic Social and Cultural Rights* released in April 2002, commenting on the Fourth Report presented by the United Kingdom, which is the result of the cooperation of 18 NGOs, under the coordination of Justice. The list of these NGOs includes: Anti-Slavery International, ATD Fourth World, Children's Rights Alliance for England (CRAE), Committee on the Administration of Justice (CAJ), Democratic Audit, Disability Awareness in Action, Justice, Low Pay Unit, Medact, NICIE, Northern Ireland Women's European Platform, Oxfam, Parity, Physicians for Human Rights UK, Prison Re-

more reports, with the same object (the level of implementation of human rights within a country), but coming from different entities (one from the member state, the other from one or more NGOs, separately or jointly), and having different legal force (only the official one is provided for by the ICCPR).

These two or more reports are made available to the HRC, together with a further document (which is not made public), referred to as 'country – analysis', prepared by the Secretariat itself, with the aim of giving a first general view of the situation within the country under consideration.

Taking into account the differences which will inevitably have emerged, the HRC will prepare a so-called list of issues, based on all the information collected, later distributed both to the government involved and to the NGO or NGOs which have contributed with a submission.

This list of issues performs several functions, which include that of directly involving the government under report, which is asked for further information and clarifications, and it can also be viewed as a sort of indirect control on the information submitted by NGOs.[34]

The members of the HRC will have the opportunity to verify how substantiated the information submitted by non-state actors is, taking into consideration the answers given by the state. This phase is called 'pre-session'. The government, to which the NGO directly addressed its concerns, formally answers the questions raised by the Committee, further elaborating on the report which will be discussed during the public session.

On the day of the public session, the informal work of NGOs continues through an informal lunch meeting, during which NGO activists hold discussions with one or more members of the HRC,[35] to whom they provide further information or comments which may be useful, as well as suggestions on how to lead the debate and the issues on which to focus.

In this way, the NGO can shape a public report, which is published on its website for it to be available to the greatest number of people and to circulate at the international level. It is then distributed to the local networks,[36] whose task (not an easy one) will be to try to create, within the state, a movement of public opinion that will put pressure on a government unwilling to give full implementation to civil and political rights.

---

form Trust, Refugee Council, Terrence Higgins Trust, Women's International League for Peace and Freedom (WILPF).

[34] This kind of verification, however, is within the HRC, which is officially the only source of the requests made to the state.

[35] Clearly these discussions will be held with those members more directly involved in the specific report. In fact, the HRC manages its workload on the basis of some workgroups, called Country Task Forces, so as to facilitate the analysis of all the various reports.

[36] We will see below the importance of the ramification of local networks for the success of the intervention.

During the public session, NGOs do not play any official role, in that, though public, the discussions do not allow any participants other than the members of the HRC and the state delegations involved.

Accordingly, the representatives of so-called 'civil society', though physically present where the report is being discussed, have to sit among the public, without any possibility of intervention of any kind. In this way NGOs are even prevented from acting in an indirect way, i.e., by means of friendly states, more responsive to these issues, to whom to pass the information on the state in breach of its international obligations under the ICCPR: the only actors entitled to take part in the discussion are, as we have already noted, the members of the HRC and of the delegations from the states under consideration.

The discussion begins with the presentation by the delegation of the state under consideration of the report on the implementation of civil and political rights within that country.

The members of the HRC, sometimes expressly mentioning NGOs as the source of their information, at other times resorting to the rather ambiguous expressions we have referred to above, put questions to the state representatives, and comment upon the answers they receive, with the possibility of further rebutting point by point where the answers are deemed unsatisfactory, in a spirit of cooperation and reciprocal stimulus.

At the end of the discussion, the HRC gathers in a closed meeting[37] and draws up its final observations, jointly with a series of concerns and recommendations, relating to situations in which the position of the state does not appear to be perfectly in line with the provisions of the ICCPR.

At this stage, the NGO delivers a press release, in which it briefly summarizes the situation, sends a letter to the government involved, denouncing the points that denote an ineffective or incomplete implementation of the ICCPR, and finally provides the local networks with all the necessary information to continue their campaigning and advocacy action.

The procedure we have just outlined is not to be considered as a predetermined series of steps, always the same in every case; it will be the specific circumstances of each situation which suggest the best way to operate and the level of involvement of NGOs, since each case has its own peculiarities and therefore needs a specific treatment.

What we have tried to illustrate is the whole range of actions which in theory may be developed within the system centred on the ICCPR and on the rules of procedures of the HRC; the problem of the choice, by the individual NGO of whether and how to intervene is outside the analysis carried out in this chapter.

If this is therefore the role that NGOs have been able to gain within a procedure that does not mention any official participation of any kind, it is just this absence of specific rules of law granting them a role that may raise more than a

---

[37] See Rule of Procedure 33: 'The adoption of concluding observations under article 40 shall take place in closed meetings'.

doubt as to the future of this informal cooperation. What guarantee is there that in the future NGOs will continue to be allowed, before a Committee with other members, to take part actively in the analysis of national reports, making their comments, providing the kind of information that states are usually rather opposed to disclosing, if this system, devised in order to create a bilateral intercourse between Committee-member and state and never updated according to the new reality of international relations, does not protect the non-state actors?

From a strictly legal standpoint, the answer is clearly 'none', in the sense that while ever the ICCPR or the rules of procedure themselves do not expressly state the right of NGOs to take part in the mechanism (with all the problems related to this, in terms of effectiveness and enforcement of the right granted, in a system such as public international law), the situation is always subject to possibly significant changes.

But if we add to a merely legalistic perspective, more broadly political considerations, we cannot but reflect on the fact that the prestige and effectiveness of the HRC itself depend on the independence and authoritativeness of the members who are called to be part of it. If the Committee were perceived to be excessively indulgent and inclined towards the standpoint of states, and therefore not able to make a contribution to the more widespread diffusion and fuller respect of human rights, the entire system enshrined in the ICCPR would lose its meaning.

We can therefore maintain that the best guarantee for NGOs lies in the high moral profile, in the absolute degree of independence from national governments which the members of the HRC have so far shown in carrying out their duties pursuant to the ICCPR, and which we have no reason to doubt will remain paramount characteristics in the choice of future members.

2.2 The actual influence of the work of NGOs in the reporting procedure

To appreciate fully the important contribution offered by the submissions of NGOs in the reporting process, it may be interesting to see how the concerns and problems there raised are taken into considerations by the members of the HRC in the drafting of their concluding observations. If we consider, for instance, the concluding observations of the HRC on the Socialist Republic of Viet Nam,[38] we may notice that the basic topics raised can also be found in a document submitted by the NGO Amnesty International.[39]

The structure of this submission is very well thought out: there is first an introduction, where the state's compliance with the reporting process is welcomed, but

---

[38] See Concluding Observations of the Human Rights Committee: Viet Nam. 26/07/2002, CCPR/CO/75/VNM (Concluding Observations/Comments), available on the website <www.unhchr.ch>.

[39] The reference is to a submission by Amnesty International, *Socialist Republic of Viet Nam: A Human Rights Review Based on the International Covenant on Civil and Political Rights. Amnesty International's briefing to the UN Human Rights Committee on the Socialist Republic of Viet Nam,* submitted in May 2002, and available on Amnesty International website <www.amnesty.org>.

where we also find a clear statement of what the most serious concerns are (in this case, the massive number of sentences to death[40] and the implications of the charge of crime against national security).[41] The second part of the submission deals in more detail with violations of specific articles of the ICCPR. Though it is expressly stated that the aim is not to 'attempt to cover all the failures to implement the ICCPR by the Vietnamese authorities, but rather to address some of the most serious breaches',[42] a thorough list of specific violations follows, comprising 11 articles of the Covenant:

(i)   Article 2 (obligations of the state to ensure all individuals enjoy the rights of the ICCPR, without distinctions of any kind): in the Socialist Republic of Viet Nam 'individuals are imprisoned on the basis of political or other opinion that questions the political supremacy of the Communist Party of Viet Nam'.[43]

(ii)   Article 6 (right to life): although in 1999 the number of offences punishable by death were reduced to 27, this is still a high number, and the death penalty is widely applied.

(iii)   Article 7 (torture and cruel, inhuman or degrading treatment or punishment): the crime of torture is not defined in law, and Amnesty International received reports of beating and ill-treatment.

(iv)   Article 9 (liberty and security of person): an article of the Penal Code dealing with the offence of 'undermining the unity policy' is used by the Vietnamese authorities 'to criminalize peaceful political and religious dissent from government policy, and leads to the arbitrary arrest, detention and sentencing of those who ... oppose government policy on a variety of issues'.[44] A number of cases of abuse by the Vietnamese authorities is also provided.

(v)   Article 10 (humane treatment of those deprived of their liberty): individuals deprived of their liberty suffer ill-treatment, and the problem is exacerbated by denial of access to independent monitors.

(vi)   Article 12 (right to freedom of movement): legal restrictions on freedom of movement are normally applied against people who are considered socially

---

[40] In Amnesty International's submission we can read that 'according to the statistics provided by the Supreme People's Court, during the period from 1997 to 2002, 931 people were sentenced to death. ... It is noteworthy that of the 931, 535 were related to violations of the right to life, 310 were convicted of drug crimes, 24 were cases of corruption, and five were cases of violations of the right to property'.

[41] The concern of Amnesty International is that 'the charges of crime against national security, which include such categories as high treason, subversion and espionage, are vague, ill defined, and operate in a "catch-all" manner with the risk that those who disagree with State doctrine may find themselves detained for doing no more than exercising their rights to freedom of expression as set forth in Article 19 of the ICCPR'.

[42] See submission, para. 1.1

[43] See submission, para. 2.1

[44] See submission, para. 2.4.

undesirable or able to undermine the policy unity of the state, and this is particularly true for religious dissidents.

(vii) Article 14 (right to a fair trial): the concerns raised by Amnesty International relate in particular to the lack of guarantees for the right to a fair and public hearing, by a competent, independent and impartial tribunal; the right to be presumed innocent until proven guilty; the right to have adequate time and facilities for the preparation of a defence, and to communicate with counsel of one's own choosing, and the right to call and question witnesses.

(viii) Article 17 (right to privacy): there are several violations of the privacy of people who are considered political suspects.

(ix) Article 18 (right to freedom of thought, conscience and religion): although according to the Vietnamese Constitution all religions are equal before the law, 'the Vietnamese government still insists on control over religious institutions' and 'all religious organizations have to be affiliated to the Communist Party-run Fatherland Front',[45] otherwise they face persecution.

(x) Article 19 (right to freedom of opinion and expression): the situation denounced by Amnesty International is particularly serious, since 'Vietnamese law criminalizes the right to freedom of opinion and expression. Individuals are harassed, detained, and imprisoned because of their conscientiously held peaceful opinions, and their attempts to share them with others. ... Anyone whose political views differ from those of the Communist Party of Viet Nam, and who dares to say so, has committed a criminal offence in Viet Nam'.[46]

(xi) Article 21 (right of peaceful assembly): there are several violations of the right of people to gather to protest, since gatherings are not officially permitted.

The work of the NGO is also extremely valuable because it refers to concrete cases, while the official reports by states tend to be more on a purely theoretical and legislative level, ignoring the actual implementation of the rules in the daily situations affecting the lives of individuals.

This great attention paid to specific cases of citizens emerges even more clearly in other submissions, relating to states where NGOs operate in a more structured way. It is evident that the more possibilities a state gives to NGOs to be able to collect complaints, verify them and extend their efforts, the more detailed the description of the situation of respect for human rights will be.

It is therefore only apparently a paradox that, e.g., in the submission relating to a state which is not under question for the general application of and respect for human rights, such as the United Kingdom,[47] we can find a far longer and more

---

[45] See submission, para. 2.9.

[46] See submission, para. 2.10.

[47] The reference is to a submission by Amnesty International, *United Kingdom: Summary of Concerns Raised with the Human Rights Committee,* available on Amnesty International website <www.amnesty.org>.

detailed list of cases of violations compared to, e.g., the situation in Viet Nam, here under analysis, where on the contrary it is the general denial of basic fundamental rights itself which hinders a full report of the great amount of abuses that take place in that country.

Returning to the case of Viet Nam, we can notice that the concluding observations of the HRC have taken into great consideration the submissions from NGOs, and this is clear right from the introduction, where, besides welcoming Viet Nam's second periodic report as well as regretting the considerable delay in its submission which was due in 1991, the Committee:

> also regrets the lack of information on the human rights situation in practice, as well as the absence of facts and data on the implementation of the Covenant. As a result, a number of credible and substantiated allegations of violations of Covenant provisions which have been brought to the attention of the Committee could not be addressed effectively and the Committee found it difficult to determine whether individuals in the State party's territory and subject to its jurisdiction fully and effectively enjoy their fundamental rights under the Covenant. [48]

It is clear that the reference is to the alternative source of NGOs' submissions (Amnesty International in this case), which become a valuable instrument for balancing the national reports and for providing the members of the HRC with a fact-based series of issues deserving further analysis.

After a couple of sentences underlining the positive aspects compared to the previous report (in the spirit of what we have called the dialectical process), the list of concerns and recommendations appears. As far as this part of the document is concerned, we can notice the massive influence that the work of NGOs has had in several respects.

First of all, it is quite obvious how the concerns raised by the members of the HRC coincide with those highlighted by Amnesty International (and this is definitely evidence of the thoroughness and reliability of its submission). Of course, the Committee framed the text as a whole in a different form, taking into consideration more broad political aspects and implications, not mentioning individual cases unless in an indirect way[49] and focusing more or less on certain issues considered more or less relevant,[50] in accordance with its role of ethical guidance for the whole international community of states.

---

[48] See Concluding Observations, n. 38 above, at para. 2.

[49] This is particularly evident, to give another example, in the Concluding Observations of the Human Rights Committee: United Kingdom of Great Britain and Northern Ireland 06/12/2001, CCPR/CO/73/UK, CCPR/CO/73/UKOT (Concluding Observations/Comments), available on the website <www.unhchr.ch>, where the Committee, while referring to the serious situation of Northern Ireland, documented by a series of cases of abuses and violations, infers its causes of concerns from the concrete situation as presented by NGOs, but limits its analysis to a general comment, without the need to mention expressly individual episodes.

[50] For instance, in the Committee's document there is no reference to the concerns, raised by Amnesty International, relating to the rights of privacy (ICCPR, Article 17) and of liberty of move-

However, at another level it is interesting to note that the HRC referred to the work of NGOs on at least four occasions. In denouncing the obsessive and overwhelming control and repression operated by the Communist Party, it expresses concern 'at reported obstacles imposed on the registration and free operation of non-governmental human rights organisations and political parties'[51] and furthermore it wishes that 'non-governmental organisations and other human rights monitors should be granted access'[52] to some regions of the state, in order to report on the situations of certain minorities. In this way, the Committee welcomes and wishes to enhance the role of NGOs in the monitoring of the degree of respect for human rights within individual states.

Finally, the HRC acknowledges the function of NGOs as an alternative source of information to use in the analysis of state reports. In fact, both in an indirect way ('in the light of information available to the Committee',[53] which is in line with the cautious tendency we have mentioned above), and also in a more direct way ('small number of recorded complaints, in contrast to the information about large numbers of violations received from non-governmental sources'[54]) the members of the Committee admit their recourse to external, additional information, thus making clear that we have reached a point where it is no longer possible to deny the importance for the protection of human rights of the participation in the reporting mechanisms of such actors as NGOs.

3.   INTER-STATE COMMUNICATIONS

The second mechanism of protection provided by the ICCPR concerns the resolution of controversies that can arise between member states. Article 41 provides that:

> a State Party to the present Covenant may at any time declare under this article that it recognizes the competence of the Committee to receive and consider communications to the effect that a State Party claims that another State Party is not fulfilling its obligations under the present Covenant. Communications under this article may be received and considered only if submitted by a State Party that has made a declaration recognizing in regard to itself the competence of the Committee. No communication shall be received by the Committee if it concerns a State Party which has not made such a declaration.

---

ment (Article 12), while reference is made to additional articles of the Covenant, relating to the equal rights of men and women (Article 3), the right of participation in public life (Article 25), the right of equality before the law (Article 26) and the rights of minorities (Article 27).

[51] See para. 20.
[52] See para. 19.
[53] See para. 16.
[54] See para. 11.

The main purpose of this procedure is to reach a friendly solution of the controversy. The organ of control, however, does not have the power to take legally binding decisions, being limited to introducing a summary of the facts.

In the concrete praxis, the substantial failure of this procedure has been recorded,[55] both because of its inability to supply adequate protection (due to the non-binding powers of the HRC), and because of the tendency of states to tolerate less serious violations in order not to compromise the often delicate balance of international relations. Consequently, NGOs have not dedicated resources to this mechanism.

4.   INDIVIDUAL COMMUNICATIONS

4.1   Scope and functions of individual communication

The third mechanism of protection of human rights is provided by the First Optional Protocol,[56] Article 1 of which states that:

> A State Party to the Covenant that becomes a Party to the present Protocol recognizes the competence of the Committee to receive and consider communications from individuals subject to its jurisdiction who claim to be victims of a violation by that State Party of any of the rights set forth in the Covenant. No communication shall be received by the Committee if it concerns a State Party to the Covenant which is not a Party to the present Protocol.

The possibility of a direct claim from an individual gave rise to lively debates,[57] as is easily understandable for an issue that in the end cannot but erode, though only partially, the national sovereignty of states.

According to Article 2 of the Protocol, 'individuals who claim that any of their rights enumerated in the Covenant have been violated and who have exhausted all available domestic remedies may submit a written communication to the Committee for consideration'. In this way, the system outlined in the ICCPR is completed, and in addition to the procedures that are directly managed by states, we now have a mechanism of protection in which it is the individual victim who acts in order to have his or her rights granted.[58]

---

[55] See Sands, Mackenzie and Shany, n. 8 above, at p. 171 ('No inter-state communication has ever been lodged with the HRC').

[56] Adopted and opened for signature, ratification and accession by General Assembly Resolution 2200A (XXI) of 16 December 1966, it entered into force on 23 March 1976.

[57] See McGoldrick, n. 9 above; M. Nowak, *U.N. Covenant on Civil and Political Rights. CCPR Commentary* (N.P. Engel Publisher, Kiel, 1993).

[58] On the First Optional Protocol and the right to individual communications see P.R. Ghandhi, *The Human Rights Committee and the Right to Individual Communication, Law and Practice* (Dartmouth, 1998); A. de Zayas, J.T. Moller and T. Opsahl, 'Application of the International Covenant on Civil and Political Rights under the Optional Protocol by the Human Rights Committee'

4.2 NGOs: inclusion or exclusion?

What could be the role of NGOs in such a procedure? First, we have to consider whether the concept of 'individual' can be construed in such a way as to include an individual NGO as well as a single person.

During the negotiations on the First Optional Protocol, some drafts circulated extending the right to submit communications to groups of people or expressly to NGOs.[59] From such documents at least three ways to extend the right to initiate proceedings before the HRC emerged.[60] A first option was to favour unconditionally the right of NGOs to file petitions; a second option was to limit it only to certain selected NGOs, particularly those having consultative status with ECOSOC; and a last option was to allow individuals or groups of individuals to file petitions through NGOs.[61] Various reasons can be put forward to extend the right to petition to NGOs, based on the necessity of a close cooperation with the HRC, including:

(a) NGOs are more flexible as regards their objectives, scope and modalities, and do not suffer from bureaucratic burdens and red tape;[62]

(b) NGOs can boast long-running experience in the preparation of reports as well as in the settlement of bilateral disputes concerning human rights;[63]

(c) the HRC, as we have already seen as far as state reports are concerned, has no power to make on-the-spot investigations, having to rely solely on information that comes from either the state or the individual involved (who is usually in a weaker position and often is not able to supply adequate information to verify his or her charges);

(1985) 28 *Ger. YB Int'l L.* 9; T. Zwart, *The Admissibility of Human Rights Petitions: The Case Law of the European Commission of Human Rights and the Human Rights Committee* (Dordrecht, 1994); M.J. Bossuyt, 'Le règlement intérieur du Comité des droits de l'homme' (1978–79) 1 *Rev. Bel. Dr. Int.* 104.

[59] Respectively, the original Dutch draft to Article 2 of the Protocol and a draft protocol presented by the USA, which stated 'With respect to states Parties to this Protocol, the Human Rights Committee established pursuant to the International Covenant on Human Rights shall also have jurisdiction to receive written petitions submitted by ... non-governmental international organizations ... alleging that a state Party to this Protocol is not giving effect to a provision of the Covenant' (See Report of the Commission on Human Rights, 7th Session, 13 UN Escor Supp., No. 9, at 18, UN Doc. E/1992 (1951).

[60] For a reconstruction of the negotiations and of the various positions see Y.K. Tyagi, 'Cooperation Between the Human Rights Committee and Nongovernmental Organizations: Permissibility and Propositions' (1983) 18 *Texas Int'l L. J.* 273 and A.K. Lindblom, *The Legal Status of Non-Governmental Organisations in International Law* (Uppsala University, 2002).

[61] See Tyagi, n. 60 above, at pp. 278–279.

[62] As Waldheim remarked, NGOs 'can afford to be, and are, much more forthright in their approach' (K. Waldheim and R.L. Schiffer (eds.), *Building the Future Order: The Search for Peace in an Independent World* (New York, 1980)).

[63] It no longer seems to be acceptable to raise the consideration (reported in Tyagi, n. 60 above, at p. 275) according to which the Committee lacks adequate experience.

(d) NGOs now enjoy a more valuable status in international law compared to some decades ago;[64]

(e) NGOs, aiming at defending the interests of humanity as a whole, owe no allegiance to any state, while individuals may fear a negative reaction from their own government, when they challenge it at the international level.

On the other hand, there has always been some opposition to granting the right of petition to such non-state entities as NGOs, in particular on grounds such as:[65]

(i)   fear of a violation of the concept of state sovereignty;

(ii) risk of infringement of sovereign equality, due to the possibility that states not parties to the ICCPR might invite NGOs to submit complaints against states parties;

(iii) fear of an excessive role for NGOs, if they were not limited to giving expert technical advice but even allowed to sponsor individual petitions;

(iv) fear of abuse of right by NGOs, through irresponsible and mischievous allegations, mainly for political or propaganda purposes;

(v)   risk of a proliferation of submissions and consequently of a paralysis of the whole procedure.

As we can see, the implications of a more active involvement of NGOs were clear, and, as remarked in academic opinion, 'these discussions on the right to petition demonstrate that the restriction to individuals in the text finally adopted in 1966 by the General Assembly was intentional'.[66]

This choice has been confirmed by the HRC's jurisprudence relating to the rights of organizations (including but not only NGOs) under the First Optional Protocol.

In this respect, it is worthwhile to give some concrete examples of the views expressed by the HRC:[67]

• *J.R.T. and the W.G. Party v Canada*[68] (submission by a political party): the conclusion of the HRC was that the communication was inadmissible due to the fact that an association as such could not submit communications.

• *A Group of Associations for the Defence of the Rights of Disabled and Handicapped Persons in Italy etc. v Italy*:[69] the submission was from both an NGO

---

[64] NGOs play a role under other international agreements for the protection of human rights (the most important being the European Convention on Human Rights 1950).

[65] See Tyagi, n. 60 above, at pp. 280–282.

[66] See Lindblom, n. 60 above, at p. 217.

[67] As far as this jurisprudence is concerned, see Lindblom, n. 60 above, at p. 217 *et seq.*

[68] Communication No. 104/1981, A/38/40, Report of the Human Rights Committee, 1983, p. 236.

[69] Communication No. 163/1984, A/39/40, Report of the Human Rights Committee, 1984, pp. 197–198.

(Coordinamento) made up of a group of associations and the representatives of those organizations. The view of the Committee is that 'according to art. 1 of the Optional Protocol, only individuals have the right to submit a communication. To the extent, therefore, that the communication originated from the Coordinamento, it has to be declared *inadmissible because of lack of personal legal standing*'.[70]

- *Lubicon Lake Band v Canada*,[71] relating to the collective right of self-determination as set out in Article 1 of the Covenant:[72] the Committee declared that 'the author, as an individual, could not claim under the Optional Protocol to be a victim of a violation of the right to self-determination enshrined in article 1 of the Covenant, as it dealt with rights conferred upon peoples as such', adding also that there is 'no objection to a group of individuals, who claim to be similarly affected, collectively to submit a communication about alleged breaches of their rights'.[73]

From these cases we can infer that, according to HRC practice:

(a) NGOs cannot submit communications under Article 1 of the First Optional Protocol for the violation of an individual right (only the victim of the breach of the individual right is so entitled);

(b) in cases of violation of collective rights,[74] NGOs could play a role through communications submitted by one or more individuals duly authorized.

4.3 Possibilities pursuant to Rule of Procedure 90(b)

Two other possible ways to achieve a more direct involvement of NGOs are to be found in the provisions of Rule of Procedure 90(b).

First there is the possibility of acting on behalf of an alleged victim 'when it appears that the individual in question is unable to submit the communication personally'. For such submissions to be accepted, however, the link between the victim and the author of the communication must be particularly strong, as in the

---

[70] Communication No. 163/1984, A/39/40, Report of the Human Rights Committee, 1984, p. 198, emphasis added.

[71] Communication No. 167/1984, (1994) 96 ILR 668.

[72] ICCPR, Article 1: '1. All peoples have the right of self-determination. By virtue of that right they freely determine their political status and freely pursue their economic, social and cultural development. 2. All peoples may, for their own ends, freely dispose of their natural wealth and resources without prejudice to any obligations arising out of international economic co-operation, based upon the principle of mutual benefit, and international law. In no case may a people be deprived of its own means of subsistence. 3. The States Parties to the present Covenant, including those having responsibility for the administration of Non-Self-Governing and Trust Territories, shall promote the realization of the right of self-determination, and shall respect that right, in conformity with the provisions of the Charter of the United Nations'.

[73] Communication No. 167/1984, (1994) 96 ILR 668 at 702.

[74] See, e.g., ICCPR Article 21 (right of assembly) and Article 22 (right of association).

case of close family connection. The analysis of the practice of the HRC in this regard shows that other types of link are not deemed adequate to grant a right of action on behalf of the victim:

- *L.A. on behalf of U.R. v Uruguay*:[75] the HRC did not accept the communication submitted by a member of the Swedish Section of Amnesty International on behalf of the victim, imprisoned in Uruguay.
- *X. on behalf of S.G.F. v Uruguay*:[76] the HRC declared the communication (submitted by an NGO on behalf of an Uruguayan citizen living in Sweden) inadmissible, on the ground that 'no written evidence with regard to the authority of the organisation... or act on behalf of the alleged victim has been provided'.

We can conclude from the practice above[77] that the possibility for an NGO to submit communications on behalf of a victim unable to do so exists at least in theory, subject to the concrete demonstration of a genuine, strong link between the two actors.

The second possibility offered by Rule 90(b) concerns the case of an NGO acting as the 'individual's representative'. In this case we are not dealing with a difficulty faced by the alleged victim, but with the specific authorization by the victim of the NGO to act in his or her behalf, as a legal representative. This provision was clearly conceived to cover hypotheses other than the involvement of NGOs,[78] but the concrete practice before the HRC (the London-based human rights organization Interights has acted as the victim's representative in some cases)[79] shows us that it is a viable, although difficult and as yet uncommon, device to enlarge the participation of NGOs.

4.4   Friends of the court?

A last possibility to grant NGOs participation in individual communications is connected with the role of so-called 'friends of the court'. Besides the presence of third parties, who can submit views due to the legal interest they have in the outcome of the case, which may affect their rights, the theory of legal procedure admits the possibility of an *amicus curiae* brief. By this we mean a submission by a third actor, who has no direct interest in the litigation, but decides to give his or

---

[75] Communication No. 128/1982, (1990) 2 *Selected Decisions of the Human Rights Committee* 40.

[76] Communication No. 136/1983, (1990) 2 *Selected Decisions of the Human Rights Committee* 43.

[77] For other cases leading to the same conclusion see Lindblom, n. 60 above, at p. 220.

[78] 'A lawyer with a written power of attorney was what the Committee primarily had in mind here', notes Lindblom, n. 60 above, at p. 220.

[79] For an analysis and evaluation of these cases (all relating to death sentences and unfair trials) see Lindblom, n. 60 above, at p. 221.

her contribution on the basis of a public or general interest.[80] The *amicus curiae* brief first appeared at national level,[81] where it developed and from where it spread into international jurisdictions, though with different outcomes. The acceptance of *amicus curiae* briefs is seen as a sign of openness towards 'civil society', i.e., a whole, complex series of entities, corporations, associations, NGOs, each one with its concept of what the public interest is, which are normally prevented from taking part in international litigation. An *amicus curiae* brief presents a whole series of advantages and can serve the purposes of international litigation in several ways.[82] The fact that they are not bound by the legal and factual framework determined by the parties to the dispute allows the friends of the court to give a significant contribution as far as different legal perspectives or even further factual data are concerned. This is particularly true in complex cases, where the implications of the possible outcomes of the dispute might go beyond the private interests directly involved and influence a broader number of stakeholders that would normally be left without the possibility of having their voice heard, or might raise questions of public interest.

Besides the extremely valuable role of these briefs in matters where there is no clear and established path for the court to follow (and where they can be even more appreciated because of the highly qualified advice they may give), it is important to underline that the position they have in the dispute allows a friend of the court, at least in theory, to be seen as a neutral player, with neither allies to help nor enemies to fight, and therefore able to give a contribution solely in the interest of justice. Of course, this particular status they enjoy in the process prevents the friends of the court from taking a more active part, since they are not granted the same rights as parties (they consequently have a more limited access

---

[80] On the concept of *amicus curiae* and the possible role of NGOs in this respect, see E. Angell, 'The Amicus Curiae: American Development of English Institutions' (1976) 16 *Int'l & Comp. L. Q.* 1017; H. Ascensio, 'L'Amicus Curiae devant les juridictions internationales' (2001) 5 *Rev. Gén. Dr. Int. Pub.* 897; R. Baratta, 'La legittimazione dell'amicus curiae dinnanzi agli organi giudiziali della Organizzazione Mondiale del Commercio' (2002) 3 *Riv. Dir. Int.* 549; O. De Schutter, 'Sur l'émergence de la société civile en droit international: le role des associations devant la Cour Européenne des droits de l'homme' (1996) 7 *Eur. J. Int'l L.* 372; S. Krislov, 'The Amicus Curiae Brief: From Friendship to Advocacy' (1963) 72 *Yale L. J.* 694; Lindblom, n. 60 above; E. Nchema, 'Le role des organisations non gouvernementales dans la promotion et la protection des droits de l'homme' *Bulletin des Droits de l'Homme*, No. 90/2; M. A. Olz, 'Non Governmental Organizations in Regional Human Rights System' (1997) 28 *Colu. Hum. Rts. L. Rev.* 307; P. Palchetti, 'Amici Curiae davanti alla Corte Internazionale di Giustizia ?' (2000) 4 *Riv. Dir. Int.* 965; J. Razzaque, 'Changing Role of Friends of the Court in the International Courts and Tribunals' (2001) 1 *Non-State Actors & Int'l L.* 169; D. Shelton, 'The Participation of Non-governmental Organizations in International Judicial Proceedings' (1994) 88 *Am. J. Int'l L.* 611, and P. Sands, 'International Law, the Practitioner and Non-State Actors' in M. Anderson (ed.), *The International Lawyer as a Practitioner* (London, 2000), pp. 103–124.

[81] It is within common law systems that the *amicus curiae* brief is mostly deployed, especially at the appeal level, whenever the litigation involves matters of common interests, such as the exercise of fundamental rights.

[82] See Razzaque, n. 80 above, at p. 170 *et seq.*

to documents, are excluded from the possibility of examining and cross-examining witnesses), and their presence being itself possible only by express leave of the court. In the absence of a precise rule on the role of the *amicus curiae*, the practice before the HRC has been non-existent in this regard,[83] and this probably reflects the hostility of sovereign states towards submissions which come from non-state actors and which can require an extra effort to address all the questions raised.

5. CONCLUSION

We have tried to analyse the possibilities which the various mechanisms for the implementation of the ICCPR offer to the participation of NGOs.

The first procedure, the system of periodic reports, has been widely deployed by non-state actors to enhance their role, and the outcome of this cooperation between the HRC and the world of NGOs may certainly be deemed to be a positive one. As we have tried to underline, NGOs' submissions play a fundamental role, with their in-depth analysis of the concrete cases of violations and abuses which will never be mentioned in the official reports of states, with their network of relations which is of paramount importance in the spread of information as well as in the furtherance and dissemination of public awareness of issues concerning human rights.

The most notable feature of this active participation is that it has managed to develop within a legal framework which lacks any reference to it; however, the NGOs themselves believe that this is not in practice a problem since it is first of all in the interests of the Committee, of its independence and of its prestige, to continue and to make the most of this cooperation.

It is worth highlighting the positive attitude that NGOs have assumed in undertaking their task: they do not want to be seen as a player acting against the states, but as a sort of stimulating partner, willing to cooperate but not overwhelmed, authoritative and independent but not seeking to oppose just for the sake of opposition.

Coming to the other two mechanisms we have examined, it is just from this perspective that granting NGOs the right to submit communications under the procedures established in the First Optional Protocol might not be the best solution. By such a move, in fact, the opposition between states and NGOs could be exacerbated beyond what may be seen as an acceptable point: to lift non-state actors to the same level as sovereign states would imply massive changes in the structure and balance of international relations, which we are probably not yet ready to cope with.

---

[83] See Sands, Mackenzie and Shany, n. 8 above, at p. 178 ('So far the Committee has not admitted such submissions').

The main issue, in our view, is the lack of democratic control on NGOs.[84] We do accept that the arguments[85] for expanding their participation are all extremely valuable ones, but the risk of abuses of rights and of politically biased actions still exist and must be taken seriously into consideration.

If we grant NGOs the same rights as sovereign states, where are the checks and balances for such great powers? Very often NGOs begin their work by virtue solely of the strong beliefs and commitment of a few people, who are accountable only to their conscience and beliefs. We doubt that this model can be expanded so as to become the commonplace and universally accepted way to deal with these situations.

One could argue that 'democratic control' and the idea that a state is politically accountable for its actions, and judged by its citizens by means of democratic elections, often does not in fact apply in practice, and moreover that under customary international law the concept of 'reserved domain' is dramatically shrinking and there is an undeniable tendency not to consider matters such as respect for the human rights of citizens as a merely internal problem.[86] However, what in the present system of international relations is becoming the exception, in the NGO world would still be the rule.

On the other hand, trying to structure NGOs in such a way as to grant a sort of democratic control or accountability to citizens is simply impossible. We would not be able to prevent in any way a certain NGO from being established through the financial contribution of a particular group in order to pursue only a particular type of issues and cases, even just towards only a particular state. This is, of course, absolutely acceptable, and a sign in itself of democracy; but how could we pretend that sovereign states would accept to be put on the same level, and be

---

[84] On this subject there is a lively debate in academic writing: on the one hand such authors as Anderson maintain that 'it is no exaggeration to regard the international NGOs ... as not merely undemocratic, but as profoundly antidemocratic' (see K. Anderson, 'The Limits of Pragmatism in American Foreign Policy: Unsolicited Advice to the Bush Administration on Relations with International Nongovernmental Organizations' (2001) 2 *Chicago J. Int'l L.* 371), while on the other hand others claim that the problem of the lack of accountability has been exaggerated (see P.J. Spiro, 'The Democratic Accountability of Non-Governmental Organizations: Accounting for NGOs' (2002) 3 *Chicago J. Int'l L.* 161, where the author writes that 'in what might be called the inclusion paradox, the accountability challenge may be better answered by formally and fully recognizing NGO power in international institutional architectures'). Other views on this subject are expressed in P. Wapner, 'The Democratic Accountability of Non-Governmental Organizations: Defending Accountability in NGOs' (2002) 3 *Chicago J. Int'l L.* 197, B. Kingsbury, 'The Democratic Accountability of Non-Governmental Organizations: First Amendment Liberalism as Global Legal Architecture: Ascriptive Groups and the Problems of the Liberal NGO Model of International Civil Society' (2002) 3 *Chicago J. Int'l L.* 183, C.L. Taylor, 'A Critique of State/NGO Relations' (2002) 29 *Syracuse J. Int'l L. and Commerce* 303 and D. Spar and J. Dail, 'Of Measurement and Mission: Accounting for Performance in Non-Governmental Organizations' (2002) 3 *Chicago J. Int'l L.* 171.

[85] See above.

[86] Consider, e.g., the idea of the legality of use of force on the basis of so-called 'humanitarian intervention', which, though not universally accepted and subject to criticism in many respects, nonetheless can give the sense of the increasing importance of respect for human rights and democratic principles within the jurisdiction of a state.

granted the same rights and possibilities, as a group of private individuals, pursuing interests which one may define as 'public' but which can also seem to be serving just a minority?

We believe that in the end, trying to equate states with NGOs would mean structuring these organizations in such a way as to make them a sort of 'copy' of states, thus losing one of their most important features, i.e., their flexibility, the possibility of acting more freely and with fewer restraints, and furthermore burdening them with a whole series of obligations which inevitably arise when we shift from a role of campaigning/advocacy to the more complete and legally binding one of litigation.

The best solution, in the interests of both the states and the NGOs (and consequently of the cause of human rights) would seem to be in the role played by international independent bodies such as the HRC. It is their ability to act as a filter that allows the system to work and to give good results. This is true also in the case of *amicus curiae* briefs: allowing all of them indiscriminately would not necessarily mean giving more possibilities to the weaker party,[87] since often the friends of the court turn out to be more simply those who have the capacities (financial, human, etc.) to prepare a submission.

The HRC can grant a right of participation to NGOs by using to the full the absolutely valuable work they do, for instance in the analysis of states' reports, but by being the only official counterpart of the state, the Committee can equally reassure the state that partial, biased, propagandistic or merely political accusations will not be taken into consideration.

---

[87] This applies particularly in commercial cases.

Chapter 6

Some Concluding Remarks on NGOs and the European Court of Human Rights

Nina Vajic*

1. INTRODUCTION

In a slightly different context from the one we are dealing with here, Nitin Desai has affirmed the important role that NGOs play in the contemporary world by saying that 'They have increasingly assumed the role of promoters of new ideas, they alerted the international community to emerging issues, and they have developed expertise and talent which, in an increasing number of areas, have become vital ...'.[1]

The same is definitely true also of the important role most human rights NGOs play in promoting and protecting human rights – I refer, of course, only to those NGOs that are independent of governmental and political groups.[2] In this chapter we shall deal with the different ways in which such NGOs are involved in proceedings before the European Court of Human Rights (ECHR) and thus exert influence on the development of its case law.

The term 'non-governmental organization' covers a broad category of organizations of a different nature. Therefore, when speaking about the role of NGOs in relation to the ECHR it should be kept in mind that, although this chapter concerns mainly human rights NGOs, they are, of course, not the only NGOs who play a role in ECHR proceedings, depending on the subject matter of the complaint and the Convention rights invoked.

As to the category of non-governmental organizations, it is accepted case law that they must be private organizations and that municipalities, other local gov-

---

* The views expressed herein are solely those of the author.

[1] UN Under-Secretary General for Policy Coordination and Sustainable Development. Remarks at the Meeting of the Organizational Session of the Open-Ended Working Group of ECOSOC on the Review of Arrangements for Consultation with Non-Governmental Organizations (17 February 1994), quoted from K. Appiagyei-Atua, 'Human Rights NGOs and their Role in the Promotion and Protection of Rights in Africa' (2002) 9 *Int'l J. Minority & Group Rts* 265.

[2] A human rights NGO is defined by Laurie Wiseberg as 'A private association which devotes significant resources to the promotion and protection of human rights, which is independent of both governmental and political groups that seek political power, and which does not itself seek such power', ibid.

T. Treves et al., eds., *Civil Society, International Courts and Compliance Bodies*
© 2005, T·M·C·ASSER PRESS, The Hague, The Netherlands, and the Authors

ernment organizations or semi-state bodies, such as governmental organs or local public authorities, cannot be included, since they are performing official functions in the name of the state.[3] Political parties or organizations, on the other hand, are regarded as NGOs or groups of individuals.[4]

Article 34 of the European Convention for the Protection of Human Rights and Fundamental Freedoms 1950 ('the European Convention'), requires that the applicants to the ECHR be victims of an alleged violation of one of the rights recognized by the European Convention. They must prove that they are directly affected by the matter complained of, which means that for professional associations and NGOs to be regarded as victims they must show that they themselves are in some way affected by the measure complained of.[5] They can only act on behalf of their members if they identify them and provide evidence of authority to represent them.

Church bodies or associations with religious or philosophical objectives,[6] me-

---

[3] See *Commune Rothenthurm v Switzerland*, No. 13252/87, Commission decision of 14 December 1988, (1988) DR 59, p. 251; *Province of Bari, Sorrentino and Messeni Nemagna v Italy*, No. 41877/98, decision of 22 March 2001; *Municipal Section of Antilly v France*, No. 45129/98, decision of 23 November 1999, (1999-VIII) ECHR Reports; *Ayuntamiento de Mula v Spain*, No. 55346/00, decision of 1 February 2001, (2001-I) ECHR Reports; and *Danderyds Kommun v Sweden*, No. 52559/99, decision of 7 June 2001.

[4] *Freedom and Democracy Party (ÖZDEP) v Turkey* [GC], No. 23885/94, judgment of 8 December 1999, (1999-VIII) ECHR Reports; *Refah Partisi (the Welfare Party) and others v Turkey* [GC], Nos. 41340/98, 41342/98, 41343/98 and 41344/98, judgment of 13 February 2003, (2003-II) ECHR Reports; *Presidential Party of Mordovia v Russia*, No. 65659/01, decision of 9 September 2003; *Yazar and others v Turkey*, Nos. 22723/93, 22724/93 and 22725/93, judgment of 9 April 2002, (2002-II) ECHR Reports; *Stankov and United Macedonian Organisation Ilinden v Bulgaria*, Nos. 29221/95 and 29225/95, judgment of 2 October 2001, (2001-IX) ECHR Reports; *Partidul Comunistilor (Nepeceristi) and Ungureanu v Romania*, No. 46626/99, decision of 16 December 2003; *Freiheitliche Partei Österreichs, Landesgruppe Niederösterreich v Austria*, No. 65924/01, decision of 9 October 2003; *The Russian Conservative Party of Entrepreneurs and others v Russia*, Nos. 55066/00 and 55638/00, decision of 18 March 2004.

[5] *Èeskomoravská myslivecká jednota v Czech Republic*, No. 33091/96, decision of 23 March 1999; *Association Les amis de Saint-Raphaël et de Fréjus and others v France*, No. 45053/98, decision of 29 February 2000; *Asociación Ramón Santos de Estudios sobre el Cannabis (ARSEC) and others v Spain*, No. 42916/98, decision of 15 June 1999; *Association Ekin v France*, No. 39288/98, decision of 18 January 2000; *VgT Verein gegen Tierfabriken v Switzerland*, No. 24699/94, decision of 6 April 2000; *Association of Polish Teachers v Poland*, No. 42049/98, decision of 9 December 2003; *Helsinki Committee for Human Rights in the Republic of Moldova v Moldova*, No. 67300/01. So, e.g., in *Èonka v Belgium* No. 51564/99, decision of 13 March 2001, the Ligue des droits de l'homme could not claim to be itself a victim of the measures taken against the Èonka family and its claim was dismissed as being incompatible *ratione personae* with the provisions of the European Convention; see also *Asselbourg and others and Greenpeace-Luxembourg v Luxembourg*, No. 29121/95, decision of 29 June 1999, (1999-VI) ECHR Reports.

[6] *Cha'are Shalom Ve Tsedek v France, Cha'are Shalom Ve Tsedek v France* [GC], No. 27417/95, judment of 27 June 2000, (2000-VII) ECHR Reports; *Metropolitan Church of Bessarabia and others v Moldova*, No. 45701/99, judgment of 13 December 2001, (2001-XII) ECHR Reports; *Johannische Kirche and Peters v Germany*, No. 41754/98, decision of 10 July 2001, (2001-VIII) ECHR Reports; *Christian Federation of Jehovah's Witnesses in France v France*, No. 53430/99, decision of 6 November 2001, (2001-XI) ECHR Reports; *Islamische Religionsgemeinschaft e.V. v Ger-*

dia organizations[7] or trade unions[8] may, of course, be directly affected in their own right. Companies can also claim to be victims of infringements of some Convention rights, such as property rights or the right to a hearing within 'a reasonable time'; not all the rights in the European Convention are, however, of relevance to them.[9]

Over time, the so-called 'indirect victim' concept has been developed in the ECHR's case law to encompass not only persons personally affected (direct victims), but also close relatives (spouses, parents or family members); in other words, those who are also prejudiced by the violation, as well as those who may have a valid personal interest in having the violation established. Conceptually, the indirect victim is to be distinguished from the representation of a direct victim by a third party (where there is no personal link),[10] or the continuation of Convention proceedings by an heir or a personal representative. While this development does not directly concern NGOs, it is an indication of a possible evolution of the ECHR's practice with regard to the role of representatives before the ECHR.

---

many, No. 53871/00, decision of 5 December 2002, (2002-X) ECHR Reports; *Synod College of the Evangelical Reformed Church of Lithuania*, No. 44548/98, decision of 5 December 2002; *Supreme Holy Council of the Muslim Community v Bulgaria*, No. 39023/97, decision of 8 July 2003; *The Zagreb Archdiocese (Nadbiskupija Zagrebaèka) v Slovenia*, No. 60376/00, decision of 27 May 2004.

[7] *Verdens Gang and Aase v Norway*, No. 45710/99, decision of 16 October 2001, (2001-X) ECHR Reports; *Tele 1 Privatfernsehgesellschaft mbH v Austria*, No. 32240/96, judgment of 21 September 2000; *Pasalaris and Fondation de Presse v Greece*, No. 60916/00, decision of 4 July 2002; *Radio France and others v France*, No. 53984/00, decision 23 September 2003; *Independent News and Media plc and Independent Newspapers (Ireland) Ltd v Ireland*, No. 55120/00, decision of 19 June 2003; *Bladet Tromsø and Stensaas v Norway* [GC], No. 21980/93, judgment of 20 May 1999, (1999-III) ECHR Reports; *Bergens Tidende and others v Norway*, No. 26132/95, judgment of 2 May 2000, (2000-IV) ECHR Reports; *Krone Verlag GmbH & Co. KG v Austria* (No. 2), No. 40284/98, judgment of 6 November 2003; *Scharsach and News Verlagsgesellschaft v Austria*, No. 39394/98, judgment of 13 November 2003, (2003-XI) ECHR Reports; *Ukrainian Media Group v Ukraine*, No. 72713/01, decision of 18 May 2004.

[8] *Unison v United Kingdom*, No. 53574/99, decision of 10 January 2002, (2002-I) ECHR Reports; *Federation of Offshore Workers' Trade Unions and others v Norway*, No. 38190/97, decision of 27 June 2002, (2002-VI) ECHR Reports.

[9] *Comingersoll v Portugal* [GC], No. 35382/97, judgment of 6 April 2000, (2000-IV) ECHR Reports; *Bielectric Srl v Italy*, No. 36811/97, decision of 4 May 2000; *ITC (Isle of Man), P.S.W.H. and A.G.S. v United Kingdom*, No. 45619/99, decision of 29 February 2000; *AB Kurt Kellermann v Sweden*, No. 41579/98, decision 1 July 2003; *Belvedere Alberghiera S.r.l. v Italy*, No. 31524/96, judgments of 30 May 2000, (2000-VI) ECHR Reports, and 30 October 2003 (just satisfaction).

[10] An exceptional and very interesting situation arose in *Karner v Austria*, No. 40016/98, judgment of 24 July 2003, (2003-IX) ECHR Reports, where after the applicant's death his legal representative was allowed to continue the proceedings, since the ECHR found that respect for human rights as defined in the European Convention and the Protocols thereto required a continuation of the examination of the case.

2. ROLE OF HUMAN RIGHTS NGOs

Although human rights NGOs do not have the right to lodge an application with the ECHR unless they are themselves victims of violations of the European Convention they have, nevertheless, an important role to play in proceedings before the ECHR by providing assistance and advice to the victims.[11] Effective use of the European Convention requires specialized legal knowledge, in particular of the Convention and the voluminous case law complementing and developing it. By this kind of assistance, specialized NGOs assist both the victims and the ECHR itself and are an essential adjunct to all systems of human rights protection.

The assistance they provide may take various forms, depending on whether they:

(a) participate in the proceedings more actively, i.e., appear directly before the ECHR representing the applicants, or appointing lawyers to assist them,[12] or
(b) only support the applicants, sponsor them, yet refrain from directly taking part in the proceedings.[13] With this kind of intervention, which is a 'hidden-face intervention', they may influence proceedings by providing professional legal assistance in the proceedings, i.e., helping the applicants to draw up applications through advice on how to draft a petition and how to answer government replies and questions put by the ECHR, etc.[14]

As already mentioned, such assistance rendered by NGOs is of extreme importance both for the applicants and the ECHR:

- by bringing important cases to the ECHR they draw attention to important infringements of human rights and systemic violations;
- their assistance to applicants helps to reduce the inequality of parties to the proceedings (specially trained lawyers, top experts);

---

[11] See generally, M.A. Nowicki, 'Non-Governmental Organisations (NGOs) Before the European Commission of Human Rights' in M. de Salvia and M.E. Villiger (eds.), *The Birth of European Human Rights Law, Liber Amicorum C.A. Nørgaard* (Nomos, Baden-Baden, 1998), pp. 267–273.

[12] In the mid-1990s, many applications concerning the infringement of human rights in South Eastern Turkey to the detriment of the Kurdish minority were thus lodged with the Human Rights Commission by the Human Rights Association, Turkey, the Kurdish Human Rights Project, London, and the Human Rights Centre, University of Essex. For more details, see Nowicki, n. 11 above, at p. 270.

[13] Some of these organizations never appear themselves before the ECHR, as happened for instance in numerous cases against French authorities by persons infected with HIV during a blood transfusion, Association française des hémophiles, Association de défense des transfusés, Associations des polytransfusés. Ibid., p. 271.

[14] Ibid., p. 269; F. Ermacora, 'Non-governmental Organizations as Promoters of Human Rights' in F. Matscher, H. Petzold and C. Heymanns (eds.), *Protecting Human Rights: The European Dimension, Studies in honour of G.J. Wiarda* (Verlag KG, Köln, 1988), p. 174.

- they can help to reduce the number of petitions to the ECHR by giving advice to applicants as to the conditions of admissibility, the scope of the rights protected, the existing case law, etc.

In this respect, it should, however, be noted that not all NGOs behave equally responsibly. In the current situation where the ECHR is faced with an enormous volume of clearly inadmissible cases, it is particularly important that NGOs do act responsibly and do not create unjustified expectations for applicants whose hopes will inevitably be frustrated. The mass of inadmissible cases makes it increasingly difficult for the ECHR to deal with substantial, potentially well-founded cases.

However, the main focus for human rights NGOs is to achieve changes in domestic legislation or general practice following an ECHR judgment finding a state to be in breach of the Convention. Therefore, NGOs often choose for their intervention cases which are capable of drawing attention to laws or practices of state organs of particular importance for the protection of human rights. Bringing cases before the ECHR is but one facet of their everyday activities and efforts to strengthen human rights guarantees in a country. It has been suggested that the influence of NGOs might diminish with the increased use made by the individual petition system.[15] This has, however, not proved to be the case. On the contrary, given the ever-increasing workload of the ECHR and its consequent inability to deal with individual applications within a reasonable time, the role of NGOs may become even more important in identifying situations of structural violation.

3. THIRD PARTY INTERVENTION (DIRECT INTERVENTION)

NGOs may also take part in the proceedings by making a third party intervention according to Article 36(2) of the Convention. Article 36(2) states that any person concerned who is not a party to the proceedings and who is not the applicant may submit written comments or take part in hearings. It has been suggested that the rationale behind this provision is that the ECHR's judgments affect the rights and obligations of everyone within the jurisdiction of a state.[16] However, the practice indicates that the two main categories of intervention are, first, persons or organizations who are in some way involved in the subject matter of the proceedings,[17] and secondly organizations who are able to shed light on the general factual and legal issues before the ECHR.

The European Convention in its original version made no provision for third party intervention. Since 1 January 1983, the Rules of ECHR have allowed for

---

[15] Ermacora, n. 14 above, at p. 174.

[16] See A. Lester, '*Amici Curiae*: Third Party Intervention before the European Court of Human Rights' in Matscher, Petzold and Heymanns, n. 14 above, at p. 342.

[17] *V. v United Kingdom* [GC], No. 24888/94, judgment of 24 July 2003, (1999-IX) ECHR Reports; *Öcalan v Turkey*, No. 46221/99.

such intervention,[18] which was subsequently enshrined in Protocol No. 11 amending the Convention.

The former Rule 61 (in Title II (Procedure))[19] dealt with this topic, while as from 1 November 2003 the new Rule 44 (Chapter I (General Rules)) relates to third party intervention. Rule 44(2)[20] is relevant to intervention by NGOs.

The new rule enables third party intervention at an early stage, i.e., from the moment of the communication of the application to the respondent government,[21] and not only after admissibility, as before. Thus account was taken of the possible wish of a potential intervener to address an issue coming within the scope of admissibility, especially as there is no rule in Article 36 of the European Convention excluding such interventions. Furthermore, when a hearing is held prior to admissibility it normally concerns both admissibility and the merits of the case. The ECHR was of the view that not allowing intervention in such cases until after the admissibility decision has been delivered, when the Chamber will often already have deliberated on the merits and arrived at a provisional conclusion, substantially reduces the utility that the intervention might have for the process of adjudication, quite apart from leaving the intervener with a sense of frustration.[22] It may also entail delays, since a further exchange of written observations is required after the hearing, on issues already presented at the hearing.[23]

A potential intervener must show an interest in the outcome of the proceedings (person concerned) and that the intervention is in the interests of the proper administration of justice (in the interests of justice), in the sense that it should assist the ECHR in the carrying out of its task. Before inviting, or granting leave to, any

---

[18] For the *amicus curiae* brief before the old ECHR, see Rules of ECHR, 1997, Rule 37(2) which read: 'The President may, in the interests of the proper administration of justice, invite or grant leave to any Contracting State which is not a party to the proceedings to submit written comments within a time-limit and on issues which he shall specify. He may extend such an invitation or grant such leave to any person concerned other than the applicant'.

[19] Rules of ECHR, October 2002.

[20] Rule 44(2) reads as follows: '(a) Once notice of an application has been given to the respondent Contracting Party under Rule 51(1) or Rule 54(2)(b), the President of the Chamber may, in the interests of the proper administration of justice, as provided in Article 36(2) of the Convention, invite, or grant leave to, any Contracting Party which is not a party to the proceedings, or any person concerned who is not the applicant, to submit written comments or, in exceptional cases, to take part in a hearing. (b) Requests for leave for this purpose must be duly reasoned and submitted in writing in one of the official languages as provided in Rule 34(4) not later than twelve weeks after notice of the application has been given to the respondent Contracting Party. Another time limit may be fixed by the President of the Chamber for exceptional reasons'.

[21] There would appear to be little sense in having intervention prior to communication of the application to the respondent government. Interventions will now normally take place prior to the decision on admissibility but not before communication of the application to the respondent government.

[22] These changes are in line with the comments by Interights, and a number of other NGOs.

[23] This happened in the case of *Hatton v United Kingdom* [GC], No. 36022/97, judgment of 8 July 2003, (2003-VIII) ECHR Reports, and also in *Brumărescu v Romania* [GC], No. 28342/95, judgment of 23 January 2001, (1999-VII) ECHR Reports, where not an NGO but an individual was given leave to intervene.

person concerned who is not the applicant, to submit written comments or, in exceptional cases, to take part in a hearing, the President of the Chamber must be satisfied that these conditions are satisfied. The mere demonstration of an interest in the outcome of the proceedings will not suffice.

Requests for leave for this purpose must be duly reasoned and submitted in writing in one of the official languages not later than 12 weeks after notice of the application has been given to the respondent state party. Another time limit may be fixed by the President of the Chamber only for exceptional reasons.[24]

Any third party in the procedure before the Chamber retains that status before the Grand Chamber, without being obliged to make a fresh request for leave to intervene. This is not spelt out in the Rule but would be confirmed to the third party when the latter is advised by the Registrar of the referral of the case to the Grand Chamber.[25]

Some commentators have asked whether there should be 'a right' to intervene or whether it should be entirely within the discretion of the President in consultation with other members of the ECHR to decide on such requests.

Personally, I agree with the view that there should be some kind of judicial control over the circumstances in which, and of the extent to which, third parties are permitted to intervene, i.e., that the ECHR should have the last word in this respect. I do not, however, think that – if one day intervention became a right *per se*, with little or no discretionary power on the ECHR's part – this would represent a real danger for the ECHR and would 'open the flood gates' so that the ECHR would be overwhelmed with such briefs.

While that might happen at the beginning, most probably it would not continue after a certain time, in view of the strict rules elaborated and the approach applied by the ECHR so far. First, the request has to be strictly limited to matters directly connected with the issues before the ECHR,[26] it has to be concise and submitted within very strict time limits – which shows that considerable skill and expertise are needed to comply with these conditions. In addition, no legal aid is available for such briefs or for possible participation in a hearing.

In any event, it seems, as stated below, that in practice the new ECHR does not turn down requests for third party intervention, in the sense that it prevents

---

[24] According to Rule 44(4), any invitation or grant of leave referred to in Rule 44(2)(a) must be subject to any conditions, including time limits, set by the President of the Chamber. Where such conditions are not complied with, the President may decide not to include the comments in the case file or to limit participation in the hearing to the extent that he or she considers appropriate.

[25] Potential interveners are allowed to submit comments for the first time when a case goes before the Grand Chamber, either on pre-judgment relinquishment of jurisdiction or for a post-judgment rehearing (Articles 30 and 43 of the European Convention). That means that a time limit for new interventions runs as from referral of the case to the Grand Chamber. In this connection, the 'decision of the Chamber' that triggers the time limit is the actual decision to relinquish jurisdiction (Rule 72(1)), see Rule 44(3).

[26] Leave to intervene was refused by the President of the ECHR in *Leander v Sweden*, No. 9248/81, judgment of 26 March 1987, ECHR A116, as the connection between the matters that would have been dealt with in the third party submissions and the issues before the ECHR was considered too remote. For more details, see Lester, n. 16 above, at p. 348.

any NGO participating in a given case. That might explain why the proposal to give NGOs a right to intervene was not further pursued.

Even if the ECHR is sometimes criticized for being excessively cautious in allowing third party intervention, and for not always making reference to unsuccessful requests, the information for the period until October 2003 shows that the new ECHR has practically never refused NGO requests for third party intervention. It has only done so in respect of requests that were either premature (before admissibility) or too late in the proceedings (out of time) – which means that either the Rules of ECHR or the established practice were not followed, or when it was of the opinion that the requested submissions would duplicate already accepted NGO briefs, and thus not be in the interests of the proper administration of justice.

Thus, since 1 November 1998, when the new permanent ECHR came into being, I have been able to trace only five[27] cases in which NGOs were refused leave. Out of these, in two cases leave was refused because the requests were premature, i.e., they were lodged before the applications had been declared admissible: *Asprogerakas-Grivas and others v Greece* (No. 58683/00), and *Comitato promotore del referendum maggioritario del 18 aprile 1999; Comitato promotore del referendum antiproporzionale del 21 maggio 2000 v Italy* (No. 56507/00). Both applications were subsequently declared inadmissible by the ECHR, in accordance with Article 35 of the European Convention.[28] There has, however, been at least one request for intervention prior to admissibility that has been granted.[29]

One further request was refused because it had not been submitted 'within a reasonable time'. In his letter the Section Registrar also referred to the fact that such an intervention would not serve 'the interests of the proper administration of justice' (*Phillips v United Kingdom*, No. 41087/98).

In *Senator Lines GmbH v 15 States Members of the European Union* (No. 56672/00) leave to intervene was granted to the Council of the Bars and Law Societies of the EU (CCBE) and the European Company Lawyers Association (ECLA), but not to the German Bar Association, because there were similarities between its proposed submissions and those of the CCBE of which the German Bar Association is a member. The request was therefore refused as not being necessary in 'the interests of the proper administration of justice'.[30]

Similarly, in *Öcalan v Turkey* (No. 46221/99), the Mothers of Martyrs Association and Istanbul Analare Dayamişma Derneği were granted leave to intervene with written submissions, while the Izmir Branch of the Association of Families

---

[27] This figure has to be taken with a certain amount of caution because of the difficulties encountered during such research.

[28] The first one by a Committee (Article 28 of the European Convention) and the second by a Chamber.

[29] *Fretté v France*, No. 36515/97, decision of 12 June 2001.

[30] It is interesting to note that a request from the European Commission to intervene in the proceedings at the admissibility stage was accepted after the communication of the application.

of Martyrs and the Turkish Law Institute were refused, having regard to the state of proceedings in the case, because their request had not been submitted 'within a reasonable time'.

Cases in which NGOs intervened before the ECHR either as a third party or by representing the applicants, between 1 November 1998 and October 2003, are numerous[31] and confirm the above assertion. They include:

- *Pretty v United Kingdom* (No. 2346/02): Voluntary Euthanasia Society and the Catholic Bishops' Conference of England and Wales;
- *Nikula v Finland* (No. 31611/96): Interights (International Center for the Legal Protection of Human Rights);
- *Stafford v United Kingdom* (No. 46295/99): Justice;
- *Fretté v France* (No. 36515/97): ILGA-Europe (International Lesbian and Gay Association, European Region);
- *Karner v Austria* (No. 40016/98): ILGA-Europe, Liberty, Stonewall;
- *I v United Kingdom* (No. 25680/94) and *Goodwin v United Kingdom* (No. 28957/95): Liberty;
- *Wilson, National Union of Jornalists and others v United Kingdom* (Nos. 30668/96, 30671/96 and 30678/96): jointly Trades Union Congress and Liberty;
- *Kress v France* (No. 39594/98): Court of Cassation and Conseil d'Etat Bar (L'ordre des avocats à la Cour de cassation et au Conseil d'Etat);
- *Sadak and others v Turkey* (No. 1) (Nos. 29900/96, 29901/96, 29902/96 and 29903/96): IPU (Inter-Parliamentary Union);
- *Sadak and others v Turkey* (No. 2) (Nos. 25144/94, 26149/95 to 26154/95, 27100/95 and 27101/95): KHRP (Kurdish Human Rights Project);
- *T. v United Kingdom* (No. 24724/94): Justice;
- *V. v United Kingdom* (No. 24888/94): Justice;
- *Hatton and others v United Kingdom* (No. 36022/97): Friends of the Earth;
- *Pedersen and Baadsgaard v Denmark* (No. 49017/99): Danish Union of Journalists;
- *Yusupova, Isayeva, Bazayeva v Russia* (Nos. 57947/00, 57948/00, 57949/00): Memorial;
- *Akhmadova and Sadulayeva v Russia* (No. 40464/02): SCJI (The Stichting Chechnya Justice Initiative);
- *M.C. v Bulgaria* (No. 39272/98): Interights;
- *Nachova and others v Bulgaria* (Nos. 43577/98 and 43579/98): the European Roma Rights Centre;
- *Koons v Italy* (No. 68183/01): National Center for Missing and Exploited Children;

---

[31] The following list of cases does not purport to be exhaustive: it is subject to a certain amount of caution because of the difficulties encountered during the research.

- *Pini and Bertani v Romania* (No. 78028/01) and *Manera and Atripaldi v Romania* (No. 78030/01): CEPSB (Complexe éducatif Poiana Soarelui de Brasov, filiale de la Fondation pour l'accueil des enfants, Bucarest);
- *Mamatkulov and Abdurasulovic v Turkey* (Nos. 46827/99 and 46951/99): ICJ (International Commission of Jurists), HRW (Human Rights Watch) and AIRE Centre (Advice on Individual Rights in Europe).

It follows from the above that the practice of the new ECHR is to accept rather than to refuse requests by NGOs for third party intervention, the ECHR being well aware of the impact of NGOs' participation in proceedings before it, as such interventions have often had an important effect upon its judgments.

4. PROSPECTS FOR POSSIBLE CHANGES

The question is often asked whether participation of NGOs before the ECHR should be further encouraged by changing the provisions of the European Convention so as to give NGOs more rights, or whether it might be more realistic to envisage in the future a new, evolving, approach by the ECHR itself.

As to possible changes of the Convention, it is thought by some that the system of protection under the European Convention would be strengthened by widening the scope of Article 34 so as to allow applications by NGOs on behalf of their members when it is not the organization itself but its members who are victims of violations of Convention rights. Some authors find it advisable to use Article 44 of the American Convention on Human Rights as a possible model in this respect.[32]

Indeed, unrestricted *locus standi* before the ECHR does not seem to be widely advocated or realistic to expect. The situation might, however, be different as to the likelihood that NGOs might in the future be granted a kind of limited *actio popularis*, at least in some circumstances, as for instance if they can show that they have an interest in the proceedings which, of course, could then be challenged before the ECHR. Such a development, even if for some it might be difficult to foresee at the moment, is not to be completely ruled out given that the cooperation of NGOs and the ECHR is constantly evolving and subject to new developments.

Another possible way to open up the participation of NGOs might be to go in the direction of having NGOs represent a 'collective interest', in the sense of bringing something close to so-called 'class actions' before the ECHR, i.e., for similar groups of cases involving numerous applicants in the same situation (e.g.,

---

[32] See Nowicki, n. 11 above, at p. 273, Article 44 reads: 'Any person or group of persons, or any nongovernmental entity legally recognized in one or more member states of the Organization, may lodge petitions with the Commission containing denunciations or complaints of violation of this Convention by a State Party'.

the environment); it might well prove to be also in the interests of the proper administration of justice. In such situations, however, there is the already existing practice of 'pilot cases' or 'pilot judgments', whereby a first judgment, or a leading case, in a situation where a group of similar, repetitive, cases is pending before the ECHR is subsequently to be followed for all cases of the same type, yet in a simplified procedure; this might make new approaches for dealing with similar groups of cases questionable or even superfluous.

In any event, because a difficult reform of the control system of the European Convention is now embodied in a new additional protocol, with a view to helping the ECHR to cope with its ever-increasing caseload[33] – the moment does not seem to be well chosen for such novel approaches that might even increase the number of cases brought to the ECHR. However, this new reform does not foresee any changes in relation to the participation of NGOs in the proceedings.

Is there, nevertheless, another possible new approach in sight?

An important question has recently been decided by the ECHR that might possibly lead to some changes in attitude towards NGOs. It was raised in a Spanish case which related to the construction of a dam that caused the flooding of several villages.[34] The applicants in the case are an association and five individual applicants, members of the association. The interesting point is that the individual applicants did not themselves participate in the domestic proceedings but were represented by the applicant association, which was created precisely in order to represent them before the national fora. Traditionally, in such circumstances, the ECHR does not accept applicants who did not themselves exhaust domestic remedies. Thus, the Spanish government raised preliminary objections as to the victim status of the applicant association and of the individual applicants and of the exhaustion of domestic remedies by them.

It is interesting to see that the ECHR in deciding this question did not take a purely formalistic approach to the 'victim' concept, set out in Article 34 of the European Convention, but an evolving one, which in the present case might also be considered a fairer one. It accepted that the individual applicants can be considered victims of the alleged violations of the European Convention and that they have themselves exhausted domestic remedies. In this respect the ECHR noted that, like the other provisions of the Convention, the term 'victim' in Article 34 must also be interpreted in an evolutive way in the light of the conditions of life today. It continued by stating:

And indeed, in modern-day societies, when citizens are confronted with particularly complex administrative decisions, recourse to collective bodies such as associations is one of the accessible means, sometimes the only means, available to them whereby they can defend their particular interests effectively. Moreover, the standing of asso-

---

[33] Protocol No. 14, amending the European Convention, adopted and opened for signature on 13 May 2004.

[34] *Gorraiz Lizarraga and others v Spain*, No. 62543/00, judgment of 27 April 2004.

ciations to bring legal proceedings in defence of their members' interests is recognised
by the legislation of most European countries. That is precisely the situation that obtained in the present case. The Court cannot disregard that fact when interpreting the
concept of 'victim'. Any other, excessively formalist, interpretation of that concept
would make protection of the rights guaranteed by the Convention ineffectual and illu-
sory. [35]

Such a decision might have important repercussions on the ECHR's case law in
general, but also some interesting ones as to the rights of NGOs under Article 34
in the future.[36]

As, however, it is never wise – and I am also not allowed – to speculate as to
possible future developments of the ECHR case law, for the time being, let us
wait and see.

It has become widely accepted nowadays that the work of human rights NGOs
makes a valuable contribution to the protection of human rights in Europe, not
least because of the various ways in which they take part in the proceedings before the ECHR. With their cooperation and with the help of the ECHR various
procedures have been found to enable them to participate in the ECHR's work.
By doing so, they promote both the achievements of the ECHR and the protection
of human rights and thus provide a substantial input to the development of human
rights law.

The increasing role of human rights NGOs before the ECHR may undoubtedly
have an influence also on the practice of other international courts and tribunals
(depending on their respective fields and areas of jurisdiction) when reviewing
possible forms of participation by NGOs in proceedings before them, as it becomes every day more difficult not to take account of their activities and impact
on the development of international law.

---

[35] Ibid., para. 38.

[36] As to the applicant association, in line with what was mentioned at the beginning of this comment, the ECHR decided that it could be considered a victim within Article 34 of the alleged
breaches of the right to a fair trial under Article 6(1) of the European Convention.

Part II

NGOs and International Criminal Courts and Tribunals

Chapter 7

The Experience of No Peace Without Justice

Mariacarmen Colitti

1. NPWJ AND THE NGO COALITION FOR AN ICC

No Peace Without Justice (NPWJ)[1] is an international committee of parliamentarians, mayors and citizens, founded in 1994 as a campaign of the Transnational Radical Party,[2] to promote the creation of an effective system of international criminal justice, through support for the activities of the *ad hoc* Tribunals for the former Yugoslavia and Rwanda and the establishment of the International Criminal Court (ICC). Ever since its creation, NPWJ has been engaged in activities to raise public awareness of the ICC as well as to put pressure on parliaments, governments and other decisional bodies with the aim of accelerating the institution of the first international permanent jurisdiction on war crimes, genocide and crimes against humanity.

On 25 February 1995, No Peace Without Justice, together with a small group of NGOs monitoring the UN General Assembly debate on a Draft Statute for an International Criminal Court elaborated by the International Law Commission, got together in New York and formed the NGO Coalition for an ICC (CICC)[3] with the purpose to advocate the establishment of an effective and just international court. The Coalition established an informal steering committee that included basically those groups involved in the earliest stages of negotiations of the Statute: Amnesty International,[4] FIDH,[5] Human Rights Watch,[6] the International Commission of Jurists,[7] the Lawyers Committee for Human Rights,[8] Parliamentarians for Global Action,[9] the World Federalist Movement[10] and, obviously, NPWJ.

---

[1] See <www.npwj.org>.

[2] The Transnational Radical Party is an NGO with general consultative status at the UN ECOSOC. See <www.radicalparty.org>.

[3] See <www.iccnow.org>.

[4] See <www.amnesty.org>.

[5] See <www.fidh.org>.

[6] See <www.hrw.org>.

[7] See <www.icj.org>.

[8] See <www.lchr.org>.

[9] See <www.pgaction.org>.

[10] See <www.wfm.org>.

T. Treves et al., eds., Civil Society, International Courts and Compliance Bodies
© 2005, T·M·C·ASSER PRESS, *The Hague, The Netherlands, and the Authors*

At the beginning of the Rome Diplomatic Conference, the CICC included some 800 NGOs. Members formed sectorial caucuses and working groups on specific aspects of the Statute, such as gender issues, the rights of the victims, peace and disarmament, protection of children. Regional networks were established in Latin America, Africa, Europe, Asia and then in the Arab Region and in the USA.

In Rome, 236 NGOs were accredited, with 450 individuals. The CICC served as a link between the United Nations and the NGOs, and in coordination of NGOs. It also established 12 monitoring teams that covered all aspects of negotiations. A service of public information was provided with the publication of *Terra Viva*, as a result of cooperation between the International Press Service (IPS) and NPWJ. Other publications redacted by the CICC were *On the Record* and the *CICC Monitor*. In addition, reports on government positions on particular issues were drafted by the CICC.[11]

After the Rome Diplomatic Conference, the NGOs of the CICC launched International Campaigns for the Worldwide Ratification and Implementation of the Rome Statute.[12]

Immediately after the night of 17 July 1998, when the Rome Statute was adopted, we started to plan new phases of our campaign in order to obtain the prompt entry into force of the Statute. A few months after the Diplomatic Conference, we launched at the UN Headquarters in New York the 'Ratification Now!' international campaign to obtain the 60 ratifications required for the ICC to enter into force in the shortest possible time, and eventually not later than June 2002. In the first phase, the campaign focused its attention only on ratification, to build on the momentum generated at the Rome Conference, asking governments to ratify first and then adopt due implementing legislation. At a later stage, NPWJ started working also on the promotion of implementing legislation to be adopted by states parties in order for them to be able to cooperate fully with the International Criminal Court. The NPWJ international activities on ratification have involved a series of conferences targeting particular regions of the world, namely, the Caribbean, Western Africa, Southeast Asia and the Pacific, Central and Eastern Europe, the Mediterranean and Latin America.[13]

---

[11] See W.R. Pace and M. Thieroff, 'Participation of Non-Governmental Organizations', in R.S. Lee (ed.), *The International Criminal Court. The Making of the Rome Statute* (Kluwer Law International, The Hague, etc., 1999), pp. 391-398.

[12] For the campaigns of each NGO, see the websites referred to above nn. 1 to 10.

[13] NPWJ targeted particular regions of the world, namely the Caribbean (Port of Spain, 15–17 March 1999); Western Africa (Bamako, 2–3 December 2000; Accra, 21–23 February 2001); Europe (Rome, 16–17 July 2000); Asia and the Pacific (Manila, 16–18 October 2001); Central and Eastern Europe (Prague, 7–8 December 2002); the Mediterranean (Seville, 8–9 February 2002); Latin America (Mexico City, 7–8 March 2002). Since the entry into force of the Rome Statute, NPWJ continued its ratification campaign in order to widen the jurisdiction of the ICC and to promote the process of internal implementation of the Statute, through conferences in Phnom Penh (9–10 October 2002), Maseru (20–24 January 2003), Nottingham (16–25 June 2003).

2. NPWJ AND GOVERNMENTS

Since the beginning of our activities, which have always tried to put together the public, opinion leaders and decision-makers as well as experts, we realized that the best approach for the promotion of the ICC was to work together with governments and not in open confrontation with them. For over nine years, building on this conviction, we targeted decision-makers, in particular those of the original group of the so-called 'like-minded[14] countries', through regional conferences, designed to provide international fora for governmental and independent experts to share information, experience and expertise on the Statute and its various aspects, but also to provide opportunities for decision-makers to commit publicly to the prompt establishment of the permanent ICC. In fact, all these conferences were concluded with the public adoption of declarations endorsed by participants, clearly stating their strong commitment and concrete engagement in the process.

3. JUDICIAL ASSISTANCE PROGRAM

At the same time, recognizing the need to speed up the negotiations aimed at securing a fair, independent and effective institution, we launched the so-called Judicial Assistance Program through which, since the Rome Diplomatic Conference, we provided legal assistance to several governmental delegations. For over five years now, some 40 lawyers, jurists and international law professors were seconded through the Permanent Missions in New York to official delegations participating in the works of the Preparatory Commission and then of the Assembly of States Parties of the International Criminal Court. The NPWJ legal advisers have the specific mandate to assist delegates in their work, without replacing them.[15]

Since August 2000, the NPWJ Judicial Assistance Program for Sierra Leone has been extended with the provision of legal experts to the Sierra Leone Mission to the UN in New York and to the Office of the Attorney-General and Minister of Justice in Freetown.[16] The legal experts provided advice to the Sierra Leone government on the negotiations for the establishment of a Special Court to prosecute violations of international humanitarian law committed in Sierra Leone.[17] NPWJ decided to establish an office in Freetown, in order also to educate the public on the importance of re-establishing the rule of law in the country.

---

[14] The 'like-minded countries' are a group of some 40 states that since the beginning of the process have worked together for the establishment of the ICC. The group is now known as the 'Friends of the Court'.

[15] See A. Tanzi, *Introduzione al Diritto Internazionale contemporaneo* (Cedam, Padova, 2003), p. 242.

[16] See <www.npwj.org/modules.php?name=Sections&op=listarticles&secid=1>.

[17] See SC Res. 1315, 14 August 2000. The Special Court for Sierra Leone was established by an agreement between the United Nations and the Government of Sierra Leone, signed on 16 January 2002. See <www.sc-sl.org>.

4. AWARENESS RAISING

NPWJ established a series of initiatives aimed at involving the public all over the world and sensitizing them to the need and importance to put an end to impunity for the most heinous crimes through the establishment of the International Criminal Court. In the first part of our international activities, we campaigned for the actual convening of the Diplomatic Conference in 1998, in Rome, with the offer by Italy to host the Conference. By organizing regional conferences in Africa, Europe, Latin and North Americas and gathering more than 80 global leaders who signed two solemn Appeals calling for the convening of a Diplomatic Conference by the year 1998, we contributed to fostering the awareness of the need for an ICC. When the Rome Diplomatic Conference was finally convened in 1998, from 15 June to 17 July, we were not expecting the perfect court, but an institution able to create and implement a new dimension in international law to overcome the principle of non-interference in national affairs, when heinous crimes are committed. In Rome, more than in other fora, it was fundamental to work with delegations in such a manner as to ensure that the largest possible number of them was provided with the necessary knowledge of the various legal aspects of the Statute.

With the objective of raising public awareness of the entire process towards the establishment of the International Criminal Court, with particular attention to governments, experts, media and students considered likely to become future potential experts in international criminal law and human rights, NPWJ published a series of materials, which are available on the Internet. NPWJ's website provides a complete documentation on all initiatives, conferences and documents related to the ICC.

During the different phases of the campaigns made by NPWJ, various international appeals, published in the international press, were launched. They are also available on the Internet.

5. NPWJ AND THE ICTY: THE KOSOVO MISSION

In August 1998, immediately after the Rome Diplomatic Conference, NPWJ decided to send a team of legal experts to the Balkans to prepare a dossier on violations of international humanitarian law in the region. In October 1998 a team composed of six members travelled to Kosovo and other parts of the Federal Republic of Yugoslavia, as well as to Macedonia and Albania, in order to conduct the necessary field research. In November and December 1998, a second field mission was conducted to follow up on the initial contacts which had been established. A smaller team again visited Kosovo, as well as Belgrade, and gathered some new material, in addition to confirming existing information and the conclusions that had been formulated on the basis of the previous visit. A final Report on Serious Violations of International Humanitarian Law in Kosovo in

1998 was submitted to Justice Louise Arbour, Prosecutor of the International Criminal Tribunal for the former Yugoslavia,[18] asking for the indictment of President Slobodan Milosevic. The aim of the Report was to demonstrate the existence of a campaign organized from within the state structure of the Federal Republic of Yugoslavia, which involved the widespread commission of violations of international humanitarian law. In particular, the report sought to ensure that they would be fully investigated and discussed in order to assess the criminal responsibility of those who directed the violence, destruction and suffering of the whole Kosovo conflict, from the highest level. The Prosecutor of the ICTY was thus called upon to focus the efforts of her staff on establishing the criminal responsibility of Milosevic and his chain of command for the violations of international humanitarian law committed in Kosovo in 1998. The Report, issued after four months of researches by the NPWJ Kosovo team, was presented at the Rambouillet Peace Talks, in February 1999 and to the UN Commission on Human Rights in Geneva.

6. CONCLUSION

The entry into force of the Rome Statute on 1 July 2002 has opened a new phase for the international community. NPWJ intends to continue its international activities to universalize the jurisdiction of the ICC, enlarging the group of states parties to the Statute.

At this stage[19] 92 countries have ratified the Rome Statute, meaning that less than half of the UN member states are parties to such an important treaty. That is why we are now focusing on regions where the number of ratifications is still very low.

We strongly believe that the International Criminal Court is a fundamental instrument to promote the rule of law within states and prevent atrocities. Our intention is thus to continue promoting ratification of the Rome Statute as one of the conditions for a state to be considered free and democratic.

---

[18] Under Article 18 of the Statute of the ICTY. For the report, see <www.npwj.net/documents/kosovo.shtml>.

[19] 25 October 2003.

Chapter 8

NGOs and the Activities of the *Ad Hoc* Criminal Tribunals for Former Yugoslavia and Rwanda

Patrizia De Cesari

1. FUNCTIONS OF NON-GOVERNMENTAL ORGANIZATIONS IN THE ACTIVITIES OF *AD HOC* CRIMINAL TRIBUNALS

The participation of NGOs in the activities of the *Ad hoc* International Criminal Tribunals for the former Yugoslavia (ICTY) and Rwanda (ICTR) has developed along four main lines.

First, non-governmental organizations (NGOs) have played a major part in the creation and functioning of these tribunals. From the very beginning their response to the serious crimes committed in the former Yugoslavia was to call on the international community to intervene and punish those responsible. They were also authorized to take an active part in the work of the Kalshoven Commission of Experts, whose reports were fundamental in the setting up of the Tribunal for the former Yugoslavia.

Secondly, they carried out investigations in the territory to find evidence and subsequently prepare the reports presented to the Prosecutor, the Tribunals and to the public at large. We need only think of the work performed by NGOs in seeking the indictment of Slobodan Milosevic for the crimes committed in the Balkans and in the preparation of the report on Kosovo published by No Peace Without Justice.

In this respect, NGOs have made an important contribution as a result of the humanitarian assistance they provide in areas of conflict and crisis where the crimes dealt with by international criminal tribunals are most frequently perpetrated. In order to exercise their function the courts must conduct investigations and need testimonies and evidence which they also gather from those working in the territory such as NGOs, who have direct contact with the victims or who may also have witnessed the crimes committed.

Thirdly, NGOs have performed the activity of monitoring the work of the Criminal Tribunals and cooperation by states with international institutions, and have worked hard to raise awareness and mobilize international civil society.

T. Treves et al., eds., Civil Society, International Courts and Compliance Bodies
© 2005, T·M·C·ASSER PRESS, The Hague, The Netherlands, and the Authors

Lastly, in some cases NGOs have intervened as *amici curiae*[1] in judicial proceedings before these courts. In this chapter I will focus attention on this last role, one which still presents many unclear aspects.[2] However, from the first hearing before the Criminal Tribunal for the former Yugoslavia, a number of non-governmental organizations have made use of the possibility of taking part as *amici curiae*.

---

[1] On the increasingly important role of NGOs in international litigation and on the concept of *amicus curiae* see B. Arts, M. Noortmann and B. Reinalda (eds.), *Non-State Actors in International Relations* (Aldershot, 2001); H. Ascensio, 'L'amicus curiae devant les juridictions internationales' (2001) 5 *Rev. Gén. Dr. Int. Pub.* 897; Y. Beigbeder, *Le rôle international des organisations non gouvernementales* (Bruxelles-Paris, 1992); M. Bettati and P.M. Dupuy, *Les O.N.G. et le droit international* (Paris, 1986); C. Chinkin, *Third Parties in International Law* (Oxford, 1993); L. Boisson De Chazournes, C. Romano and R. Mackenzie (eds.), *International Organisations and International Dispute Settlement: Trends and Prospects* (New York, 2002), in particular in this volume see C. Chinkin and R. Mackenzie, 'Intergovernmental Organizations as "Friend of the Court"' at p. 135; A.K. Lindblom, *The Legal Status of NGOs in International Law* (Uppsala University, 2002), p. 291; P. Mavroidis, *Amicus Curiae Briefs Before the WTO: Much Ado About Nothing*, Harvard Jean Monnet Working Paper 2/2001; F. Orrego Vicuña, 'Individual and Non-State Entities before International Courts and Tribunals' (2001) 5 *Max Planck YB UN L.* 53; J. Razzaque, 'Changing Role of Friends of the Court in the International Courts and Tribunals' (2001) 1 *Non-State Actors & Int'l L.* 169; D. Shelton, 'The Participation of Nongovernmental Organizations in International Judicial Proceedings' (1994) 88 *Am. J. Int'l L.* 611. A group of NGOs on 25 February 1995 formed an NGOs Coalition whose main purpose was to advocate the establishment of an effective and just international criminal court. On the involvement of NGOs in the process of the establishment of the ICC see W. Pace and M. Thieroff, 'Participation of Non-Governmental Organizations' in R.S. Lee (ed.), *The International Criminal Court: The Making of the Rome Statute: Issues, Negotiations, Results* (The Hague/London/Boston, 1999); W. Pace and J. Shense, 'The Role of Non-Governmental Organizations' in A. Cassese, P. Gaeta and J.R.W.D. Jones, *The Rome Statute of the International Criminal Court: A Commentary*, vol. I (Oxford, 2002), pp. 105–143; Leonetti, 'La contribution des organisations non gouvernementales dans la création du statut de Rome' in M. Chiavario (ed.), *La justice pénale internationale entre passé et avenir* (Milano, 2002); see also the documents listed by Amnesty International, 10 February 1995 (AI Index: Ior 40/18/00). On the role of NGOs before the European Court of Human Rights, see O. De Schutter, 'Sur l'émergence de la société civile en droit international: le rôle des associations devant la Cour Européenne des droits de l'homme' (1996) 7 *Eur. J. Int'l L.* 372; A. Lester, 'Amici Curiae: Third Party Intervention before the ECHR' in F. Matscher and H. Petzold (eds.), *Protecting Human Rights: The European Dimension* (1988). On the participation of NGOs in the WTO dispute settlement system, see R. Baratta, 'La legittimazione dell'amicus curiae dinanzi agli organi giudiziali della organizzazione mondiale del commercio' in (2002) 85 *Riv. Dir. Int.* 549; B. Stern, 'L'intervention des tiers dans le contentieux de l'OMC' (2003) 107 *Rev. Gén. Dr. Int. Pub.* 257.

[2] The participation of NGOs in international litigation continues to present many problems, not only related to the issue of whether they are or not part of proceedings, but also related to the treatment of witnesses. Recently, for example, the ICTY Trial Chamber in the *Milosevic* case refused to grant the requested closed session for three witnesses who were employees of a humanitarian organization, considering that Rule 75 of the Rules of Procedure and Evidence of the Tribunal for the former Yugoslavia protection can be provided only to persons related to or associated with a victim or witness. See the public version of the confidential decision filed on 13 March 2003 on Prosecution Motion for Protective Measures (concerning a humanitarian organization) in (2003) 41 *Judicial Supplement* (June) 15. On the problems related to the protection of NGO witnesses see S. Sanna, 'La testimonianza dei delegati del Comitato internazionale della Croce Rossa davanti ai tribunali penali internazionali' in (2001) *Riv. Dir. Int.* 393.

2. KEY PROVISIONS OF THE STATUTES AND OF THE RULES OF PROCEDURE AND EVIDENCE

I will start by analysing the norms regulating the participation of NGOs in the proceedings before the International Criminal Tribunals.

Rule 74 of the Rules of Procedure and Evidence of the Tribunal for the former Yugoslavia states that:

> A Chamber may, if it considers it desirable for the proper determination of the case, invite or grant leave to a State, organisation or person to appear before it and make submissions on any issue specified by the Chamber.

The same rule applies in the case of the Tribunal for Rwanda. A similar provision is contained in Rule 103 of the Rules of Procedure and Evidence for the International Criminal Court.[3] Rule 103.1 is identical to Rule 74 for the ICTY, but it specifies that the request can be made at any stage of the proceedings, as has been accepted in the ICTY and the ICTR, including appellate proceedings. Rule 103.2 provides that 'The Prosecutor and the defense shall have the opportunity to respond to the observations submitted to the Court under sub rule 1', meeting in this manner the requirements of a fair trial.

Likewise, Rule 61B of the Rules of Procedure of the Tribunal for the former Yugoslavia is relevant for the participation of an NGO as an *amicus curiae* in proceedings. In the case of failure to execute a warrant, this Rule provides that the Prosecutor or the Trial Chamber may call any witness whose statement has been submitted to the confirming judge.

A non-governmental organization may participate under another provision: Article 18(1) of the Statute of the Tribunal for the former Yugoslavia. This provision states that 'the Prosecutor shall initiate investigations *ex officio* or on the basis of information obtained from any source'. Among these sources Article 18 includes non-governmental organizations. However, the provision does not require those in possession of information that may prove sufficient to initiate proceedings to transmit it to the Prosecutor. However, the Prosecutor is free to act insofar as Article 18 grants him the power to initiate official investigations.[4]

---

[3] A similar rule is contained in Article 36.2 of the European Convention on Human Rights which provides that 'the President of the Court may in the interest of the proper administration of justice invite ... any person concerned who is not a party to the proceedings to submit written comments or take part in hearings'. In this way also the European Convention on Human Rights is open to the participation of *amici curiae* in its proceedings.

[4] The Prosecutor will assess the information so received or obtained and decide whether there is sufficient basis to proceed. He or she has a general power to interrogate suspects, victims and witnesses and gather evidence as well as conduct investigations on the scene. Specific limits to this power are contained in Rule 66 of the Rules of Procedure and Evidence of the Tribunal for the former Yugoslavia which requires the Prosecutor to provide the defence access to all documents and evidence related to the trial, except where such communication would prejudice current investigations, the public interest or the security of a state. NGOs therefore continue to face problems related

Article 17(1) of the Statute of the ICTR is identical. A similar rule has been adopted in the text of Article 15 of the Statute of the International Criminal Court which provides in para. (1) that 'The Prosecutor may initiate investigations *proprio motu* on the basis of information on crimes within the jurisdiction of the Court' and in para. (2): 'The Prosecutor shall analyse the seriousness of the information received'. For this purpose, the Prosecutor may also seek additional information from non-governmental organizations.

3.   THE PRACTICE OF THE TRIBUNALS

If we examine the practice of the Tribunals for the former Yugoslavia and Rwanda, the role of NGOs is mentioned in judgments in very few cases. In other cases it emerges from the Tribunal orders that briefs were submitted by NGOs.

In the *Tadic* case, a coalition of NGOs submitted an *amicus* brief to the Trial Chamber of the ICTY to point out the Prosecutor's failure to treat rape as a crime against humanity in order to have the case transferred from the German national court to the ICTY.[5]

During the same case in 1995 a preliminary status conference was held in open session in the presence of the accused to discuss procedural and other matters relating to the case. An NGO submitted reports on the anonymity and protection of the witnesses and of the victims. In September 1995, Juristes Sans Frontières was granted leave by the Appeal Chamber to file a brief on the jurisdiction and legality of the setting up of the ICTY by the Security Council.[6] These briefs were not mentioned in the judgment of the Trial Chamber or in the judgments of the Appeal Chamber.

In the *Furundzija* case, on 9 November 1998 representatives of non-governmental organizations and human rights scholars submitted a brief to the Trial Chamber requesting the ICTY to reconsider its decision having regard to the rights of witnesses to equality, privacy and security of the person.[7]

In the *Blaskic* case, NGOs were invited to submit *amicus curiae* briefs on a number of legal issues and to give their opinion on these matters at the hearing.[8] The Prosecutor successfully sought a decree requiring the Croatian government to turn over government documentation to the ICTY through the *sub poena duces tecum* clause. This procedure had raised the question of the validity of such an act with respect to a sovereign state.

---

to the need for confidentiality and problems related to the risks deriving from testimony or the transmission of confidential documents in their possession.

[5] *Prosecutor v Tadic* IT-94-I, Opinion and judgment of Trial Chamber I, 7 May 1997, para. 11.

[6] Ibid., para. 15.

[7] *Prosecutor v Furundzija*, Orders granting leave to appear as *amicus curiae*, 10 and 11 November 1998.

[8] *Prosecutor v Blaskic*, Case No. IT-95-14-PT, Order submitting the matter to Trial Chamber II and inviting *amicus curiae*, 14 March 1997.

On this particular question judge McDonald invited some organizations to request authorization to intervene in the trial as *amici curiae*. The invitation was taken up by Juristes Sans Frontières in the person of Professor Alain Pellet. The opinions expressed by Juristes Sans Frontières were not shared by the Trial Chamber, which held that the procedure followed was lawful and hence that Croatia should comply with the requests of the ICTY. Juristes Sans Frontières did not appear in court but did file a brief. This brief was not mentioned in the judgment of the Trial Chamber.[9]

Croatia appealed against the decision. The Appeal Chamber invited the NGO to submit a request to participate as an *amicus curiae* on these same questions.[10] Juristes Sans Frontières reiterated its position. On that occasion the Appeals Chamber shared the opinions of Juristes Sans Frontières and annulled the *sub poena* orders since it held that such orders could only be issued against individuals and not against sovereign states.

The involvement of NGOs was very significant in the first trial of the International Criminal Tribunal for Rwanda in the case of *Jean Paul Akayesu*. In those proceedings[11] the Prosecutor did not initially charge Akayesu with sexual violence crimes despite reports by several NGOs that Rwandan women had been subjected to sexual violence during the genocide in general and particularly in Taba commune, near Kigali, where Akayesu was mayor. During the trial testimonies were given about Akayesu's prominent role in rapes.

A coalition of NGOs submitted an *amicus curiae* brief to the ICTR. The brief was signed by over 45 international human rights organizations. The NGOs urged the Prosecutor to include rape and other sexual crimes in the indictment.[12] Following the brief the indictment was amended but on the basis of the witnesses' testimonies, and not as a result of the *amicus curiae* brief. However, the *amicus curiae* brief forms an official part of the *Akayesu* file even though NGO participation is not mentioned in the Trial Chamber's judgment.[13]

In the *Alfred Musema* case, a brief on restitution of property to the victims was submitted to the Trial Chamber of the ICTR by the NGO African Concern. The Chamber rejected the request because leave to appear was requested by an *amicus curiae* and not by the victims.[14]

---

[9] *Prosecutor v Blaskic*, judgment of the Trial Chamber, 3 March 2000.

[10] *Prosecutor v Blaskic*, Appeals Chamber Order granting extension of time, 17 September 1997, and A/52/375, Report of the International Tribunal, 18 September 1997, para. 52.

[11] ICTR, Chamber I, *Prosecutor v Akayesu*, 2 September 1998.

[12] See R. Copelon, 'Gender Crimes as War Crimes: Integrating Crimes against Women into International Criminal Law'(2000) 46 *McGill L. J.* 225. Rhonda Copelon was one of the authors of the brief.

[13] At the appeals stage of the *Akayesu* case, the International Criminal Defence Attorney applied for leave to submit an *amicus curiae* brief. This brief was not mentioned in the judgment of the Appeals Chamber (ICTR Appeals Chamber *Prosecutor v Akayesu*, 1 June 2001), but it is stated in the Annual Report of the petitioning NGO that this brief was submitted in June 1999.

[14] Decision on an application by African Concern for leave to appear as an *amicus curiae*, Case No. ICTR- 96-13-T (17 March 1999).

4.   CONDITIONS FOR THE PARTICIPATION OF NGOs AS *AMICI CURIAE* IN
     PROCEEDINGS

The Tribunal for the former Yugoslavia has set out the conditions for the admission of an *amicus curiae*. Naturally these conditions also apply to NGOs. In a
note dated 27 March 1997[15] it was stated that an *amicus curiae*:

(a)   must be an actor that can guarantee objectivity and independence;
(b)   must intervene to uphold the general interest of the international community
      and not a particular interest;
(c)   must intervene on being granted leave by a judge or at his request by virtue
      of its technical expertise and with a view to solving a question.

These conditions are based on a set of reasons.

4.1   The interests of NGOs

Non-governmental organizations must not pursue their own interests, they must
appear to uphold the interests of the international community.[16] This is what distinguishes them from witnesses, experts and parties to the case.

Confusion should be avoided between the interests of NGOs and those of the
parties in the trial. In the Appeal Chamber of the ICTY in the *Furundzija* case the
defence sought the disqualification of the trial judge Mumba due to her links with
three authors of an *amicus curiae* brief.[17]

Other objectives of the *amicus curiae* intervention by NGOs can be to contribute to the development of international law as far as possible and to raise the attention of public opinion.

4.2   Authorization from the Tribunal

The judge has the discretionary power to grant an NGO leave to submit *amicus
curiae* briefs or in any case to appear before the court. In the event of denying
leave he or she must state the reasons for his or her refusal.

This discretionary power is founded on the idea of the good administration of
justice. The Tribunal can grant a non-governmental organization leave to take
part in the trial if it holds that the contribution of this actor would really be useful
and will not delay the trial.

---

[15] IT 122, 27 March 1997.

[16] On the main objectives of the *amicus curiae* intervention by NGOs see O. De Schutter and
P. Sands in Workshop Report by E. Rebasti, *A Legal Status for NGOs in Contemporary Interna-
tional Law? A Contribution to the Debate on Non-State Actors and Public International Law at the
Beginning of the Twenty-First Century, 15-16 November 2002*.

[17] The defence had cited the *Pinochet* case during which Lord Hoffmann was disqualified for his
links with Amnesty International, which had taken part in the trial as an *amicus curiae*.

4.3   Form of participation

The usual form of participation is through the submission of written briefs and, where necessary, through oral argument at a hearing. The method of participation may be stated more precisely in the authorization.

If the authorization does not indicate exactly the amount of information required, the NGO must try not to broaden the scope of its opinion, thereby creating delays. Leave is normally granted for technical and limited support and not recommendations or suggestions. The aim of *amicus curiae* participation is to assist the judicial process and not to attempt to put pressure on it.

Elements of fact and of law are to be submitted to the court on the basis of their objective and extrinsic value.

5.   NEED TO CLARIFY THE INVOLVEMENT OF NGOs AS *AMICI CURIAE* BEFORE *AD HOC* CRIMINAL TRIBUNALS

In attempting to sum up the involvement of NGOs as *amici curiae* in proceedings before the Tribunals of the former Yugoslavia and Rwanda we must observe that there have been few interventions in trials and that it is not easy to evaluate to what extent their participation has determined the proceedings.

Generally, the intervention of an NGO is not mentioned in the judgment. In any event, when the NGO brief is in respect of facts, it makes available to the Tribunal information gathered throughout the country. It is not easy for the Tribunal to gather this information and so the participation of NGOs helps to form the Tribunal's conclusions, as in the *Akayesu* case.

Whenever NGOs have submitted briefs containing elements of law it is even more difficult to understand to what extent these briefs have influenced judgments. Their effect is clearer when the Chamber mentions these briefs among the reasons for its ruling. This happened in the *Tadic* case. In the ICTY Appeal Chamber's decision of 2 October 1995, the judge mentioned the brief of Juristes Sans Frontières in support of the Prosecutor's reasoning.

As we have seen, the participation of NGOs as *amici curiae* is informal in character. They perform many functions in the interests of international criminal justice, but these actors cannot yet be considered parties to the proceedings. The participation of NGOs in proceedings before International Criminal Courts is still cloaked in some uncertainty and this will have to be clarified in future.

Chapter 9

NGOs and the Activities of the International Criminal Court

Francesca Trombetta-Panigadi

1. EXPLICIT REFERENCES TO NGOs IN THE STATUTE AND SUBSIDIARY DOCUMENTS

As far as the Rome Statute and its subsidiary documents are concerned, NGOs have been explicitly referred to in a limited number of rules.

The Rome Statute expressly mentions NGOs in Article 15 which provides for the role of the Prosecutor in initiating investigations *proprio motu* on the basis of information on crimes within the jurisdiction of the ICC (International Criminal Court). According to Article 15(2) the Prosecutor analyses the seriousness of the information received and for this purpose he or she may seek additional information from states, organs of the United Nations, intergovernmental organizations and also NGOs. Therefore, this paragraph lays the ground for an important contribution NGOs may provide at an early stage of the proceeding before the ICC. Indeed, it recognizes them as potential sources in the jurisdiction triggering phase. Article 15 recalls the provisions of Article 18 of the *Ad Hoc* Criminal Tribunal for the former Yugoslavia (ICTY) and of Article 17 of the Tribunal for Rwanda (ICTR).

NGOs are also mentioned in Article 44(4) in Part 4 of the Statute (Composition and administration of the Court). This provision relates to personnel and provides for a possibility for the ICC, in exceptional circumstances, to:

> employ the expertise of gratis personnel offered by States parties, intergovernmental organizations or NGOs to assist with the work of any of the organs of the Court. The Prosecutor may accept any such offer on behalf of the Office of the Prosecutor. Such gratis personnel shall be employed in accordance with guidelines to be established by the Assembly of States Parties.

These guidelines have not yet been discussed.

The Rules of Procedure and Evidence, on their part, do provide a legal basis for NGOs to act as *amici curiae*: Rule 103(1) states that:

> At any stage of the proceeding, a Chamber may, if it considers it desirable for the proper determination of the case, invite or grant leave to a State, organization or per-

T. Treves et al., eds., Civil Society, International Courts and Compliance Bodies
© 2005, T·M·C·ASSER PRESS, *The Hague, The Netherlands, and the Authors*

son to submit, in writing or orally, any observation on any issue that the Chamber deems appropriate.

According to Rule 103(2), the Prosecutor and the defense shall have the opportunity to respond to such submissions. Here again, the ICTY and ICTR models (Rule 74 of the ICTY and of the ICTR) have been adopted, with the difference that Rule 103 explicitly specifies that such a request or invitation can be made at any stage of the proceedings: this has been accepted in the ICTY and ICTR, including in appellate proceedings (*Tadic* case).[1] It should be noted that the simple designation 'organization' in Rule 103 (as in the same rules of the ICTY and ICTR) does not specify whether the Rule deals with either an international organization or a NGO or if it makes no distinction between them. Therefore it is likely they will be treated similarly, which begs the question as to whether this approach is appropriate. It remains to be seen how the rule will be applied in practice, but it is certain that the ICC is free to accept written or oral submissions also from NGOs.

NGOs are also explicitly mentioned in the Rules of Procedure of the Assembly of States Parties (ASP).[2] Rules 93 and 95 authorize the participation of representatives of NGOs at meetings of the ASP and its subsidiary bodies, and give them the opportunity to receive copies of official documents and to make oral and written statements strictly related to their activities, with the provision that the written statements 'shall not be issued as official documents' (Rule 95(2)).[3]

---

[1] *Prosecutor v Tadic*, IT-94-I, Opinion and judgment of Trial Chamber I, 7 May 1997, para. 11.

[2] The Rules of Procedure of the Assembly of States Parties were included in the mandate of the Preparatory Commission for the Establishment of an International Criminal Court. The Preparatory Commission was established by Resolution F of the Final Act of the United Nations Diplomatic Conference of Plenipotentiaries on the Establishment of an International Criminal Court. Resolution F established the mandate for the Commission. The task of the Preparatory Commission was to prepare proposals for practical arrangements for the establishment and coming into operation of the ICC, including the draft texts of: (a) Rules of Procedure and Evidence, (b) Elements of Crimes, (c) a relationship agreement between the ICC and the United Nations, (d) basic principles governing a headquarters agreement to be negotiated between the ICC and the host country, (e) financial regulations and rules, (f) an agreement on the privileges and immunities of the ICC, (g) a budget for the first financial year, (h) Rules of Procedure of the Assembly of States Parties.

[3] Rule 93 states as follows: 'Non-governmental organizations invited to the Rome Conference, registered to the Preparatory Commission for the International Criminal Court, or having consultative status with the Economic and Social Council of the United Nations whose activities are relevant to the activities of the Court and other non-governmental organizations invited by the Assembly may, through their designated representatives: (a) Attend meetings of the Assembly and meetings of its subsidiary bodies under the conditions laid down in rule 42 of the present Rules of Procedure; (b) Receive copies of official documents; (c) Upon the invitation of the President and subject to the approval of the Assembly, make oral statements through a limited number of representatives on questions relating to their activities at the opening and closing meetings of the Assembly; (d) Make oral statements through a limited number of representatives on questions relating to their activities at the opening and closing meetings of subsidiary bodies, when the subsidiary body concerned deems it appropriate'. Rule 95 provides that: 'Written statements submitted by the designated representatives referred to in rules 92, 93 and 94 shall be made available by the Secretariat to representatives of the States Parties and Observer States in the quantities and in the language or languages in which the

2. NGO Coalition for an ICC and the Recognition of its Role by the Assembly of States Parties and the Organs of the ICC

It is generally recognized that NGOs have played a very important, active and decisive role in the negotiation of the Rome Statute, both before and during the Conference. The adoption of the Rome Statute has been the culmination of three and a half years of intense efforts of cooperation and coordination among NGOs themselves and between NGOs and governments and the United Nations Secretariat. NGOs used a variety of techniques and strategies for asserting influence on the negotiations, which are now well known[4] and will not have further attention turned on them here. In general, the role of NGOs was to exercise pressure for the establishment of the ICC and to create an atmosphere favourable to this. In this regard, NGOs' influence has been particularly strong during each Preparatory Commission session and it contributed to the adoption of most of the documents provided by Resolution F of the Rome Conference's Final Act[5] and to the achievement of the number of ratifications necessary to the entry into force of the Rome Statute on 1 July 2002.

Among the NGOs which played a decisive role throughout the negotiations was the NGO Coalition for an ICC. Originally, a small group of NGOs monitoring the United Nations General Assembly debates on the International Law Commission's Draft Statute for an International Criminal Court in New York subsequently formed the NGO Coalition for an International Criminal Court (CICC).[6]

From February 1995, the CICC has grown to a movement involving more than 800 organizations throughout the world. It sought to bring together a broad-based network of NGOs and international law experts to develop strategies on substantive legal and political issues relating to the proposed Statute. The main purpose of the CICC was and is to give support for the ICC among a wide range of civil society organizations, including those focusing on human rights, international law, humanitarian issues, peace, the rights of women and children, religion and many other sectors.[7]

---

statements are made available to it, provided that a statement submitted on behalf of a non-governmental organization is related to the work of the Assembly and is on a subject in which the organization has a special competence. Written statements shall not be made at the expense of the Assembly and shall not be issued as official documents'.

[4] A.K. Lindblom, *The Legal Status of Non-Governmental Organizations in International Law* (Uppsala, 2001), p. 423 *et seq.*

[5] See n. 2 above.

[6] The Coalition for an International Criminal Court (CICC) established an informal steering committee comprised largely of groups involved in these earliest stages of cooperation, including Amnesty International, Fédération Internationale des Ligues des Droits de l'Homme (FIDH), Human Rights Watch, the International Commission of Jurists, the Lawyers Committee for Human Rights, No Peace Without Justice, Parliamentarians for Global Action and the World Federalist Movement.

[7] W. Pace and M. Thieroff, 'Participation of Non-Governmental Organizations' in R.S. Lee, *The International Criminal Court: The Making of the Rome Statute: Issues, Negotiations, Results* (The

A clear example of strong NGO influence on the negotiations of the Rome Statute is the recognition of the role and independence of the Prosecutor. Besides this, NGOs played and continue to play an important and considerable role in promoting a global education and awareness campaign about the ICC. They launched a global campaign for signatures and ratifications of the Rome Statute before and after the entry into force of the Rome Statute, and at present, the CICC is mainly advocating for the support of implementation processes in ratifying countries, against the threats to the integrity of the Statute, in particular the campaign of bilateral immunity agreements launched by the USA, recalling Article 98(2) of the Rome Statute.

An official recognition of the powerful role gained recently by NGOs, in particular the CICC, is granted by a resolution adopted during the 2nd Session of the Assembly of States Parties on 11 September 2003. The draft resolution, submitted by Sierra Leone, entitled 'Recognition of the coordinating and facilitating role of the NGO Coalition for the ICC' was adopted by consensus by states parties.[8] The resolution expresses the appreciation for the activities undertaken by the CICC during recent years in a variety of fields concerning the establishment of the ICC, mainly for the coordinating role the organization played between civil society and the Court and between civil society and governments, and in this official forum gives full recognition to the work the CICC will develop in the same direction in the future. The resolution recalls that Rules 93 and 95 of the Rules of Procedure of the Assembly of States Parties (ASP) provide for the participation of NGOs in the meetings of the ASP and its subsidiary bodies.

Introducing that draft resolution Mr Pemagbi from Sierra Leone stressed that from the beginning of efforts to establish an International Criminal Court, NGOs had been supporting the work of governments and the United Nations in an extremely constructive and coordinated manner, thanks to the role of the CICC. The draft resolution reconfirmed a long-term basis for the continued role of the CICC, and the NGO community in general. He stressed that this official recognition of the coordinating role of the CICC did not intend to grant any kind of privileges to the CICC, and that the liaison role was of a non-exclusive nature.

Indeed, it has to be borne in mind that there are other NGOs particularly influential on the international framework which have always taken a stand for the ICC and which are not members of the CICC, such as the International Committee for the Red Cross.

Another example showing official recognition of the role played by NGOs is a seminar meeting organized by the ICC between the Registry and NGOs, held in The Hague on 22 September 2003, entitled 'Challenges Lying Ahead: Cooperation with NGOs'. The seminar was aimed at discussing various issues of mutual

---

Hague, 1999), p. 392; W. Pace and J. Schense, 'The Role of Non-Governmental Organizations' in A. Cassese, P. Gaeta and J.R.W.D. Jones (eds.), *The Rome Statute of the International Criminal Court: A Commentary*, vol. I (Oxford, 2002), p. 108.

[8] Resolution ICC-ASP/27Res. 8 has been adopted at the 4th Meeting of the ASP.

interest and concern. It was intended to inform the NGOs present about the structure and functions of the Registry, its major projects accomplished and its goals and priorities. During the open discussion some of the issues touched upon included the usefulness of regularized meetings between the ICC and the NGOs and possibilities of future dialogue. On the 6-7 April 2004, in fact, a second general strategy consultation between the ICC Registry and representatives of NGOs was held in the Hague. The main purpose of the meeting was to discuss modalities of dialogue and cooperation between the Registry and NGOs. Particular issues addressed at the meeting were, among others, the ICC's budget, communications and outreach, victims, witnesses and defence, the Headquarters Agreement and the Agreement and the ICC–UN Relationship Agreement. The diverse roles and mandates of the different NGOs were discussed as well as how these NGOs can relate to the Registry and its different sections and units.[9]

On 16 July 2003,[10] the Prosecutor himself, Mr Moreno Ocampo, giving his first public analysis of the communications that the ICC has received since the Rome Statute entered into force, stressed that, out of the nearly 500 situations communicated to the Court since July 2002, many reports were submitted by individuals and NGOs located in a total of 66 countries. The Office of the Prosecutor has received in particular six communications regarding the situation in Ituri, in the Democratic Republic of Congo, as a situation referred to the ICC which the Office would 'follow closely'. These six communications included two detailed reports from NGOs, whose names have not been disclosed. The Prosecutor announced that he will begin a preliminary examination before launching a formal investigation. He said that the Office and selected staff are analyzing the information available. Notwithstanding the fact that the Prosecutor did not officially express his intention to seek additional information from NGOs in particular, it is likely that this will happen considering the terms of his presentation of the two detailed reports by NGOs. In any event, if this does not happen on this occasion it is likely it will happen in future, since at his first press conference, the Prosecutor fully recognized that it is vital for the ICC to have the support of the international community and international organizations.

3. NGOs' ACTIVITIES TODAY: THE POLICY OF THE COALITION

During the ceremony for the solemn undertaking of the Chief Prosecutor on 16 June 2003, the Convenor of the CICC, Mr Pace, stressed that international, national and local NGO members of the Coalition have been working for years at the state level to support the development of implementing legislation allowing for cooperation with the ICC and the exercise of complementarity. Indeed, one of the primary goals of the CICC has been to build the capacity of national and local

---

[9] (2004) 'The International Criminal Court Monitor', 6.
[10] Press Release pids 009.2003-EN.

NGOs to participate in the drafting of complementarity legislation, not only so as to ensure a strong output, but so the groups will understand the legislation and be in a position to play an invaluable role in the application of that law in national investigations and prosecutions. The involvement of civil society will not end once an investigation has been initiated. Indeed, the Office of the Prosecutor anticipates a role for NGOs in the collection of tangential information to substantiate or avert prosecutions. The monitoring and facilitation of national investigations and prosecutions will be an enormous task, and one in which the Office of the Prosecutor must be assisted by the efforts of civil society. The CICC has also been pleased by the dedication of the Prosecutor to ensuring that the rights of victims are respected in the process of investigations and prosecutions. Indeed, one of the most active caucuses within the Coalition is the Victims Rights Working Group. The CICC strongly encourages close and frequent consultation with the Victims Rights Working Group about how victims and victims' issues should be handled.

It is to be underlined, however, that the CICC has recently adopted a formal policy entitled 'CICC's Policy on the Referral and Prosecution of Situations before the ICC'. According to this policy, the CICC as a whole, and its Secretariat, will not be directly involved in the promotion or development of situations before the ICC.[11] Jennifer Schense,[12] the Legal Adviser to the CICC, explained:

> the policy was taken in consultation with the Steering Committee. Please do distinguish here between the Coalition as a whole and our individual members. The Coalition as a whole won't be involved in the promotion of particular cases, but our members will. The Coalition as a whole will not because any action we take ostensibly represents all of our members. Therefore, we can only take the broadest actions which we are confident will have the support of all our members. At the same time, limited action by the Coalition as a whole is coupled with freedom for Coalition members to follow their own mandates and pursue their own activities, as long as it is consistent with promotion of a fair, effective and independent permanent ICC ... This division of labour, between the Coalition as a whole and its members, has characterized all of the Coalition's work. For example, in the recent election of the judges, the Coalition did not support or oppose any particular candidates, but only supported an open, fair and transparent election process and the need for a balanced bench. Our members, however, were free to campaign for or against specific candidates, if they so chose.

---

[11] The full policy states as follows: 'The Coalition is dedicated to the establishment of the International Criminal Court as a fair, effective, and independent international organization. The Coalition will continue to provide the most up-to-date information about the ICC and to help coordinate global action to effectively implement the Rome Statute of the ICC. The Coalition as a whole, and its secretariat, will not be directly involved in the promotion or development of situations before the ICC. The Coalition will endeavour though to respond to basic queries and to raise awareness about the ICC's complaint system, as it develops. In addition, many individual CICC members will provide legal and other support on investigations and will develop partnerships with local and other organizations in the course of their efforts'. In the same policy the CICC states that: 'Communications to the ICC can be sent to: ICC, P.O. Box 19519, 2500 CM The Hague, The Netherlands'.

[12] This interview has been released in a private context at the end of August 2003.

A clear example of this analysis is the fact that Fédération Internationale des Ligues des Droits de l'Homme (FIDH) on 13 February 2003 during a press conference, presented a first report entitled *War Crimes in the Central African Republic*, aimed at bringing formally the occurrence of alleged war crimes in this region before the ICC. FIDH is a member of the Steering Committee of the CICC, but in this instance it acted as a single NGO and not as a member of the Coalition.[13]

In different circumstances NGOs have given proof of their prominent role in the ICC supporting process on a worldwide basis. They have organized and they still continue to plan many conferences, seminars, workshops and training courses tackling different issues concerning the ICC.

Among the goals the CICC has fixed for the future are activities such as assisting the ICC bodies and other organizations aimed at developing rules and regulations regarding legal aid; following closely the Victims and Witnesses Unit; supporting the Victims Trust Fund (as announced by Mr. Pace at the ceremony for the solemn undertaking of the Office of the Prosecutor), and collaborating to create an international bar association.[14]

Limiting our analysis to the European region, and the relevant events planned in recent months, the CICC attended the Human Dimension Implementation Meeting, held in Warsaw from 6–17 October 2003. This is an event organized by the OSCE Office for Democratic Institutions and Human Rights (ODIHR) every year.[15] This seminar represented one of the opportunities for the Coalition to widen its range of action, attending the meeting on an equal footing with governments. During a two-hour side event, addressed to NGOs and states' delegates, the CICC discussed the new challenges the ICC is facing, it encouraged OSCE non-ratifying countries to become state parties to the Court and called for national implementing legislation among OSCE ratifying members. The role of NGOs in this new phase has also been discussed, together with the need to strengthen civil society presence and support in certain regions of the world.

At the end of September 2003, FIDH held a three-day regional seminar in partnership with the Human Rights Association of Turkey and in collaboration with the Human Rights Foundation of Turkey in Ankara. At its conclusion, there was adopted a declaration in which the participants urged states of the region, *inter alia*, to accede to the Statute of the ICC, in order to repress and deter genocide, crimes against humanity and war crimes, and to adopt ICC implementing legislation at the domestic level. On this occasion, FIDH launched a regional

---

[13] The full report of this case has been published on FIDH website <www.fidh.org>.

[14] See the Coalition Report on Resolution ICC-ASP/2/Res. 8, adopted during the 2nd Session of the ASP.

[15] The meeting gathers hundreds of government representatives, human rights activists and international experts from the 55 participating states of the OSCE, as well as the six Mediterranean Partners for Co-operation and the Partners for Co-operation from Asia. The meeting aims at scrutinizing the human rights records of all participating states and provides a unique forum for NGOs, which can participate and make their voices heard.

campaign for the ratification and implementation of the ICC in the Eastern and Southern Mediterranean countries.

In other circumstances, even where the CICC did not directly attend relevant events focusing on the ICC and other topics in the human rights field, and taking into consideration the role of NGOs, it contributed strongly to raising the profile of these events. On 14 July 2003, the European Commission held a Special Seminar with human rights NGOs in Brussels. The goal of the seminar was to meet with NGOs in order to strengthen relation between the latter and the European Commission in the formulation of EU policy on human rights. Among the issues which have been touched upon was international justice. In this context, it has been highlighted that the European Union has always supported the ICC since it was established and that the European Union has always opposed the signature of ICC bilateral immunity agreements. It has been decided that other seminars like this one will follow in order to keep the dialogue open with NGOs.

The CICC did not directly attend but contributed to publicizing the 109th General Assembly of the Inter-Parliamentary Union held in Geneva on 3 October 2003. Also on this occasion the main topics were international justice, international peace and security, terrorism and core crimes. The Resolution adopted by consensus entitled 'The role of Parliaments in assisting multilateral organizations in ensuring peace and security and in building an international Coalition for peace' calls for acceding to and/or ratifying international instruments such as the Protocols additional to the Geneva Conventions and the Rome Statute and it explicitly encourages parliaments to support NGOs which seek to promote peace throughout the world.

4.   Concluding Remarks

As the previous analysis shows, the relevance of NGOs throughout the ICC negotiation process has grown from a mere logistic support to an officially recognized role gained in this framework. Therefore, from the first Preparatory Commissions in which NGOs could only listen to the plenary sessions,[16] their important contribution has been recently crystallized in the above-mentioned Resolution ICC-ASP/2/Res.8 adopted during the 2nd Session of the Assembly of States Parties.

In addition to what NGOs have achieved so far, it is expected that they will proportionally widen their range of action as the ICC begins to be fully effective.

---

[16] See Lindblom, n. 4 above, at p. 419.

Chapter 10

NGOs and the East Timor Special Panels for Serious Crimes

*Chiara Ragni**

1. THE ROLE OF NGOs IN JUDICIAL SYSTEM RECONSTRUCTION IN EAST TIMOR

The purpose of the present chapter is to examine the role that non-governmental organizations (NGOs), especially those concerned with justice and human rights, played in post-conflict judicial system reconstruction in East Timor. In fact, in this context, NGOs made an important contribution in identifying the appropriate form of justice to be established in the territory, and the challenges to be faced in order to implement it.[1]

The chapter will deal in particular with the importance that civil society organizations had in criminal proceedings before UN-supported internationalized Criminal Special Panels. Regarding this issue, emphasis will be placed on the crucial role played by the Judicial System Monitoring Programme (JSMP), a Timorese NGO set up in Dili in 2001. This project was concerned with monitoring the respect for human rights standards in Timorese criminal proceedings, and with the development of the local judicial system by identifying areas of concern, and the making of recommendations for reform. Before going further, it is important to illustrate briefly the historical context that accompanied the creation of Timorese Special Panels and the legal framework within which they operate, in order to appreciate the challenges posed by the current situation in East Timor.

2. HISTORICAL BACKGROUND

East Timor was a Portuguese colony until 1975, when it was invaded by the Indonesian army. Under the pressure of the United Nations, which has never recognized its rule over the area,[2] Indonesia was bound to agree to a referendum,

---

* I would like to thank Mr Mark Bastick (Legal Research Coordinator of JSMP) and Mrs Caitlin Reiger (Co-founder and former Legal Research Coordinator of JSMP) for the information on JSMP they provided to me by answering my email requests.
[1] See N. Roth-Arriaza, 'Civil Society in Process of Accountability' in M.C. Bassiouni (ed.), *Post-Conflict Justice* (Ardsley, 2002), p. 100.
[2] See Security Council Resolution 384 (1975), UN Doc. S/INF/31 (1975).

T. Treves et al., eds., Civil Society, International Courts and Compliance Bodies
© 2005, T·M·C·ASSER PRESS, The Hague, The Netherlands, and the Authors

monitored by UN representatives, to determine the future status of East Timor. In the period before the popular consultation, the Indonesian army spread a climate of intimidation and fear in order to force Timorese people to vote for the autonomy of the territory within Indonesia.[3] To deal with the situation the Security Council, acting under Chapter VII of the United Nations Charter, authorized the establishment of a multinational force (UNAMET), which was empowered to use all necessary means to restore order, to facilitate humanitarian assistance and to monitor elections.[4] On 30 August 1999 almost 75 per cent of the Timorese people voted for independence, but this was just the first step towards the creation of a viable system of self-government.

Indeed, the situation that the United Nations found in East Timor upon their arrival was the dramatic result of years of civil war: houses and buildings were almost completely destroyed; the legislative and administrative system and the judiciary had totally collapsed.[5] In order to rebuild basic institutions, the Security Council created an interim administration with a very broad mandate, which included the exercise of all legislative and executive authority in East Timor and the administration of justice.[6] The United Nations Transitional Administration for East Timor (UNTAET) took on all the functions typically run by organs of state while aiming in the long term to transfer all its powers to Timorese independent institutions.

One of the most difficult and urgent challenges that UNTAET had to face was the prosecution and trial of people involved in abuses and crimes committed in East Timor before and during the popular consultation in 1999. Indeed, on the one hand, people who have endured years of violence and war seek to obtain reparations and justice for what they have suffered; on the other hand they tend to believe that no form of justice can exist in their society, and they totally lack either the resources or the know-how to address past and present abuses. The second challenge UNTAET had to face was, therefore, to rebuild the judicial system out of the vacuum that the Indonesian administration had left, and to re-establish the rule of law.[7] East Timor lacked a working judiciary. Moreover, the very

---

[3] See Report of the Secretary General on the Question of East Timor, UN Doc. S/1999/803 (20 July 1999).

[4] See Security Council Resolution 1264 (15 September 1999), UN Doc. S/RES/1264 (1999), in (2000) ILM 232.

[5] H. Strohmeyer, 'Collapse and Reconstruction of a Judicial System: The United Nations Missions in Kosovo and East Timor' in (2001) 95 *Am. J. Int'l L.* 46; S. Linton, 'Rising from the Ashes: The Creation of a Viable Criminal Justice System in East Timor' in (2002) 25 *Melbourne U. L. Rev.* 122.

[6] When the United Nations Transitional Administration for East Timor (UNTAET) was established on 25 October 1999 by the UN Security Council it was mandated to 'exercise all legislative and executive authority, including the administration of justice'. See Security Council Resolution 1272, UN Doc. S/RES/1272 (1999), in (2000) ILM 240.

[7] See United Nations Development Programme, East Timor Human Development Report, 2002, available at <www.undp.east-timor.org> which states: 'The Indonesian government suborned the legal system to its own ends and corrupted both courts and the judiciary in East Timor effectively turn-

weakened and politicized one that existed under Indonesian rule facilitated abuses, crimes and the violation of human rights. In addition to that, there were no court buildings because they were all destroyed during the war and almost all the judges and lawyers had left the country in 1999 since they had supported the Indonesian administration.[8]

To reconcile the need for the prosecution of serious crimes with the urge to restore and enhance the fledging judicial system in East Timor, UNTAET, by Regulation 15/2000, decided to establish within the District Court in Dili mixed panels composed of both international and East Timorese judges,[9] and with exclusive jurisdiction over crimes against humanity, war crimes, genocide, as well as over murder and sexual offences under the Indonesian Penal Code.[10]

3. NGO COALITION FOR AN INTERNATIONAL TRIBUNAL FOR EAST TIMOR

The creation by the United Nations of internationalised Panels did not meet the expectations of Timorese people and of local NGOs, which had supported, from the very start of UNTAET, the institution of an international tribunal rather than just a mixed one, in accordance with the conclusions reached by the UN-sponsored Commission of Inquiry, set up in 1999 in order to investigate the situation of justice in East Timor.[11] Since the end of 1999, East Timorese NGOs, orga-

---

ing the legal system into a servile extension of the executive. As a result many East Timorese had little faith in legal institutions. Then in 1999 the courts were destroyed along with much of the legal infrastructure and archives'.

[8] As has been remarked by Hansjoerg Strohmeyer, who served both as Principal and Deputy Principal Legal Adviser to UNTAET: 'administering a justice system is no easy task when there is no system left to be administered' in H. Strohmeyer, 'Policing the Peace: Post-Conflict Judicial System Reconstruction in East Timor' (2001) 24 *U. New South Wales L. J.* 172.

[9] The idea was that international judges, due to their experience in international law, could give an essential contribution both to the correct application of international criminal law and to verify the implementation and the respect of human rights standards by local judges, lawyers and prosecutors. See S. Linton, 'Cambodia, East Timor and Sierra Leone: Experiments in International Justice' (2001) 12 *Crim. L. Forum* 185 at 186.

[10] See Regulation 2000/15 on the Establishment of Panels with Exclusive Jurisdiction over Serious Criminal Offences (6 June 2000), UN Doc. UNTAET/REG/2000/15; Regulation 2000/11 on the Organization of Courts in East Timor, UN Doc. UNTAET/REG/2000/11 (6 March 2000). For more detailed comments on the issue see S. Linton, 'Prosecuting Atrocities at the District Court of Dili' (2001) 2 *Melbourne J. Int'l L.* 414; 'New Approaches to International Justice in Cambodia and East Timor' (2002) 84 *Int'l Rev. Red Cross* 93; Y. Beigbeder, *Judging Criminal Leaders* (The Hague, 2002), pp. 194–205; L.A. Dickinson, 'The Promise of Hybrid Courts' (2003) 97 *Am. J. Int'l L.* 295; C. Romano, 'Mixed Jurisdiction for East Timor, Kosovo, Sierra Leone and Cambodia: The Coming of Age of Internationalised Criminal Bodies?' in *The Global Community* (2003) 97; C. Romano and T. Boutruche, 'Tribunaux pénaux internationalisés: état des lieux d'une justice "hybride"'(2003) 107 *Rev. Gén. Dr. Int. Pub.* 109; S. Katzenstein, 'Hybrid Tribunals: Searching for Justice in East Timor' (2003) 16 *Harvard Hum. Rts. J.* 245.

[11] The Commission of Inquiry was established with the main purpose to gather and compile systematically information on possible violations of human rights and acts that might constitute

nized in a NGOs Forum,[12] and global activists have placed a high priority on supporting East Timorese demands for justice, while UNTAET was blamed for having failed to argue the case for an international tribunal.

The concern of NGOs was that the Special Panels could not satisfy the expectations of local people to see perpetrators of the worst crimes committed during the civil war being brought to justice, because of the resource limitations and lack of cooperation of Indonesia, where most of the suspects of crimes within the jurisdiction of the tribunal found shelter. Only a Tribunal created by the Security Council, as the ones for the former Yugoslavia and for Rwanda, could provide justice for Timorese people since it would have the power to bind third states to cooperate with it.

Immediately after the institution of Special Panels for serious crimes, a coalition of global activists[13] and NGOs, supported by Timorese people, started a

---

breaches of international humanitarian law committed in East Timor since January 1999, advocated for the need to set up an International criminal tribunal, with the participation of local jurists. An international tribunal could have the power to bind Indonesia to extradite people responsible of grave violations of international and domestic criminal law (UN Doc. A/54/726). Accordingly, the Special Rapporteurs of the Commission on Human Rights to East Timor (with which the Commission was requested to cooperate) stated that: '... The Security Council should consider the establishment of an international criminal tribunal for the purpose. This should preferably be done with the consent of the Government, but such consent should not be a prerequisite. Such a tribunal should then have jurisdiction over all crimes under international law committed by any party in the Territory since the departure of the colonial Power.' UN Doc. A/54/660. But, since the high cost of a United Nations Tribunal and the limits of the other international ones, the Security Council preferred to invest UNTAET of the task to administer justice. The Secretary General, in its Report on the situation in East Timor, expressed the view that: 'UNTAET will endeavour to fill the justice system with professionals recruited from among East Timorese, to the largest extent possible'. (See Report of the Secretary General on the Question of East Timor, UN Doc. S/1999/1024 (4 October 1999). Accordingly UNTAET decided to set up internationalised panels with mixed jurisdiction.

[12] In 1998 Timorese Non-Governmental Organisations organised themselves in a Forum in order to give support and assistance to local communities. In the years of the Indonesian occupation Timorese NGOs were replaced with pro-government ones and they were persecuted as they acted in the interest of local population and of its right to self determination. It was only towards the end of 1999 that the NGOs Forum could re-establish itself with the support of the UN's Office for the Coordination of Humanitarian Affairs (OCHA). Now the NGOs Forum plays a very important role in the challenge of rebuild the nation; it takes part in donors conference and its advice is taken into account when the Transitional Administrator makes its own decisions. In 2001 the NGO Forum realised the need for Timorese civil society organisations to register themselves and to be cover by appropriate regulation. Now most Timorese NGOs (including Judicial System Monitoring Programme) included, have been formally registered by the NGO Forum.

[13] Indeed in several countries mounted a solidarity campaign backing the idea that only an international tribunal could have provided justice for East Timor. In the United States, the *East Timor Action Network* (ETAN) advocated for a congressional resolution supporting an international tribunal. Earlier, the intensive lobbying of U.S. activists was key to enacting a law that prohibited the financing and training of the Indonesian military by Washington (the Leahy amendment). The legislation blocked the U.S. from resuming bilateral military cooperation until those responsible for violence in East Timor were brought to justice. The law is still in effect, although ETAN and other U.S. activists must continually defend it against the attempts made by the Bush administration to restore the U.S.-Indonesia military-to-military ties. East Timor support groups in Asia also pressed for the

campaign to promote the institution of an international tribunal for East Timor.[14] In May 2000, activists from Europe, the USA and Indonesia met in the Netherlands, and reaffirmed that they would encourage efforts to hold the Indonesian military to account for their crimes, and call for a special international tribunal for East Timor. As a result, the International Federation for East Timor (IFET)[15] and over 80 organizations and human rights campaigners from around the world wrote to UN Secretary General Kofi Annan in July 2000. Similar letters were sent to national governments and to the European Union.

On 13 June 2001, IFET published a statement entitled 'Justice for East Timor', concerning the administration of justice for crimes against humanity committed in the territory of East Timor. The aim of the statement was essentially to express great concern about the performance of Special Panels in delivering justice, and accordingly to call upon the international community (especially the Security Council) to set up an international tribunal for East Timor.[16]

Since they had no answer from the United Nations, in October 2001 NGOs organized a seminar to discuss the problems of the Timorese judicial system in order to find a joint solution. During the seminar all the NGO participants emphasized the need for the victims to obtain reparation and justice, and the responsibility of the international community to bring to justice perpetrators of crimes during the Indonesian occupation, which the United Nations had never recognized. The result of the meeting was again that the international community should be involved in the constitution of a working and credible tribunal for East

---

institution of an international tribunal. The Free East Timor Japan Coalition recently made this a priority for its campaigning, focusing its efforts on the Japanese government and the members of the UN Security Council. In the Netherlands, human rights and pro-democracy groups have launched a major campaign to highlight the scourge of impunity in Indonesia and encourage bringing leading generals responsible for atrocities in Indonesia and East Timor to justice. IFET groups in many countries also continue to make the justice campaign a top priority.

[14] The demand of the international civil society directed towards the creation of accountability mechanisms for violations of human rights had in the past important consequences, since it influenced the creation of the International Tribunal for the Former Yugoslavia (ICTY), the International Tribunal for Rwanda (ICTR) and the International Criminal Court (ICC). See for example on this issue W.R. Pace, M. Thieroff, 'Participation of Non-Governmental Organisations', in R.S. Lee (ed.), *The International Criminal Court. The Making of the Rome Statute. Issues, Negotiations, Results* (The Hague, 1999), pp. 391-398; W.R. Pace, J. Schense, 'The Role of Non-Governmental Organisations', in A. Cassese, P. Gaeta, J.R.W. Jones (eds.), *The Rome Statute of the International Criminal Court. A Commentary* (Oxford, 2002), pp. 105-143.

[15] The International Federation for East Timor was founded in 1991 by groups pleading Timorese cause coming from all over the world. It was set up with the aim to coordinate on the international level non-governmental organisations' initiatives on East Timor and to support those initiatives to United Nations. Indeed IFET is accredited with the UN Department of Public Information an has a UN Representative in New York. Upon its establishment IFET included NGOs with an interest in the decolonisation process of East Timor; then, after pro-independence vote, it provided support for various activities aimed to promote international protection of Timorese rights. IFET has never received direct funding and depends on membership contributions.

[16] See S. Pritchard, 'United Nations involvement in Post-Conflict reconstruction efforts: new and continuing challenges in the case of East Timor', (2001) 24 *U. New South Wales L. J.* 183.

Timor since the violations perpetrated in East Timor during Indonesian rule were not committed just against the East Timorese people, but because of their gravity they were to be considered as crimes against humanity. These considerations were expressed to the United Nations Security Council in a letter dated 24 October 2001.[17] Again, the Organization did not reply. Indeed, it is extremely unlikely that the Security Council will set up any new international criminal tribunals, both for political and financial reasons.

In any event, the coalition of NGOs has continued its campaign for an international tribunal for East Timor by writing letters to the Security Council and to the Secretary General and trying to awake the international community to the need to provide justice for Timorese people in the face of uncertain international political will.[18] In the meantime, the NGOs Forum, considering that one of the most difficult obstacles to an international tribunal was the financial one, managed to take part in June 2001 in the Canberra International Donors' Conference on Justice and Human Rights issues. In a briefing paper presented to the Conference, NGOs Forum expressed disappointment and concern about the slow progress of prosecution, in relation to crimes committed in East Timor, by emphasizing the fact

---

[17] The letter states: 'East Timorese NGOs came together on the 16 October 2001, and unanimously concluded that an international mechanism of accountability for those responsible for the death, violence and humiliation in East Timor must be urgently established. The same conclusion was reached by the International Commission of Inquiry on East Timor established by the United Nations in January 2000. However, with 2002 close at hand, neither process has brought us nearer to realizing this objective. The situation is made even more critical by the coming end of the UNTAET mission. Under the stewardship of UNTAET was the time when the impunity of the past was needed to be replaced by the rule of law and justice, necessary for the nation building process of and reconciliation for East Timor. Instead, we are facing the dark reality of such impunity characterizing our future. We urge the United Nations not to leave East Timor alone with the consequences of the crimes so terrible that they are characterized as against all humanity. It is time to take immediate steps to establish an International Tribunal for East Timor. This is the only mechanism that could address the current need for justice, the missing element so far, in the process of nation building for East Timor and worldwide respect for human dignity'.

[18] In a recent letter, sent on the 25 July 2003 to main the bodies of the United Nations and to the Special Representative of the Secretary General for East Timor, NGOs strongly criticised the performance of UNTAET and of the international community in general in providing justice for East Timorese people. The letter states: 'East Timor still suffers from the legacies of 24 years of crimes against humanity, for which the international community has largely failed to hold the perpetrators accountable. ... the world owes some honesty and consideration to the people of East Timor, who were neglected for so many years, and were then subject to pioneering projects in transitional government and post-conflict reconstruction, development and justice. Where those experiments are failing, the responsibility remains with the international community to set them right ... If the international community is not willing to compel Indonesia to cooperate with justice, there is no reason to continue a hypocritical charade. We continue to believe that an international tribunal for East Timor would be the best option. However, we offer some observations on the justice process as currently constituted, and about some of its problems. ... Although the Serious Crimes Unit was slow getting started, it has now indicted more than 300 people, including some Indonesian generals who masterminded crimes here during 1999. Unfortunately, more than 70% of those indicted enjoy impunity in Indonesia, which refuses to honour its commitment to cooperate with investigations and extradition'.

that none of the high level Indonesian militia leaders had yet been tried. As a consequence the Forum, representing the opinion of a great number of NGOs and of the Timorese community, recommended the financing and organization of a conference in Dili (to be organized by the NGOs Forum) to examine the possibility of an International Criminal Tribunal for East Timor. In addition the NGOs Forum proposed that a priority for the international donors' community should be the creation of a court administration, which required the funding and appointment of experienced administrative court staff, the appointment of at least seven additional interpreters able to speak the working languages used by the Special Panels, and of experienced lawyers, and financial support for the basic facilities needed for the proper administration of justice.

At the International Donors' Conference held in Dili on the 14 and 15 May 2002, education and health were highlighted as priority areas for human development, while it was stressed that justice, although it was an important aspect to be considered in the development of East Timor, was not the major challenge to be dealt with. This conclusion disappointed those NGOs that took part in the meeting. On 9 and 10 December 2002, another conference took place in Dili, but NGOs did not have the opportunity to provide a formal statement to it. Only in an informal paper could they express their disappointment and stress again the need to improve and develop the judicial system in East Timor, even if the demand for an international tribunal was not mentioned.

Whatever the result of NGOs' efforts, it clearly emerges from their statement and letters that their campaign was aimed at calling upon the international community to take into consideration the demands for justice of Timorese people. That implies not only the establishment of an International Criminal Tribunal for East Timor, but also the development and the improvement of the local judicial system. Regarding this matter it is important to stress the contribution that NGOs made in identifying the challenges posed by the need to build a functioning court system and a valid legal framework within which the courts could operate, by proposing suggestions for reforms.

4. NGOs AND THE SPECIAL PANELS FOR SERIOUS CRIMES

In order to establish a valid legal framework within which the Special Panels could operate, the Transitional Administrator decided by Regulation 1999/1 that the applicable law in the territory would be Indonesian in so far as it was consistent with international human rights standards, and it was not replaced by UNTAET Regulations.[19] In practice, however, this provision proved rather difficult to apply because it did not specifically identify the laws that were inconsistent with internationally recognized human rights standards. The task to interpret

---

[19] See section 3 of UNTAET Regulation 1999/1 on the Authority of the Transitional Administration in East Timor (27 November 1999), UN Doc. UNTAET/REG/1999/1.

Indonesian criminal provisions through the lens of human rights standards was referred to the judges and lawyers of the Special Panels, only a few of whom have some experience in international law.[20] In this context, international and especially local NGOs played an important role in denouncing the situation to the international community, in organizing training for young and inexperienced lawyers and in assisting them.[21] No Peace Without Justice (NPWJ), for example, as well as other international NGOs, has seconded defence lawyers experienced in international criminal law and procedure to assist the Public Defender's Office. This is intended to improve the quality of the defence, and to provide assistance to local jurists to represent defendants in crimes against humanity, war crimes and genocide trials.

But the problems of the Special Panels are not only limited to the lack of experienced lawyers or judges, since UNTAET failed meaningfully to build East Timorese capacity to run a judicial system; as the NGOs Forum stressed during the Canberra Conference, the East Timorese Special Panels system faces significant problems also in terms of lack of court administration and basic facilities (as, e.g., courtroom and research facilities). This had serious impact on the rights of defendants to a fair trial, and on public confidence in the new judicial system.[22]

In this context several NGOs, including Amnesty International and the International Commission of Jurists, have called for independent observers of the judicial system. They stressed that a monitoring and reporting mechanism is essential to promote respect for international human rights standards in criminal proceedings and is required to identify where ongoing reforms are needed.[23] Up to now, UNTAET has not made provision for carrying out judicial system analysis through trial observation. Therefore this important task has been fulfilled, since the birth of the Special Panels, at non governmental level by the Judicial System Monitoring Programme (JSMP).[24]

---

[20] H. Strohmeyer, above n. 5.

[21] On 3 June 2001 a coalition of NGOs wrote to Colin Powell arguing that the Special Panels' lack of experienced judges and lawyers had had a bad influence on the opportunity to conduct criminal proceedings in the respect of due process standards. Indeed the right of the defendants to legal assistance, as well as many other rights related to fair trials, resulted compromised by the paucity of human and material resources.

[22] For example Special Panels were considered to violate the right to an appeal due both to the lack of an adequate number of judges to constitute a Panel within the Appellate Court of Dili and to the lack of resources required to make transcripts of the proceeding, recognised as an indispensable prerequisite to exercise the right for the accused to have its conviction reviewed, accordingly to what the ICCPR stated in Article 14(5).

[23] It was noted that: 'human rights law is the ideal lens for investigating the structures and functioning of international criminal justice', S. Zappalà, Human Rights in International Criminal Proceedings (Oxford, 2003), p. 1. The author stresses that NGOs could made an important contribution in monitoring the respect of human rights standards even in international judicial criminal bodies. Ibidem, p. 14.

[24] It seems important to stress that in very similar context, such as in Kosovo, the Interim Administration created by Security Council Resolution (UNMIK) and OSCE realised the importance of setting up their own monitoring programmes (the Legal System Monitoring Programme was estab-

4.1 Judicial System Monitoring Programme and its activities

JSMP, as stated above, is an East Timorese non-governmental organization set up in Dili in April 2001 by Christian Ranheim and Caitlin Reiger, two international lawyers. The project really came about quite spontaneously and was not formally connected with the birth of the Special Panels. Christian Ranheim attended (as an interested observer) the first hearings of the Special Panels. The poor quality and organization of the proceedings, and the lack of any media and public attendance, prompted him to develop the idea of providing high quality legal observation of the trials. Immediately afterwards other lawyers joined the idea to attend the hearings before the Special Panels in order to monitor the respect of human rights standards and due process within them. As the trials had already begun, they simply started sitting in court and setting up a website and an email list to initiate the information flow.[25]

After being entirely dependent upon volunteer contributions for several months, JSMP has been fully funded by assessed contributions since August 2001. At the beginning it was the Australian Section of the International Commission of Jurists[26] that covered most urgent financial needs, such as those related to office requirements, and that hosted the organization within its premises. Then the project received funds also from the United States Agency for International Development (USAID),[27] which is, to date, the major donor to the organization and which is administered locally by the Asia Foundation, a San Francisco-based NGO. JSMP also receives substantial funding from the Australian Agency for International Development (AusAid), as well as additional project-specific grants from other donors.

---

lished to the end of monitoring and reporting the respect of human rights standards in criminal proceedings in the Kosovo district courts). This means that it does exist the possibility to monitor respect of human rights in international proceedings even at an institutional level.

[25] The website is updated daily with a lot of useful information about proceedings before the Special Panels of Dili and the Human Rights Court of Jakarta, with thematic reports on the justice system and with any other resource or documentation related to the topic of justice in East Timor.

[26] The International Commission of Jurists (ICJ) was set up in Berlin in 1952. It is an independent, non-profit and non-governmental organisation supported entirely by voluntary contributions and grants from governments, foundations, other non-governmental organisations and individuals. The mandate of ICJ is to promote and implement protection of human rights by providing legal expertise at both the international and national levels to ensure that developments in international law adhere to human rights principles and that international standards are implemented at the national level. The main body of the Commission is the International Secretariat, based in Geneva, which is responsible for realising the aims and objectives of the organisation. The International Secretariat benefits from a network of autonomous national sections and affiliated organisations located in all continents. The Australian Section was established in 1958.

[27] USAID is the principal U.S. agency to extend assistance to developing countries trying to escape poverty or engaging in the democratic reforms. In the case of East Timor USAID program was finalised to support the transition of the country to a democratic government and to a market economy. Since JSMP give an important contribution to democratize justice system monitoring and promoting the respect of international human rights standards in criminal proceedings USAID has always supported and financed the project.

The project started with limited ambitions, but it has grown considerably since then. JSMP is now a large, well-staffed and structured NGO.[28] Even though it has a mixed composition since its members are half local and half international, it does not reflect its nature; actually JSMP is a fully local NGO. It is independent from the government, but also from the United Nations. It was set up just in response to the need identified by local and international observers for a monitoring presence in the Special Panels which was independent of UNTAET.

As its name suggests, JSMP's purpose is to provide independent comment on and analysis of the development of the judicial system in East Timor through its three key activities: trial observation, judicial system analysis and public outreach. Trial observation includes attendance and monitoring most of the hearings held before the Special Panels. JSMP sends legal observers to assist at the proceedings, and to interview judges, lawyers and all the people involved in the East Timor judicial system in a professional capacity. Detailed notes are taken by legal observers and entered into the organization's database which contains information about all the trials and reports on specific cases or decisions.[29] Through trial observation, JSMP is able to gain a first-hand impression of the developments taking place in the East Timor judicial system and to point out the reforms needed.

The second activity of the organization is to analyse all the notes taken during the proceedings and all the decisions of the Special Panels, with the aim of assessing the functioning of the judicial system by identifying the main areas of concern. The assessment criteria used by JSMP are internationally recognized standards that include, for example, access to justice, promptness of processing cases, the fairness of the proceedings, integrity and independence of judges, equality of arms. In fact, all those standards are expressed in the international human rights Conventions; JSMP actually believes that it is important to assess the level of the development in the new system on the basis of qualitative compliance with international provisions concerning fair trial. This approach derives from the consideration that:

---

[28] JSMP has one international Director and one Timorese Deputy Director and Outreach Coordinator, one international Legal Research Coordinator, three East Timorese Legal Researchers and one East Timorese Office Manager. The Legal Research Coordinator and two of the three Legal Researchers each hold law degrees and/or are qualified practising lawyers. The third researcher is currently studying law at the University. In addition, JSMP has been assisted in the past by a number of volunteer lawyers and law students who have spent periods of three to six months working with the organisation, and it has also employed an international media professional to work as Outreach Advisor to JSMP and to develop the organisation's website and outreach activities. JSMP has recently planned to move in wider offices and expand its staffing levels. E-mail Interview with Mark Bastick, Legal Research Coordinator of JSMP (May 2003).

[29] See for example 'Trial Observation Report: General Prosecutor v. Joni Marques (the Los Palos Case)' (March, 2002); 'Interim Report on the Dili District Court' (April, 2003); 'Report on the Court of Appeal Decision on the Applicable Subsidiary Law in Timor-Leste' (August, 2003); 'Report on the Court of Appeal Decision in the Case of Armando Dos Santos' (August, 2003).

If the new judicial system fails to meet international human rights standards, it will not be able to fulfil its important role in establishing the rule of law and overcoming the legacy of impunity and selective justice that characterized the Indonesian occupation.[30]

In addition, as mentioned above, UNTAET, pursuant to its mandate and to its role within the United Nations, has to promote respect for human rights standards and so has established that the law applicable in the territory would be the local one, as long as it was consistent with them.

All the findings reached by JSMP during the judicial system analyses are included in Thematic Reports,[31] published on the organization's website and delivered to government and UNTAET representatives. In fact, JSMP's third key activity, public outreach, includes the dissemination of information to the international and domestic media, and the community, generally via Internet and radio.[32]

4.2 Relationship between JSMP and public institutions

JSMP's role is limited strictly to observing, monitoring and reporting proceedings before the courts. Accordingly, the organization does not have any standing to intervene in cases before either the Special Panels or other Divisions of the Dili District Court. To date JSMP has not considered submitting *amicus curiae* briefs[33] (nobody has at all in East Timor), holding that it may conflict with

---

[30] JSMP Thematic Report on 'Human Rights in Court Administration' (November, 2001).

[31] Thematic Reports published by JSMP up to now are: 'Human Rights in Court Administration' (November, 2001); 'JSMP Position Paper on the Issue of an International Tribunal for East Timor' (February, 2002); 'The Right to Appeal in East Timor' (October, 2002).

[32] JSMP also has a close and very productive working relationship with both the local and international media through outreach program. JSMP's activities are widely reported in the local press here in East Timor while international media briefed by JSMP includes Time Magazine, the BBC, the Boston Globe, the Guardian ....

[33] The *amicus curiae* intervention is a way for a Non-Governmental Organization to participate to a proceedings before an international court of tribunal without having the stand of a party. In general an *amicus curiae* is a person, but more often an organisation experienced in specific matters related to the case that ask or is asked to submit a brief to the court suggesting a view of the facts or of the law in order to influence the outcome of the case involving matters of wide public interest. NGOs can participate in the proceeding both on the basis of a general interest, but even to protect the human rights of a victim or of a unrepresented person. *Amici curiae* can not offer evidence or examine witness, they just give an opinion to the court, but even if they act on the basis of a specific interest, they have not the arms to control the management of the action. The participation of the amicus curiae to the proceedings rests on to an authorization of the judges who can decide discretionally on the ground of an interest of the organisation in the case. See, e.g., D. Shelton, 'The participation of Nongovernmental Organisations in International Judicial Proceedings', (1994) *Am. J. Int'l L.* 611. The Rules of Procedure of the International Criminal Tribunal for the former Yugoslavia (rule 74) and the International Tribunal for Rwanda (rule 74) both admit *amicus curiae* interventions. The Statute of the International Criminal Court does not include any provision on the participation of non-governmental organization to the proceedings, even if the Rules of Procedure

JSMP's role as an independent observer and not as a direct participant at trials.[34]

In any event, JSMP enjoys a very positive working relationship with the judges and staff of the Special Panel for Serious Crimes, the Serious Crimes Unit, the Public Defenders for Serious Crimes and the court staff. Being able to have good relationships with members of the Panel is very important for the organization, since they are the only way to gain access to information about the proceedings and to any documents related to the trials (e.g., copies of judgments and indictments), since there is still no official publication system. Members of JSMP are now allowed as observers to attend all the proceedings, and even the hearings that are closed to the public.

The organization also works cooperatively with the many other international and local NGOs active in East Timor, particularly those concerned with justice and human rights. For example, JSMP works closely with Amnesty International in monitoring proceedings before the Indonesian Jakarta Tribunal for Human Rights, a judicial institution set up by Indonesia under the pressure of the international community, with the official purpose to prosecute crimes committed during Indonesian rule in East Timor, but indeed established just to show the international community that justice is being done. On 15 August 2002, Amnesty International and JSMP issued a joint statement expressing their deep disappointment with respect to the trials of the first East Timor cases in Indonesia.[35]

In addition, JSMP submits reports and critiques to the government and donors with recommendations for reforms.[36] These reports are published electronically on the website and distributed to subscribers via e-mail. Some reports, for example those issued by the JSMP on trials before Dili District Court, are translated into multiple languages (English, Portuguese, Indonesian) and delivered in person to relevant individuals and bodies.[37] In the case of the Dili District Court Report this included East Timorese parties such as the Minister for Justice and the Presi-

---

states: 'at any stage of the proceedings, a Chamber may, if it considers it desirable for the proper determination of the case, invite or grant leave to a State, organisation or person to submit, in writing or orally, any observation n any issue specified by the Chamber' (rule 103, paragraph 1).

[34] E-mail interview with Caitlin Reiger, an Australian lawyer, co-founder and former Legal Research Coordinator of JSMP (May 2003).

[35] The findings of the two organizations show that the trials were seriously flawed and were not performed in accordance with international human rights standards. As a consequence they delivered neither truth nor justice.

[36] JSMP issued a presentation at a NGO seminar in Oslo, Norway during the East Timor Donor's Conference in December 2001. In addition it contributed to the NGO Forum briefing paper to the Canberra Donor's Conference on Justice and Human Rights issues. Regarding this it is important to stress that one of the proposals put forward in the Briefing was that international donors took into consideration the opportunity to fund JSMP and other such initiatives, involving Timorese participation to monitor judicial proceedings in East Timor.

[37] According to what the First Annual Report (March 2002) states: 'JSMP's main objective for 2001 was to provide high quality reports and analysis of the developments within the judicial sector of East Timor. The first major report is a testament to that policy; it has not only been widely cited and circulated within East Timor and abroad, but is now being used as an important source for policy development within the final months of the Transitional Administration'.

dent of the Court of Appeal and Superior Council of the Judiciary, judges, public prosecutors and public defenders. It was also distributed to a number of UN Agencies, including the Special Representative of the Secretary General and the heads of the UN Human Rights Unit and others. JSMP has also developed good relationships with many members of the UN Mission in East Timor, and is frequently called on to provide independent briefings on the progress of the judicial system, for example, to the United Nations Development Program, which in its reports made reference to the conclusions reached by JSMP.[38] That is important because the findings of UNDP are taken into consideration and included in the official documents and planning of the United Nations. In a report of the Secretary General to the General Assembly issued on 13 August 2003, a whole paragraph concerns 'the development of the Justice Sector in East Timor', and emphasis is placed on 'the need for technical assistance and support from the international community' and on the opportunity to assess 'strategies to improve access to justice for Timorese citizens'.[39]

5. AN ASSESSMENT OF THE RESULTS ACHIEVED BY NGOs IN THE EAST TIMOR CONTEXT

As mentioned above, the aim of the activities of NGOs, in supporting East Timorese demands for the prosecution of crimes committed during Indonesian rule, was to promote the institution of an international tribunal, and to point out flaws in the judicial system created by UNTAET in order to suggest necessary reforms. Civil society campaigns for justice in East Timor went therefore in two main directions: some organizations, such as NPWJ and especially the Timorese JSMP, focused their actions on the internal domain of East Timor, by aiming to develop the Special Panels judicial system; other NGOs acted on the international level with the purpose of setting up an International Tribunal for East Timor. The two activities had different outcomes.

The efforts made by NGOs for the establishment of an International Tribunal did not achieve the result hoped for. However, even if they did not obtain any response from the United Nations, NGOs should continue to ensure that demands for international justice do not disappear. Indeed, if they gave up their support for the East Timorese people's need for justice, Indonesia would have even less incentive to reform its judicial system, while the international community would be likely reduce its post-UNTAET support for the Serious Crimes work of East Timor's judicial system.

---

[38] For example a Joint Assessment of the Justice System issued in November 2002 by the United Nations Development Programme and East Timor Ministry of Justice, while explaining problems of the Serious Crimes Panels of Dili made explicit reference to the JSMP Report entitled: 'The Right of Appeal' (See Joint Assessment, p. 8, note 12).

[39] See Report of the Secretary General on 'Assistance for humanitarian relief, rehabilitation and development for Timor-Leste' (13 August 2003), UN Doc. A/58/280.

On the other hand, the feedback JSMP have received from all sectors has been extremely positive; local NGOs concerned with criminal law and human rights law should therefore best consider the essential role that they can play in aiding the democratization process of local institutions, by identifying areas of concern for the judicial system, monitoring the respect of international fair trail standards in criminal proceedings and suggesting reforms to be implemented, even with the necessary support of the international community.

In addition to these two main activities, organizations such as NPWJ have also played a fundamental role in promoting the accession of East Timor to the Rome Statute of the International Criminal Court, once the territory officially became an independent state on 20 May 2002. To this end NPWJ, at the request of East Timor, obtained accreditation for UNTAET to take part in the Preparatory Commission for the International Criminal Court (ICC) and provided legal experts to attend the 8th and the 9th Session of the Preparatory Commission in New York in September/October 1999 on behalf of UNTAET. At the 10th Session of the Preparatory Commission for the ICC, held in July 2002, where East Timor was for the first time recognized as an independent country, the Timorese delegation expressed its gratitude to NPWJ for giving them the opportunity to participate as observers at the previous sessions and to express to the international community their strong will not only to protect the people of East Timor from being the victims of future crimes, but also to stand in solidarity with fellow human beings living in very difficult situations similar to what the East Timorese went through for over half a millennium. East Timor therefore showed its commitment to ratify the ICC soon and join the international community in ensuring the establishment of an independent, fair and effective international criminal court.

The activities described above are not new ones for NGOs. In the past, the demand of international civil society directed towards the creation of accountability mechanisms for violations of human rights had important consequences, since it influenced the creation of the International Tribunal for the former Yugoslavia (ICTY), the International Tribunal for Rwanda (ICTR) and the ICC. Therefore, since the establishment of a permanent international criminal body and for the reasons explained above, it is unlikely that in the future similar campaigns would obtain the hoped-for result. However, NGOs, as stressed in the case of East Timor, played and continue to play a considerable role in promoting a global education and awareness campaign about the ICC and in helping coordinate global action to implement effectively the Rome Statute.

Finally, the experience of East Timor demonstrates once again the central role that NGOs have in human rights monitoring. For many years groups such as the International Commission of Jurists, Amnesty International, the Lawyers Committee for Human Rights and Human Rights Watch have provided very detailed, objective reports on situations they have observed at very close range. Within the scope of criminal justice, NGOs can make a very important contribution in monitoring respect for international human rights standards, especially those related to due process, in international criminal proceedings, and, following the example of JSMP and of NPWJ, in internationalized ones.

Chapter 11

Some Concluding Remarks on the Role of NGOs in the ICC

Mauro Politi

1. THE ROLE OF NGOs IN THE INTERNATIONAL LEGISLATIVE PROCESS

There is no doubt that one of the major aspects of the current evolution in the life and structure of the international community is represented by the tremendous growth in the presence and relevance of new actors, who are neither states nor intergovernmental organizations. This has already been described as yet another consequence of globalization at all levels. There are in fact a number of issues (concerning in particular the social, economic and humanitarian fields) that clearly cross national boundaries, and cannot be adequately addressed on the basis of the traditional concept of state sovereignty. Participation of entities that are perceived as truly representative of community interests in the elaboration of international norms and, more generally, in the governance of today's world society, has then become increasingly important.

The most striking example of this phenomenon is the unprecedented role played by non-governmental organizations (NGOs) in the international legislative process, especially in areas affecting the protection of the environment, human rights and respect for humanitarian law. From the Rio Conference of 1992 on Environment and Development to the other recent UN world conferences on human rights (population, habitat or the condition of women); from the debates on the Kyoto Protocol of 1997[1] to the negotiations that led to the Ottawa Treaty of 1997on the ban on land-mines,[2] representatives of civil society have been in the forefront both of the campaigns aimed at achieving certain objectives, and in promoting the adoption of legal norms and political solutions that would be consistent with these goals.

However, according to a widespread opinion, the most evident case in point is the process of establishment of the International Criminal Court, culminating in the adoption of the Rome Statute of 17 July 1998. Contrary to what had happened

---

[1] 1997 Kyoto Protocol to the 1992 United Nations Framework Convention on Climate Change (UNFCCC).

[2] 1997 Ottawa Convention on the Prohibition of the Use, Stockpiling, Production and Transfer of Anti-Personnel Mines and on their Destruction (Mine-Ban Convention).

T. Treves et al., eds., Civil Society, International Courts and Compliance Bodies
© *2005, T·M·C·ASSER PRESS, The Hague, The Netherlands, and the Authors*

in the preparation and drafting of the statutes of the *ad hoc* Tribunals for the former Yugoslavia and for Rwanda (where the final texts basically resulted from close-door experts' discussions at the United Nations and negotiations within the Security Council), the ICC process was characterized by the continuous and active participation of NGOs. It is not exaggerated to say that without the impulse and pressure exercised by the world's civil society the successful conclusion of the Rome Conference and the actual creation of the ICC would not have been possible; and the international community would have probably lost the momentum for setting up a revolutionary judicial institution against impunity for the most heinous crimes known to humankind.

2. ACTION OF NGOs IN SUPPORT OF THE ICC

One may distinguish three phases in the ICC process, in which action by NGOs in support of the Court was undertaken and developed, although with different connotations. The first phase went from the beginning of the discussions in the *ad hoc* Committee in 1995 until the Rome Conference and the end of the work of the Preparatory Commission on the Rules of Procedure and Elements of Crimes (June 2000). The second went from June 2000 to the election of the 18 judges of the ICC in February 2003. The third phase is the present one, characterized by the fact that the Court has become fully operational and ready to deal with the first situations and cases brought to its attention.

During the first period, and aside from offering strong political support to the process, the main concerns of NGOs were to speed up the preparatory works and ensure that the Statute was adopted, as well as to encourage the timely preparation of subsidiary documents such as the Rules of Procedure and the Elements of Crimes. From the beginning, coordinating this action was the task carried out by the NGO Coalition for an International Criminal Court (CICC), whose membership progressively increased from 25 NGOs to almost 1,000 as of today. The ways and means utilized by the CICC in this respect were extremely various and, at the same time, ended up by being particularly effective. Contacts with delegates were constant, recalling their responsibilities towards public opinion, preparation of documents and proposals and lobbying the countries who were still sceptical, as a reflection of a common feeling shared by world public opinion, not only states.

The main element was pressure on states to conclude the legislative process in Rome – we wanted concrete results.

The second phase was from June 2000 to February 2003. Action focused on the ratification process and on the concrete setting up of the ICC. Countless initiatives to foster ratification were taken, in particular regional conferences sponsored by No Peace Without Justice (NPWJ); meetings in New York; beginning of the work aimed at helping countries with their implementing legislation; the same lobbying exercised with the US government (vigilance over the attempts to jeopardize the integrity of the Statute: Security Council and Article 16, bilateral agreements under Article 98); control exercised over the process of the election of judges. The phase included a questionnaire and interviews with the candidates – for me, one of the most difficult steps.

The third phase is the present phase. The ICC is essentially ready to meet its challenges. The importance of the role of NGOs is unchanged and will remain unchanged. The main areas for NGO involvement are:

- encouraging the adoption of implementing legislation (complementarity): the assistance provided by NGOs remains crucial;
- future role in the proceedings: Prosecutor's initiative (Article 15), cooperation with the Registrar (Victims and Witnesses Unit), interaction with the OTP;
- role in investigations, and fact-finding missions (field experience) (Article 54(3)).

In essence, the new role for the NGOs is a role of scrutiny and vigilance over the activity of the ICC. The world will be watching us very closely, and will be doing that mainly through the eyes of the NGOs. Hopes and expectations are very high. We will do our best to meet these expectations.

Part III

NGOs and International Environmental Disputes and Compliance Mechanisms

Chapter 12

The Experience of Greenpeace International

*Duncan E.J. Currie**

1. INTRODUCTION

Most international environmental disputes arise in the context of multilateral environmental agreements (MEAs) and this chapter will primarily address the Greenpeace experience of compliance mechanisms with respect to MEAs.[1] This chapter interprets compliance to mean fulfilment by a party of its obligations under a MEA and is not restricted to compliance mechanisms *strictu sensu* within MEAs but rather addresses mechanisms for achieving compliance with MEAs. Thus, national tribunals and courts and arbitral tribunals are included as possible means for achieving compliance.[2]

This chapter discusses the roles NGOs can play in enforcing MEAs, some problems with enforcing MEAs, and then gives some examples of MEA compliance issues, focusing on illegal logging, scientific whaling, illegal, unreported and unregulated fishing and the IMO.

2. INTERNATIONAL DEVELOPMENTS ON ENFORCEMENT OF MEAs

While the theoretical distinctions between international law and domestic law are clear, the interface is not and is becoming increasingly important. Greenpeace in the vast majority of cases has to resort to domestic courts to address enforcement issues. The role of NGOs in international dispute resolution mechanisms is normally one of lobbying, information and publicity. A decision of a state to bring a case before an international tribunal is predicated on diplomatic and political considerations as much as by legal and policy considerations, and it is the political and publicity arena that NGOs normally inhabit.

---

* The views noted here are these of the author and do not necessarily reflect the views of Greenpeace International or any Greenpeace entity.

[1] There are, of course, also disputes between states on an environmental matter but not one necessarily involving an MEA. However such disputes would normally be resolved by dispute resolution mechanisms rather than compliance mechanisms.

[2] This chapter does not address enforcement and dispute resolution issues with respect to the WTO, NAFTA or other trade bodies.

T. Treves et al., eds., Civil Society, International Courts and Compliance Bodies
© 2005, T·M·C·Asser Press, The Hague, The Netherlands, and the Authors

The World Summit on Sustainable Development (WSSD) Plan of Implementation[3] called for urgent action at all levels to actively promote corporate responsibility and accountability, based on the Rio Principles, including through the full development and effective implementation of intergovernmental agreements and measures. On forests specifically, the WSSD Plan of Implementation noted that achievement of sustainable forest management, nationally and globally, including through partnerships among interested governments and stakeholders, including the private sector, indigenous and local communities and non-governmental organizations, is an essential goal of sustainable development.[4] This included actions to:

> take immediate action on domestic forest law enforcement and illegal international trade in forest products, including in forest biological resources, with the support of the international community, and provide human and institutional capacity-building related to the enforcement of national legislation in those areas.

This amounts to a direct mandate for NGOs to participate in actions to stop illegal logging with the support of the international community. Yet the practical opportunities to do so are still limited.

The role implied by the Aarhus Convention[5] for NGOs[6] with respect to rights of access to information, public participation in decision-making and access to justice in environmental matters[7] is regrettably still an aspiration even on the domestic level. Procedures are to be fair, equitable, timely and not prohibitively expensive.[8] Even if the former two were to be satisfied, most legal litigation would fall at the latter two hurdles. Of course on the international plane, access to jus-

---

[3] Plan of Implementation of the World Summit on Sustainable Development, para. 45ter, see <www.johannesburgsummit.org/html/documents/summit_docs/2309_planfinal.htm>.

[4] Plan of Implementation of the World Summit on Sustainable Development, para. 43, see <www.johannesburgsummit.org/html/documents/summit_docs/2309_planfinal.htm>.

[5] Convention on Access to Information, Public Participation in Decision-Making and Access to Justice in Environmental Matters, Aarhus, Denmark, 25 June 1998, entered into force 30 October 2001 <www.unece.org/env/pp/treatytext.htm>. The UNECE (United Nations Economic Commission for Europe) website lists 26 parties. Aarhus Convention, Articles 2(5) and 9(1).

[6] NGOs will be discussed in terms of ECOSOC Resolution 1996/31 <www.un.org/esa/coordination/ngo/df/res96-31.pdf>, as organizations that are not established by a governmental entity or intergovernmental agreement (para. 12), but are not necessarily restricted to international NGOs: they can encompass NGOs at the national, subregional, regional or international level. The International Law Commission (ILC) recently adopted a definition of 'international organization' at its 2776th meeting, held on 16 July 2003, following the report of the Drafting Committee on Responsibility of International Organizations (A/CN.4/L.632), see <http://daccess-ods.un.org/access.nsf/Get?Open Agent&DS=A/CN.4/L.631&Lang=E>. That definition was that the term 'international organization' refers to an 'organization established by treaty or other international instrument governed by international law and possessing its own international legal personality. International organizations may include as members, in addition to States, other entities'.

[7] Aarhus Convention, Articles 1 and 9.

[8] Aarhus Convention, Article 9(4).

tice is even more limited. NGOs thus act more often as facilitators, investigators and publicists than actors in respect of international environmental disputes. NGOs may provide advice, assistance and support to governments, may from time to time attempt to achieve outcomes by suggesting, advising or promoting certain courses of action, and may take steps to achieve facilitation by other actors such as international organizations or states. Yet opportunities for direct participation in dispute resolution are very limited. While the role of MEAs in international environmental disputes has without doubt increased over the last two decades, the opportunities for participation of NGOs and other civil society actors in international decision-making and dispute resolution has not kept pace. The primary avenues of NGOs for legal enforcement are still domestic tribunals and NGOs in international dispute enforcement are still largely relegated to advisory and publicity roles. Even in submitting *amicus curiae* briefs to dispute resolution mechanisms the opportunities for NGOs are sharply limited.

2.1 UNEP Guidelines

In 2002, the UNEP Governing Council[9] adopted guidelines on compliance with multilateral environmental agreements and on the capacity-strengthening, effective national environmental enforcement. The UNEP Guidelines are to assist governments, Secretariats of MEAs, relevant international and regional organizations, NGOs and the private sector in enhancing and supporting compliance with agreements.[10] The Guidelines[11] recommend regular exchange of information among states about environmental issues that are the subject of negotiations and about the ability of the states to address those issues, as well as informal consultations on issues that could affect compliance among states between negotiating sessions, workshops involving governments, NGOs, the private sector and relevant international and regional organizations. Cooperation is a key theme in the Guidelines and some developments underlying the importance of international cooperation in the enforcement of MEAs are outlined below. Greenpeace and other NGOs have a role to play in assisting with such cooperation, monitoring and reporting and ensuring that governments carry out their consultative and cooperative functions.

2.2 Reporting, monitoring and verification of compliance and capacity-building

NGOs frequently monitor and publicize reporting, monitoring and verification reports and functions and can assist states parties and Secretariats of MEAs in as-

---

[9] UNEP Governing Council, 15 February 2002, Decision VII/4. Compliance with and enforcement of multilateral environmental agreements, see <www.unep.org/governingbodies/gc/special sessions/gcss_vii/Reports.htm>.

[10] UNEP Guidelines I.A., see <www.unep.org/governingbodies/gc/specialsessions/gcss_vii/>.

[11] UNEP Guidelines D(1).

sessing such reports and suggesting responses to such reports. NGOs assist with disseminating information through the media about issues, obligations under MEAs and remedial steps that can be taken by parties.[12] Where non-compliance is due to capacity issues, NGOs can assist through information, training and technical assistance.[13]

At the same time as the Governing Council adopted the UNEP Guidelines, the Council passed a resolution on enhancing civil society engagement in the work of the United Nations Environment Programme[14] in which the Governing Council agreed to make efforts to meaningfully consider the views of representatives of major groups and NGOs, including the private sector, giving them clear channels for providing governments with their views, within the established rules and modalities of the United Nations system.

2.3   *Locus standi*

The participation of NGOs in the enforcement of MEAs is dogged by problems of access to tribunals, typified by restrictive standing provisions. A clear example of the exclusion of NGOs from enforcement procedures was seen in the decision of the European Court of Justice to refuse standing to Greenpeace International in *Greenpeace v Commission*.[15] There the Court of First Instance in 1995, upheld by the European Court of Justice,[16] held that Greenpeace International had no standing to challenge a decision adopted by the Commission in 1993 to fund assistance in relation to the construction of two power stations in the Canary Islands,[17] since Greenpeace International was not individually affected by the decision. This decision stands in stark contrast to the decision in the previous year by the English High Court that Greenpeace Ltd (Greenpeace UK) was a 're-

---

[12] UNEP Guidelines E(1).

[13] The 8th Meeting of the Conference of the Contracting Parties to the Ramsar Convention on Wetlands in 2002 noted the difficulties in implementing MEAs, including the Ramsar Convention, include limited institutional capacity and resources in the areas of reporting, monitoring and verification. Resolution VII.24, see <www.ramsar.org/key_res_viii_24_e.pdf>. Ramsar Convention (Convention on Wetlands of International Importance especially as Waterfowl Habitat), Ramsar, Iran, 2 February 1971, as amended by the Protocol of 3 December 1982 and the Amendments of 28 May 1987, text at <www.ramsar.org/key_conv_e.htm>.

[14] UNEP Governing Council Decision VII/5 of 15 February 2002, see <www.unep.org/governingbodies/gc/specialsessions/gcss_vii/Documents/K0260448.doc>.

[15] *Greenpeace International v Commission*, Case T-585/93, [1995] ECR II-2205, judgment of the Court of First Instance, see <www.eel.nl/cases/t_585_93.htm>.

[16] Case C-321/95, 2 April 1998, [1998] ECR I-165, see <www.curia.eu.int/en/content/juris/index.htm>. See IMPEL, *Complaint Procedures and Access to Justice for Citizens and NGOs in the Field of the Environment within the European Union, Final Report*, see <europa.eu.int/comm/environment/impel/pdf/access_to_justice.pdf> and D.L. Torrens, 'Locus Standi and Access to Justice under EC Law – Where to Go after Greenpeace?' (1999) 1 *ELNI Rev.* 15.

[17] Council Directive 85/337 of 27 June 1985 on the assessment of the effects of certain public and private projects on the environment.

sponsible and respected body with a genuine concern for the environment' and thus had standing to challenge the construction of a nuclear power plant.[18] This is not the place for a comprehensive discussion of *locus standi* but it is clear that the implementation of the Aarhus aspirations has a long way to go.

2.4 *Amicus curiae* briefs

The Permanent Court of International Justice (PCIJ) had specific powers to permit international NGOs to furnish information concerning the subject matter of advisory opinions. The current provision is contained in Article 66(2) of the Statute of the International Court of Justice (ICJ) [19] which provides that the Registrar may notify any state entitled to appear before the ICJ or international organization considered by the Court or the President as likely to be able to furnish information on the question, that the ICJ will be prepared to receive written statements, to hear oral statements relating to the question. The ICJ has interpreted this language to permit it to receive statements from an international NGO, specifically the International League for Human Rights.[20] Unfortunately, while the procedure was often used by the PCIJ, particularly in proceedings involving the interpretation of ILO documents,[21] this procedure is all too seldom invoked in the practice of the ICJ.

2.5 Consultation and cooperation

As noted in the UNEP Guidelines,[22] consultation and cooperation has become increasingly important in the field of international environmental law and litigation. As the ICJ observed in its Advisory Opinion on the Legality of the Threat or Use of Nuclear Weapons, trust and confidence are inherent in international cooperation, in particular in an age when this cooperation in many fields is becoming increasingly essential.[23] The need for international cooperation for conservation

---

[18] *R v Inspectorate of Pollution, ex parte Greenpeace Ltd (No. 2)* [1994] 4 *All ER* 329 (High Court, per Otton J).

[19] Formerly contained in Article 73 of the Rules of the Permanent Court of International Justice.

[20] ICJ, Pleadings, *International Status of South West Africa* (1950) at 327; also see R. Clark, 'The International League for Human Rights and South West Africa 1947–1957: The Human Rights NGO as Catalyst in the International Legal Process' (1981) 3(4) *HRQ* 101 at 120–122.

[21] K. Keith, *The Extent of the Advisory Jurisdiction of the International Court of Justice* (Leyden, 1971), pp. 189-190.

[22] UNEP Guidelines IF(34) notes that there is a recognized need for a commitment by all countries to the global process of protecting and improving the environment. This may be furthered by the United Nations and other relevant international organizations, as well as through multilateral and bilateral initiatives for facilitating compliance. UNEP Guidelines II(35) similarly with respect to domestic enforcement notes that consistent with relevant provisions in multilateral environmental agreements, national enforcement of laws and regulations implementing multilateral environmental agreements could be supported through international cooperation and coordination that can be facilitated by, *inter alia*, UNEP.

[23] Legality of the Threat or Use of Nuclear Weapons, Advisory Opinion of 8 July 1996, (1996) ICJ Reports 226.

has long been recognized.[24] A number of Conventions and international instruments specifically provide for cooperation. To name a few examples:

- The Rio Declaration[25] requires states and people to cooperate in good faith and in a spirit of partnership in the fulfilment of the principles embodied in the Declaration and in the further development of international law in the field of sustainable development.
- The 1993 Chemical Weapons Convention requires each party to cooperate with other states parties to facilitate the implementation of its obligations under the Convention[26] and otherwise,[27] as well as to cooperate with the Organization for the Prohibition of Chemical Weapons.[28]
- The 1959 Antarctic Treaty aims, *inter alia*, at the promotion of international cooperation in scientific investigation.
- The 1992 Convention on Biological Diversity requires parties to cooperate.[29]
- The Convention to Combat Desertification[30] contains numerous provisions requiring and enhancing cooperation, as well as promoting the involvement of NGOs.
- Numerous provisions in Law of the Sea Convention include Article 117 (the duty to take, or to cooperate with other states in taking, such measures for their respective nationals as may be necessary for the conservation of the living resources of the high seas), and Article 118 (the duty to cooperate with

---

[24] *Fisheries Jurisdiction (Spain v Canada)*, Judgment of 4 December 1998, (1998) ICJ Reports 432, Judge Oda separate opinion, para. 11, see <www.icj-cij.org/icjwww/idocket/iec/iecjudgment(s)/iec_ijudgment_981204.htm>.

[25] UN Declaration on Environment and Development, 14 June 1992, UN Doc. A/CONF.151/5/Rev.1 (1992), reprinted in (1992) 31 ILM 876 (1992), Principle 27, see <www.unep.org/documents/default.asp?DocumentID=78&ArticleID=1163>. See also Principle 7 ('States shall cooperate in a spirit of global partnership to conserve, protect and restore the health and integrity of the Earth's ecosystem').

[26] Article VII(2).

[27] Article IX.

[28] Article VII(7).

[29] Convention on Biological Diversity, concluded 5 June 1992, entered into force 29 December 1993, (1992) 31 ILM 818, see <www.biodiv.org/convention/articles.asp>. Article 5 provides that each contracting party shall, as far as possible and as appropriate, cooperate with other contracting parties, directly or, where appropriate, through competent international organizations, in respect of areas beyond national jurisdiction and on other matters of mutual interest, for the conservation and sustainable use of biological diversity. Other provisions require cooperation in financial and other support for *in situ* and *ex situ* conservation (Articles 8 and 9) and require states to encourage cooperation between its governmental authorities and its private sector in developing methods for sustainable use of biological resources (Article 10(3e)).

[30] United Nations Convention to Combat Desertification in those Countries Experiencing Serious Drought and/or Desertification, particularly in Africa, adopted 17 June 1994, opened for signature 14 October 1994, entered into force 26 December 1996, UN Doc. A/AC.241/15/Rev.3, (1994) 33 ILM 1328, see <www.unccd.int/convention/text/convention.php>.

each other in the conservation and management of living resources in the areas of the high seas.)[31]

The duty of states to cooperate to avoid transboundary environmental harm can be traced as early as the 1957 *Lac Lanoux Arbitration*.[32] The International Tribunal for the Law of the Sea (ITLOS) has stated very clearly that the duty to cooperate is a fundamental principle which gives rise to enforceable rights. In its Order in the *Southern Bluefin Tuna (SBT)* case,[33] the Tribunal stated that:

> under Article 64, read together with Articles 116–119, of the Convention, States parties to the Convention have the duty to co-operate directly or through appropriate international organizations with a view to ensuring conservation and promoting the objective of optimum utilization of highly migratory species.[34]

More recently, in the *MOX Plant Case (Ireland v United Kingdom)*, ITLOS stated that:

> the duty to cooperate is a fundamental principle in the prevention of pollution of the marine environment under Part XII of the Convention and general international law and that rights arise therefrom which the Tribunal may consider appropriate to preserve under article 290 of the Convention.[35]

ITLOS ordered Ireland and the United Kingdom to cooperate and enter into consultations in order to exchange further information with regard to possible consequences for the Irish Sea arising out of the commissioning of the MOX plant, monitor risks or the effects of the operation of the MOX plant for the Irish Sea and devise, as appropriate, measures to prevent pollution of the marine environment which might result from the operation of the MOX plant. Accordingly, in a decision of the MOX Arbitral Tribunal on 24 June 2003 on provisional measures[36] the Tribunal expressed concern that cooperation and consultation may not

---

[31] United Nations Convention on the Law of the Sea, signed at Montego Bay, Jamaica, 10 December 1982, entered into force 16 November 1994, UN Doc. A/CONF.62/122 (1982), (1982) 21 ILM 1261 ss., see <www.un.org/Depts/los/convention_agreements/texts/unclos/closindx.htm>.

[32] *Lac Lanoux Arbitration (France v Spain)* (1957) 24 ILR 101, at 127–128. The tribunal held that France had complied with its obligation to consult and negotiate in good faith with Spain before diverting a common watercourse.

[33] *Southern Bluefin Tuna (New Zealand v Japan; Australia v Japan)*, Order of 27 August 1999, Provisional Measures, (1999) 38 ILM 1624, para. 48, see <www.itlos.org/cgi-bin/cases/case_detail. pl?id=3&lang=en>.

[34] *SBT* Order, para. 48.

[35] *MOX Plant case (Ireland v United Kingdom)*, Order of 3 December 2001, Provisional Measures, (2001) ITLOS 2, see <www.itlos.org/cgi-bin/cases/case_detail.pl?id=10&lang=en>, para. 82.

[36] Permanent Court of Arbitration: Arbitral Tribunal constituted pursuant to Article 287, and Article 1 of Annex VII, of the United Nations Convention on the Law of the Sea for the Dispute concerning the MOX Plant, International Movements of Radioactive Materials, and the Protection of the Marine Environment of the Irish Sea (*Ireland v United Kingdom*) (the 'MOX Plant' case), Order No. 3, suspension of proceedings on jurisdiction and merits, and request for further provisional measures, 24 June 2003.

always have been as timely or effective as it could have been[37] and recommended that the United Kingdom reviews with Ireland the whole system of intergovernmental notification and cooperation in respect of the concerns of Ireland as to the Sellafield plant.[38]

More recently, ITLOS again restated the duty to cooperate in the *Case Concerning Land Reclamation by Singapore in and around the Straits of Johor (Malaysia v Singapore)*[39] and prescribed provisional measures requiring that Malaysia and Singapore cooperate and enter into consultations to establish a group of independent experts to study the effects of Singapore's land reclamation, prepare a report on infilling, exchange information and consult.

NGOs have a vital role to play in the facilitation of coordination and consultation in these matters. NGOs have access to information, expertise, experience and advice that is often invaluable to states, and their participation in international conferences and negotiating sessions provides access to NGOs to states that assists NGOs in carrying out these functions of coordination and the provision of information.

3. SOME EXAMPLES OF MEA COMPLIANCE ISSUES UNDER INDIVIDUAL INSTRUMENTS

3.1 CITES and illegal logging

Enforcement of bans on illegal logging and on the international trade in forest products arising is one area where there is a lively interface between domestic and international law. The dispute resolution provision in the Convention on International Trade in Endangered Species of Wild Fauna and Flora (CITES)[40] are brief, with Article XVIII providing for the submission of disputes to arbitration by mutual consent. Parties are required to take appropriate measures to enforce the provisions of CITES and to prohibit trade in specimens in violation. These are to include measures to penalize trade in, or possession of, such specimens, or both and to provide for the confiscation or return to the state of export of such specimens.[41] CITES has an enforcement assistance unit to assist with enforce-

---

[37] Ibid., para. 66.

[38] Ibid., paras. 66, 67, ref. para. 48; Order, para. 7. The Tribunal buttressed its recommendation by imposing reporting requirements.

[39] *Case concerning Land Reclamation by Singapore in and around the Straits of Johor (Malaysia v Singapore)*, Order of 8 October 2003, Provisional Measures, see <www.itlos.org/cgi-bin/cases/case_detail.pl?id=12&lang=en>, para. 92 citing para. 82 of the ITLOS Order in the *MOX Plant case*, n. 35 above.

[40] Convention on International Trade in Endangered Species of Wild Fauna and Flora (CITES), adopted 3 March 1973, entered into force 1 July 1975, 993 UNTS 243, see <www.cites.org/eng/disc/text.shtml>.

[41] CITES Article VIII(1).

ment, yet NGOs have an important role to play in ensuring the enforcement of CITES provisions.

Illegal logging occurs when timber is felled, processed or traded in violation of national laws and is known to occur in as many as 70 countries. The World Bank has estimated that illegal logging results in an annual loss of revenue to governments of around US$5 billion with an additional US$10 billion lost to the economies of producer countries.[42] In 1998 at the Birmingham summit[43] the G8 countries recognized that illegal logging robs national and sub-national governments, forest owners and local communities of significant revenues and benefits, damages forest eco-systems, distorts timber markets and forest resource assessments, and acts as a disincentive to sustainable forest management. They agreed a set of actions designed to deter illegal logging and trade in illegal timber, which included identifying and assessing the effectiveness of their internal measures to control illegal logging and international trade in illegally harvested timber and identify areas needing improvement.[44]

A recent case study will illustrate difficulties NGOs have faced in assisting the enforcement of MEAs and shows the relevance of domestic litigation.

Under CITES Article V.3 (for Appendix III) or Article V.2 (for Appendix II) and CITES Resolution Conf. 10.2,[45] parties should require a valid export permit which complies with CITES requirements. The Brazilian government suspended the trading of mahogany in October 2001, pending investigations into illegalities and corruption exposed by Greenpeace in its report, *Partners in Mahogany Crime*.[46] Following investigations by the Brazilian Environment Agency (IBAMA), a further ban was imposed, halting the logging of mahogany in December.[47] Despite this ban, a number of timber companies in Brazil managed to continue exporting through obtaining preliminary Brazilian court rulings on a without notice basis[48] which were completed without the necessary findings of legality required by CITES Article V.2(a).[49] IBAMA was required to issue

---

[42] WWF, *The Timber Footprint of the G8 and China: Making the Case for Green Procurement by Government*, June 2002, see <www.wwfchina.org/english/downloads/Forest/timberreport.doc>.

[43] See <usinfo.state.gov/topical/econ/group8/summit98/98summit/forests.htm>

[44] See D. Brack, K. Gray and G. Hayman, *Controlling the International Trade in Illegally Logged Timber and Wood Products*, (Royal Institute of International Affairs Sustainable Development Programme, February 2002), see <www.illegal-logging.info/papers/1_ControllingTrade.pdf>, N. Scotland and S. Ludwig, 'Deforestation, the Timber Trade and Illegal Logging', paper for EC Workshop on Forest Law Enforcement, Governance and Trade (April 2002), see <www.illegal-logging.info/papers/FLEGT_background_0402.rtf.doc>.

[45] Resolution Conf. 10.2, <www.cites.org/eng/resols/10/10_2.shtml>, states in part that the Conference of the Parties recommends at II(h) that parties not authorize the import of any specimen if they have reason to believe that it was not legally acquired in the country of origin.

[46] See <www.greenpeace.org/~forests/forests_new/html/content/reports/Mahoganyweb.pdf>.

[47] IBAMA Decree No. 17, 19 October 2001.

[48] Eight of these companies have exported over 15,000 cubic metres between 20 December 2001 and March 2002, with an export value of around US$11 million, see <http://archive.greenpeace.org/pressreleases/forests/2002mar27.html>.

[49] IBAMA Decree, 5 December 2001, instrução normative No. 22 ordered the cessation of mahogany logging and invalidated the management plans under which mahogany logging took place.

CITES export permits in respect of substantial quantities of timber owned by those companies, even though IBAMA had not been satisfied that the timber had been acquired lawfully, as required by CITES Article V(2)(a). On the strength of such CITES export permits, the timber companies concerned shipped consignments of mahogany from Brazil to the USA, Canada, Belgium, Germany, the Netherlands and England. IBAMA made it clear that, when issuing all such CITES export permits, it had *not* been satisfied that the specimens of mahogany concerned were not illegally logged. The CITES Secretariat stated that in the light of the existence of reasonable doubt as to whether IBAMA had been satisfied that the specimens had not been obtained in contravention of national conservation legislation, the export permits were issued contrary to CITES and should not be accepted.[50]

In *R (Greenpeace Ltd) v Secretary of State for the Environment, Food and Rural Affairs and another*,[51] Greenpeace had asked the High Court to make declarations that the importation by Alan Thomas Craig Ltd of a cargo of mahogany from Brazil contravened the European Union's regulatory regime for endangered species in Council Regulation 338/97, which implements CITES. On appeal the English Court of Appeal held by two to one, with a strong dissenting decision by Laws LJ, that where an importing state was presented with an export permit which complied with Article VI of CITES it was entitled to treat the permit as sufficient documentary evidence of its validity unless it had been set aside by agreement or a court, or cancelled by the issuing authority. The importing state was not obliged to satisfy itself that before the permit had been issued the requisite conditions had been properly met even when they know that the exporting state's management authority issued an export permit for those specimens without any belief that the preconditions for issuing a permit were met, and therefore on a false basis. The CITES Secretariat itself had advised affected state parties that, under the Convention, they should not accept export permits in such circumstances.

This series of cases shows the difficulties NGOs face in enforcing MEAs. The decision by contracting parties to CITES to list mahogany on CITES Annex II is an important step in the right direction.[52] Appendix II includes species for which it has been determined that trade may be detrimental to the survival of the species if that trade is not strictly controlled. Trade in these species is regulated through the use of export permits. Any shipment of mahogany must be accompanied by

---

[50] The Environment-Directorate of the EC Commission notified the management authorities of all the EC member states of its view that member states should not accept export permits for specimens of bigleaf mahogany from Brazil until further notice without first obtaining a statement that those specimens were legally acquired, and the United States Fish and Wildlife Service detained more than 20 shipments arriving at its ports on similar grounds.

[51] *R (Greenpeace Ltd) v Secretary of State for the Environment, Food and Rural Affairs and another* [2002] EWCA Civ 1036, see <www.lawreports.co.uk/civjulb2.6.htm>.

[52] See <www.greenpeaceusa.org/media/press_releases/2002/11132002btext.htm>.

an export permit affirming that it was legally harvested in a way that is not detrimental to the survival of the species.

FSC certification schemes would be of further assistance.

3.2 'Scientific whaling'

The controversy over so-called 'scientific whaling within the 1946 International Whaling Convention[53] involves issues as to whether the practice of 'scientific whaling' by Japan is incompatible with Article VIII of the Convention and whether Japan is cooperating with the International Whaling Commission (IWC) as required by Articles 65 and 120 of the 1982 Law of the Sea Convention. Article VIII allows contracting governments to grant special permits to its nationals authorizing that national to kill, take and treat whales 'for purposes of scientific research'. Whales caught in Japan's special permit operations provide over 3,000 tonnes of edible products per year that are sold for commercial purposes, despite IWC resolutions that expressed serious concern at the possibility of whaling for scientific purposes assuming the characteristics of commercial whaling[54] and have stated that the meat and products of special permit whaling should be utilized entirely for domestic consumption.[55] The IWC has issued resolutions concerning scientific whaling permits in a series of over 30 resolutions[56] from the adoption of the moratorium on commercial whaling in 1985/1986 through to this year.[57] The IWC this year called on the Japanese government to halt its Antarctic JARPA[58] programme, or to revise it so that it is limited to non-lethal research methodologies.[59] This record has given rise to concerns that Japan's issuance of scientific permits may be for purposes other than scientific research and accord-

---

[53] International Convention for the Regulation of Whaling, opened for signature at Washington, 2 December 1946, entered in force 10 November 1948, 161 UNTS 72. Amended 19 November 1956. 338 UNTS 366, see <http://ourworld.compuserve.com/homepages/iwcoffice/Convention. htm>.

[54] IWC Resolution 1985/2.

[55] IWC Resolution 1994/7.

[56] The IWC has stated that special permit whaling should: only be permitted in exceptional circumstances (1995/8 and 1995/9); meet critically important research needs (1987); satisfy criteria established by the Scientific Committee; be consistent with the Commission's conservation policy (1987/1); be conducted using non-lethal research techniques (1995/9); and ensure the conservation of whales in sanctuaries (1995/8). See most recently IWC Resolution 2003/2 <www.iwcoffice.org/Resolutions2003/Resolution%202003.htm>.

[57] In 2003, the IWC restated its deep concern that the provision permitting special permit whaling enables countries to conduct whaling for commercial purposes despite the moratorium on commercial whaling, stated that the current and proposed special permit whaling operations represent an act contrary to the spirit of the moratorium on commercial whaling and to the will of the Commission and that Article VIII of the Convention is not intended to be exploited in order to provide whale meat for commercial purposes and shall not be so used and urged any country conducting or considering the conduct of special permit whaling to terminate or not commence such activities and to limit scientific research to non-lethal methods only: IWC Resolution 2003/2.

[58] Japan's Whale Research Program under Special Permit in Antarctica.

[59] IWC Resolution 2003/3.

ingly not be consistent with the requirements of Article VIII(1), that Japan's issuance of permits under Article VIII could constitute an abuse of rights,[60] and that Japan is not cooperating with other states and working through the IWC as required under Law of the Sea Convention, including in particular Article 65 which requires that states shall cooperate with a view to the conservation of marine mammals and in the case of cetaceans, shall in particular work through the appropriate international organizations for their conservation, management and study.[61]

Yet there are no dispute resolution provisions in the International Whaling Convention and, while dispute resolution provisions in Part XV of the Law of the Sea Convention could be resorted to, no state has invoked them to date. This is perhaps a good example of a situation where in the absence of domestic or international remedies the resolution of disputes is relegated to the diplomatic arena. The *SBT* Arbitral Tribunal observed[62] that, to the extent that the search for resolution of the dispute were to resort to third party procedures, those listed in Article 16 of the Convention for the Conservation of Southern Bluefin Tuna[63] are labels that conform to traditional diplomatic precedent and suggested in addition to third-party binding settlement rendered in the form of an arbitral award, other ways in which an independent body can be configured to interact with the states party to a dispute, including a combination or alternation of direct negotiations, advice from expert panels, benevolent supervision and good offices extended by a third party body, and recourse to a third party for step-by-step aid in decision-making and for mediation.

Whether this dispute can be resolved through these or more formal dispute resolution mechanisms remains to be seen. The jurisprudence of the International Tribunal for the Law of the Sea (ITLOS) has been growing since the *Saiga* decision in 1997.[64] ITLOS is open to non-state entities in very limited circumstances.[65] ITLOS may give an advisory opinion on a legal question if an interna-

---

[60] The Law of the Sea Convention specifically incorporates the obligation to act in good faith and not to abuse the rights in Article 300. In the *SBT* Arbitral Award, the Tribunal did allow for the possibility that there might be instances in which a party to UNCLOS and fisheries treaty implementing it would be so egregious and risk consequences of such gravity that a Tribunal might find that the obligations of UNCLOS provide a basis for jurisdiction, having particular regard to the provisions of UNCLOS Article 300, which requires good faith and prohibits abuse of rights (*SBT Case (Australia and New Zealand v Japan)*, Award on Jurisdiction and Admissibility, 4 August 2000, (2000) 39 ILM 1359, see <www.worldbank.org/icsid/bluefintuna/award080400.pdf> ('*SBT* Arbitral Award'), para. 64.

[61] Article 120 of the Law of the Sea Convention provides that Article 65 also applies to the conservation and management of marine mammals in the high seas.

[62] *SBT* Arbitral Award, n. 60 above.

[63] 1819 UNTS 360, see <www.ccsbt.org/docs/pdf/about_the_commission/convention.pdf>.

[64] *M/V 'Saiga' (Saint Vincent and the Grenadines v. Guinea)*, judgment of 4 December 1997, Prompt Release (1998) 37 ILM 360, see <www.itlos.org/cgi-bin/cases/case_detail.pl?id=1&lang=en>.

[65] ITLOS is open to entities other than states parties in any case expressly provided for in Part XI (relating to the sea-bed) or in any case submitted pursuant to any other agreement conferring juris-

tional agreement related to the purposes of the Convention specifically provides for the submission to ITLOS of a request for such an opinion.[66] If an opinion was sought, or contentious proceedings issued, then NGOs may wish to submit an *amicus curiae* brief. The Statute of the Tribunal is silent on the receipt of *amicus curiae* briefs as such. Article 31 of the Statute provides for intervention by additional states upon request to the Tribunal.[67] Article 84 of the Rules provide that ITLOS may, at any time prior to the closure of the oral proceedings, at the request of a party or *proprio motu*, request an appropriate intergovernmental organization to furnish information relevant to a case before it.[68] ITLOS has discretion in regulating its procedure. Under Article 45 of the Rules of the Tribunal, the President is to ascertain the views of the parties with regard to questions of procedure. To the best of the author's knowledge, an *amicus brief* has yet to be submitted to ITLOS.

3.3   Illegal, unregulated and unreported fishing

Greenpeace International has been actively involved in identifying and facilitating the arrest of 'pirate' fishing vessels and exposing illegal, unregulated and unreported (IUU) fishing activities. Pirate vessels commonly use shell companies to hide their owners' identities and go to extraordinary lengths to conceal their activities. The vessels commonly fly flags of convenience and sometimes, like the *Salvora* discovered by Greenpeace in 1999 near the Kerguelen Islands, carry concealed or no markings to mask their identities at sea. Yet despite international

---

diction on the Tribunal which is accepted by all the parties to that case (ITLOS Statute, Article 20(2)). An application for prompt release may be made by a person authorized by the flag state (Law of the Sea Convention, Article 292 and Rules of the Tribunal, Article 110, which make it clear that states may authorize persons to make applications for the prompt release of a vessel on behalf of the flag state). There are, however, provisions for NGO involvement with respect to the sea-bed. The Secretary General, on matters within the competence of the International Sea-Bed Authority, is to make suitable arrangements with the approval of the Council for consultation and cooperation with NGOs recognized by ECOSOC (Law of the Sea Convention, Article 169(1)). Such NGOs can attend meetings of the organs of the Authority as observers and submit written reports on subjects in which they have special competence and which are related to the work of the Authority (Law of the Sea Convention, Article 169(2) and (3)). The Sea-Bed Disputes Chamber has jurisdiction over natural or juridical matters such as the interpretation or application of a contract (Law of the Sea Convention, Article 187).

[66] ITLOS Rules, Article 138(1).

[67] ITLOS Statute, Article 31 (request to intervene): '1. Should a State Party consider that it has an interest of a legal nature which may be affected by the decision in any dispute, it may submit a request to the Tribunal to be permitted to intervene. 2. It shall be for the Tribunal to decide upon this request. 3. If a request to intervene is granted, the decision of the Tribunal in respect of the dispute shall be binding upon the intervening State Party in so far as it relates to matters in respect of which that State Party intervened'.

[68] 'Intergovernmental organization' is not defined, other than as 'an intergovernmental organization other than any organization which is a party or intervenes in the case concerned' (ITLOS Rules, Article 52(4), although Article 52 of the Rules uses the words 'international organization and any other intergovernmental organization'.

concern about illegal fishing activities, and associated effects such as by-catch of albatrosses,[69] positive action to close ports to vessels engaged in IUU fishing and their support vessels, close markets to fish caught from IUU fishing activities and take enforcement action on the international level against such activities has not been forthcoming.

The FAO's International Plan of Action to deter, prevent and eliminate IUU fishing[70] stresses deterrence. The requirement to consider the need for deterrence has yet to be fully implemented by ITLOS in its assessment of the reasonableness of the bond. A bond should not be held to be unreasonable if it is reasonably necessary for a coastal state to ensure the effective enforcement of fisheries laws. Judge Anderson noted in the *Monte Confurco* case that 'where there is persistent non-observance of the law, deterrent fines serve a legitimate purpose'.[71]

For its part, ITLOS has been frequently asked to decide applications for prompt release of vessels under Article 292 of the Law of the Sea Convention. After the *Camouco*[72] and *Monte Confurco*[73] cases in which ITLOS reduced the amount of the bond, the *Grand Prince* case marked a turning point where ITLOS held that 'in the view of the tribunal, the assertion that the vessel is "still considered as registered in Belize" contains an element of fiction, and does not provide sufficient basis for holding that Belize was the flag State of the vessel for the purposes of making an application under article 292 of the convention'.[74] As the author noted at the time, the entire flag of convenience system contains an element of fiction, and the *Grand Prince* decision is an important step towards closing the loophole.

---

[69] Greenpeace has estimated that up to 93,000 Southern Ocean seabirds (including endangered species of albatross) have been caught and drowned as by-catch by pirate fishers in 2002 alone, see <www.greenpeace.org/international_en//press/release?item_id=89498&campaign_id=4022>.

[70] Food and Agriculture Organization, International Plan of Action to Prevent, Deter and Eliminate Illegal, Unreported and Unregulated Fishing (IPOA-IUU), adopted by consensus at the 24th Session of COFI on 2 March 2001 and endorsed by the 120th Session of the FAO Council on 23 June 2001, see <www.fao.org/DOCREP/003/y1224e/y1224e00.HTM>. Para. 21 provides that 'States should ensure that sanctions for IUU fishing by vessels and, to the greatest extent possible, nationals under its jurisdiction are of sufficient severity to effectively prevent, deter and eliminate IUU fishing and to deprive offenders of the benefits accruing from such fishing'. Paragraph 22 states that 'All possible steps should be taken, consistent with international law, to prevent, deter and eliminate the activities of non-cooperating States to a relevant regional fisheries management organization which engage in IUU fishing'.

[71] 'Monte Confurco' Case (Seychelles v France), judgment of 18 December 2000, Prompt Release, Dissenting Opinion of Judge Anderson, see <www.itlos.org/cgi-bin/cases/case_detail.pl?id=5&lang=en>.

[72] In the 'Camouco' Case (Panama v France), judgment of 7 February 2000, Prompt Release, see <www.itlos.org/cgi-bin/cases/case_detail.pl?id=4&lang=en> the bond of FF20,000,000 was reduced to FF8,000,000 (about €1,200,000).

[73] In the 'Monte Confurco' Case, n. 71 above, the bond of FF56,400,000 was reduced to FF18,000,000 (about €2,700,000).

[74] The 'Grand Prince' Case (Belize v France), judgment of 20 April 2001, Prompt Release, see <www.itlos.org/cgi-bin/cases/case_detail.pl?id=7&lang=en>, para. 85.

Most recently, the *Volga* case *(Russian Federation v Australia)*[75] involved a long-line fishing vessel flying the Russian flag which was boarded in February 2002 by the Australian navy outside the EEZ of the Australian Territory of Heard Island and the McDonald Islands with over 131 tonnes of Patagonian toothfish (*Dissostichus eleginoides*). Australia sought a bond of AU$3,332,500 which included AU$1,920,000 as security to cover the assessed value of the vessel, fuel, lubricants and fishing equipment, AU$412,500 to secure payment of potential fines and a security of AU$1,000,000 related to the carriage of a fully operational VMS and observance of conservation measures under the Convention on the Conservation of Antarctic Marine Living Resources (CCAMLR). ITLOS held the first to be reasonable, and decided that the second would serve no practical purpose, since the crew had been granted bail so they could return to their native Spain. In doing so, ITLOS held that a 'good behaviour bond' to prevent future violations of the laws of a coastal state cannot be considered as a bond or security within the meaning of Article 73(2) of the Law of the Sea Convention, read in conjunction with Article 292 of the Convention.[76] The Russian Federation argued that the proceeds of the sale of the catch should be considered as security given by the owner for the release of the vessel and its crew. If accepted, this argument could be analogous to the fruits of an alleged crime being considered as security.[77] ITLOS, however, held that the proceeds have no relevance to the bond to be set for the release of the vessel and the members of the crew. In doing so, ITLOS moved forward from its previous position in *Monte Confurco.*

ITLOS did, however, expressly note that it 'understands the international concerns about illegal, unregulated and unreported fishing and appreciates the objectives behind the measures taken by States, including the States Parties to CCAMLR, to deal with the problem'.[78] Judge Anderson in his dissenting opinion stated that:

> In my opinion, the duty of the coastal State to ensure the conservation of the living resources of the EEZ contained in article 61 of the Convention, as well as the obligations of Contracting Parties to CCAMLR to protect the Antarctic ecosystem, are relevant factors when determining in a case under article 292 whether or not the amount of the bail money demanded for the release of a vessel such as the *Volga* is 'reasonable'.[79]

Judge Anderson found that Article 73 contains no explicit restriction upon the imposition of non-financial conditions for release of arrested vessels. Indeed, the reasonableness of a good behaviour bond bearing in mind the risk of re-offending does seem fully consistent with the object and purpose of Article 73 and of the

---

[75] *The 'Volga' Case (Russian Federation v Australia)*, judgment of 23 December 2002, Prompt Release, see <www.itlos.org/cgi-bin/cases/case_detail.pl?id=11&lang=en>.

[76] Ibid., para. 80.

[77] Ibid., Dissenting Opinion of Judge *ad hoc* Shearer, para. 15.

[78] *Volga* judgment, n. 75 above, para. 68.

[79] Ibid., Dissenting Opinion of Judge Anderson, para. 2.

Law of the Sea Convention as a whole. If the gravity of the alleged offences is a factor to be taken into account in assessing reasonableness, as it was in the *Monte Confurco* judgment and recognized in the *Volga* judgment[80] then *a fortiori* the imposition of a good behaviour bond should not be considered as unreasonable. Indeed, Article 73(1) itself empowers coastal states to take such measures as are 'necessity to ensure compliance' with its laws and regulations.[81]

Similarly, Judge Nelson in his separate opinion in the *Camouco* case said that:

> in my opinion, this Tribunal ... should also take account of what, in the introduction to the Statement in Response of the French Republic, was referred to as 'the context of illegal, uncontrolled and undeclared fishing in the Antarctic Ocean and more especially in the exclusive economic zone of the Crozet Islands where the facts of the case occurred'. This material constitutes part of the 'factual matrix' of the present case – the factual background surrounding the case. In my view this factor ought to have played some part, not by any means a dominant part, but a part nevertheless in the determination of a reasonable bond.[82]

Judge Nelson was right to be concerned about deterrence. After its bond was reduced by ITLOS, the *Camouco* was reflagged under the Uruguay flag and renamed the *Arvisa 1* and continued to fish for Patagonian tooth-fish. *Arvisa 1* was one of two vessels found fishing inside the CCAMLR Area by an Australian research vessel in January 2002 and was yet again caught, this time by the French Navy, in July 2002, this time having apparently been reflagged to the Netherlands Antilles. Clearly, its owners are not deterred by the previous arrests.

In summary, the author suggests that there is already sufficient authority in the Law of the Sea Convention for ITLOS to treat the need for deterrence, prevention and innovative bonding arrangements as relevant matters for assessing whether bonds are reasonable under Article 73. Nonetheless, additional compliance mechanisms are required, such as including increased powers for port states, better regulation of markets, enforcement of the genuine link requirement of flag states and mechanisms to ensure the application of fisheries laws to flags of convenience.

3.4 The IMO

While the International Maritime Organization (IMO) is an international organization rather than an MEA, the experience of Greenpeace in highlighting environmental abuses relevant to the purposes of the IMO shows hazards facing NGOs in the international arena. The experience of Greenpeace International in the IMO shows the lengths some states may go when faced with what they may consider to be excessive or embarrassing involvement of NGOs in demanding compliance of states with international law and environmental standards.

---

[80] *Volga* judgment, n. 75 above, para. 63.
[81] See ibid., Dissenting Opinion of Judge Anderson, para. 16.
[82] *Camouco* judgment, n. 72 above, Separate opinion of Vice-President Nelson.

Greenpeace has participated in the IMO as an organization with consultative status since 1991. The IMO Council in June[83] recommended that Greenpeace International's observer status be withdrawn and it is for the General Assembly in November to accept or reject that recommendation. The suggestion is that Greenpeace International has not complied with the Collision Regulations 1972 (COLREGS).[84] Greenpeace International has repeatedly reaffirmed that it in fact does comply with the COLREGS and has not been charged with any breaches of the COLREGS.

The IMO Council, subject to approval by the Assembly, may grant consultative status to any NGO which is able to make a substantial contribution to the work of the IMO.[85] The Council undertakes periodic review of the list of NGOs with consultative status with the IMO.[86] No complaint has been made as to the contribution of Greenpeace to the work of the IMO,[87] and no changes have occurred in the nature, purposes, membership or activities of Greenpeace International which could be said to make continuance of consultative status inappropriate or incompatible with the Rules or Guidelines.[88] Greenpeace has repeatedly reaffirmed its 1991 undertaking that 'Greenpeace observes and will continue to observe "rules of good seamanship". This, of course, includes Greenpeace's commitment to comply with the international regulations concerning collisions at sea'.[89] The primary flag state of Greenpeace vessels, the Netherlands, has informed the IMO that it not aware of any verdict or sentence by another flag state or coastal state because of irresponsible navigational behaviour of Greenpeace vessels.

The Council's decision was taken following complaints received by Australia in 2003[90] and Turkey and Greece in 2002. In contrast, with respect to one of the complaints by Australia, protesters from a protest flotilla, well prepared for the conditions, entered the water to the port side of the nuclear transports that were subject of the protest, and held up a sign whilst in the water. The vessels were contacted before the protest. The swimmers were not in front of the vessel, no navigational rule or other law was broken and no vessel was at any risk of colli-

---

[83] Summary of Decisions, IMO Doc C90/D, 1 July 2003. The record of decision stated '29(b).2 The Council further decided to withdraw the consultative status of Greenpeace International in line with Rule 10 of the Rules Governing Relationship with Non-Governmental International Organizations'.

[84] Convention on the International Regulations for Preventing Collisions at Sea, 1972 (COLREGS), adopted 20 October 1972, entered into force 15 July 1997, see <www.imo.org/Conventions/contents.asp?doc_id=649&topic_id=257>.

[85] Rules Governing Relationship with Non-Governmental International Organizations, amended in IMO Doc. A1/A/6.02, Circular Letter No. 2348, 30 November 2001, Rule 1.

[86] Rule 10.

[87] Thus, Council cannot have recommended the withdrawal of consultancy status on the basis of para. VI of the IMO Guidelines on the Grant of Consultative Status, A/22/28(C) ('IMO Guidelines') para. VI.

[88] IMO Guidelines, para. VIII.

[89] Letter dated 4 November 1991 by Roger Wilson for Greenpeace International.

[90] IMO Doc. C90/29(b)/Add.1 and Greenpeace response in IMO Council Decision 86/D, para. 22(b).

sion. Greenpeace is aware of no proceedings that were brought against any members of the flotilla following the protest, nor was there any breach of the COLREGS or danger to shipping involved in any of the other protests. It appears that the real issue is that Greenpeace's activities in exposing the polluting practices of industries such as ocean incineration, dumping, nuclear shipment, the dumping of toxic decommissioned ships on Asian shores, illegal fishing and substandard shipping, in particular oil tankers, are inconvenient for the industries and states supporting them. Following the *Prestige* oil spill there have been no moves to expel any responsible organization or state.

The moves by the IMO are in contrast to the comments made by the United Nations Secretary General, Kofi Annan, who has recognized the role of NGOs as essential, stating that NGOs were 'our best defence against complacency, our bravest campaigners for honesty and our boldest crusaders for change'.[91] Greenpeace International has Category II consultative status with the UN Economic and Social Council, and takes part as an official observer at a wide range of political conferences and conventions. If the IMO Assembly confirms the decision made by the Council, such a decision would represent a reverse of developments towards the participation of civil society in international decision-making seen in the Aarhus Convention and signalled by the Secretary General.[92]

4. CONCLUSION

The rapid development in MEAs and international environmental law in the past 20 years has been accompanied by a rise in the number and involvement of NGOs at the international level. However, issues of access, standing, cost and a far from perfect interface between the international and domestic litigation mean NGOs have had to resort to innovative methods to bring their influence to bear on enforcement and compliance issues. The development of law on consultation and cooperation does leave the door open to the contribution of NGOs with respect to information, advice, assistance, support or publicity. However, the reality that corporations are often responsible for or have an important role to play in compliance issues, suggests a more direct role for NGOs than has until now been evident. Standing to initiate dispute resolution procedures on the international as well as domestic levels, the right to submit *amicus curiae* briefs and access to negotiating and decision-making bodies, as well as the implementation of cost-effective, timely and effective procedures, are all important issues to address to enable compliance and enforcement to catch up with the norms that have been put in place.

---

[91] See AFP, 'Annan Says NGOs Essential to the Work of the UN', 29 August 2000 <www.globalpolicy.org/msummit/millenni/ngoconf1.htm>.

[92] In November 2003, the 23rd IMO Assembly decided to retain the consultative status of Greenpeace International. See Resolution A/938(23) <www.imo.org/Newsroom/mainframe.asp?topic_id=144&doc_id=3440>.

Chapter 13

NGOs and the Aarhus Convention

*Jeremy Wates**

This chapter is presented in four parts. The first two parts provide some general information about the Aarhus Convention, the first describing its origin and evolution and the second giving a summary of its content. The third part addresses the question of the role of NGOs in the Convention processes, both during the negotiation phase and now in the implementation phase. The final part describes the innovative compliance mechanism developed under the Convention and the role of civil society in relation to the mechanism.

1. ORIGIN AND EVOLUTION OF THE AARHUS CONVENTION

The Aarhus Convention – or to give it its full name, the United Nations Economic Commission for Europe (UNECE) Convention on Access to Information, Public Participation in Decision-making and Access to Justice in Environmental Matters[1] – has been described by the UN Secretary General Kofi Annan as 'the most ambitious venture in environmental democracy undertaken under the auspices of the United Nations [whose] adoption was a remarkable step forward in the development of international law'.

The Convention was adopted at the 4th Ministerial 'Environment for Europe' Conference, held in the Danish city of Aarhus in June 1998. It was signed by 39 states and the European Community and entered into force on 30 October 2001.

The origins of the Aarhus Convention can be traced back to the Rio Declaration on Environment and Development, whose Principle 10 promotes the notion that individuals should have appropriate access to information, opportunities for participation in decision-making and effective access to judicial and administrative proceedings. This rather general principle was taken up by governments within the framework of the Environment for Europe process,[2] initially leading

---

* Any opinions expressed in this chapter are those of the author in his personal capacity.

[1] Reprinted in 38 ILM 517. Also available at <www.unece.org/env/pp/treatytext.htm>.

[2] A UNECE-wide process of cooperation on environmental issues, established following the collapse of communism in Eastern Europe at the end of the 1980s and punctuated by a series of Ministerial Conferences (Dobris, Czechoslovakia, 1991; Luzern, Switzerland, 1993; Sofia, Bulgaria, 1995; Aarhus, Denmark, 1998; and Kiev, Ukraine, 2003).

T. Treves et al., eds., Civil Society, International Courts and Compliance Bodies
© 2005, T·M·C·ASSER PRESS, *The Hague, The Netherlands, and the Authors*

to the preparation by a UNECE Task Force on Environmental Rights and Obligations of a set of draft guidelines on access to environmental information and public participation in environmental decision-making. The guidelines were adopted at the 3rd Ministerial 'Environment for Europe' Conference in Sofia in October 1995 and hence became known as the Sofia Guidelines.[3]

At the same time as adopting the Guidelines, the Ministerial Conference agreed that the development of a regional convention on public participation with 'appropriate involvement of NGOs' should be considered.[4] In January 1996, the UNECE Committee on Environmental Policy mandated the start of negotiations and established an *ad hoc* working group for the purpose. The negotiations began in June 1996 and were concluded in March 1998, in due time for the new Convention to be adopted and opened for signature at the Ministerial Conference.

The adoption and signing of the Convention was one of the key outcomes of the Aarhus Conference. In parallel with adopting the Convention, the signatories adopted a resolution establishing, *inter alia*, a Meeting of the Signatories.[5] This and other subsidiary bodies operated under the authority of the Committee on Environmental Policy during the following years and carried out important preparatory work paving the way for the entry into force and the first Meeting of the Parties. The Convention entered into force on 30 October 2001, following the deposit of the 16th instrument of ratification with the UN Secretary General, and the 1st Meeting of the Parties to the Convention took place in Lucca, Italy, in October 2002.

With the Lucca Meeting, the Convention entered a new phase. A wide range of decisions establishing the basic institutional 'architecture' of the Convention, including decisions on Rules of Procedure, financial arrangements, work programmes, reporting and compliance, were adopted. Working groups and task forces were established to work on issues such as genetically modified organisms, access to justice and electronic information tools among others. The Meeting also resulted in the adoption of the 'Lucca Declaration',[6] an important policy statement encapsulating the key elements of other decisions of the Meeting and in addition sowing some seeds for future initiatives.[7] The Declaration was adopted not only by parties, signatories, other states but also by NGOs and other stakeholders represented in Lucca, reflecting the ability of a diverse range of stakeholders to cooperate in producing a text acceptable to all despite obvious differences.

---

[3] UNECE Guidelines on Access to Environmental Information and Public Participation in Environmental Decision-making, Doc. ECE/CEP/24/Rev.1.

[4] Declaration of the 3rd Ministerial 'Environment for Europe' Conference, para. 48.

[5] Resolution on Access to Information, Public Participation in Decision-making and Access to Justice in Environmental Matters, Doc. ECE/CEP/43/Add.1/Rev.1, para. 10(a).

[6] Doc. ECE/MP:PP/2/Add.1.

[7] See, e.g., para. 31 of the Declaration which prompted the Working Group of the Parties to establish an expert group to look into the feasibility of developing guidelines on promoting the application of the principles of the Convention in international environment-related bodies and processes as required under Article 3(7) of the Convention.

At Lucca, the negotiations on the preparation of a Protocol on pollutant release and transfer registers that had started under the authority of the Committee on Environmental Policy were brought under the authority of the Meeting of the Parties. Seven months later, the Protocol was adopted at an extraordinary Meeting of the Parties held within the framework of the 5th Ministerial 'Environment for Europe' Conference (Kiev, May 2003) and signed by 36 states and the European Community.

As of 20 October 2003, there were 26 parties to the Aarhus Convention, the bulk of these being countries with economies in transition or EU accession countries. While some of these countries face significant challenges in giving full effect to the Convention's provisions, the fact that so many have ratified or acceded to the Convention – often before ratifying or acceding to other international or regional treaties which have been in the queue for longer – is an important political signal which shows that at some level, the issues addressed by the Convention are seen as being of particular importance in such countries.

Just five of the European Union countries were parties by that date. This should not, however, be interpreted as reflecting a lack of activity or interest in the Convention in that part of the region. Rather it stems partly from the requirement in most Western countries that the implementing legislation must be in place before a treaty is ratified (whereas in several Eastern countries, international treaties have direct effect and can therefore be ratified without necessarily requiring implementing legislation to be developed in advance); and partly from the complexity of the EU decision-making processes combined with the fact that some member states have chosen to defer ratification until the European Community as a whole is ready to ratify.

2. CONTENT OF THE AARHUS CONVENTION

As its title suggests, the Convention contains three broad themes or 'pillars': access to information, public participation and access to justice. However, before describing these, it is worth referring to a number of important general features of the Convention.

2.1 General features

(a) Rights-based approach

The Convention adopts a rights-based approach. Article 1, setting out the objective of the Convention, requires parties to guarantee rights of access to information, public participation in decision-making and access to justice in environmental matters. It also refers to the goal of protecting the right of every person of present and future generations to live in an environment adequate to health and well-being, which represents a significant step forward in international law. These rights underlie the various procedural requirements in the Convention.

(b) A 'floor', not a 'ceiling'

The Convention establishes minimum standards to be achieved but does not prevent any party from adopting measures which go further in the direction of providing access to information, public participation or access to justice. Nor does it require any derogation from existing rights in this area.[8]

(c) Non-discrimination

The Convention prohibits discrimination on the basis of citizenship, nationality or domicile against persons seeking to exercise their rights under the Convention.[9]

(d) Definition of public authorities

The main thrust of the obligations contained in the Convention is towards public authorities, which are defined so as to cover governmental bodies from all sectors and at all levels (national, regional, local, etc.), and bodies performing public administrative functions. Although the Convention is not primarily focused on the private sector, privatized bodies having public responsibilities in relation to the environment and which are under the control of the aforementioned types of public authorities are also covered by the definition. Bodies acting in a judicial or legislative capacity are excluded.[10]

(e) Inclusion of EC institutions

The definition of 'public authority' also covers the institutions of regional economic integration organizations that become a party to the Convention. Therefore, if the European Community ratifies the Convention, the provisions of the Convention will apply to its institutions. The main impact of this would probably be on the European Commission but it would also apply to the Council when it is not acting in a legislative capacity, and to the European Environment Agency.[11]

(f) International bodies

Apart from the special case of regional economic integration organizations such as the EU, the Convention contains a more general requirement on parties to promote the application of its principles within the framework of international pro-

---

[8] Article 3(5) and (6).
[9] Article 3(9).
[10] Article 2(2).
[11] Article 2(2)(d).

cesses and bodies in matters relating to the environment. The inclusion of this provision would appear to show some recognition of the need to prevent any loss of transparency and public accountability as decision-making moves onto an international level.[12]

(g) Non-compliance mechanism

The Meeting of the Parties to the Convention is required to establish, on a consensus basis, optional arrangements for reviewing compliance with the provisions of the Convention. Such arrangements are to allow for 'appropriate public involvement'.[13] This aspect of the Convention is discussed in further detail in section 4 below.

(h) Non-ECE countries:

Finally, the Convention is open to accession by non-ECE countries, subject to approval of the Meeting of the Parties.[14]

2.2   Access to information

The information pillar covers both the 'passive' or reactive aspect of information, i.e., the obligation on public authorities to respond to public requests for information, and the 'active' aspect dealing with other obligations relating to information, such as collection, updating, public dissemination and so on.
The passive aspect is addressed in Article 4, which contains the main essential elements of a system for securing the public's right to obtain information on request from public authorities:

(a) Presumption in favour of access

Any environmental information held by a public authority must be provided when requested by a member of the public, unless it can be shown to fall within a finite list of exempt categories.[15]

(b) 'Any person' right

The right of access extends to any person, without his or her having to prove or even state an interest.[16]

---

[12] Article 3(7).
[13] Article 15.
[14] Article 19(3).
[15] Article 4, in particular 4(1), (3) and (4).
[16] Articles 2(4) and 4(1).

(c) Broad definition of 'environmental information'

The scope of information covered is quite broad, encompassing a non-exhaustive list of elements of the environment (air, water, soil, etc.); factors, activities or measures affecting those elements; and human health and safety, conditions of life, cultural sites and built structures, to the extent that these are or may be affected by the aforementioned elements, factors, activities or measures.[17]

(d) Time limits

The information must be provided as soon as possible, and at the latest within one month after submission of the request. However, this period may be extended by a further month where the volume and complexity of the information justify this. The requester must be notified of any such extension and the reasons for it.[18]

(e) Form of information

The definition of environmental information covers information in any material form (written, visual, aural, electronic, etc.). There is a qualified requirement on public authorities to provide it in the form specified by the requester.[19]

(f) Charges

Public authorities may impose a charge for supplying information provided the charge does not exceed a 'reasonable' amount.[20]

(g) Exemptions

Public authorities may withhold information where disclosure would adversely affect various interests, e.g., national defence, international relations, public security, the course of justice, commercial confidentiality, intellectual property rights, personal privacy, the confidentiality of the proceedings of public authorities; or where the information requested has been supplied voluntarily or consists of internal communications or material in the course of completion. There are, however, some restrictions on these exemptions, e.g., the commercial confidentiality exemption may not be invoked to withhold information on emissions which is relevant for the protection of the environment.[21]

---

[17] Article 2(3).
[18] Article 4(2).
[19] Articles 2(3) and 4(1)(b).
[20] Article 4(8).
[21] Article 4(3) and (4).

(h) Public interest test

To prevent abuse of the exemptions by over-secretive public authorities, the Convention stipulates that most of the aforementioned exemptions are to be interpreted in a restrictive way, and in all cases may only be applied when the public interest served by disclosure has been taken into account.[22]

(i) Refusals

Refusals, and the reasons for them, are to be issued in writing where requested. A similar time limit applies as for the supply of information: one month from the date of the request, with provision for extending this by a further month where the complexity of the information justifies this.[23]

(j) Onward referral of requests

Where a public authority does not hold the information requested, it should either direct the requester to another public authority which it believes might have the information, or transfer the request to that public authority and notify the requester of this.[24]

The Aarhus Convention also imposes active information duties on parties. These include quite general obligations on public authorities to be in possession of up-to-date environmental information that is relevant to their functions, and to make information 'effectively accessible' to the public by providing information on the type and scope of information held and the process by which it can be obtained.[25] It also contains several more specific provisions:

- *Internet access:* parties are required 'progressively' to make environmental information publicly available in electronic databases which can easily be accessed through public telecommunications networks. The Convention specifies certain categories of information (e.g., state of the environment reports, texts of legislation related to the environment) which should be made available in this form.[26]
- *State-of-the environment reporting:* parties are required to produce national reports on the state of the environment at regular intervals not exceeding four years.[27]

---

[22] Ibid.
[23] Article 4(7).
[24] Article 4(5).
[25] Article 5, in particular 5(1) and (2).
[26] Article 5(3).
[27] Article 5(4).

- *Pollutant release and transfer registers* (PRTRs): the Convention requires parties to take steps progressively to establish such registers.[28] It also requires the issue to be on the agenda of the 1st Meeting of the Parties, where further steps are to be considered, including the elaboration of an appropriate instrument that could be annexed to the Convention.[29] These provisions provided the legal basis for the negotiation and adoption of the Protocol on PRTRs.
- *Emergency situations:* public authorities are required immediately to provide the public with all information in their possession that could enable the public to take measures to prevent or mitigate harm arising from an imminent threat to human health or the environment.[30]

2.3   Public participation

The Aarhus Convention sets out minimum requirements for public participation in various categories of environmental decision-making.

(a) Specific projects or activities

Article 6 of the Convention establishes certain public participation requirements for decision-making on whether to license or permit certain types of activity listed in Annex I of the Convention. This list is similar to the list of activities for which an environmental impact assessment or integrated pollution prevention and control licence is required under the relevant EU legislation. The requirements also apply, albeit in a slightly more ambivalent form, to decision-making on other activities which may have a significant effect on the environment. Activities serving national defence purposes may be exempted.[31] Activities involving genetically modified organisms (GMOs) are not included in Annex I, but parties are required to apply provisions of the article to decision-making on the deliberate release of GMOs to the environment 'to the extent feasible and appropriate'.[32] Furthermore, the issue of GMOs is given emphasis in both the Preamble and the accompanying Resolution.[33] A working group is looking into options for further developing the application of the Convention in this area.

The public participation requirements include timely and effective notification of the public concerned; reasonable time frames for participation, including provision for participation at an early stage; a right for the public concerned to inspect information which is relevant to the decision-making free of charge; an obligation on the decision-making body to take due account of the outcome of the public participation; and prompt public notification of the decision, with the text

---

[28] Article 5(9).
[29] Article 10(2)(i).
[30] Article 5(1)(c).
[31] Article 6(1)(c).
[32] Article 6(11).
[33] Preamble, para. 20, and Doc. ECE/CEP/43/Add.1/Rev.1, para. 15.

of the decision and the reasons and considerations on which it is based being made publicly accessible.[34] The 'public concerned' is defined as 'the public affected or likely to be affected by, or having an interest in, the environmental decision-making', and explicitly includes NGOs promoting environmental protection and meeting any requirements under national law.[35]

(b) Programmes, plans and policies

Article 7 requires parties to make 'appropriate practical and/or other provisions for the public to participate during the preparation of plans and programmes relating to the environment'. It can be argued that the term 'relating to the environment' is quite broad, covering not just plans or programmes prepared by an environment ministry, but also sectoral plans (transport, energy, tourism, etc.) where these have significant environmental implications. Though the Convention is less prescriptive with respect to public participation in decision-making on plans or programmes than in the case of projects or activities, the provisions of Article 6 relating to reasonable time frames for participation, opportunities for early participation (while options are still open) and the obligation to ensure that 'due account' is taken of the outcome of the participation are to be applied in respect of such plans and programmes. Article 7 also applies, in more recommendatory form, to decision-making on policies relating to the environment.

(c) General rules and regulations

Article 8 applies to public participation during the preparation by public authorities of executive regulations and other generally applicable legally binding rules that may have a significant effect on the environment. Although the Convention does not apply to bodies acting in a legislative capacity, this article clearly would apply to the executive stage of preparing rules and regulations even if they are later to be adopted by parliament.

2.4 Access to justice

The third pillar of the Aarhus Convention (Article 9) aims to provide access to justice in three contexts:

- review procedures with respect to information requests;
- review procedures with respect to specific (project-type) decisions which are subject to public participation requirements;
- challenges to breaches of environmental law in general.

---

[34] Article 6.
[35] Article 2(5).

Thus the inclusion of an 'access to justice' pillar not only underpins the first two pillars; it also points the way to empowering citizens and NGOs to assist in the enforcement of the law.

(a) Access to information appeals

A person whose request for information has not been dealt with to their satisfaction must be provided with access to a review procedure before a court of law or another independent and impartial body established by law (the latter option being included to accommodate those countries which have a well-functioning office of Ombudsperson). The Convention attempts to ensure a low threshold for such appeals by requiring that where review before a court of law is provided for (which can involve high costs), there is also access to an expeditious review procedure that is free of charge or inexpensive. Final decisions must be binding on the public authority holding the information, and the reasons must be stated in writing where information is refused.[36]

(b) Public participation appeals

The Convention provides for a right to seek a review in connection with decision-making on projects or activities covered by Article 6. The review may address either the substantive or the procedural legality of a decision, or both. The scope of persons entitled to pursue such an appeal is similar to, but slightly narrower than, the 'public concerned', involving a requirement to have a 'sufficient interest' or maintain impairment of a right (though the text also states that these requirements are to be interpreted in a manner which is consistent with 'the objective of giving the public concerned wide access to justice').[37]

(c) General violations of environmental law

The Convention requires parties to provide access to administrative or judicial procedures to challenge acts and omissions by private persons and public authorities which breach laws relating to the environment. Such access is to be provided to members of the public 'where they meet the criteria, if any, laid down in ... national law' − in other words, the issue of standing is primarily to be determined at national level, as is the question of whether the procedures are judicial or administrative.[38]

(d) Other access to justice requirements

The procedures in each of the three contexts referred to above are required to be

---

[36] Article 9(1).
[37] Article 9(2).
[38] Article 9(3).

'fair, equitable, timely and not prohibitively expensive'. Decisions must be given or recorded in writing, and in the case of court decisions, made publicly accessible. Assistance mechanisms to remove or reduce financial and other barriers to access to justice are to be considered.[39]

3.   THE ROLE OF NGOs IN THE AARHUS CONVENTION

Non-governmental organizations have been involved in the Aarhus Convention since its inception. Indeed, the initial idea of developing a UNECE convention on the theme was introduced by environmental NGOs at the very first session of the Task Force that developed the Sofia Guidelines.[40] The pan-European coalition of environmental citizens' organizations (ECOs), later to become known as the European ECO Forum, had established an issue group on public participation, led by the European Environmental Bureau (EEB), and the theme of public participation, including the demand for a convention, became a central plank of the ECOs' demands to the Ministerial Conference.[41] There was little support from government experts within the task force, but the ECOs' call for a convention was taken up by other voices (e.g., the rapporteur of the Environment Committee of the European Parliament, GLOBE Europe, the European Greens). This undoubtedly helped to persuade some of the more progressive governments, notably Denmark which was due to host the next conference, to push for the issue to be on the agenda for the next phase of the process.

3.1   The negotiating phase

When the Committee on Environmental Policy established the mandate of the *ad hoc* working group charged with the task of preparing the draft Convention, it deemed that NGOs, particularly those involved in the Environment for Europe process, would be invited to participate 'as appropriate', and that as regards the involvement of major groups, the practice established in the preparations for the Sofia Conference would be followed.[42]

Even before the negotiations on the Aarhus Convention got under way, this stipulation was taken up by the UNECE Secretariat which convened a small group of 'friends of the Secretariat' to assist it in preparing a first draft of the Convention (officially termed 'draft elements'). The European ECO Forum (through the EEB) was represented among the 'friends of the Secretariat', enabling ECOs to provide input into the very first draft of the Convention. This had

---

[39] Article 9(3) and (4).

[40] Task Force on Environmental Rights and Obligations, Geneva, February 1994.

[41] See, e.g., the NGO Position Paper on Public Participation and Access to Environmental Information adopted by the NGO Working Group on the Pan-European Environment following the NGO Strategy Meeting held in Groznjan, Croatia, 23–25 June 1995 (Groznjan Declaration).

[42] Doc. ECE/CEP/18, Annex I.

the effect of ensuring that various ideas of importance to civil society organization were reflected in the working document which formed the basis of the negotiations, and while some of these ideas did not survive the negotiating process and other new ones were introduced along the way, it was certainly an impressive example of 'early public participation, when all options are open and effective participation can take place'.[43]

When the actual negotiations began, NGOs were invited by the Chairman, Prof. Willem Kakebeeke (Netherlands), to participate on a basis more or less equal to that on which government delegations participated, and availed fully of this opportunity. Kakebeeke generally took the flags in the order in which they were raised, only occasionally restricting the right to intervene to governmental delegations. In practice, the ECO delegation probably intervened more than any other single delegation in the course of the negotiations. While from a formal point of view, it might seem anomalous that an observer delegation should participate more actively in a negotiating process than voting delegations, the latter (or at least their Chairman) seemed to accept the logic that it would not make sense to negotiate a convention on public participation without a significant measure of participation in the negotiating process. There may also have been a perception that the environmental organizations, as the subset of the public most likely to exercise its rights under the Convention, were in some sense the main 'clients' of the process.

The way in which the environmental NGOs prepared for and participated in the negotiations was crucial to the success of the process, whether measured from the perspective of governments or from that of the NGOs themselves. A key factor was the fact that the NGOs worked as a coalition under the umbrella of the European ECO Forum and presented coordinated positions on each issue. These positions had been worked out through an extensive consultation process using an open-ended network of a couple of hundred interested organizations and individuals and a resource group of some 15 to 20 experts, and were put forward by a delegation of four NGO representatives. This consultative process not only ensured that the ECO positions enjoyed broad support; it also contributed to the robustness of the positions put forward, in the sense that proposals which had not been well thought through would be weeded out before they reached the negotiating forum.

The perceived legitimacy of the NGO input came not so much from the fact that large formal federations were involved (even though some were, such as the EEB and Friends of the Earth) as from the open-ended consultative process that was followed. Interestingly enough, the European ECO Forum itself was not accredited with the UN and indeed, it was such a loose framework that it might have been difficult for it to meet the accreditation criteria, even though some of the participating organizations were accredited with the UN. However, it served a useful purpose both for the environmental organizations and for the governments.

---

[43] Aarhus Convention, Article 6(4).

Had civil society been represented in the negotiations by a plethora of diverse or even conflicting voices, the process would have been more difficult for all concerned. As it was, the ECOs aired their differences in their preparatory discussions and generally managed to find common positions before entering the negotiating forum with governments.

Other important factors in the success of the participatory process were the supportive attitude of the Chairman of the Working Group, Prof. Willem Kakebeeke, and the fact that certain donor governments provided sufficient funds to finance the participation of ECOs, including to a certain extent the ECO preparatory processes.

In practice, many of the ideas put forward by the ECOs were taken up and incorporated in the Convention text, albeit usually in modified form. The involvement of civil society representatives greatly increased the relevance of the resulting text to the real problems which the Convention aimed to tackle.

It is worth mentioning that other non-governmental stakeholders, such as business, were also invited to participate in the negotiation of the Convention but remained relatively uninvolved. It seems that environmental organizations were recognized as the natural representatives of the concerned public in relation to the particular issues addressed by the Convention. This was not the case with respect to the negotiation of the PRTR Protocol: in that instance, the chemical industry, represented by the European Chemical Industry Federation (CEFIC) played an active role, equal in significance to that played by the European ECO Forum, throughout most of the negotiating process.

3.2 The implementation phase

The tradition of NGO participation continued uninterrupted into the implementation phase. NGOs participated in the meetings of the signatories as well as in each of the working groups and task forces set up to prepare for the 1st Meeting of the Parties. The situation did not change following the formal establishment of subsidiary bodies under the Convention, and indeed, active participation of NGOs remains a feature of the processes under the Convention up to the present day.

Once the Convention entered into force and the parties held the 1st Meeting, there were more formal grounds for allowing and facilitating the participation of NGOs in the activities under the Convention.

First, those parts of the text of the Convention referring to the participation of NGOs took on legal effect with the entry into force. Article 10(5) of the Convention entitles 'any non-governmental organization qualified in the fields to which [the] Convention relates' to participate as an observer in the Meetings of the Parties unless one-third of the parties present in the Meeting raise objections. The definition of 'the public concerned', although not used specifically in the text of the Convention in connection with the processes under the Convention, is also significant in the fact that it identifies 'non-governmental organizations promot-

ing environmental protection and meeting any requirements under national law'
as automatically falling within the scope of the definition.

Secondly, Rules of Procedure of the Meetings of the Parties were adopted at
the 1st Meeting of the Parties, establishing in more detail the terms for the participation of NGOs both in those meetings and in meetings of subsidiary bodies. As
well as establishing certain transparency requirements, these rules provide for 'a
representative of non-governmental organizations established for the purpose of,
and actively engaged in, promoting environmental protection and sustainable development' to attend Bureau meetings as an observer. The Rules of Procedure do
not require the establishment of an accreditation procedure for Meetings of the
Parties, and so far the Secretariat has not found it necessary to establish one.

Thirdly, several other decisions of the Meeting of the Parties specify a role for
the public or NGOs in the respective processes under the Convention. Perhaps
the most significant references providing for the involvement of NGOs are those
in Decision I/7 on review of compliance, discussed below, but there are others.[44]

It is beyond the scope of this chapter to analyse the various ways in which
NGOs are referred to in these different texts, but it is quite apparent that they differ significantly. Whereas Article 10(5) more or less follows a formula found in
other UN treaties and does not distinguish between the various different types of
stakeholder (e.g., environmental groups, academic institutes, business federations, etc., the definition of the 'public concerned' clearly singles out registered
environmental organizations. Rule 22(2) goes even further in that direction:
whereas the definition of the 'public concerned' leaves it open for stakeholders
other than registered environmental organizations to argue that they fall within
that definition, the role of observer at bureau meetings is restricted to a representative of environmental organizations. This may be seen as a reflection of the idea
that for this particular Convention, such organizations are the subset of 'the public' most likely to exercise the rights which the Convention seeks to guarantee
and therefore to represent the interests of the wider public *vis-à-vis* those rights.

At a practical level, the resources of the Aarhus Convention trust fund have
been used to support the participation of ECOs in meetings held under the auspices of the Convention. As a general rule, support for four ECO participants is
provided for each meeting of a subsidiary body. The selection is made by the
Secretariat but this is almost always done on the basis of a recommendation from
the European ECO Forum: partly because it is considered more appropriate that
the environmental organizations should choose who will represent them at the
meetings than that this should be done by a Secretariat official (in reality, the provision of financial support is a pre-requisite for participation for most ECOs); and
partly because for the Secretariat to evaluate competing requests for financial

---

[44] E.g., Decision I/8 on reporting requirements, Doc. ECE/MP.PP/2/Add.9, paras. 3 and 7; Decision I/9 on Designation of National Focal Points, Doc. ECE/MP.PP/2/Add.10, para. 2; and Decision
I/10 on the clearinghouse mechanism and capacity-building service, Doc. ECE/MP.PP/2/Add.11,
para. 5.

support would imply an even greater commitment of Secretariat time to the process of providing financial support. This is an example of how the existence of a coordination framework for the ECOs streamlines the work of the Secretariat.

4. THE COMPLIANCE MECHANISM

Perhaps one of the most significant areas where NGOs may play an important role under the Aarhus Convention is in relation to the compliance mechanism, which was put in place by the parties at the 1st Meeting.

4.1 The structure and function of the Aarhus Convention compliance mechanism

The Convention requires the Meeting of the Parties to 'establish, on a consensus basis, optional arrangements of a non-confrontational, non-judicial and consultative nature for reviewing compliance with the provisions of [the] Convention'. These arrangements are to allow for 'appropriate public involvement and may include the option of considering communications from members of the public on matters related to the Convention'.[45]

This provision of the Convention, coupled with a provision in the Resolution of the Signatories,[46] led to the establishment of first a task force and then a working group, the latter charged with the task of preparing a draft decision establishing a compliance mechanism for adoption at the 1st Meeting of the Parties.[47]

The outcome was Decision I/7 on review of compliance, adopted by the Parties at the 1st Meeting.[48] Decision I/7 establishes a Compliance Committee consisting of eight members serving in a personal capacity (rather than as representatives of parties). These individuals are to be nationals of parties or signatories to the Convention who are 'persons of high moral character and recognized competence in the fields to which the Convention relates'.

The compliance mechanism may be triggered in four ways: (i) a party may make a submission to the Committee about compliance by another party;[49] (ii) a party may make a submission to the Committee concerning its own compliance;[50] (iii) the Secretariat may make a referral to the Committee;[51] and finally, (iv) communications may be made to the Committee, via the Secretariat, by one or more members of the public concerning a party's compliance with the Con-

---

[45] Doc. ECE/CEP/43, Article 15.
[46] Doc. ECE/CEP/43/Add.1/Rev.1, para. 12.
[47] Doc. CEP/WG.5/2000/2, para. 23.
[48] Doc. ECE/MP.PP/2/Add.8.
[49] Doc. ECE/MP.PP/2/Add.8, Annex, para. 15.
[50] Doc. ECE/MP.PP/2/Add.8, Annex, para. 16.
[51] Doc. ECE/MP.PP/2/Add.8, Annex, para. 17.

vention.[52] The last trigger may only be applied following the expiry of a 'grace' period of one year from the date of the decision or the entry into force of the Convention for the party in question, whichever is the later.

In addition, the Committee may examine compliance issues on its own initiative and make recommendations; prepare reports on compliance with or implementation of provisions of the Convention at the request of the Meeting of the Parties; and monitor, assess and facilitate the implementation of and compliance with the reporting requirements under Article 10(2) of the Convention.

In line with the 'soft' nature of the mechanism as stipulated in Article 15 of the Convention, the powers of the Committee to act directly to address specific compliance issues with respect to a particular party are rather limited. It may take certain actions either in consultation with or with the agreement of the party concerned,[53] but its primary function is to prepare the way for decisions by the Meeting of the Parties, which may take somewhat more extensive measures but still subject to the overall requirement that they be non-confrontational, non-judicial and consultative in character.[54]

The requirement under Article 15 that the arrangements be 'optional' was implemented in Decision I/7 through a time-limited opt-out option. The interpretation of the requirement tends to discourage opting out, in at least three ways: first, the very fact that it is an 'opt-out' mechanism rather than an 'opt-in' mechanism means that a party has to take definite action in order not to be covered by the mechanism, and such action may be seen by observers as tantamount to a concession by the party that it has or expects to have compliance problems; secondly, the party may only opt out of the part of the mechanism concerning communications from the public (Chapter VI of Decision I/7); and thirdly, the party may only opt out for a limited period of up to four years, and it must notify the Depositary that it is opting out before the 'grace' period expires.

4.2 NGO participation in the mechanism

It will be clear from the foregoing description that the Aarhus Convention compliance mechanism is unusual among multilateral environmental agreement (MEA) compliance mechanisms in the extent to which it allows for the possibility of civil society involvement. In some respects, the approach is closer to a human-rights type model. Formally, there are two main ways in which NGOs feature in the Aarhus Convention compliance mechanism.

First, as already mentioned, members of the public are entitled to make communications to the Committee with respect to compliance by any party which has not exercised the 'opt-out' option. The scope of the public entitled to make such communications may be taken to be that covered by the definition in the Conven-

---

[52] Doc. ECE/MP.PP/2/Add.8, Annex, para. 18.
[53] Doc. ECE/MP.PP/2/Add.8, Annex, paras. 36 and 37(a) to (d).
[54] Doc. ECE/MP.PP/2/Add.8, Annex, para. 37.

tion, which embraces 'any natural or legal person'. There is no requirement that the member of the public must be from the state alleged not to be in compliance. The Committee has started to elaborate more detailed procedures for processing such communications. These are described in an information sheet on 'Communications from Members of the Public'[55] along with summary information on the communications being processed by the Committee.

Secondly, Decision I/7 provides that, as well as parties and signatories, 'non-governmental organizations falling within the scope of article 10, paragraph 5, of the Convention and promoting environmental protection' may nominate candidates for the Committee.[56] It is the Meeting of the Parties which actually elects the Committee, and it has no obligation to elect candidates put forward by NGOs, but the right of NGOs to nominate candidates is already significant.[57]

There is a third possible connection between NGOs and the compliance mechanism of a more informal nature, namely that members of the Committee may themselves be members of NGOs or have connections with NGOs. There has been an underlying assumption, which is not spelled out in Decision I/7, that Committee members should be independent, and that this independence implies that they should not be too closely associated with the parties themselves,[58] or with NGOs who might be involved in making communications. This has found expression in agreement by the Committee that normal principles of conflict of interest would apply,[59] and in a recommendation by the Committee to its members that they should generally only participate in Aarhus Convention bodies in their capacities as members of the Compliance Committee (rather than, for example, as a member of or adviser to a governmental or NGO delegation).[60]

The independence 'requirement' has certain financial implications: travel and subsistence costs of Committee members related to participation in Committee meetings are all covered from the Convention's trust fund. Even if a government or NGO were willing to provide the necessary funding for a Committee member, this might raise questions as to whether the Committee member was really independent.

The possibility for members of the public to trigger the mechanism by making a communication to the Committee is accompanied by certain rights of participation in the Committee's processes. A member of the public having made such a communication (the communicant) is entitled to participate in the discussions of the Committee with respect to that communication. The communicant is also en-

---

[55] Which may be found at <www.unece.org/env/pp/pubcom.htm>.

[56] Doc. ECE/MP.PP/2/Add.8, Annex, para. 4.

[57] Two of the present members of the Committee were in fact nominated by NGOs.

[58] For example, when Prof. Veit Koester (who was later elected as the Committee's first Chairman) was nominated by Denmark at the 1st Meeting of the Parties for membership of the Committee, the Danish delegate underlined Prof. Koester's suitability as a candidate by emphasizing that he (Prof. Koester) would shortly be retiring from the Danish Ministry.

[59] Doc. MP.PP/C.1/2003/2, para. 22.

[60] Doc. MP.PP/C.1/2004/2, para. 38.

titled to receive a copy of any draft findings, measures or recommendations of the Committee prepared in connection with the communication, and to provide comments which the Committee must take into account when finalising those findings, measures or recommendations. However, the communicant is not entitled to take part in the preparation and adoption of any findings, measures or recommendations of the Committee.[61]

The Committee has given explicit consideration to the issue of cooperation with NGOs. At its 2nd Meeting, it agreed that NGOs present at the beginning of its meetings should be invited to present specific points for discussion during the meeting, and that the Committee would try to accommodate these points within its agenda. The possibility of holding meetings of the Committee outside Geneva in order to make the Committee more visible and more accessible to national NGOs was considered. Compliance Committee members could make themselves available to present the compliance mechanism at NGO events such as conferences and workshops. Draft findings, measures or recommendations could be sent to appropriate national NGOs for comment. Finally, in the preparation of recommendations, the Committee would as a general rule consider whether the implementation of a recommendation would benefit from the involvement of intergovernmental, non-governmental or regional organizations and would include this in the recommendation.[62]

Apart from making significant provision for civil society involvement, the mechanism bears some other hallmarks of the Convention. For example, Decision I/7 spells out a number of limited circumstances in which information held by the Committee may be kept confidential. The Committee may not keep any other information confidential.[63]

4.3   Relevance of the Aarhus Convention model

Whether or not the Aarhus Convention model is considered to be relevant and useful for other instruments will depend to some extent on what weight is given to the various possible reasons for having adopted such a model. If the accessibility to NGOs of the Aarhus mechanism is seen as flowing from the fact that the Convention explicitly seeks to guarantee certain individual rights and that a violation of the provisions of the Convention may therefore often involve a violation of those individual rights, then it can be argued that the model is not necessarily applicable to MEAs which are not so linked to questions of individual rights.

On the other hand, if the rationale for involving NGOs in the Aarhus mechanism has more to do with effectiveness than to do with the substantive content of the Convention – with the fact that NGOs are more likely to root out cases of

---

[61] Doc. ECE/MP.PP/2/Add.8, Annex, paras. 32 to 34. The party whose compliance is the subject of the communication enjoys the same participation rights, with the same limitations.

[62] Doc. MP.PP/C.1/2003/4, paras. 28 to 32.

[63] Decision I/7, Annex, paras. 26 to 31.

non-compliance and less likely to remain silent about them for reasons of diplomacy – then it could indeed be relevant to a wider range of instruments.

At this stage, it is probably premature to draw firm conclusions about the wider relevance and applicability of the Aarhus Convention model, given the lack of experience with applying it. What is clear is that it provides a distinct reference point in the widening landscape of MEA compliance mechanisms.

Chapter 14

The World Bank Inspection Panel: About Public Participation and Dispute Settlement

Laurence Boisson de Chazournes

1. INTRODUCTION: EVOLUTION OF THE INSPECTION PANEL'S MANDATE

The World Bank Inspection Panel[1] was created by the Board of Executive Directors of the World Bank ('the Bank')[2] in September 1993 in the year of that Organization's 50th anniversary. It is in many regards an original institution. It is an unprecedented mechanism in the world of international organizations, insofar as it provides a direct means of controlling the Bank's operations, thus enabling certain actors to question the legitimacy of Bank activities. In addition, the Inspection Panel reveals the World Bank's complexity in regard to the institution's legal and structural characteristics, as much as in regard to the nature of its relations with its partners.

Moreover, the Inspection Panel reflects the evermore urgent need to build 'public spaces' – in the meaning attributed to that concept by the philosopher Jürgen Habermas[3] – enabling unusual connections between partners of different stature, who need to exchange information, work together and even negotiate.

---

[1] The Inspection Panel was created in September 1993, by the adoption of two identical resolutions emanating from the Executive Board of the International Bank for Reconstruction and Development (IBRD No. 93-10) and the International Development Association (IDA No. 93-6). These resolutions provide the framework within which the Panel is to exercise its functions. The Panel has in addition itself adopted Operating Procedures to implement these resolutions. For the text of these instruments see I. Shihata, *The World Bank Inspection Panel: In Practice* (2nd edn., Oxford University Press, Oxford/New York, 2000), pp. 271–277 and 373 *et seq.* Moreover, in 1996 and 1999 the Board of Executive Directors issued further clarifications in respect of the Panel's functioning. These instruments are reproduced in Shihata, ibid., pp. 320–328.

[2] The 'World Bank Group' is made up of five institutions: the International Bank for Reconstruction and Development (IBRD) established in 1944; the International Finance Corporation (IFC) and the International Development Association (IDA), respectively established in 1956 and in 1960; the International Center for the Settlement of Investment-related Disputes (ICSID) and the Multilateral Investment Guarantee Agency (MIGA), set up in 1965 (Washington Convention) and 1985 (Seoul Convention) respectively.

[3] J. Habermas, *L'espace public: archéologie de la publicité comme dimension constitutive de la société bourgeoise* (trad. M.B. de Launay) (Payot (coll. 'Critique de la politique'), Paris, 1993), p. 324. For relatively recent developments – notably at the European level – see by the same author,

---

T. Treves et al., eds., Civil Society, International Courts and Compliance Bodies
© 2005, T·M·C·Asser Press, The Hague, The Netherlands, and the Authors

Within the World Bank, borrower states are obviously privileged partners, as the vast majority of loan operations are made with them or with related entities. Nevertheless, some grant programmes have been created, allowing the Bank to supply non-states entities, such as foundations or associations, with funds. Within the context of the preparation and implementation of operational activities, other actors may, even if they are not a party to the transactional operations, wish to intervene in order to put forward their point of view or because they advocate interests related to the development of Bank-financed operations. Such is often the case for non-governmental organizations (NGOs), be they local, national or international.

The Inspection Panel procedure is a formalization of the type of interrelation contemplated by Habermas' model: it has created for both individuals and collectivities within the borrower states' jurisdictions, a means of intervening before the World Bank and in particular, a means of coming into relation with the Board of Executive Directors, the Bank's privileged decision-making body. Thus, the Inspection Panel procedure connects individuals with the very core of the international decision-making process within this institution.

The creation of the Inspection Panel is the result of a comprehensive maturation process, the World Bank having been through important changes, especially since the end of the 1980s. At the dawn of the twenty-first century, the Bank is no longer what it was when first established in the aftermath of the Second World War. At that time, the reconstruction of the European economic systems was the primary concern. When in the 1950s, talk of 'development' first emerged to adjust activities to other regions around the world (the results in Europe of the Marshall Plan having gone beyond expected forecasts) it was mostly in macroeconomic terms, with particular concern for domestic growth, via the financing of infrastructure projects. The mandate of financial institutions has since extended progressively to the extent of today embracing matters such as social development, the fight against poverty and against corruption.[4]

Development is now conceived first and foremost as a societal problem, one requiring that sustained attention be given to institutional aspects. These changes demonstrate that a new vision of development is emerging: development can no longer be based on the vertical 'trickle-down effect', but must be distributive and involve participation. If economic growth can still be considered the spearhead for development, one must nonetheless acknowledge additionally, the needs of various concerned populations and issues of redistribution.

These ideas have blossomed within the World Bank, notably thanks to the large international conferences hosted under the auspices of the United Nations

---

Après l'état-nation: une nouvelle constellation politique (trad. R. Rochlitz) (Fayard, Paris, 2000), p. 157.

[4] See L. Boisson de Chazournes, 'Issues of Social Development: Integrating Human Rights into the Activities of the World Bank' in *World Trade and the Protection of Human Rights: Human Rights in the Face of Global Economic Exchanges* (Institut René Cassin, Bruylant, Brussels, 2001), pp. 47–70.

(UN). These conferences also showed that there were an increasing number and diversity of actors on the international stage. It is true that states remain the first and foremost subjects of the contemporary legal order; nevertheless, other entities have emerged internationally, be they international organizations (which, whilst established by states, have emancipated themselves to a greater or lesser extent from their control, depending on their activities), NGOs, private sector companies, or again, even private persons.

The hydroelectric construction projects at Narmada[5] in India and in the Arun Valley in Nepal,[6] for which World Bank financing had been solicited, and the protest that followed, have shown that the financial institution could not avoid a debate with actors with which it had not previously established any contact, such as NGOs and local populations. Thus the concepts of public participation, transparency and empowerment have progressively found their right to exist within the context of the preparation and implementation of the activities financed by the World Bank, enabling concerned groups to be heard during the elaboration phase of projects, and even to be a party to the project's execution.

New control and dispute settlement procedures accompany these changes, paving the way for consultations, negotiations and readjustments between 'traditional' partners of the international legal order, but also between the latter and a growing number of other actors who are becoming, to a lesser or greater extent, endowed with international legal capacities. The mechanism established by the World Bank Inspection Panel fits within this context.

Thus, the World Bank Inspection Panel is one of the answers given to the criticisms made by those who wanted the Bank to be more involved with non-state actors. This procedure provides individuals with a means of intervening in an international organization, enabling them to influence the latter's decision-making process (section 2 below). It also presents characteristics that demonstrate new trends in respect of compliance and dispute settlement (section 3 below).

2. PUBLIC PARTICIPATION AND THE INTERNATIONAL DECISION-MAKING PROCESS: THE PATH OPENED BY THE WORLD BANK INSPECTION PANEL

The Inspection Panel is a subsidiary body of the World Bank's Board of Executive Directors (the Board). It has been established to ensure, by the means of an investigation mechanism, better quality in the projects financed by the Organization. It has jurisdiction over the operational activities of two of its affiliates, the

---

[5] On this question, see B. Morse and T.R. Berger, *Sardor Sarovar: The Report of the Independent Review* (1992); and T.R. Berger, 'The World Bank's Independent Review of India's Sardor Sarovar Projects' (1993) 9 *Am. U. J. Int'l L.& Pol'y* 33. See also Shihata, n. 1 above, at pp. 5–8.

[6] From A. Umaña Quesada (ed.), *The World Bank Inspection Panel: The First Four Years (1994-1998)* (World Bank Publications, Washington DC, 1998); see also Shihata, n. 1 above, at pp. 102–105.

International Bank for Reconstruction and Development (IBRD) and the International Development Association (IDA). Two other affiliates of the World Bank group, the International Finance Corporation (IFC) and the Multilateral Investment Guarantee Agency (MIGA) maintain a privileged relationship with the private sector. Despite strong pressure, they have not yet created this type of mechanism. They have opted for an organ fulfilling advisory functions as well as an ombudsman's role,[7] enabling them to avoid setting up a formalized supervisory mechanism.

Conceived as an independent body, it consists of three members,[8] chosen mostly for their professional abilities, integrity and independence from Bank Management. They are appointed for five-year mandates by the Board, on the President's nomination. They can only be relieved of their functions by a reasoned decision of the Board. Lastly, in order to fulfil their functions, Panel members are independent of any hierarchy in their work despite being Bank civil servants.[9]

2.1   The Bank's operational policies and the promotion of the principle of public participation

The Inspection Panel procedure rests on the concept of public participation[10] and, more specifically, aims at taking due account of local populations in borrower

---

[7] The Office of the Compliance Advisor/Ombudsman (CAO), or 'mediating adviser' for the application of the IFC and MIGA policies. Its function, mandate and the applicable procedural requirements are to be found on the IFC website <www.ifc.org/cao/index.html>. Its task is described as follows: The CAO has three roles: 1. To advise and assist IFC/MIGA to address Complaints by people directly impacted by projects in a manner that is fair, objective and constructive (Ombudsman) 2. To oversee compliance audits of IFC/MIGA, overall environmental and social performance, and specific projects (Compliance auditor.) 3. To provide independent advice to the President and management on specific projects as well as broader environmental and social policies, guidelines, procedures and resources (Advisor) The Ombudsman role is the most innovative of the three. It is aimed at resolving issues by providing a context and process for parties to find mutually satisfactory solutions. It is focused on identifying problems, recommending actions, using conflict resolution and mediation approaches and addressing systemic issues, where necessary. An external review of the CAO was completed in July 2003: B. Dysart, T. Murphy and A. Chayes, *Beyond Compliance? An External Review Team Report on the Compliance Advisor/Ombudsman Office of IFC and MIGA* (24 July 2003).

[8] Every year the Inspection Panel nominates a President from among its members. The President's function is to supervise the Panel's standard activities.

[9] See paras. 2–10 of the Resolution establishing the Panel.

[10] Principle 10 of the Rio Declaration on the Environment and Development (Rio de Janeiro, 13 June 1992) states: 'Environmental issues are best handled with the participation of all concerned citizens, at the relevant level. At the national level, each individual shall have appropriate access to information concerning the environment that is held by public authorities, including information on hazardous materials and activities in their communities, and the opportunity to participate in decision-making processes. States shall facilitate and encourage public awareness and participation by making information widely available. Effective access to judicial and administrative proceedings, including redress and remedy, shall be provided'. See Report of the United Nations Conference on Environment and Development, UN Doc. A/CONF.151/26 (vol. 1) Annex I (1992).

countries. This principle, that blossomed at the end of the 1980s, has become a key concept in efforts to ensure the effective application of projects and that they produce the expected results. The World Bank operational policies and procedures rank among the most important vehicles to promote the enforcement of this principle.

The latter are documents, elaborated and adopted by Bank Management, indicating to the Organization's staff the behaviour to be adopted in respect of the preparation and implementation of Bank-financed projects. They deal notably with subjects having social and environmental implications, such as requirements in respect of the conduct of environmental impact assessments, indigenous populations, or compensation to be paid to populations that have been resettled as a result of a project. Another requirement is that local populations be informed and consulted and be given an opportunity to put forward their point of view. Respecting the operational policies and procedures is one of the quality guarantees of Bank-financed operations.

The operational policies are internal documents and the vast majority of them are binding on Bank employees, who are required to follow their prescriptions when dealing with borrower countries.[11] Operational policies nonetheless have external effects, since they shape both the Bank's, and its partners' behaviour within the context of their mutual relationship during design, appraisal and implementation phases of a project. Besides, they are more and more frequently used as an assessment criterion for the Bank's projects by a civil society avid for international actors' accountability, thus becoming parameters for good conduct. This is all the more important if one keeps in mind that the World Bank acts increasingly as a facilitating body in projects uniting public and private financial actors: its operational policies can then influence the behaviour of other creditors who may be implicated in the process.

An underlying question is the legal nature of the Bank's operational policies and procedures. The scale of normativity, ranging from soft to hard, and the question of the extent to which one or other is to prevail in assessing the impact of legal norms and rules, are well known. In the context at hand, this question remains unsettled, to say the least. The same problem exists for other instruments, such as the UN Secretary General's circulars.[12] Whilst they present certain char-

---

[11] On the significance of the World Bank's operational policies, see L. Boisson de Chazournes, 'Policy Guidance and Compliance Issues: The World Bank Operational Standards' in D. Shelton (ed.), *Commitment and Compliance: The Role of Non-Binding Norms in the International Legal System* (Oxford University Press, Oxford/New York, 2000); see also in the same volume, the chapter by D.A. Wirth, 'Commentary: Compliance with Non-Binding Norms of Trade and Finance' at pp. 330–344.

[12] See, e.g., the UN Secretary General's Bulletin of 6 August 1999, 'Observance by United Nations Forces of International Humanitarian Law' (ST/SGB/1999/13), reproduced in (1999) 81 *Revue Internationale de la Croix-Rouge* [*International Review of the Red Cross*] 812, in English. For a commentary, see L. Condorelli, 'Les progrès du droit international humanitaire et la Circulaire du Secrétaire Général des Nations Unies du 6 août 1999' in L. Boisson de Chazournes and V. Gowlland-Debbas (eds.), *The International Legal System in Quest of Equity and Universality*

acteristics of an administrative character within the organization in which they are to be implemented, operational policies also produce external effects, by 'shaping' the behaviour of the Bank's partners. In so doing, some of them contribute to the creation of norms of general international law or codify existing norms of general international law. They may also acquire the status of conventional law when their stipulations are re-used in loan and credit agreements binding both the borrower and the Bank.[13]

The creation of the Inspection Panel has made it possible to reinforce both the enforcement and impact of these policies, since they constitute the 'applicable law' in requests before the Inspection Panel. Policies and procedures determine the Panel's jurisdiction *rationae materiae*, insofar as they are one of the conditions for a request's eligibility. Thus, in the event that a local population representative in a borrower country deems the interest of that population to be affected, or even that their legitimate demands have been ignored in the process of a project's design and during implementation, and after having tried to gain satisfaction from the Bank – a step which draws on the condition of 'exhausting diplomatic remedies' in dispute settlement practice – they may seize the Inspection Panel with a complaint for the non-application of the relevant operational policies, invoking serious damage caused by this situation.

2.2   The concepts of public participation, transparency and accountability at the heart of the Inspection Panel procedure

The Inspection Panel procedure enables groups of persons affected by a Bank-financed project to seize the Panel in order to request that the Organization assess, and even correct, its own behaviour. The Panel decides on the complaint's eligibility, as well as on the merit of asking the Board for the authorization to undertake an investigation of Bank action with regard to the application of its operational policies. In the event of an investigation, the Bank may be led to enact an action plan in order to correct the litigious situation.

This process is innovative, if not a precursor, since it gives civil society a place at the core of the international decision-makers' considerations, and paves the way for ensuring accountability for the latter's decisions. This procedure also plays the role of institutional bridge between the World Bank's executive organ and the ultimate beneficiaries of the financed project. Thus, the Inspection Panel makes possible a contact between the Board and affected individuals. It is true that before the Inspection Panel was created, persons affected by Bank-financed projects could write to Bank Management, stipulating any damage which they

---

[*L'ordre juridique international en quête d'équité et d'universalité*] *Liber amicorum Georges Abi-Saab* (Kluwer Law International, The Hague, 2001), and, by the same author, 'Le azioni dell'O.N.U. e l'applicazione del diritto internazionale umanitario: il "bollettino" del Segretario generale del 6 agosto 1999' (1999) 82 *Riv. Dir. Int.* 1049.

[13] On the legal nature of these agreements, see A. Broches, 'International Legal Aspects of the Operations of the World Bank' (1959-III) 98 *RdC* 297 *et seq.*

considered they might suffer or had suffered, but no institutionalized and independent mechanism enabled them to articulate their concerns and complaints; moreover, whilst such communications were addressed to Bank Management and staff, the Board was not informed.

The Inspection Panel's jurisdiction only extends to Bank activities. Thus, the borrower states' behaviour does not fall within its jurisdiction. The Board re-iterated this imperative in 1999, when Conclusions aimed at clarifying the Resolution establishing the Inspection Panel were adopted.[14] This question had provoked ferocious discussions within the Board, since developing countries saw, under the cover of the Inspection Panel procedure, a means of circumventing respect for their sovereignty, enabling interference in their domestic affairs. They particularly opposed the use of the Panel as a tribune by non-state actors apparently without any legitimacy to do so. This situation of mistrust among members of the Board and between some Executive Directors and the Inspection Panel, which became apparent as soon as the mechanism was established, resulted with a few exceptions in a clear departure in the Panel's functioning from what was originally conceived in the Resolution.[15] The situation returned to normal with the adoption of the above-mentioned Conclusions in 1999.

It is true that the distinction to be made between the World Bank's behaviour and that of the borrower is likely to raise problems in practice, because of the permeable nature of the relationship that prevails between the World Bank and its borrowers. The notion of 'project cycle' highlights this aspect of the very close relationship, not to say dependency, between these actors in the conduct of operational activities. In its beginnings, the Bank required that borrower countries submit loan or credit requests, accompanied by a description of the projects ready to be undertaken. However, the institution soon realized that borrower countries often lacked the means and human resources necessary to elaborate such documents. It thus established a practice involving Bank staff in the design and preparation of the projects it was to finance. The project cycle then requires the

---

[14] The Executive Directors re-iterated as follows: 'The profile of Panel activities, in-country, during the course of an investigation, should be kept as low as possible in keeping with its role as a fact-finding body on behalf of the Board. The Panel's methods of investigation should not create the impression that it is investigating the borrower's performance. However, the Board, acknowledging the important role of the Panel in contacting the requesters and in fact-finding on behalf of the Board, welcomes the Panel's efforts to gather information through consultations with affected people. Given the need to conduct such work in an independent and low-profile manner, the Panel – and Management – should decline media contacts while an investigation is pending or underway. Under those circumstances in which, in the judgment of the Panel or Management, it is necessary to respond to the media, comments should be limited to the process. They will make it clear that the Panel's role is to investigate the Bank and not the borrower'.

Cf., Conclusions of the Board's Second Review of the Inspection Panel, 20 April 1999, reproduced in Shihata, n. 1 above, at pp. 323–328.

[15] Some investigations requested by the Inspection Panel have not been authorized by the Board and disagreements have arisen regarding the extent of the Inspection Panel's authority during the various phases in the procedure. On this question, see Shihata, n. 1 above, at pp. 99–154.

negotiation of a loan or credit agreement between the borrower and the Bank, containing a description of the project and the conditions in which it is to take place: loans or credits may be subject to conditions to be implemented either upon entry into force of the loan or credit agreement or upon disbursement of the funds allocated for the project. During the implementation phase of the project, the institution is under an obligation of oversight and of 'due diligence' to ensure that the funds intended for a loan are used by the borrower exclusively for the purposes for which they were disbursed.[16] The Inspection Panel's recommendations at the conclusion of any investigation must be approved by the Board before they can have any effect. The Inspection Panel's conclusions may shed light on weaknesses in the Bank's functioning, compelling the financial institution to correct its behaviour by means of action plans. Undertaking such a procedure may also reveal deficiencies attributable to the borrower country. However, such behaviour does not formally belong to the procedure before the Panel, and it is therefore in parallel to the latter that borrower countries may have to decide on a future course of action in concert with the Bank. Any such action nonetheless remains external to the review process before the Panel and is not subject to supervision by the Inspection Panel.

A concession was made in 1999 in terms of extending the Panel's powers to the Bank and state actions after its recommendations had been approved. It was not, however, granted a general oversight role in elaboration and implementation of action plans. It was only granted jurisdiction to allow it to assess the nature of the consultations undertaken with affected populations during the elaboration of an action plan between the borrower and the Bank.[17] It remains to be seen whether these subtle distinctions can be applied in practice: evaluating the extent to which the process of public participation has been carried out may indeed nec-

---

[16] This oversight is performed when the borrower withdraws the sum needed for the project's execution. The loan resources can only be withdrawn piecemeal as the project progresses and with the financial institution's agreement. The latter prepares reports and sends assessment missions to the borrower country, notably as a means of initiating communication with the beneficiaries and of assessing the conditions of a project's implementation.

[17] See Conclusions of the Board's Second Review of the Inspection Panel, 20 April 1999, reproduced in Shihata, n. 1 above, at pp. 323–328. 'A distinction has to be made between Management's report to the Board (Resolution para. 23), which addresses Bank failure and possible Bank remedial efforts and "action plans", agreed between the borrower and the Bank, in consultation with the requesters, that seek to improve project implementation. The latter "action plans" are outside the purview of the Resolution, its 1996 clarification, and these clarifications. In the event of agreement by the Bank and borrower on an action plan for the project, Management will communicate to the Panel the nature and outcomes of consultations with affected parties on the action plan. Such an action plan, if warranted, will normally be considered by the Board in conjunction with the Management's report, submitted under Resolution paragraph 23. The Panel may submit to the Executive Directors for their consideration a report on their view of the adequacy of consultations with affected parties in the preparation of the action plans. The Board should not ask the Panel for its view on other aspects of the action plans nor would it ask the Panel to monitor the implementation of the action plans. The Panel's view on consultation with affected parties will be based on the information available to it by all means, but additional country visits will take place only by government invitation'.

essarily imply that the entity conducting the evaluation addresses the very content of that which is the object of the process. Moreover, the acts of both the Bank and the borrower being so closely connected, it is difficult to conceive that one of them would not be tempted to offload its responsibility onto the other. The Bank's Board would then have to fulfil the function conferred upon it by the Resolution establishing the Inspection Panel; namely, to make a final decision, at the stage when the Panel recommendations are being discussed and approved, about the attribution of responsibilities.

Thus, although they are not party to the Bank's contractual relationship with its borrowers, individuals are given the possibility of defending their interests in the event that the requirements of the operational policies – which are internal Bank documents – have not been respected. They can thereby exercise a certain control on the financial institution's activities. This contributes to the emergence of concepts of accountability and transparency. One can note, however, that one is dealing with a new type of accountability, since it has been traditionally understood that an international organization need only be accountable to its member states. With the Inspection Panel, private persons have become agents of this transparency within the decision-making process. The characteristics of this vehicle for transparency will now be analyzed.

3. THE INSPECTION PANEL: A *SUI GENERIS* SETTLEMENT PROCEDURE

The aim of the Inspection Panel procedure is to conduct investigations. It is characterized by flexibility and the fact that it is non-judicial in nature. Moreover, the nature of the procedure is administrative, finding application mostly within the relevant international organization itself. Established by the Bank's Board of Executive Directors and entrusted with the task of examining the organization's activities in the light of the prescriptions elaborated by the former, the Inspection Panel is an autonomous body whose independence is guaranteed in various ways.[18]

What is more, this procedure is both preventive, as well as curative. The Inspection Panel may be seized in a 'preventive' manner during a project's preparation phase, in order to lodge a complaint in respect of potential damages (as was for instance the case in the Arun Valley project).[19] It may also be seized during the implementation phase of a project, when the contemplated (and potentially damaging) activities have not yet begun. The Panel may be seized in a 'curative' sense as well, when the damage has already occurred, be it during the project's preparation or implementation phase. Such is the case, for instance, when groups of persons must be displaced before a, or part of a project begins.

---

[18] On the guarantees securing the Panel's independence, see above.
[19] See Umaña Quesada, n. 6 above.

Considering these various possibilities, one readily understands that the Inspection Panel performs its work along the breadth of a continuum, a period of time that goes from a project's conception to its implementation, which generally covers an eight to 10-year time span.[20]

3.1   Seizing the World Bank Inspection Panel

The favoured method of seizing the Inspection Panel is based on the complaints formulated by private persons who consider that they have been adversely affected by a project. Thus, the Resolution establishing the Inspection Panel foresees, in its Article 12, that:

> 12. The Panel shall receive requests for inspection presented to it by an affected party in the territory of the borrower which is not a single individual (i.e., a community of persons such as an organization, association, society or other grouping of individuals), or by the local representative of such party or by another representative in the exceptional cases where the party submitting the request contends that appropriate representation is not locally available and the Executive Directors so agree at the time they consider the request for inspection. ... The affected party must demonstrate that its rights or interests have been or are likely to be directly affected by an action or omission of the Bank as a result of a failure of the Bank to follow its operational policies and procedures with respect to the design, appraisal and/or implementation of a project financed by the Bank (including situations where the Bank is alleged to have failed in its follow-up on the borrower's obligations under loan agreements with respect to such policies and procedures) provided in all cases that such failure has had, or threatens to have, a material adverse effect.

As early as 1996, the Bank's Board thought it necessary to specify that an affected party is 'a community of persons such as an organization, association, society or other grouping of individuals including 'any two or more persons who share some common interests or concerns'.[21]

The crucial issue is to identify the individuals who may lodge a complaint. It cannot be a country's entire population; but must rather be groups of private persons living in the project zone (or representatives of persons living there) and who run the risk of suffering damage by activities related to Bank-financed projects.[22] They must allege and prove on the one hand, that the Bank has not followed its own operational policies and procedures, and on the other hand, that

---

[20] Note that para. 14(c) of the Resolution establishing the Panel states: '14. In considering requests under paragraph 12 above, the following requests shall not be heard by the Panel: (c) Requests filed after the Closing Date of the loan financing the project with respect to which the request is filed or after the loan financing the project has been substantially disbursed. This will be deemed to be the case when at least ninety five percent of the loan proceeds have been disbursed'.

[21] See *Review of the Resolution Establishing the Inspection Panel: Clarifications of Certain Aspects of the Resolution*, 17 October 1996, reproduced in Shihata, n. 1 above, at pp. 320–322.

[22] Affected persons may ask for their anonymity to be preserved, under the condition, naturally, that they give (confidentially) their identity to the Panel itself.

this has provoked, or may provoke, material adverse effects. They must have previously expressed their concerns to Bank representatives and not be satisfied with the consequences. One of the problems that has only been partially dealt with to date is that of knowing whether the criterion relative to the place of implementation is essential, or whether other inhabitants of the concerned borrower country are also entitled to bring a request due to the fact that the project deals with state-wide interests and issues. In the case relative to the construction of the Yacyreta dam, the Panel even went as far as to point out the global nature of the interests involved, but did not draw any explicit consequence as to the lodging of a request in such circumstances.[23]

According to paragraph 12 of the Resolution, NGOs can submit requests to the Panel, as the local representatives of an 'affected party', if they prove that the concerned populations have duly entitled them to do so. It can be pointed out that international NGOs may also play the role of 'another representative in the exceptional cases where the party submitting the request contends that appropriate representation is not locally available'. Nevertheless, the Board must approve this mode of representation during their evaluation of the request for inspection brought to their attention by the Panel. This would implicitly mean that the Board assesses a country's domestic situation, and the extent to which fundamental freedoms are respected, such as freedom of association and freedom of assembly.

A World Bank Executive Director (or the whole Board of Executive Directors) may also seize the Inspection Panel. The same paragraph 12 reads:

> In view of the institutional responsibilities of Executive Directors in the observance by the Bank of its operational policies and procedures, an Executive Director may in special cases of serious alleged violations of such policies and procedures ask the Panel for an investigation, subject to the requirements of paragraphs 13 and 14 below. The Executive Directors, acting as a Board, may at any time instruct the Panel to conduct an investigation.

On one occasion, the Board of Executive Directors asked the Inspection Panel to conduct an investigation into a project in China. The request for investigation had in fact been initiated by international NGOs, thus raising the problem of the Board's authorization for doing so. In order to obviate this issue, and because the Chinese representative had agreed to this arrangement, the Board asked the Panel to undertake an investigation.

In this situation one is not within the context of a given group of persons' specific interests having been affected. What is at issue here is enabling representatives of the World Bank's main decision-making body to verify the quality of the projects financed by this organization. They are therefore acting in the name of a collective interest covering both the interests of private persons affected by a project and those of the institution.

---

[23] See *Request for Inspection: Argentina/Paraguay: Yacyretá Hydroelectric Project* (RQ 96/2, 30 September 1996), discussed in Shihata, n. 1 above, at pp. 117–124.

In the first case, namely seizure of the Panel by a group of individuals, persons external to the Bank may access the Inspection Panel. 'External persons' means persons who are neither agents of the Organization, nor parties to a contractual relationship with the Organization. In the second case, it is an organ of the Organization, or a member of the latter, which requests an investigation. Private persons put forward their own interests, having to prove that they would have been or might be the victims of damage to their own interests. On the other hand, the Board of Executive Directors or one of its members will request an investigation in the name of the protection of an institutional collective interest.

3.2 Course of the procedure

Once initiated, the procedure has several phases, and is accompanied by time limits. A political dimension is added to the technical and factual assessment of the circumstances evoked by the complaint. Indeed, the investigation cannot be undertaken on the Panel's own initiative: it must have been previously approved by the Board. Similarly, the Board will have to adopt the recommendations and conclusions of the Inspection Panel at the end of the investigation before they can result in any effects, notably insofar as Management and Bank staffs are concerned.

First, the Panel must decide whether it has *prima facie* jurisdiction over the claim. This is then recorded, which is a mere administrative formality. The claim is then transmitted to Bank Management, which has 21 working days to answer the claim's allegations. The Panel then has 21 working days to assess whether the claimants have standing and whether their request is eligible.

If the Panel does not recommend an inspection and if the Executive Directors accept this view, the case is classified. Should they deem it necessary, the Executive Directors, may, despite the Panel's opinion, nonetheless require that an inspection investigation be undertaken. Three days after the Board has made a decision on whether an investigation is required or not, the Panel report, including the inspection enquiry and the answer from the Management, is made public through the Bank Public Information Centre (PIC) in Washington DC as well as in its offices located in the relevant member states.

If the Panel recommends an inspection and if the Board approves this recommendation, the Panel proceeds to a detailed inspection, with no specific time limit. Once the Panel has finished its inspection, its findings and conclusions are recorded concerning the allegations in the request for an inspection, which are then transmitted to the Board and the Bank Management. Bank Management then has six weeks to submit to the Board their recommendations on the measures that should be taken by the Bank in response to the Panel's findings and conclusions.

The Board then adopts a final decision concerning the measures to be taken, given the Panel's findings and Bank Management recommendations. Three days after the Board's decision, the Panel report and the Management's recommendation are made public through the Bank Public Information Center and the Bank offices located in the relevant member countries.

The country concerned by a request for an investigation is informed that the request has been lodged, and the Panel takes its opinion into account in the course of its inspection. If the Panel wishes to visit the country concerned, it must obtain its prior approval. This has raised a number of problems, due to the tensions (referred to above) associated with the fears held by some countries regarding foreign control of the conduct of their domestic affairs. Several investigation claims presented by the Panel have therefore not been authorized. In 1999, under cover of the diplomatic formula 'gentlemen's agreement', the Board committed itself to clarifying its role, by accepting that field visits would be authorized if the Panel deemed them to be necessary:

> The Board recognizes that enhancing the effectiveness of the Inspection Panel process through the above clarifications assumes adherence to them by all parties in good faith. It also assumes the borrowers' consent for field visits envisaged in the Resolution. If these assumptions prove to be incorrect, the Board will revisit the above conclusions.[24]

Once a claim has been lodged, private persons are no longer formally involved in the procedure. Their fate concerning access to information is the same as that of any person external to the Bank. Nevertheless, the Panel may question them and take their views into account. The Panel, in addition, has the ability to do so with any person of its choice. Individuals, groups of persons, national and international NGOs, may also transmit documents and reports related to an investigation to the Panel.[25] This practice is quite similar to the submission of *amicus curiae* briefs, which may operate in other dispute settlement fora.

3.3 Specific features of the Inspection Panel procedure and subsequent practice

The novelty of the Inspection Panel procedure is more striking when one thinks, for instance, about the issue of external disputes in which international organizations are involved and the difficulty of finding fora enabling claims for accountability from these organizations.[26] Of course, one must remember that the Inspection Panel is not a contentious dispute settlement procedure, nor is it by any means a mechanism challenging or asserting the international organization's legal responsibility, no more than that of the borrower countries or their decision-making bodies.

---

[24] See *Conclusions of the Board's Second Review of the Inspection Panel*, 20 April 1999, reproduced in Shihata, n. 1 above, at pp. 323–328.

[25] R.E. Bissel, 'Recent Practice of the Inspection Panel of the World Bank' (1997) 91 *Am. J. Int'l L.* 743.

[26] On this issue see in general L. Boisson de Chazournes, C. Romano and R. Mackenzie (eds.), *International Organizations and International Dispute Settlement: Trends and Prospects* (Transnational Publishers, New York, 2002).

Nonetheless, in the event of a dysfunction within the system, the Inspection Panel procedure enables problems to be 'objectivized' by way of a control mechanism and may result in a correction of behaviour by the financial organization, for the benefit of the affected populations, through the implementation of corrective actions. This leads one to think that such a mechanism will have its followers, and may be a model for other such mechanisms within the world of international organizations – not only financial – at a time when the latter are blossoming, not to say proliferating, and when their focus on various operational activities within member states' territories is multiplying.

Indeed, the Inter-American Development Bank (IDB) and Asian Development Bank (AsDB) had set up similar procedures,[27] but reviewed them at the turn of the twenty-first century. It is interesting to note that an emphasis in the new system has been put on a first stage of consultation and problem solving prior to recourse to compliance review.

The IDB created an Independent Investigation Mechanism in 1994, which was reviewed in 2001.[28] The mechanism enables a Permanent Coordinator to receive complaints by individuals who consider, in a manner similar to the World Bank's Inspection Panel procedure, that their rights have been or will be materially adversely affected by an IDB-financed activity as a result of the latter not having followed one or several of its operational procedures. The matter may then be addressed to a panel whose membership is drawn from a permanent roster. The IDB mechanism differs from the Bank's Inspection Panel in that investigators, drawn from a roster, participate in the process only after the Coordinator, working in collaboration with the Bank's Legal Department, has decided that an allegation warrants further consideration. A single expert drawn from the roster and appointed by the IDB President will ascertain whether the claim is eligible and warrants an inspection. If so, three other experts will be appointed to conduct an investigation.[29]

Pursuant to a decision taken in May 2003,[30] the AsDB replaced in December 2003 its Inspection Function (itself created in 1995) with a mechanism modelled on the Investigation Mechanism of the IDB. One reason for this change was because of difficulties faced by the Board in reaching decisions on whether or not to authorize inspections under the 1995 mechanism. The new mechanism provides for a 'non-objection' decision-making formula for the Board in its function of authorizing reviews. The mechanism is comprised of two phases: a consultation phase, which involves the appointment of a Special Project Facilitator (SPF) and

---

[27] A similar mechanism has been established with the Inter-American Bank for Development (in 1994), and the Asian Bank for Development (in 1999). For a comparison of the three institutions, see Shihata, n. 1 above, at pp. 491–500.

[28] See <www.iadb.org/aboutus/iii/independent_invest/independent_invest.cfm?Language=English> (site visited July 2004).

[29] *Accountability at the World Bank* (IBRD, Washington DC, 2003), pp. 15–16.

[30] See <www.adb.org/Documents/Policies/ADB_Accountability_Mechanism/default.asp> (site visited July 2004).

a compliance review phase, to which matters will be directed if they cannot be resolved by the SPF. Requests can be submitted to the SPF regardless of whether the complaint alleges that the AsDB has complied or not with its operational procedures but must nonetheless stipulate that the two or more persons submitting their request will be, or are likely to be, affected by the project, this requiring direct material harm or a likelihood of such harm in the future. The consultation phase takes several months and is aimed at arriving at a consensus based problem-solving course of action. An interesting feature is that monitoring is envisaged of any agreement reached in that regard. The creation of a Compliance Review Panel (CRP) may nonetheless be deemed necessary at various stages of the consultation phase (which may therefore be abandoned) but this requires an allegation of a breach of one of the AsDB's operational policies and procedures. The CRP may investigate not only the AsDP's activities but also those of the borrowing country, executing agency or private partner, but only to the extent that their acts are directly relevant to the project.

In 2003, the European Bank for Reconstruction and Development (EBRD) created in like fashion its own mechanism, with the expectation that it will be operational by April 2004. The Independent Recourse Mechanism (IRM) was created after considerable public and internal consultation, and consists of a 'system of processes and procedures designed to provide a venue for an independent review of complaints or grievances from groupings that are, or are likely to be, directly and adversely affected by a Bank-financed project'.[31] On receipt of a complaint and a consideration of its eligibility, an independent EBRD-appointed Chief Compliance Officer (CCO) will ascertain whether it is useful to have recourse to problem-solving techniques (fact-finding, mediation, conciliation, etc.).[32] The President has the final say on whether such a problem-solving initiative should be pursued. This procedure is quite independent of the Compliance Review Procedure. In the latter context, complainants (being two or more individuals with a common interest who are, or are likely to be, adversely affected by an EBRD-financed project) are assessed by the CCO, who may register it (this will not occur if the complaint is manifestly frivolous or malicious or no good faith attempts have been made to resolve the issue with the relevant EBRD department) and an independent expert, taken from a roster, will be appointed. The latter will assist the CCO in evaluating the eligibility of the complaint.[33] Complaints that challenge, *inter alia*, the adequacy or suitability of the EBRD policies themselves will be ineligible.[34] To be eligible for Compliance Review, the CCO and independent expert must consider that there is a possibility that a mandatory provision of an EBRD policy within the scope of the IRM has not been complied

---

[31] See EBRD, Independent Recourse Mechanism as Approved by the Board of Directors on 29 April 2003, Annex 1, para. 2.

[32] Ibid., para. 27.

[33] Ibid., para. 12.

[34] Ibid., para. 13.

with.[35] It is significant that only environmental and public information disclosure policies can be reviewed. Should compliance review be considered necessary, an expert will be appointed and he or she has as long as they consider necessary to fulfil this function.

As noted, the IFC and MIGA have established a Compliance Officer/Ombudsman (CAO) mechanism. The significant difference when compared to other models is that this mechanism only deals with private sector projects. The CAO has three functions, the first being its ombudsman's role, using mediation and other dispute settlement techniques to address complaints by people who feel that they are or will be affected by MIGA or IFC supported projects; the second is as compliance auditor to verify selected projects; and finally the CAO provides independent advice to Senior Management either with regard to specific projects or more generally on the application and effectiveness of policies. Whilst functionally independent, the CAO nonetheless reports to the President of the Bank.[36]

Finally, one can note that the African Development Bank is contemplating the creation of its own compliance review procedure.[37]

4. CONCLUSIONS: OF THE ENDOGENOUS AND INNOVATING NATURE OF THE INSPECTION PANEL PROCEDURE

The innovative aspects of the World Bank Inspection Panel procedure must not make one forget that this mechanism's endogenous aspects are linked to the peculiarities of the organization within which it was established. The World Bank structure, together with the type of activities it conducts, has strongly influenced the shape of the mechanism. It is obvious that no perfect solution exists, and the Panel has not escaped criticism. Ever since it began, the procedure has caused tensions, as the different actors involved have not always been satisfied with the process or its results. For instance, Bank Management does not appreciate being questioned, nor do borrower countries appreciate being pinpointed, nor complaining private parties not achieving their pursued goals because of blockages or slowness in the course of the procedure.

The Inspection Panel procedure is a prism enabling one to apprehend the Organization's inner life and the difficulties attaching to the setting-up of control mechanisms. The ambiguous relationship between the privileged political decision-making body and an Inspection Panel body whose role is to investigate dysfunctions in the Organization's activities, are thus singled out within the financial

---

[35] Ibid., para. 16.

[36] *Accountability at the World Bank*, n. 29 above, at p. 16.

[37] A. Rigo Sureda, 'Process Integrity and Institutional Independence in International Organizations: The Inspection Panel and the Sanctions Committee of the World Bank' in Boisson de Chazournes, Romano and Mackenzie, n. 26 above, at pp. 180–187. See also D. Bradlow, 'Study on an Inspection Function for the African Development Bank' (24 November 2003, unpublished, on file with author).

institution. It is difficult for the political body – the Board – to accept that the very investigation body it has established – the Panel – should invoke its independence to ask its creator to make decisions that risk neglecting the sacrosanct harmony within its walls, established, notably, by the generalized recourse to consensus. Private persons, for their part, wish to participate more in the course of the procedure initiated, whereas Bank authorities are becoming painfully used to the presence of these new actors, who assert ever more firmly that the principles of public participation, transparency and accountability are to be acknowledged for their benefit.

The Panel's experience (23 claims have been declared eligible)[38] nonetheless shows that the implementation of this investigation procedure has contributed to improve the quality of Bank-financed operations. The institution has decided to withhold the implementation of certain projects, if not to renounce them. It has also enforced corrective measures, premised largely on the contribution of local populations and has established within the Organization a series of mechanisms and procedures to ensure a supervision of the quality of operations during the projects' preparation and implementation.[39]

The Inspection Panel procedure also sheds light on new trends in the contemporary legal order, especially on the need to build public spaces enabling the relationships between partners destined to work side by side, and with each other. The World Bank has joined this emerging trend by establishing the Inspection Panel, and by taking part in the implementation of other innovative mechanisms in the field of international decision-making process.

---

[38] As at 17 February 2004, out of 30 requests received, the Panel registered 26. Out of the 26, the Panel found three to be not eligible, because either the harm did not exist, or it was not related to a Bank project. Out of the 23 requests found eligible, the Panel recommended an investigation in 14 cases.

[39] See Boisson de Chazournes, n. 11 above, at pp. 289–292; D. Freestone, 'The Environmental and Social Safeguard Policies of the World Bank and the Evolving Role of the Inspection Panel' in A. Kiss, D. Shelton and K. Ishibashi (eds.), *Economic Globalization and Compliance with International Environmental Agreements* (Kluwer Law International, The Hague, 2003), pp. 139–156.

Chapter 15

NGOs in Non-Compliance Mechanisms under Multilateral Environmental Agreements: From Tolerance to Recognition?

*Cesare Pitea**

1. Reviewing Compliance and the Role of NGOs: Introduction

The increasing participation of non-governmental organizations (NGOs) in the process of international law, particularly in the field of environment, can nowadays be considered an *acquis* of international legal practice and doctrine.[1] Such participation, however, often takes hidden or informal forms, remaining outside formal mechanisms of international law-making, administering and enforcing.[2] The resistance to recognition of formal rights is two-sided: NGOs are jealous of

* I would like to thank Prof. Tullio Treves, Prof. Attila Tanzi and Prof. Laura Pineschi for their invaluable comments on early drafts of the present chapter. Special thanks are due to Mr Jeremy Wates, Dr Veit Koester and Mr Nicholas Bonvoisin for their suggestions and precious insights. Needless to say, any error or omission which may remain, rests on my sole and full responsibility.
[1] Such view, which does not imply in any way the recognition of NGOs as subjects of international law, is endorsed in recent international law and international environmental law textbooks, see P.M. Dupuy, *Droit International Public* (6th edn., Paris, 2000), p. 1; A. Tanzi, *Introduzione al Diritto Internazionale Contemporaneo* (Padova, 2003), p. 239; P. Birnie and A. Boyle, *International Law and the Environment* (2nd edn., Oxford, 2002) p. 66; P. Sands, *Principles of International Environmental Law*, (2nd edn., Cambridge, 2003) pp. 112-120. Indeed, it is increasingly the object of specific scholars' attention, see P. Sands, 'The Environment, Community and International Law' (1989) 30 *Harv. Int'l L. J.* 393; P. Sands, 'The Role of Non-Governmental Organizations in Enforcing International Environmental Law' in W.E. Butler (ed.), *Control over Compliance with International Law* (Dordrecht, 1991), pp. 61–68; W.E. Burhenne, 'The Role of NGOs' in W. Lang (ed.), *Sustainable Development and International Law* (London, 1995), pp. 207–211; J. Cameron, 'Compliance, Citizens and NGOs' in J. Cameron, J. Werksman and P. Roderick (eds.), *Improving Compliance with International Environmental Law* (London, 1996) (hereinafter *Improving Compliance*), p. 29; S. Charnovitz, 'Two Centuries of Participation: NGOs and International Governance' (1997) 18 *Mich. J. Int'l L.* 183; R. Ranjeva, 'Les Organisations non gouvernementales et la mise en œuvre du droit international' (1997) 270 *RdC* 9–106; U. Beyerlin, 'The Role of NGOs in International Environmental Litigation' (2001) 61 *ZaöRV* 357; A. Tanzi and C. Pitea, 'Emerging Trends in the Role of Non-State Actors in International Water Disputes' in International Bureau of the Permanent Court of Arbitration (ed.), *Resolution of International Water Disputes* (2003), pp. 259–297, H. Gherari and S. Szurek (eds.), *L'émergence de la société civile internationale, vers la privatisation du droit international?* (Paris, 2003).
[2] See A. Alkoby, 'Non-State Actors and the Legitimacy of International Environmental Law' (2003) 3 *Non-State Actors & Int'l L.* 23, at 25.

T. Treves et al., eds., Civil Society, International Courts and Compliance Bodies
© 2005, T·M·C·Asser Press, *The Hague, The Netherlands, and the Authors*

their independence and freedom of action as much as states are of their sovereignty.[3]

This chapter deals with the issue of NGO participation in relation to non-compliance mechanisms (NCMs) established, or undergoing a process of negotiation, under multilateral environmental agreements (MEAs). Following the example given by the procedure established under the Montreal Protocol, several recent MEAs have developed, often on the basis of an explicit treaty provision, special institutions and procedures to respond to non-compliance by states parties.[4] Notwithstanding the analogy they apparently bear with quasi-judicial procedures well known in other branches of international law,[5] the mechanisms established under MEAs are meant to differ significantly from those models, since they are designed mainly to prevent and avoid, rather then resolve, disputes and to do so in a non-judicial, non-confrontational and cooperative manner. This formula is used to underline two aspects of the procedure. First, it takes into account theories according to which non-compliance with international environmental obligations is largely due to inability rather than to lack of commitment.[6] Secondly, it is in-

---

[3] As observed by Alkoby, n. 2 above, at p. 46, the regulation of NGO activities, bringing a degree of control on sources of financing and internal structure, is sometimes perceived as a way to limit, rather than increase, their influence. One may also add that 'institutionalization' of NGOs may change the perception of them as outsiders in the realm of international diplomacy and bureaucracy.

[4] The scope of the present chapter is restricted to mechanisms designed to deal with individual non-compliance issues, through the action of a dedicated permanent body, rather then through *ad hoc* action or exercise of Conference of the Parties (COP) or Meeting of the Parties (MOP) prerogatives. This aspect, although considered by some the most influential for compliance purposes (see D.G. Victor, *The Early Operation and Effectiveness of Montreal Protocol's Non-Compliance Procedure*, IIASA Paper ER-96-2 (1996) (available at <www.iiasa.ac.at/Publications/Documents/ER-96-002.pdf> (visited July 2004), p. 37) is only one step of a larger compliance review strategy which comprises at least reporting requirements and, on this basis, a mechanism of general review and monitoring. On the other hand, approaches to compliance are different in different contexts; see, generally, *Improving Compliance*, n. 1 above, and R. Wolfrum, 'Means of Ensuring Compliance with and Enforcement of International Environmental Law' (1999) 272 *RdC* 9-154, and, for reference to particular mechanisms, V. Koester, 'Pacta Sunt Servanda' (1996) 26 *Envt'l Pol'y & L.* 78 and R. Reeve, *Policing International Trade in Endangered Species: The CITES Treaty and Compliance*, (London, 2002). The list of the mechanisms considered is annexed to this chapter (see section 6 below). On NCMs, see generally, M. Koskenniemi, 'Breach of Treaty or Non-Compliance? Reflections on the Enforcement of the Montreal Protocol' (1992) 3 *YB Int'l Envt'l L.* 123; G. Handl, 'Compliance Control Mechanisms and International Environmental Obligations' (1997) 5 *Tul. J. Int'l & Comp. L.* 29; M.M. Goote, 'Non-compliance Procedures in International Environmental Law: The Middle Way between Diplomacy and Law' (1999) 1 *Int'l L. Forum* 82; M. Fitzmaurice and C. Redgwell, 'Environmental Non-Compliance Procedures and International Law' (2000) 31 *Neth. Yb Int'l L.* 35; M. Ehrmann, 'Procedures of Compliance Control in International Environmental Treaties' (2002) 13 *Colo. J. Envt'l L. & Pol'y* 377; L. Pineschi 'Non-compliance Mechanisms and the Proposed Center for the Prevention and Management of Environmental Disputes' (2004) to be published in *Anuario de Derecho Internacional* (on file with the author).

[5] This label is in fact used by some authors also in relation to NCMs, see V. Röben, 'Institutional Developments under Modern International Environmental Agreements' (2000) 4 *Max Planck Y.B. U.N.L.* 363, at 412; Handl, n. 4 above, at p. 45.

[6] See R.B. Mitchell, 'Compliance Theory: An Overview' in *Improving Compliance*, n. 1 above, at pp. 1–28.

tended to overcome political and legal limitations suffered by invocation of state responsibility through traditional dispute settlement procedures.[7]

Within this framework, NGO participation can be seen in two opposite ways. On the one hand, it could contribute to the cooperative spirit of the mechanisms, by helping to identify cases of, and causes for, non-compliance through both factual information and scientific and legal assessment. On the other hand, it is feared that the traditional confrontational attitude of environmental NGOs could undermine the very nature of the mechanism, turning it into a human rights-style procedure.

This chapter will describe how NGO participation is taken into account by existing instruments establishing or envisaging NCMs and will attempt to identify the major problems posed by existing approaches. The Montreal NCM leaves little room for NGO participation:[8] it neither contains specific provisions dealing with the issue, nor has any relevant practice in this respect developed under it. Therefore, the main question to be answered is whether more recent mechanisms inspired by the Montreal NCM have followed this precedent as far as NGO participation is concerned. The enquiry will focus on three aspects of the NCMs in which NGO participation may be relevant: the institutional arrangements, the triggering mechanism and the evaluation process, including fact-finding and assessment.

At the outset it is noteworthy that the Aarhus Convention and the Protocol on Water and Health mention in their provisions requiring the establishment of a NCM, a role for NGOs.[9] Considering also that the Aarhus Convention itself binds parties to it to promote the principle of public participation 'in international environmental decision-making processes and within the framework of international organizations in matters relating to the environment',[10] it is not by accident

---

[7] See K. Sachariew, 'State Responsibility for Multilateral Treaty Violations: Identifying the "Injured State" and Its Legal Status' (1988) 35 *Netherlands Int'l L. Rev.* 273; A. Kiss, 'Present Limits to the Enforcement of State Responsibility for Environmental Damage' in F. Francioni and T. Scovazzi (eds.), *International Responsibility for Environmental Harm* (Dordrecht, 1991), pp. 3–14; Koskenniemi, n. 4 above; L. Boisson de Chazournes, 'La mise an œuvre du droit international dans le domaine de la protection de l'environnement: enjeux et défis' (1995) 99 *Rev. Gén. Dr. Int. Pub.* 37, especially at 50 *et seq.*; Wolfrum, n. 4 above, at pp. 96–100; T. Scovazzi, 'State Responsibility for Environmental Harm' (2001) 12 *YB Int'l Envt'l L.* 43; Ehrmann, n. 4 above, at pp. 379–386.

[8] See O. Yoshida, 'Soft Enforcement of Treaties: The Montreal Protocol's Noncompliance Procedure and the Functions of Internal International Institutions' (1999) 10 *Colo. J. Envt'l L. Pol'y* 95, at 110.

[9] Article 15 of the Aarhus Convention and Article 15 of the Protocol on Water and Health provide that '[the arrangements for reviewing compliance] shall allow for appropriate public involvement'. The Aarhus Convention further indicates that these arrangements 'may include the option of considering communications from the public'. 'The public' is defined in Article 2(4) of the Aarhus Convention as 'one or more natural or legal persons, and, in accordance with national legislation or practice, their associations, organizations or groups'. Full references for all the treaties cited in this chapter can be found in the Annex, section 6 below.

[10] Article 3(7) of the Aarhus Convention (section 6 below).

that the role of NGOs finds unusual acknowledgment in the procedures developed in the European region generally and under the two above-mentioned instruments particularly, as will be shown below.

2.   NGO PARTICIPATION IN COMPLIANCE OR IMPLEMENTATION COMMITTEES

Several actors are involved in the institutional aspect of a NCM. The Secretariat, which serves as administrative support and, in some cases, as a necessary liaison between the Committee and other actors involved in the procedure, and the Conference of the Parties (COP), which nominates the Committee and bears final responsibility for the decisions to be taken to respond to non-compliance,[11] both play important roles in the administration of a NCM. However, the distinctive institution of the mechanism is a dedicated and standing body (Compliance or Implementation Committee)[12] created to administrate the core aspects of the procedure.

The Committee, which is normally composed of a limited number of members sitting either as state representatives or as individuals in their personal capacity, carries out, *inter alia*, the task of examining, through fact-finding and assessment, specific issues of non-compliance brought to its attention. If a situation of non-compliance is found, the Committee is to identify the reasons therefor, envisage possible solutions in cooperation with the party concerned and address recommendations to the COP.

This section will focus on NGO participation in the workings of the Committee, in the different forms it may take.

2.1   Existing practice

First of all, NGOs may passively participate, by simply attending meetings open to the public. Texts setting up NCMs often fail to address explicitly the issue of publicity of meetings, leaving its regulation to the Rules of Procedure or to the Committee's practice. The Implementation Committee under the Montreal Protocol has taken a very restrictive approach, considering confidentiality of meetings the rule, probably beyond the needs connected to the substantive obligations of

---

[11] This is the prevalent pattern, but exceptions can be found. The most egregious example is given by the mechanism under the Kyoto Protocol, where the Committee bears the responsibility for the final decision on compliance, except where appeal under Section XI is requested by the interested party, see S. Urbinati, 'Non-Compliance Procedure under the Kyoto Protocol' (2003) 3 *Baltic YB Int'l L.* 229, at 237.

[12] Other expressions may be found in practice. Under the Alpine Convention, for instance, the body established to administer the mechanism is called 'Comité de vérification', see Alpine NCM (section 6 below).

the Protocol and the related information to be provided.[13] The Basel NCM provides for the confidential nature of the Committee's meetings in which specific submissions of non-compliance are at issue, except where the Committee and the party concerned agree otherwise.[14] The meetings of the Aarhus Compliance Committee, where the information handled is less likely to justify confidentiality, should be held in public,[15] except where conventional rules on confidentiality apply.[16] The Implementation Committee established under the Espoo Convention, notwithstanding the existence and applicability of a rule of publicity in the relevant Rules of Procedure,[17] has taken a different view and has applied a rule derived from the Basel NCM.[18] This attitude has been later formalized in the proposed amendments to the mechanisms.[19]

Some of the mechanisms not yet in force or still under negotiation take into account the problem, through the inclusion of a specific provision on confidentiality/publicity. The preference for publicity is expressed in the Kyoto NCM, although with a scope limited to hearings of a party whose compliance is at issue before the enforcement branch.[20] Such hearings are to be held in public, unless a contrary decision is taken by the branch itself.[21] The draft Prior Informed Consent Convention (PIC) NCM envisages a clause applying to all meetings. At the present stage of negotiation the decision on the substantive issue has not yet been made, with both options still available.[22]

More meaningful than simple attendance, the attribution of observer status to NGOs would give them the chance to play a more active role in the process. They would be thus afforded rights to receive and submit documents and to make written and oral statements. Again, the issue of whether such participation is possible and the extent of attached rights and entitlements is left to the Rules of Procedure and to practice, with the exception of the Alpine NCM, under which observers

---

[13] See Handl, n. 4 above, at p. 40.

[14] See Basel NCM (section 6 below), para. 16.

[15] Such a rule constitutes an application *mutatis mutandis* of the Rules of Procedure of the Meeting of the Parties, which are applicable to subsidiary bodies of the Meeting of the Parties (see Rule 7 and Rule 23(2), Rules of Procedure, Decision I/1, Doc. MP.PP/2002/2 (2002), p. 4). It is not clear, however, if the application *mutatis mutandis* of the rules is due to the fact that Committee considers itself as a subsidiary body or by way of analogy, see Report of the First Meeting, Doc. MP.PP/C.1/2003/2 (2003) (hereinafter Aarhus Committee, First Report), para. 11, p. 3).

[16] See Aarhus NCM (section 6 below), Section VIII.

[17] Meeting of the Parties to the Convention on Environmental Impact Assessment in a Transboundary Context, Decision I/1, Rules of Procedure, in Report of the First Meeting, Doc. ECE/MP.EIA/2, Annex I, (1998), p. 5.

[18] See Report of the Third Meeting of the Implementation Committee, Doc. MP.EIA/WG.1/2003/8 (2003) (hereinafter Espoo Committee, Third Report) para. 12, p. 3.

[19] See Espoo NCM (section 6 below), para. 3.

[20] The Kyoto NCM (section 6 below), Section III para. 2(d) leaves to the Plenary of the Committee decisions relating to rules on confidentiality.

[21] Ibid., Section IX para. 2.

[22] See Draft PIC NCM (section 6 below), para. 7.

represented in the main subsidiary body of the COP, the Permanent Committee,[23] are allowed to delegate up to two persons to the Committee.[24]

As far as practice of other existing Committees is concerned, there are few occurrences of NGOs participating as observers. In at least one case, NGOs are reported to have unsuccessfully tried to attend the meetings of the Montreal Implementation Committee.[25] On the other hand, NGOs representatives are regularly admitted as observers to the meetings of the Aarhus Compliance Committee, with the right to participate in the discussion.[26] Such participation has extended also to the meeting dealing with specific issues of non-compliance. The Espoo Implementation Committee, after having considered the possibility of admitting observers, without settling the question, in its review of public participation issues,[27] has admitted as observer at its 4th Meeting an NGO already enjoying observer status before the Meeting of the Parties. However, the Committee made clear that this decision was taken on an *ad hoc* and experimental basis, that the view expressed by the NGO representative would not be reflected as such in the Report and that the NGO representative was bound by confidentiality rules.[28]

The Aarhus Convention provides an example, so far unique, of an even stronger role for NGOs in the non-compliance institutional mechanism. In fact, it affords qualified NGOs the right to formulate candidatures for election as full members of the Committee. Among the five NGO candidatures put forward at the 1st Meeting of the Parties, two eventually resulted in election. Although, as noted by the Espoo Implementation Committee, even in the absence of a formal entitlement, nothing prevents parties from nominating an individual from an NGO or

---

[23] On the institutional structure of the Alpine Convention see L. Pineschi, 'The Convention for the Protection of the Alps and Its Protocols: Evaluation and Expectations' in T. Treves, L. Pineschi and A. Fodella (eds.), *Sustainable Development of Mountain Areas: From Rio to Johannesburg and Beyond* (Milano, 2004), pp. 191-214.

[24] See Alpine NCM (section 6 below), section 2, para. 1.1. Observer organizations decided, however, to nominate only one person and one alternate, see T. Enderlin, 'Alpine Convention: A Different Compliance Mechanism' (2003) 33 *Envt'l Pol'y & L.* 155, at 157.

[25] See Victor, n. 4 above, at p. 6.

[26] See Aarhus Committee, First Report, n. 15 above, at para. 5, Report of the Second Meeting, Doc. MP.PP/C.1/2003/4 (2003) (hereinafter Aarhus Committee, Second Report), para. 1 and Report of the Third Meeting, Doc. MP.PP/C.1/2004/2 (2004) (hereinafter Aarhus Committee, Third Report), para. 1 and Report on the Fourth Meeting, Doc. MP.PP/C.1/2004/4 (2004) (hereinafter Aarhus Committee, Fourth Report), para. 1. According to the Rules of Procedure of the Meeting of the Parties the recognition of NGOs as observers is regulated by Rule 6(2), which allows one-third of the Committee's members to exclude them from the Meeting.

[27] The Committee did not feel it necessary to take an immediate decision on the issue of active participation, deciding that '[t]he need for such a provision would be reviewed in the light of experience and a recommendation might be made to the Parties at their fourth meeting', see Espoo Committee, Third Report, n. 18 above, at paras. 14–15, p. 3.

[28] See Report of the Fourth Meeting of the Implementation Committee, Doc. MP.EIA/WG.1/2004/3 (2003) (hereinafter Espoo Committee, Fourth Report), para. 3, p. 1.

from the private sector,[29] a formal recognition can be a decisive factor to over-come political opposition to such an occurrence. Although the United States' del-egation formally declared that it did not consider as a precedent the Aarhus NCM in relation to this and other issues of public participation,[30] NGO entitlement to put forward candidatures is currently one of the alternatives proposed under the Protocol on Water and Health.[31]

2.2 Evaluation

At the present stage, participation of NGOs in the institutional arrangements to respond to non-compliance seems to be rather limited, with the egregious excep-tion of the Aarhus Convention and, to a lesser extent, of the Espoo and Alpine Conventions. Whether this is due to lack of interest by NGOs or to resistance by states, as expressed in Rules and practices governing the matter, it is disputable. However, since the issue is often left to practice rather than to regulation, only observation of the developing practice will allow for a sound evaluation.

As a matter of policy, participation of NGOs in the institutional arrangements to address non-compliance can raise both concerns and expectations. Participa-tion of NGOs could lead to an instrumental use of the Committee's proceedings to pursue a particular political agenda of non-governmental groups.[32] Moreover, it raises serious issues as far as confidentiality is concerned. On the other hand, it seems valuable, for the proper functioning of the mechanisms, to move outside a strictly intergovernmental perspective in the composition of the administering in-stitution. At the outset it is fair to observe that, regardless of the existence and the extent of formal participatory forms, a committee composed of individuals seems to better equipped to respond to issues and arguments from the non-governmental sector. In addition, the participation in the Committee of either NGOs or indepen-dent individuals with an NGO background, can significantly strengthen the con-tinuous representation of public interest in the Committee's workings.

---

[29] See Espoo Committee, Third Report, n. 18 above, at para. 14, p. 3. Following the proposal of the Committee (see Report of the Fifth Meeting of the Implementation Committee (hereinafter Espoo Committee, Fifth Report), Doc. MP.EIA/WG.1/2004/4 (2004), para. 12, p. 3) the Meeting of the Parties agreed to include Poland among the member parties. The appointee is expected to be Dr Jerzy Jendroska who is not a government official.

[30] The delegation of the United States obtained that a written statement, expressing its concerns with respect to the compliance mechanism and the negotiating process which had led to it, be an-nexed to the Report of the First Meeting. The Statement expresses concerns, inter alia, for the 'vari-ety of unusual procedural roles that may be performed by non-State, non-Party actors, including the nomination of members of the Committee and the ability to trigger certain communication require-ments by Parties under these provisions' and 'about the efficacy of such provisions as a general policy matter'. It concludes that 'United States will not recognize this regime as precedent', see Re-port of the First Meeting of the Parties, Doc. ECE/MP.PP/2, para. 45 and Annex, reprinted in (2003) 33 Envt'l Pol'y & L 178.

[31] See proposed Water and Health NCM (section 6 below), p. 14.

[32] Handl, n. 4 above, at p. 40.

3.   TRIGGER MECHANISM: HIDDEN ACTION OR LEGAL RIGHT?

3.1 **Existing practice**

The non-confrontational nature of NCMs justifies the recognition of broader access than that provided for under formal dispute settlement mechanisms.[33] This notwithstanding, the right of individuals and NGOs to initiate the proceedings remains exceptional. NCMs can normally be triggered by a state party, in relation to another party, regardless of its position of injured state under the law of state responsibility (party-to-party triggering),[34] by a party in relation to itself (self triggering),[35] by the Secretariat and, in some cases, by the Committee *proprio motu*.

None of mechanisms set up under global instruments mention individuals and/ or NGOs among the subjects entitled to trigger the procedure. Proposals to this effect have been rejected under the Montreal NCM[36] and Basel NCM.[37] The same restrictive approach seems to be shared in ongoing negotiations under the Stockholm Convention on Persistent Organic Pollutants (POPs).[38]

In the European region, especially in the UNECE framework, early established mechanisms followed the same path. However, some important developments have taken place in newly established mechanisms, as well as in those currently under negotiation. At present, there are two examples of NCMs allowing non-state actors to initiate the proceedings. Under the Alpine NCM, the right to refer cases of non-compliance to the Reviewing Committee is limited, as far as NGOs are concerned, to those having observer status.[39] Under the Aarhus Convention, in keeping with the provision of Article 15, and notwithstanding the ini-

---

[33] See Tanzi and Pitea, n. 1 above, at p. 276.

[34] It should be noted that in the framework of the Cartagena NCM, a proposal was made by the United States' delegation in order to limit the right to submit issues of non-compliance to 'directly involved' third parties, see Compilation of Views on Compliance Procedures and Mechanisms under the Cartagena Protocol on Biosafety, Doc. UNEP/CBD/BS/COP-MOP/1/INF/4 (2004), p. 17 (hereinafter Cartagena NCM, Compilation of Views). The proposal was mentioned by the Secretariat among possible options for amendment, see Summary of Views or Understanding on the Contents in Square Brackets in the Text of the Draft Procedures and Mechanisms on Compliance under the Cartagena Protocol on Biosafety, Doc. UNEP/CBD/ICCP/3/4 (2002), p. 11.

[35] In few cases this kind of triggering is not explicitly mentioned, but may be considered implicit in a broad provision relating to the triggering rights of parties. See, with reference to the Alpine NCM (section 6 below), Section II para. 2.3, Pineschi, n. 23 above, at p. 200.

[36] See Report of the Third Meeting of the Ad Hoc Working Group of Legal Experts on Non-Compliance with the Montreal Protocol, Doc. UNEP/OzL.Pro/WG.3/3/3, Annex II (1991), p. 10.

[37] See Monitoring the Implementation of and Compliance with the Obligations set out by the Basel Convention, Doc. UNEP/CHW.6/9, Annex (2002), para. 8, p. 9.

[38] For the mechanism under the POPs Convention (section 6 below) negative views have been expressed in this respect by governments, see Synthesis of Views on Non-compliance, Doc. UNEP/POPS/INC.7/21 (2003), para. 12, p. 4.

[39] See Alpine NCM (section 6 below), Section II para. 2.3.

tial strong opposition of some delegations, the final decision on the establishment of a NCM included a far-reaching provision regarding 'communications from the public'.[40]

The role of the public in triggering the proceedings has been extensively considered in the text submitted for negotiation under the Protocol on Water and Health, but has already encountered opposition from some states.[41] Finally, the Implementation Committee set up under the Espoo Convention has considered proposals to reform the existing mechanism in order to enable the initiation of proceedings by NGOs.[42] Proposals in such matter, however, are not included in the amending decision submitted for approval to the 3rd Meeting of the Parties and have been postponed for consideration at the subsequent meeting.[43]

Direct access of the public to the proceedings poses practical problems in relation to the management of the procedure. It is feared that NGO activism could overload the agenda (and the budget) of the various committees, with consequent adverse impact on the effectiveness of the whole mechanism.[44] Several procedural safeguards can be implemented in order to avoid or limit such occurrence, as provided for in the Aarhus NCM. In the first place, arrangements providing for communications from the public can be made optional, through either an opt-out or an opt-in clause.[45] In the second place, communications from the public can be subject to additional admissibility provisions, requiring to take into account whether available and effective domestic remedies have been exhausted[46] and allowing the Committee to strike off its agenda anonymous, manifestly ill-founded

---

[40] See Aarhus NCM (section 6 below), para. 18.

[41] See proposed Water and Health NCM (section 6 below), para. 13 and Report on the Third Meeting of the Working Group on Water and Health, Doc. MP.WAT/WG.4/2004/3 (2004), paras. 16-19.

[42] See Espoo Committee, Third Report, n. 18 above, at para. 13, p. 3.

[43] See points 5 and 7 of the amending Decision (section 6 below).

[44] Concerns of this kind were expressed by the Australian delegation in the process of negotiation of the Cartagena NCM (see Cartagena NCM, Compilation of Views, n. 34 above, at p. 3), and are reflected in the decision of the Espoo Implementation Committee to postpone consideration of the issue (see Espoo Committee, Third Report, n. 18 above, at para. 13, p. 3).

[45] Under the Aarhus NCM, in addition to a general transitional period of one year (beginning from the day of approval of the decision setting up the NCM or the entry into force of the Convention for the party concerned, whichever is the later) during which the Committee may not consider communications from the public in respect to that party, each party can opt out from the procedure by making a declaration stating its inability to accept the consideration of communications from the public, for a period of no more than four years, see Aarhus NCM (section 6 below), para. 18. This solution was chosen among others which, in application of the principle of the optional nature of direct access from the public set out in Article 15 of the Aarhus Convention, envisaged either opt-in or opt-out for longer or shorter terms, see Report of the Working Group on Compliance and Rules of Procedure, Doc. CEP/WG.5/AC.1/2001/2, Annex II (2001), pp. 24–26.

[46] See Aarhus NCM (section 6 below), para. 21. The Committee has made clear that 'paragraph 21 of the decision I/7 offered considerable flexibility, but also agreed that given its limited resources, it would make sense if issues were tackled at domestic level where feasible'.

and abusive communications,[47] or those incompatible with the provisions of the relevant Decision or Convention.[48]

Notwithstanding such safeguards, however, the financial and administrative implications of the right of the public to submit compliance issues remains an outstanding issue for discussion before the Aarhus Committee. After the first five cases were submitted to it by NGOs, the Committee considered questions relating to translation of documents, additional funding and internal working procedures (including further safeguards against manifestly inadmissible submissions) and agreed to keep these matters under close review in light of the rate at which communications are received.[49]

Different approaches to this problem may be envisaged. One example is that of the Alpine NCM, where, as has already been observed, access is limited to NGOs already represented in other treaty bodies.[50] The proposal originally made for the Basel NCM tackled the issue of safeguards in a different way by submitting the continuation of proceedings initiated by a non-state actor to the explicit agreement of at least one state party.[51]

As often noted,[52] nothing prevents NGOs from bringing an issue to the attention of the Committee informally, where the Committee can act *proprio motu*, through a state party, or through the Secretariat.[53] However, only one occurrence of such kind has been reported. The Espoo Implementation Committee, after a long discussion, denied the possibility for it to consider a submission forwarded by an Ukrainian NGO concerning the project of construction of a canal to the Danube. It has found that 'considering unsolicited information from NGOs and

---

[47] However, the identity of the member of the public submitting the communication can be kept confidential when necessary, see Aarhus NCM (section 6 below), para. 29.

[48] Ibid., para. 20.

[49] See Aarhus Committee, Fourth Report, n. 26 above.

[50] See n. 39 above and accompanying text.

[51] Para. 12 of the proposed text provided as follows: 'Where a submission is made pursuant to paragraph 8(c) [specific submission from individuals or organizations] the secretariat shall, as soon as the Party whose compliance is in question has responded, but in any event not later than six months after receiving the original submission, forward the submission and the reply from the Party, if received, to the other Parties and to the members of the Committee. If one or more Parties wish the submission to be pursued further, they shall so notify the Committee in writing, through the secretariat, not later than three months after the date at which the secretariat sent the submission and, if applicable, the reply from the Party, to the other Parties, after which the Committee shall consider the submission as soon as practicable', see Monitoring the Implementation of and Compliance with the Obligations set out by the Basel Convention, Doc. UNEP/CHW.6/9, Annex (2002), p. 5.

[52] See Ehrmann, n. 4 above, at p. 397; Goote, n. 4 above, at p. 87.

[53] However, it has been submitted that under the Montreal NCM this would not be allowed, the Secretariat's task being limited to forwarding issues of non-compliance it may become aware of through government reports under Articles 7 and 9 of the Montreal Protocol, see Bothe, 'Compliance Control Beyond Diplomacy: The Role of Non-Governmental Actors' (1997) 27 *Envt'l Pol'y & L.* 293, at 296. In other cases reliance on information of a non-governmental source seems implicit. This will be the case under the Kyoto Protocol where the procedure may be triggered by the Secretariat with regard to issues of implementation indicated in the reports of expert review teams (Draft Kyoto NCM (section 6 below), Section VII.1), see Urbinati, n. 11 above, at p. 239.

the public relating to specific cases of non-compliance was not within the Committee's existing mandate'.[54] This view was not shared by a minority of members, who believed that the provision in the Espoo NCM on 'Committee Initiative' allowed the opening of proceedings *proprio motu*, whenever the Committee became aware of non-compliance and regardless of the source of the information.[55] The relevance of this precedent is, however, limited, since the Espoo NCM, contrary to most NCMs, does not afford the Secretariat the entitlement to initiate proceedings. Most interestingly, it seems that the issue forming the object of the NGO's request will be considered by the Espoo Committee since a submission regarding this issue has now been made by another party.[56]

3.2 Evaluation

In the light of existing practice, states' attitude towards the recognition of triggering rights to non-state actors can be defined as cautious. The example reported under the Espoo Convention is topical. Contrary to the decision taken by the Committee, which is composed of state representatives, the wording of the decision establishing the mechanism seems to support clearly the possibility for the Committee to consider and decide upon any non-compliance issue it becomes aware of.[57] This can be explained in several ways. Leaving aside the argument that states always tend to preserve their sovereignty, two main problems can be identified. The first relates to the very nature of NCMs. If NGOs were to be allowed to become 'parties' to the procedure, it is not unreasonable to wonder how the mechanism could maintain its non-confrontational and non-adversarial features. The second relates to practical aspects of the administration of the mechanism, as mentioned above.

On the other hand, it is hard to ignore the key role civil society may play in order to expand the Committee's ability to become aware of possible non-compli-

---

[54] See Espoo Committee, Fourth Report, n. 28 above, at paras. 7–10 and Espoo Committee, Fifth Report, n. 29 above, at paras. 9-12.

[55] Ibid., para. 7. See Espoo NCM (section 6 below), para. 6 (former para. 5): 'Where the Committee becomes aware of possible non-compliance by a Party with its obligations, it may request the Party concerned to furnish necessary information about the matter'.

[56] The other party concerned is Romania, who publicly criticized the attitude of Ukrainian authorities, see the Statement of the Romanian Secretary of State for Environment at the Third Meeting of the Parties, available at <www.unece.org/env/eia/documents/cavtat/Romania.pdf> (visited July 2004).

[57] The majority view in the Committee seems to rely on a reading of para. 5, according to which the 'Committee's initiative' refers to the action to be taken once the proceedings are initiated under para. 4 (self-triggering or party-to-party triggering). However, it should be noted that according to para. 3(a) the Committee, as part of its functions and mandate, may '[c]onsider any submission made in accordance with paragraph 4 below *or any other possible non-compliance by a Party with its obligations that the Committee decides to consider in accordance with paragraph 5*, with a view to securing a constructive solution' (emphasis added). Thus the Decision makes clear that para. 5 refers to the power of the Committee to put in motion the procedure *proprio motu*, without prior state request to this effect.

ance cases, enhancing, rather then curbing, the effectiveness of its action in facilitating and inducing compliance.

As far as 'informal' triggering is concerned, a first reason for the scarce practice may be the fact that NCMs are not yet operative in areas, such as climate change, where public opinion and public pressure are overwhelming. Apart from that, it could also be explained by a procedural deficiency in the interplay by MEAs' bodies and civil society. In two areas, improvements may be sought, without going as far as recognizing a full right for NGOs to trigger the mechanism.

First of all, the role of NGOs could be strengthened at a stage preceding the proper non-compliance proceedings, by recognizing and expanding their contribution in the process of review and evaluation of periodical reports on implementation and compliance prepared by states. The task of carrying out such review, in the first place, is often assigned to the Secretariat and in special cases other bodies such as the experts review teams under the Kyoto Protocol. NCMs normally afford these actors the right to initiate proceedings in relation to non-compliance issues they become aware of during such activity. In order to enhance civil society's role in compliance assessment, where NGOs are denied the right to trigger the NCM, they should at least be put in a position to express their comments on state reports in order to highlight possible cases of non-compliance.

In the second place, civil society could be recognized as a privileged source of information for other actors entitled to initiate proceedings, the Secretariat in particular. This could be obtained by including in the text establishing the NCM, a provision explicitly affording non-state actors the entitlement to submit information to the Secretariat. Such an option is currently under consideration for the PIC NCM, whose last draft provides, within square brackets, that the Secretariat may make a submission to the Committee 'when it receives submissions from individuals or organizations having reservations about a Party's compliance with its obligations under the Convention'.[58] An obligation for the Secretariat to give to the submitting NGO a written answer containing the reasons for its decision not to refer the issue to the Committee, were this to be the case, would further strengthen the mentioned provision.[59] An arrangement of this kind would sensibly point in the direction of the recognition of the role played by the Secretariat in the process of treaty management, from a mere administrative body to an active participant.[60]

Against this background, it is difficult to see a trend towards recognition of a right for NGOs to initiate non-compliance proceedings, except, perhaps, in the

---

[58] Draft PIC NCM (section 6 below), Annex, para. 11(c).

[59] This solution is suggested, although not included in the proposed text, in alternative to a provision tailored on the Aarhus precedent, in the proposed Water and Health NCM (section 6 below), p. 17. The non inclusion of this option in the draft text is due to its resource implications for the Secretariat.

[60] The transformation of the Secretariat's role is already a feature of NCMs, see Goote, n. 4 above, at p. 87.

European region. Where such a role is recognized or strongly envisaged, it can be justified by special features of the instrument to which it relates. The Alpine Convention, in contrast to any other instrument concerned, is composed of a small number of parties and NGOs have played a fundamental role throughout the Convention's life. As far as the Aarhus and the proposed Water and Health NCM are concerned, it cannot be ignored that non-compliance with the underlying substantive obligations is likely to affect private interests more directly than in other cases.

As a matter of policy, it is hard to ignore the impact that granting access to NGOs can have on the nature and on the overall cost of the mechanism. Those fears, however, can be balanced by accurate filters of NGO action either within the proceedings (admissibility provisions) or at a previous stage.

4.   NGOs IN FACT-FINDING AND ASSESSMENT PHASES

4.1   Existing practice

The fundamentally interstate nature of existing non-compliance procedures does not exclude NGOs from being involved in them, by putting at the Committee's disposal their expertise and knowledge. NGO contribution to fact-finding and assessment activities of the Committee, may have three distinct legal bases.

With some exceptions,[61] all NCMs contain a provision allowing the Committee to carry out on-site information-gathering activity, subject to invitation or consent of the relevant party/parties.[62] In this context, the Committee should have no limitation as far as sources of information are concerned. Such a possibility seems particularly relevant since local NGOs which can help the accomplishment of the Committee's task, especially in certain sectors such as water management or public participation, may lack knowledge and resources to participate in proceedings held abroad.

In the second place, recent NCMs enable the Committee to seek opinions from experts and advisers,[63] who will normally come from a non-state sector, including qualified environmental NGOs. More generally, almost all mechanisms endorse the idea that the Committee, in the normal course of the proceedings, should be able to seek and receive information additional to that provided by the actor submitting the issue and the concerned party.[64] In some mechanisms pos-

---

[61] Namely the Kyoto, FCCC and Cartagena NCMs (section 6 below).

[62] See Montreal NCM, para. 7(e); Basel NCM, para. 19(d); LRTAPT NCM, para. 6(b); Aarhus NCM, para. 25(b); Espoo NCM, para. 7(b) (section 6 below).

[63] See Basel NCM, para. 19(c) (but see n. 71 below and accompanying text); Kyoto NCM, section VIII, para. 5; Aarhus NCM, para. 25(d); Espoo NCM, para. 7(d) (former 6(e)) (section 6 below).

[64] The Kyoto NCM leaves to the plenary of the Compliance Committee the task of deciding on this delicate issue, see Kyoto NCM (section 6 below), Section III para. 2(d).

sible sources of information are not specifically listed.[65] In these cases, nothing seems to prevent consideration of information originating from non-governmental sources.[66] In the Espoo NCM, the phrase 'and consult other relevant sources' has been added to the existing provision allowing the Committee to seek the services of scientific experts and other technical advice as appropriate,[67] which had been in any case considered by the Committee as a sufficient legal basis to seek non-governmental information.[68] On the other hand, an exhaustive list of possible sources of information, which includes NGOs, is contained in the Kyoto NCM.[69] The text submitted for negotiation under the Protocol on Water and Health, on the other hand, mentions NGOs in a non-exhaustive list.[70]

Two exceptions may be noted to this trend of openness to NGOs as providers of information and expertise for the Committee. The first is represented by the Basel NCM. In this context, the ability of the Committee to consider 'further information from any source and draw upon outside expertise' seems to be severely reduced, since it is limited to information requested, thus not covering explicitly unsolicited information, and it can take place only 'either with the consent of the Party concerned or as directed by the Conference of the Parties'.[71] The second is the Cartagena NCM, where NGOs seem to be left with a very limited role. First, expert advice may be sought by the Committee only from experts included in the Biosafety roster established under the Protocol.[72] Secondly, after the deletion of

---

[65] An example of the first drafting technique is given by the Montreal NCM, according to which the functions of the Implementation Committee shall be, *inter alia*, '[t]o receive, consider and report on any information or observations forwarded by the Secretariat in connection with the preparation of the reports referred to in Article 12(c) of the Protocol and on any other information received and forwarded by the Secretariat concerning compliance with the provisions of the Protocol' and '[t]o request, where it considers necessary, through the Secretariat, further information on matters under its consideration' (see Montreal NCM (section 6 below), paras. 7(b) and 7(c)). The same approach as to sources of information is substantially followed by the mechanisms in place under the UNECE umbrella (see LRTAPT NCM, paras. 6(a) and 6(c); Aarhus NCM, paras. 25(a) and 25(c); Espoo NCM, paras. 7(a) and (c) (former 6(a) and 6(c)) and in the Draft PIC NCM, para. 19 (see section 6 below).

[66] See Ehrmann, n. 4 above, at p. 399. See also the informal document realised by the Aarhus Compliance Committee on 'The NGOs and the Compliance Committee' (hereinafter NGOs and the Aarhus Compliance Committee), para. 2, available at <www.unece.org/env/pp/compliance.htm> (visited July 2004), in which it is stressed that 'the Committee is not required to make any distinction between information submitted to it by individuals and States and information submitted by NGOs' under para. 25 of the Aarhus NCM.

[67] Compare Espoo NCM (section 6 below), para. 7(d) with para. 6(e) of Decision II/4, Review of Compliance, in Report of the Second Meeting of the Parties, Doc. ECE/MP.EIA/4, Annex IV, p. 75.

[68] See Espoo Committee, Third Report, n. 18 above, at para. 10, p. 3.

[69] See Kyoto NCM (section 6 below), Section VIII, paras. 3 and 4.

[70] See proposed Water and Health NCM (section 6 below), p. 20.

[71] See Basel NCM (section 6 below), para. 22(c).

[72] Cartagena NCM (section 6 below), Section V, para. 3. This qualification was included at a very late stage of negotiation during the First Meeting of the Parties (compare with the draft submitted to negotiation, Recommendation 3/2 of the Intergovernmental Committee for the Cartagena Protocol (hereinafter Cartagena NCM Draft), in Report of the Intergovernmental Committee for the Cartagena Protocol on Biosafety on the Work of its Third Meeting, Doc. UNEP/CBD/ICCP/3/10, Annex, p. 35.

an explicit reference to non-governmental organizations contained in the draft submitted to the parties for approval,[73] it is not clear whether the Committee will be able to draw any information from non-governmental sources.[74] As usually happens with controversial negotiating issues, it seems that lack of clarity reflects the impossibility to reach an agreement on the point, leaving to practice or subsequent adjustments the resolution of specific problems.[75]

A major drafting difference between the different mechanisms relates to the procedure by which such information can reach the Committee. In some mechanisms, in fact, information may be sought through the Secretariat and the information received is that forwarded by the Secretariat,[76] while in others the liaison role of the Secretariat is not mentioned.[77] Since it seems obvious that written communication between the Committee and external sources shall take place via the Secretariat, the latter being the only permanent body created by the relevant environmental treaties, the difference in drafting may reflect a different role for the Secretariat when unsolicited information is submitted. While in the latter case the Secretariat should have a mere administrative function, in the former it has an active role, filtering submitted information and forwarding only that deemed to be relevant.[78]

It is noteworthy that Committees enjoy a broad discretion in the consideration of information sought or received from NGOs. Thus, this information has a different status than that provided by the party whose compliance is at issue. The latter, as a matter of procedural fairness, has the right to have its own information fully considered by the Committee.[79]

An additional question relates to the subjective qualifications that may be required to submit unsolicited information and possible procedures to process it. Under the Kyoto NCM, information can originate from 'competent' NGOs.[80] The same requirement was mentioned in a previous draft of the Basel Conven-

---

[73] Ibid., Section V, para. 2.

[74] Section V(2) of the Cartagena NCM (section 6 below), provides that: 'The Committee may seek or receive and consider relevant information from sources, such as: (a) The Biosafety Clearing-House, the Conference of the Parties to the Convention, the Conference of the Parties serving as the meeting of the Parties to the Protocol, and subsidiary bodies of the Convention on Biological Diversity and the Protocol; (b) Relevant international organizations'. Therefore it is not clear whether the list is deemed to be exhaustive nor if 'international organizations' are those of intergovernmental character.

[75] It is noteworthy that the last provision of the Cartagena NCM is devoted to setting out explicitly the role of the Conference of the Parties in updating and modifying the mechanisms according to the needs evidenced in practice.

[76] See Montreal NCM , paras. 7(b) and 7(c); LRTAPT NCM , paras. 6(a) and 6(c); Espoo NCM , paras. 7(a) and 7(c); and Draft PIC NCM, para. 19 (section 6 below).

[77] See Aarhus NCM, para. 25; Kyoto NCM, Section VIII (section 6 below).

[78] See Handl, n. 4 above, at p. 43.

[79] This difference is well expressed in the Cartagena NCM, whose section V provides that the Committee 'shall consider' information from the Party concerned (para. 1), and 'may seek or receive' those from other sources (para. 2(b)).

[80] See Kyoto NCM (section 6 below), Section VIII, para. 4.

tion,[81] while during the negotiations of the Cartagena NCM the proposal to limit standing to 'directly involved' NGOs was made.[82] Regardless of the existence in the texts of adjectives qualifying NGOs to submit information, the issue of 'legitimacy' of the submitting NGO is likely to be common.[83] Although a case-by-case approach is possible, guidelines for submission could be useful to simplify the Committee's task and enhance the transparency of the process of selection. The drafting of such rules is indicated in the Kyoto NCM among the tasks to be accomplished by the plenary of the Committee.[84]

4.2 Evaluation

The role of NGOs in providing relevant information to the Committee seems to be less controversial than the issues treated above, it being accepted that the effectiveness of the whole compliance mechanisms largely depends on the ability of the relevant bodies to evaluate critically self-reported information provided by states under their reporting requirements.[85] Despite the different drafting solutions adopted under various mechanisms, almost all of them leave to the Committee's discretion the consideration of information coming from NGOs.

Paradoxically, some recent solutions and proposals seem to make a step backward in this field, by including explicit provisions to limit the Committee's ability to refer to external sources of information to assess compliance. Such an attempt could prove dangerous for the effectiveness of an NCM. As rightly pointed out by the European Union in its views relating to the proposed Cartagena NCM, it is difficult to understand 'how the Committee could accomplish its task if it were to disregard available compliance related information, and why ... NGOs should be prevented from transmitting such information. This would clearly put in question the very reason for the existence of the Committee'.[86]

---

[81] See Monitoring the Implementation of and Compliance with the Obligations set out by the Basel Convention, Doc. UNEP/CHW.6/9, Annex (2002), para. 20(c), p. 8.

[82] See the position of the United States in Compilation of Views on Compliance Procedures and Mechanisms under the Cartagena Protocol on Biosafety, Doc. UNEP/CBD/ICCP/3/INF/3, p. 17.

[83] See Beyerlin, n. 1 above, at p. 377.

[84] Kyoto NCM (section 6 below), Section III para. 2(d)

[85] See Bothe, n. 53 above, at p. 296; Beyerlin, n. 1 above, at p. 376. See also the Aarhus Committee, Third Report, n. 26 above, at paras. 23–26, especially para. 24 where it is observed, *inter alia*, that '[t]he Committee should adopt an approach to information gathering that is pragmatic and cost-effective, in order to ensure smooth operation of its activities .... Among other things, a pragmatic approach would mean that the Committee should aim to avoid being overloaded by too much information, and only seek additional information if necessary for the consideration of a specific matter .... This approach to information gathering also reflects the fact that the Committee should take into account all information available to it and not just the information brought to it by the parties in a specific case. If the Committee is not satisfied that it has a comprehensive, sufficiently balanced and accurate picture of the facts and the situation in a Party, it may be necessary to undertake further investigations and information gathering'.

[86] See Cartagena NCM, Compilation of Views, n. 34 above, at p. 10. A similar view is expressed emerges from the document on NGOs and the Aarhus Compliance Committee, n. 66 above, para. 3,

5.   OVERCOMING STATES' RESISTANCE: A PROSPECT FOR THE FUTURE?

There is no doubt that NGOs' involvement in NCMs can prove decisive in enhancing effectiveness and, to a certain extent, legitimacy in the joint action to ensure compliance under MEAs. In particular, NGO participation may contribute to the objectivity and impartiality of the process, avoiding selective approaches to compliance, such as targeting 'weak' states or tackling only 'politically acceptable' issues.

However, several questions and doubts are raised by extensive participation of NGOs. As expressed in different contexts throughout this chapter, the main fear is that, were NGO involvement based on rights recognized to them, it could undermine the non-confrontational and cooperative nature of the mechanisms, thus diminishing the trust states parties have in its usefulness.

Although this argument may have some basis, the possible adverse effect of NGO participation in NCMs seems be to some extent over-estimated. A positive contribution in limiting possible excesses can be provided by NGOs' self-restraint. It is not hard to imagine that NGOs, in a sort of trade-off with full participatory rights, could be willing to adapt their attitude and behaviour in pursuance of the general and common interest in enhancing compliance with the various agreements. An example of such an attitude can be found in the statement of an NGO representative at the 1st Meeting of the Compliance Committee of the Aarhus Convention, who gave assurance that 'NGOs would have an important role to play in ... helping ensure that [the Committee] would not be flooded with communications through coordinating their efforts'.[87] Besides that, procedural safeguards can be implemented to preserve the nature of the mechanism and its effectiveness. Existing NCMs provide a wide range of possible drafting examples of how to allow and enhance NGO participation without endangering the mechanism.

Notwithstanding this, at the present stage it is hard to recognize NGOs as major actors in NCMs, both on the basis of the legal text and of actual practice of existing Committees. Recent practice is somehow contradictory. On the one hand, recent mechanisms negotiated under global instruments, such as the Basel NCM and the Cartagena NCM, show the increasing diffidence of states, especially developing ones, towards the involvement of NGOs in this peculiar kind of procedures. On the other hand, in the European region, the application in international forums of the public participation principles of the Aarhus Convention may be a positive factor in enhancing recognition of participatory rights of NGOs. As far as existing NCMs are concerned, the mechanism provided for under that Convention and the Alpine Convention are two examples of how NGO participation

---

where it is recognized that 'the task of the Committee will be very difficult without the input and the knowledge of the NGO community'.

[87] Statement by Mr Yves Lador (Earth Justice), Report of the First Meeting of the Compliance Committee, Doc. MP.PP/C.1/2003/2, p. 5.

can be formally recognized. Although it might be difficult to consider them as precedents, for the reasons indicated above, some elements in the same direction come from the attempts to enhance public participation in the Espoo NCM and to promote it fully under the proposed Water and Health NCM. Whether these attempts will overcome state resistance remains to be seen.

6.   ANNEX: LIST OF RELEVANT INSTRUMENTS AND DOCUMENTS

Mechanisms already established: at the global level:

- 1987 Montreal Protocol on Substances that Deplete the Ozone Layer to the 1985 Vienna Convention on the Protection of the Ozone Layer (1987) 26 ILM 1529 and 1550 ('Montreal Protocol'), through Meeting of the Parties Decision IV/5 in 1992 (*Report of the Fourth Meeting of the Parties*, Doc. UNEP/OzL.Pro.4/15, Annex IV (1992), p. 44), subsequently amended by Decision X/10 in 1998, *Report of the Tenth Meeting of the Parties*, Doc. UNEP/OzL.Pro.10/9 (1998), Annex II, p. 23 ('Montreal NCM').
- 1989 Basel Convention on the Transboundary Movement of Hazardous Wastes and Their Disposal (1989) 28 ILM 649 ('Basel Convention'); following the decision taken at the 6th Conference of the Parties, see *Mechanism for Promoting Implementation and Compliance: Revised Text of the Annex in Doc. UNEP/CHW.6/9 Proposed by the Working Group on a Compliance Mechanism*, Doc. UNEP/CHW.6/CRP.12 (2001) ('Basel NCM').
- 1997 Kyoto Protocol to the 1992 Framework Convention on Climate Change (1998) 37 ILM 22 ('Kyoto Protocol'); the mechanism was established by the 2nd Conference of the Parties of the FCCC in 2001, see *Report of the Conference of the Parties at their Seventh Session*, Doc. FCCC/CP/2001/13/Add.3 (2001), Annex, p. 64 ('Kyoto NCM'), but is not operational pending the entry into force of the Kyoto Protocol.
- 2000 Cartagena Protocol on Biosafety to the Convention on Biological Diversity, (2000) 39 ILM 1027 ('Cartagena Protocol'); through Decision BS-I/7 (*Establishment of Procedures and Mechanisms on Compliance under the Cartagena Protocol on Biosafety*) taken at the 1st Meeting of the Parties, see *Report of First Meeting of the Conference of the Parties of the Convention Serving as the Meeting of the Parties to the Protocol*, Doc. UNEP/CBD/BS/COP-MOP/1/15 (2004), p. 98 ('Cartagena NCM').

At the regional level:

- 1979 Long-Range Transboundary Air Pollution Treaty (1979) 18 ILM 1442 ('LRTAPT'), through Executive Body's Decision 1997/2, see *Report of the Fifteenth Session of the Executive Body*, Doc. ECE/EB.AIR/53 (1997), Annex III, p. 28 ('LRTAP NCM').

- 1991 Espoo Convention on Environmental Impact Assessment in a Transboundary Context (1991) 30 ILM 802 ('Espoo Convention'), through Meeting of the Parties Decision II/4 (*Review of Compliance*) in 2001, see *Report of the Second Meeting of the Parties*, Doc. ECE/MP.EIA/4, Annex IV, p. 72). A decision amending and replacing Decision II/4, with a view, *inter alia*, to extending the mechanism to the newly adopted Protocol on Strategic Environmental Assessment, was approved at the 3rd Meeting of the Parties, see Decision III/2 (*Review of Compliance*), Doc. MP.EIA/2004/3 (2004), Annex ('Espoo NCM').

- 1998 Convention on Access to Information, Public Participation in Decision-making and Access to Justice in Environmental Matters (1999) 38 ILM 517 ('Aarhus Convention'), through Decision I/7 (*Review of Compliance*) in 2002, see *Meeting of the Parties to the Convention on Access to Information, Public Participation in Decision-making and Access to Justice in Environmental Matters, Report of the First Meeting of the Parties*, Addendum 8, Doc. ECE/MP.PP/2/Add.8 (2004) ('Aarhus NCM').

- 1991 Convention on the Protection of the Alps, BU 991:883 ('Alpine Convention'). (Since English is not one of the official languages of the Convention reference should be made to the official texts available at the official site <www.convenzionedellealpi.org>. An unofficial English translation may be found in Treves, Pineschi and Fodella (eds.), *International Law and Protection of Mountain Areas*, Milan, (2002), p. 185). Decision VII/4 of the Seventh Alpine Conference in 2002 ('Alpine NCM'); the mechanism applies to the Convention and to its Protocols.

Under the following instruments NCMs are under negotiation: at the global level:

- 1992 Framework Convention on Climate Change (1992) 31 ILM 1330 ('FCCC'); the 4th Conference of the Parties adopted in 1998 Decision 10/CP4, containing an approved text, prepared by an ad hoc group, for a consultative process envisaged in Article 13 FCCC, reserving final approval and the establishment of the Committee to a successive decision ('Draft FCCC NCM').

- 1994 United Nations Convention to Combat Desertification in Countries Experiencing Serious Drought and/or Desertification, Particularly in Africa (1994) 333 ILM 1328 ('Desertification Convention'); under this instrument an open-ended working group has been established to deal with implementation issues, which are included in the agenda for the 6th Conference of the Parties, to be held in Summer 2005. The Secretariat has prepared several notes, presented to the parties at their meetings, on the issue (see the latest version *Consideration of Procedures and Institutional Mechanisms for the Resolution of Questions on Implementation, in accordance with Article 27 of the Convention, with a view to Deciding how to Take this Matter Forward*, Doc. ICCD/COP(6)/7 (2003)).

- 1998 Rotterdam Convention on the Prior Informed Consent Procedure for Certain Hazardous Chemicals and Pesticides in International Trade (not yet in force), (1999) 38 ILM 1 ('PIC Convention'); an open-ended Working Group on Compliance was established by the Intergovernmental Negotiating Committee at its 9th Session; the latest version of a draft mechanism is contained in Draft of Procedure and Institutional Mechanism for Handling Cases of Non-compliance, by the Chair of the Working Group on Compliance, Doc. UNEP/FAO/PIC/INC.10/20, Annex (2003) ('Draft PIC NCM').
- 2001 Stockholm Convention on Persistent Organic Pollutants (2001) 40 ILM 532 ('POPs Convention'); the negotiation of the NCM under the latter instrument is at a very early stage, being limited to a background paper on existing compliance mechanism prepared by the Secretariat and comments thereon by states.

At the regional level:

- 1999 Protocol on Water and Health to the 1992 Helsinki Convention on the Protection and Use of Transboundary Watercourses and International Lakes (not yet in force), available at <www.unece.org/env/documents/2000/wat/mp.wat.2000.1.e.pdf> ('Protocol on Water and Health'). On the basis of the mandate of the Parties to the 1992 Helsinki Convention, the Working Group on Water and Health has the task of undertaking, assisted by the Working Group of Legal and Administrative Aspects, the arrangements envisaged in Article 15, taking into consideration the work of the Group of Experts set up by the Parties to the Convention. A background paper and a draft decision prepared by a consultant have been submitted to the 1st Meeting of the Legal Board of the Convention for consideration, with a view to a final decision at the 1st Meeting of the Parties (*Establishing a Compliance Review Mechanism under the 1999 Protocol on Water and Health*, Doc. MP.WAT/AC.4/2004/4) ('proposed Water and Health NCM').

All of the regional instrument listed above, except the Alpine Convention, have been concluded in the context of the United Nation Economic Commission for Europe (UNECE).

Part IV

NGOs and Inter-State and European Disputes

Chapter 16

Non-Governmental Organizations and the International Court of Justice

Eduardo Valencia-Ospina

1. THE STATUTE AND RULES: NO ROLE FOR NGOS

When approaching this subject from the strict perspective of traditional concepts of international law, as they are reflected in the governing instruments of the International Court of Justice (ICJ), a rapid reading of the relevant provisions of the Statute and the Rules of Court would lead to the conclusion that no role is envisaged for non-governmental organizations (NGOs) in the system of the ICJ.

However, some measure of elaboration is required to place such a conclusion in its proper perspective.[1] It is well known that the Charter of the United Nations (UN) has endowed the International Court of Justice with both a contentious and an advisory jurisdiction. As to its contentious jurisdiction, pursuant to Article 34(1) of its Statute, 'Only States may be parties in cases before the Court'.

The same article envisages a very specific role to be played by public international organizations when it provides, in paragraph 2 that:

> The Court, subject to and in conformity with its Rules, may request of public international organizations information relevant to cases before it, and shall receive such information presented by such organizations on their own initiative.

The corresponding provision, Article 69, in the Rules of Court, defines in its paragraph 4 the term 'public international organization' as 'an international organization of States', in other words, an 'inter-governmental Organization'.

According to Article 34(3) of the Statute:

> Whenever the construction of the constituent instrument of a public international organization or of an international convention adopted thereunder is in question in a case

---

[1] L. Boisson de Chazournes, 'Advisory Opinions and the Furtherance of the Common Interest of Mankind' in L. Boisson de Chazournes, C. Romano, R. Mackenzie (eds.), *International Organizations and International Dispute Settlement* (Ardsley on Hudson, 2002), pp. 115–118. See also C. Chinkin and R. Mackenzie, 'Inter-governmental Organizations as "Friends of the Court"' in ibid., pp. 139–145.

T. Treves et al., eds., Civil Society, International Courts and Compliance Bodies
© 2005, T·M·C·ASSER PRESS, The Hague, The Netherlands, and the Authors

before the Court, the Registrar shall so notify the public international organization concerned and shall communicate to it copies of all the written proceedings.

Under Article 69(3) of its Rules, the ICJ, or its President if the Court is not sitting, may fix a time limit within which the public international organization concerned:

> may submit to the Court its observations in writing. These observations shall be communicated to the parties and may be discussed by them and by the representative of the said organization during the oral proceedings.

The provisions referred to above make it clear that NGOs not only cannot be parties in contentious cases before the ICJ but can neither submit observations or furnish information directly to the Court in connection with those cases.

The ICJ has so held since very early in its life. In the *Asylum* case, the International League for the Rights of Man, an NGO in consultative status B with the Economic and Social Council of the UN, informed the ICJ's Registrar that:

> The League desires to take advantage of the provisions of Article 34 of the Statute of the Court, providing that the Court shall receive information presented to it by international organizations on their own initiative relevant to cases before the Court. In order to determine whether the League should present such information, [we] herewith request that the Court determine whether the League is a public international organization within the meaning of Article 34.[2]

The ICJ's decision, transmitted by the Registrar, was to the effect that Article 34 was not applicable since the League could not be characterized as a public international organization as envisaged by the Statute.[3]

No record appears to exist of subsequent attempts by NGOs to submit information to the ICJ in contentious proceedings.

2.   AN INDIRECT ROLE

In the light of the foregoing, it is clear that whatever role NGOs may play in relation to the ICJ's contentious jurisdiction can only be an indirect one. They might exert influence on a state to initiate proceedings against another state, or on international intergovernmental organizations, in particular those which have granted those NGOs a consultative or observer status, when submitting observations under Article 69(3) or furnishing information under Article 69(1) or (2), respectively.

That such an influence has been exerted is generally known. It was recently alluded to, in no uncertain terms, in a dispatch published in a daily journal, cover-

---

[2] ICJ, Pleadings, *Asylum*, vol. II, p. 227.
[3] Ibid., p. 228.

ing the ICJ's decision on the request for provisional measures in the case brought by the Republic of the Congo against France concerning *Certain Criminal Proceedings in France*. Commenting on a statement made after the reading of the ICJ's order by a representative of the Fédération Internationale des Ligues des Droits de l'Homme (FIDH), which the journal characterized as being 'à l'origine des poursuites engagées en France', the newspaper article asserted:

> Rien ne permet d'anticiper un jugement sur le fond favorable aux organisations non gouvernementales, mais ces dernières n'en ont pas moins salué comme 'symbolique' la décision.[4]

There remains to consider the role of NGOs in the context of the ICJ's advisory jurisdiction. Under Article 65(1) of the Statute:

> The Court may give an advisory opinion on any legal question at the request of whatever body may be authorized by or in accordance with the Charter of the United Nations to make such a request.

The use in this provision of the term 'body' instead of 'public international organization', 'international organization' or 'organ' thereof, as is done elsewhere in the relevant provisions of the UN Charter and the Statute is, obviously, due to reasons of style. It cannot create the impression that entities other than intergovernmental organizations were intended to be entitled to request advisory opinions of the ICJ. As expressly provided for in Article 65, any such 'body' can only be one of those authorized by or in accordance with the UN Charter. Pursuant to Article 96 of the Charter, requests for an advisory opinion of the Court can only be made by the General Assembly and the Security Council and such other organs of the UN and specialized agencies as may at any time have been so authorized by the General Assembly.

Article 66 of the Statute envisages the submission by states of written and/or oral statements relating to the question on which an opinion is asked. In addition, under Article 65(2) of the Statute, the organization or organ submitting the 'written request containing an exact statement of the question upon which an opinion is required' must accompany it 'by all documents likely to throw light upon the question'.

Furthermore, in accordance with Article 66(2) of the Statute, the ICJ Registrar must notify not only states entitled to appear before the Court but also any 'international organization considered by the Court, or, should it be not sitting, by the President, as likely to be able to furnish information on the question', that the Court will be prepared to receive in writing or hear statements relating to that question. It is to be noted that in Article 66(2), the Statute does not mention the term 'public international organization' but uses, rather, the expression 'interna-

---

[4] 'La Cour internationale de justice ne gèle pas l'instruction française sur les disparus au Congo', *Le Monde*, 18 June 2003.

tional organization'. In Article 66(4), allowing for comments to be made on written and/or oral statements presented by others, the Statute does away altogether with the adjective 'international', referring simply to 'organizations'. However, the corresponding Article 108 of the Rules reverts to the use of the term 'public international organization'.

It is debatable whether the use of different terminology in Articles 34 and 66 of the Statute was intended to draw a distinction between a role to be allowed to NGOs in advisory proceedings as opposed to no role at all in contentious proceedings. The practice of the ICJ on the point has not made matters any clearer.

3. THE PRACTICE OF THE ICJ

Early in its life, the ICJ included in its Advisory Opinion of 11 July 1950 on the International Status of South-West Africa the following passage:

> On March 7, 1950, the Board of Directors of the International League of the Rights of Man sent a communication to the Court asking permission to submit written and oral statements on the question. On March 16, the Court decided that it would receive from this organization a written statement to be filed before April 10 and confined to the legal questions which had been submitted to the Court. On the same day, the League was notified accordingly, but it did not send any communication within the time-limit prescribed.[5]

It is noteworthy that, in agreeing for the first and only time to the request made by an international non-governmental organization, the ICJ interpreted the relevant provision of the Statute in the sense that it was not required to have determined in advance which international organizations should be notified by the Registrar, on account of having been considered by the ICJ, or even its President, as 'likely to be able to furnish information on the question'.

The opening made in 1950 towards NGOs, unfortunately not taken advantage of at the time, has not been reiterated in the ICJ's subsequent practice. Among instances made public, reference has been made to one of the Advisory Opinions on the Review of the United Nations Administrative Tribunal (UNAT) Judgments, where the Court did not authorize the Federation of International Civil Servant's Associations (FICSA), to present its views.[6] Also, in the Namibia advisory proceedings, a statement by the American Committee on Africa (connected with the International League for the Rights of Man) was refused by the Registrar due to the fact that the Committee had not been included in the list of organiza-

---

[5] (1950) ICJ Reports 130.

[6] S. Rosenne, *The Law and Practice of the International Court*, vol. III (The Hague, 1997) p. 1731.

tions to which the communication provided for under Article 66(2) of the Statute was addressed.[7]

In response to an article published in an international newspaper to the effect that the Federation of American Scientists had submitted to the ICJ an *amicus curiae* brief in connection with the two requests for advisory opinions on the legality of nuclear weapons emanating, respectively, from the World Health Organization and the UN General Assembly, the Registrar wrote to the Editor in the following terms:

> I would point out that, contrary to the impression that may have been given ... the *amicus* brief has been received by the Court but has not been admitted as part of the record in those cases. It is, however, available to Members of the Court in their Library.
>
> The Court has received numerous documents, petitions and representations from non-governmental organizations, professional associations and other bodies that, while they have no formal standing in the proceedings before it, wish to communicate their views on the subject matter of these important cases.
>
> The Court would like to make it clear that all such documents are given consistent treatment and that the Federation of American Scientists has not been accorded more favorable consideration than any other body.[8]

In the Advisory Opinion on the Legality of the Threat or Use of Nuclear Weapons, Judge Weeramantry indicated in the Introduction to his dissenting opinion that:

> A multitude of organizations, including several NGOs, have also sent communications to the Court and submitted materials to it; and nearly two million signatures have been actually received by the Court from various organizations and individuals from around 25 countries. In addition, there have been other shipments of signatures so voluminous that the Court could not physically receive them and they have been lodged in other depositories. If these are also taken into account, the total number of signatures has been estimated by the Court's Archivist at over three million.[9]

The Registrar received in person many of the cartons containing those signatures, from the representatives of an NGO, the World Court Project, the most active supporter of bringing the issue to the ICJ by means of a request for an advisory opinion. Those documents were placed in the Library of the Court but none was formally regarded as an *amicus curiae* brief and no reference to any of them was made by the ICJ in the opinions themselves.

As matters still stand, the NGOs' role in the context of advisory opinions can only be an indirect one, by exerting influence through their member states on the

---

[7] ICJ, Pleadings, *Legal Consequences for States of the Continued Presence of South Africa in Namibia (South West Africa) notwithstanding Security Council Resolution 276 (1970)*, vol. II, p. 649.

[8] Letters to the Editor, *International Herald Tribune* (The Hague), 15 November 1995.

[9] (1996) ICJ Reports 438.

bodies authorized to request such opinions and express views thereon. That such an influence has also been exerted in the case of requests for advisory opinions is well known and has been recognized by the foremost authority on the Court:

> In 1994, the General Assembly, responding above all to pressure from Non-Governmental Organizations, requested an advisory opinion of the ICJ on the question: is the threat or use of nuclear weapons in any circumstances permitted under international law?[10]

In his separate opinion in the same Advisory Opinion, Judge Guillaume wrote as follows:

> The opinion requested by the General Assembly of the United Nations (like indeed the one requested by the World Health Assembly) originated in a campaign conducted by an association called International Association of Lawyers against Nuclear Arms (IALANA), which in conjunction with various other groups launched in 1992 a project entitled 'World Court Project' in order to obtain from the Court a proclamation of the illegality of the threat or use of nuclear weapons. These associations worked very intensively to secure the adoption of the resolutions referring the question to the Court and to induce States hostile to nuclear weapons to appear before the Court. Indeed, the Court and the judges received thousands of letters inspired by these groups, appealing both to the Members' conscience and the public conscience.
> I am sure that the pressure brought to bear in this way did not influence the Court's deliberations, but I wondered whether, in such circumstances, the requests for opinions could still be regarded as coming from the Assemblies which had adopted them or whether, piercing the veil, the Court should not have dismissed them as inadmissible. However, I dare to hope that Governments and inter-governmental institutions still retain sufficient independence of decision to resist the powerful pressure groups which besiege them today with the support of the mass media.[11]

In the absence of other such express pronouncements, one way or the other, it is not possible to conclude whether Judge Guillaume's view reflects the prevailing attitude among Members of the ICJ. In any event, in the light of the foregoing discussion, it would appear that, its current position notwithstanding, the Court has not completely closed the window it opened in 1950.

---

[10] S. Rosenne, 'The Perplexities of Modern International Law' (2001) 291 *RdC* 159.
[11] (1996) ICJ Reports 287.

Chapter 17

NGOs and Law of the Sea Disputes

Philippe Gautier

1. INTRODUCTION

This chapter deals with the role of non-governmental organizations (NGOs) in law of the sea disputes. In addressing this subject matter, I intend to focus on the question of participation of NGOs and other non-state entities in proceedings before the International Tribunal for the Law of the Sea (ITLOS).

As an introduction, it may be useful to comment briefly on the role of NGOs in law of the sea matters:

- There is no doubt that NGOs, although normally set up as entities under municipal law, play an important role in international relations. This is not new and it may be recalled that certain NGOs or 'learned societies' such as the Institute of International Law or the Interparliamentary Union[1] were instrumental in the nineteenth century in the move towards the establishmen of a permanent court for the settlement of international disputes.[2]
- When mention is made of NGOs in the context of international law, we usually refer to NGOs which are active in the fields of environment or human rights. But the notion of 'NGOs', legally speaking, is not limited to entities protecting those interests. It includes entities representing a wider spectrum of interests as this may be seen from the list of NGOs admitted to participate in the work of international institutions. As an illustration, we may take the example of Article 11 of the Convention for the Protection of the Marine Environment of the North-East Atlantic (the 'OSPAR Convention') of 22 September 1992, which states that 'any international governmental or any non-governmental organization the activities of which are related to the Convention' may be admitted as observer by unanimous vote of the contracting parties. According to information available on the website of the organiza-

---

[1] It should be noted that the legal status of the Interparliamentary Union is a disputed issue frequently addressed in legal writings; see, e.g., H. Schermers and N. Blokker, *International Institutional Law* (3rd edn., Martinus Nijhoff, The Hague, 1995), p. 24; J. Klabbers, *An Introduction to International Institutional Law* (Cambridge University Press, Cambridge, 2002), p. 178.

[2] See J. Scott, *The Hague Court Reports* (Oxford University Press, New York, 1916), pp. xi–xii.

T. Treves et al., eds., *Civil Society, International Courts and Compliance Bodies*
© 2005, T·M·C·ASSER PRESS, *The Hague, The Netherlands, and the Authors*

tion,[3] 28 NGOs have been granted observer status. On this basis, we may note that not only environmental NGOs such as Greenpeace, Friends of the Earth, WWF are represented, but also associations representing the interests of dredging, detergent, oil, gas and nuclear industries. In the case of the International Seabed Authority ('the Authority'), NGOs which have demonstrated their interest in matters under consideration by the Authority may be granted observer status. This applies to Greenpeace International, the International Association of Drilling Contractors, the International Ocean Institute and the Law of the Sea Institute. NGOs may also be admitted to participate as observers in the meetings of states parties to the 1982 United Nations Convention on the Law of the Sea. In 2003, representatives of WWF International and of the Center for Seafarers' Rights (from the Seamen's Church Institute) attended the 13th Meeting of States Parties. On this occasion, the representative of the Center for Seafarers' Rights delivered a statement in which he drew the attention of the delegates to the need to ensure the protection of seafarers in light, *inter alia*, of the increased number of acts of piracy and armed robbery.[4]

- Legal issues involving questions of international law are not exclusively dealt with by international tribunals. On the contrary, they are often dealt with by municipal courts. In such cases, NGOs will try to intervene at the municipal level whenever a *locus standi* is granted to them. An example of such action is the legal action brought by Greenpeace in the United Kingdom before the High Court of Justice in 1999. The case concerned the failure of the Secretary for Trade and Industry to consider the provisions of the European Directive 92/43/EEC on the Conservation of Natural Habitats and of Wild Fauna and Flora in the process of granting licences for the exploitation of oil and gas with respect to areas beyond the territorial sea.[5]

- The 1982 United Nations Convention for the Law of the Sea (UNCLOS) devotes considerable attention to non-state entities (a category to which NGOs certainly belong): mining activities of private entities in 'the Area' (i.e., 'the seabed and ocean floor and subsoil thereof, beyond the limits of national jurisdiction'[6]) are directly regulated by the Authority, and some non-state entities even have the possibility to ratify or accede to the Convention. Accordingly,

---

[3] See <www.ospar.org>.

[4] The representative proposed to place on the agenda of the next Meeting of States Parties the protection of seafarers and a review of how states parties implemented the relevant provisions of UNCLOS. While some delegations shared the concerns expressed, one delegation opposed the inclusion of this issue on the agenda (see the report of the 13th Meeting of States Parties, SPLOS/103, 25 June 2003, para. 108).

[5] High Court of Justice, Queen's Bench Division, *R v Secretary for Trade and Industry, ex parte Greenpeace Ltd*, 5 November 1999, [2002] 120 ILR 617; for a commentary, see P. Klein, 'L'action des organisations non gouvernementales pour la protection de l'environnement marin dans la zone économique exclusive: le cas de Greenpeace' in E. Franckx and P. Gautier (eds.), *The Exclusive Economic Zone and the United Nations Convention on the Law of the Sea, 1982-2000: A Preliminary Assessment of State Practice* (Bruylant, Bruxelles, 2003), pp. 133–141.

[6] Article 1(1) of UNCLOS.

this chapter will address issues relating not only to NGOs but more generally to non-state entities.

2. NON-STATE ENTITIES, UNCLOS AND THE RULES OF THE TRIBUNAL

The 1982 Convention on the Law of the Sea reveals interesting features regarding non-state entities. It contains provisions enabling non-state entities such as international organizations or self-governing associated states[7] to become parties to it. It also devotes considerable attention to the activities of non-state entities in the exploration and exploitation of the deep seabed mining area. Of course, non-state entities engaged in mining activities are mainly private companies or consortia which have few characteristics in common with NGOs defending public interests. Nevertheless, the fact that UNCLOS had to adapt its provisions in order to meet the specific situation of non-state entities had consequences on the legal regime put into place, including the provisions dealing with the settlement of disputes.

Article 187 of UNCLOS expressly recognizes that in disputes relating to the exploitation or exploration of 'the Area', the Seabed Disputes Chamber of ITLOS is competent to deal with cases involving not only states or the Authority but also public and private companies and individuals. This is echoed by Article 20 of the Statute of the Tribunal (Annex VI to UNCLOS) which states that ITLOS is open not only to states parties but also 'to entities other than States Parties in any case expressly provided for in Part XI'. This is well known but the provision goes on to say that ITLOS is also open to entities other than states parties 'in any case submitted pursuant to any other agreement conferring jurisdiction on the Tribunal which is accepted by all parties to that case'. The wording is here broader than the expression to be found in Article 288(2) of UNCLOS (applicable to all courts and tribunals to which a dispute would be submitted under Part XV of the Convention) which refers to 'any dispute concerning the interpretation or application of an *international* agreement *related to the purposes of this convention*'.[8] It is worth noting that legal writings have addressed the question as to whether a non-state entity could be entitled to appear before ITLOS, e.g., by virtue of an agreement concluded with a state or an international organization, on the basis of the reference made in Article 20 of the Statute to an 'agreement' and not to 'an international agreement'.[9]

---

[7] See Article 305 of UNCLOS.

[8] Emphasis added.

[9] See P. Chandresakhara Rao who, commenting on Article 20 of the Statute, states: 'The agreement conferring jurisdiction may be one concluded either before or after the submission of a case; it may open the Tribunal to a case in which all the parties are entities other than States Parties or some of which are States Parties and other entities which are not States Parties' in 'ITLOS: The First Six Years' (2002) *Max Planck YB UN L.* 209; R. Wolfrum, 'The Legislative History of Articles 20 and 21 of the Statute of the International Tribunal for the Law of the Sea' (1999) 63 *Rabels Zeitschrift für ausländisches und internationals Privatrecht* 345; T. Treves, 'Private Maritime Litigation and

That said, even if the interpretation based on the provision contained in Article 288 should prevail, access to ITLOS could still be open to non-state entities possessing an international legal personality. Indeed, there is no *a priori* reason to deny NGOs any international legal personality. A determination as to whether an entity possesses international personality, as the International Court of Justice stated in its 1949 Advisory Opinion in the *Reparation* case,[10] will depend upon the needs of the international community. In this respect, reference may be made to the observer status conferred on the International Union for the Conservation of Nature and Natural Resources (IUCN), the International Committee of the Red Cross and the International Federation of Red Cross and Red Crescent Societies, in the United Nations General Assembly. Such status, as well as the performing of functions at international level and the conclusion of international agreements by the entity concerned, may constitute evidence of an international legal personality.[11]

Besides contentious cases, requests for advisory opinions may also be submitted to ITLOS. UNCLOS only provides in express terms for the submission of such request to the Seabed Disputes Chamber by an intergovernmental organization, the International Seabed Authority. Nevertheless, Article 138 of the Rules of the Tribunal has added the possibility of requesting the Tribunal to give an advisory opinion 'on a legal question if an international agreement related to the purposes of the Convention specifically provides for the submission to the Tribunal of a request for such opinion'. This provision is based on Article 21 of the Statute which states that the jurisdiction of ITLOS comprises 'all matters specifically provided for in any other agreement which confers jurisdiction on the Tribunal'. However, the Tribunal took here a cautious approach by limiting the possibility of requesting advisory opinions pursuant to Article 138 to the parties to an international agreement related to the purposes of UNCLOS, a wording closer to Article 288 of the Convention than to Articles 20 or 21 of its Statute.

The fact that non-state entities may appear before ITLOS is reflected in several provisions contained in the Statute and the Rules of the Tribunal. It is therefore useful to examine these provisions to see to what extent they provide for the participation of non-state entities in cases submitted to ITLOS. Given the specific character of issues relating to mining activities in 'the Area', participation of non-state entities in proceedings before the Seabed Disputes Chamber will not be con-

---

the International Tribunal for the Law of the Sea' (1999) 63 *Rabels Zeitschrift für ausländisches und internationals Privatrecht* 352; A. Boyle, 'Dispute Settlement and the Law of the Sea Convention: Problems of Fragmentation and Jurisdiction' (1997) 46 *Int'l & Comp. L. Q.* 49; J. Noyes, 'The International Tribunal for the Law of the Sea' (1998) 32 *Cornell Int'l L. J.* 132.

[10] [1949] ICJ Reports 174.

[11] See, e.g., P. Reuter, 'La personnalité juridique internationale du Comité international de la Croix-Rouge' in *Mélanges Pictet* (Geneva/The Hague, 1984), p. 783 *et seq.*; C. Dominicé, 'La personnalité juridique internationale du C.I.C.R.' in *Mélanges Pictet* (Geneva/The Hague, 1984), p. 673 *et seq*; P. Gautier, 'O.N.G. et personnalité internationale: à propos de l'accord conclu le 29 novembre 1996 entre la Suisse et la Fédération internationale des sociétés de la Croix-Rouge et du Croissant-Rouge' (1997) 30 *Rev. Bel. Dr. Int.* 172.

sidered. On this understanding, two aspects will be discussed: non-state entities as parties or intervening parties and participation of non-state entities in proceedings before the Tribunal. In this respect, it may be added that the usefulness of developing specific procedural rules on *amicus curiae* briefs will depend on the possibility for the entity concerned to participate in the proceedings as a party or intervening party. In other words, if an NGO has access to a judicial body, there is no reason to contemplate the possibility for it to submit briefs as a 'friend of the court'.

3. NON-STATE ENTITIES AS PARTIES OR INTERVENING PARTIES

As already indicated, with the exception of disputes relating to the mining activities in 'the Area' where access of non-state entities to the Seabed Disputes Chamber is expressly granted by UNCLOS, the possibility for these entities to appear before ITLOS will depend on the interpretation of the expression 'agreement' contained in Article 20 of the Statute. Whenever such access is granted, the following provisions may be relevant:

(a) Article 52 of the Rules deals with the transmission of communications by ITLOS to the parties before they have appointed their agents. In the case of natural or juridical persons, communications will be directed 'through the Government of the State in whose territory the communication has to be received' (Article 52(2)(e)).

(b) Pursuant to Article 67 of the Rules, copies of pleadings are available to the public only at the opening of the hearing. Preferential treatment is given to states or other entities entitled to appear before ITLOS, since pleadings are available to them, upon request, as soon as possible after their filing. This latter provision would apply to a non-state entity only in the event it would be entitled to appear before the Tribunal. This could be the case where the question submitted to ITLOS relates to an agreement conferring jurisdiction on the Tribunal to which the entity is a party.

(c) If a non-state entity is successful in bringing a claim before ITLOS, it may be requested to cover to a certain extent the expenses incurred by the Tribunal in dealing with the case. According to Article 19(2) of the Statute, 'when an entity other than a State Party or the Authority is a party to a case submitted to it, the Tribunal shall fix the amount which that party is to contribute towards the expenses of the Tribunal'. It may be expected that the Tribunal, in fixing the amount of such a contribution, would take into account all circumstances of the particular dispute submitted to it.

Intervention of a non-state entity in proceedings before ITLOS does not seem to be easily accepted under UNCLOS. The term 'intervention' is here used in its procedural meaning; it refers to the procedure provided for under Articles 31 and

32 of the Statute by which a third party to a dispute is allowed to intervene in the proceedings to defend its interests. As a result, the intervening party will be bound by the decision taken by the Tribunal with respect to the matter which was the subject of the intervention. A request to intervene in a case brought before ITLOS (when the intervening party claims that its interests are affected by the dispute) is limited to states parties pursuant to Article 31 of the Statute. However, pursuant to Article 32 of the Statute, when the interpretation or application of an international agreement is in question, each party to the agreement has the right to intervene. In this connection, it has to be noted that Article 32 uses the expression 'international agreement'. The Statute then seems to adopt a restrictive approach as regards intervention and to limit recourse to it to subjects of international law which are parties to an international agreement.

It may also be useful to refer to Article 292 of UNCLOS regarding urgent proceedings for the prompt release of detained vessels and crews. These proceedings concern interstate litigation but Article 292(2) specifies that 'the application for release may be made only by or on behalf of the flag State of the vessel'. Therefore, while the flag state is the party to a dispute submitted to ITLOS under Article 292, proceedings may be instituted by any person authorized to act on behalf of the flag state. In the cases submitted to the Tribunal under Article 292, persons so authorized by the competent authorities of the flag state were not necessarily officials or nationals of that state. Nothing seems to prevent a flag state (for example, one seeking to obtain the release of the crew members of a detained ship) to obtain the assistance of non-state entities promoting, for example, the rights of seafarers.

4. PARTICIPATION OF NON-STATE ENTITIES IN PROCEEDINGS BEFORE ITLOS

When a non-state entity or an NGO is not a party to a case, it might nevertheless wish to participate in proceedings as a 'friend of the court' in order to defend the interests it promotes or to assist the court and bring relevant information to its attention. Until now, no NGO or non-state entity has sought to participate in proceedings before ITLOS as an *amicus curiae*. However, if we consider provisions in the Rules which could be relevant in this respect, the following may be mentioned:

(a) A party to a dispute may intend to call a witness or an expert to give evidence during the hearing. Nothing would prevent a party having recourse to the expertise of a member of an NGO. The party intending to do so would have to comply with the general requirements applicable in this regard (communication to the Registrar 'in sufficient time before the opening of the oral proceedings' of the particulars of the experts and the 'point or points to which their evidence will be directed' (Article 72)) and the other party would receive a copy of such communication. In addition, ITLOS can also *proprio motu* decide to 'arrange for the attendance of a witness or expert to give evidence in the proceedings' (Article 77(2)).

(b) Pursuant to Article 82 of the Rules, ITLOS may decide that it needs an independent expert opinion. This requires, after having heard the parties, a formal decision (an order), which defines the subject of the expertise, the mode of appointment of the experts and the procedure to be followed.

(c) Article 84 of the Rules seems *prima facie* a provision more likely to be used in the context of *amicus curiae*. According to it, an intergovernmental organization may furnish information to ITLOS at the request of the Tribunal or on its own initiative. The Rules here use the term 'intergovernmental organization' and not the term 'international organization' as defined in Article 1 of the Rules, or the term 'public international organization' contained in the corresponding provision (Article 69) in the Rules of the International Court of Justice. For the purposes of Article 84, an 'intergovernmental organization' is defined as 'an intergovernmental organization other than any organization which is a party or intervenes in a case' (Article 84(4)). Under Article 1(d) of the Rules, the term 'international organization' has the meaning set out in Article 1 of Annex IX to UNCLOS, i.e. an 'intergovernmental organization constituted by States to which its members States have transferred competence over matters governed by [the] Convention, including the competence to enter into treaties in respect of those matters'. Pursuant to the Convention, such an 'international organization' is entitled to become a party to it, and in this case the term 'State Party' applies to it *mutatis mutandis*.[12] Therefore, under the Rules, the terms 'international organization' or 'intergovernmental organization' have a specific meaning which does not fully correspond to the use of these terms in general international law. While the term 'international organization' is restricted to organizations which could become parties to UNCLOS, the term 'intergovernmental organization' is broader and includes all international organizations (within the meaning of this term in general international law) except when they are parties or intervening parties to a case. It is, however, difficult to see how the term 'intergovernmental organization' could cover an NGO. The term 'NGO' is literally defined by what it is not, i.e. a 'governmental organization' or an 'intergovernmental organization'. Under general international law, the term 'intergovernmental (or international) organization'[13] refers to an organization possessing an international legal personality, set up by a treaty 'with a constitution and common organs'. That said, the distinction be-

---

[12] Article 1(2)(2) of the Convention.

[13] According to the definition of G. Fitzmaurice, the 'term "International organization" means a collectivity of States established by treaty, with a constitution and common organs, having a personality distinct from that of its member-States, and being a subject of international law with treaty-making capacity' (1956) II *Yearbook ILC* 108.

tween NGOs and intergovernmental or international organizations is not always clear. International organizations are usually defined as institutions composed of states. This is not, however, an absolute requirement since more and more organizations admit as members other subjects of international law.[14] There may be borderline cases where the membership of an institution consists of governmental bodies as well as individuals or NGOs. The International Union for the Conservation of Nature[15] is a good example of an institution with one foot in public international law, and the other in municipal law.

5. PRACTICE OF ITLOS

The protection of the environment is an objective which, without any doubt, is shared by many NGOs. If we look into the practice of ITLOS, we may note that the protection of the marine environment is often the subject matter of cases dealt with by the Tribunal. This concerns cases where an allegation is made that human activities cause a risk of harm for the environment.[16] It also includes proceedings for the prompt release of vessels and crews under Article 292 of UNCLOS where vessels have been detained for fishery offences. Reference may be made in this respect to the four cases dealt with by ITLOS involving exploitation of Patagonian tooth fish stocks.[17] On the basis of the experience gained from these cases, the following comments may be made:

(a) No intergovernmental organization has furnished information on its own motion or upon request of ITLOS. However, it is interesting to note that parties to a dispute have included documents or reports from relevant international organizations in their pleadings.[18]

---

[14] See Article 305 of UNCLOS; see also Article 2 of the draft articles on responsibility of international organizations provisionally adopted by the ILC ('the term "international organization" refers to an organization established by treaty or other instrument governed by international law and possessing its own international legal personality. International organizations may include as members, in addition to States, other entities'), in Report on the Work of the 55th Session of the ILC (5 May to 6 June and 7 July to 8 August 2003), Doc. A/58/10, p. 33.

[15] The IUCN consists of states, governmental agencies, NGOs and affiliates.

[16] See *Southern Bluefin Tuna Cases (New Zealand v Japan; Australia v Japan)*; *MOX Plant (Ireland v United Kingdom)*; *Land Reclamation in and around the Straits of Johor (Malaysia v Singapore)*.

[17] *Camouco (Panama v France)*, Prompt Release, Judgment, [2000] ITLOS Reports 10; *Monte Confurco((Seychelles v France)*, Prompt Release, Judgment, [2000] ITLOS Reports 86; *Grand Prince (Belize v France)*, Prompt Release, Judgment, [2000] ITLOS Reports 17; *Volga (Russian Federation v Australia)*, Prompt Release, Judgment, [2002] ITLOS Reports 12.

[18] In the *Volga* case, for example, which concerned alleged illegal fishery activities in the Antarctic Ocean, Australia included in its written pleadings reports from the Commission for the Conservation of Antarctic Marine Living Resources (CCALMR).

(b) It is worth mentioning that states other than the parties to the dispute before ITLOS have sometimes taken steps which could be considered as a form of *amicus curiae*. For example, in the *MOX Plant* case, Ireland included in its pleadings letters sent by the Prime Minister and the Minister of Environment of Norway to their counterparts in the United Kingdom in support of the position of Ireland. It is probably not uncommon for a party to a dispute to refer to the position taken by other states in favour of its allegation.[19] What is perhaps not so common is to include in written pleadings copies of *notes verbales* sent by third states after the institution of proceedings and expressing views in favour of one of the parties to the dispute.[20] In this case, the states concerned preferred to act as 'friends of one of the parties' (as '*amicus litigandis*' if such an expression could be used) rather than to use the right of intervention under UNCLOS.

(c) While NGOs did not request to submit briefs as *amicus curiae* or did not communicate unsolicited information in cases involving environmental concerns, they nevertheless did not remain inactive. Representatives of NGOs were present in the courtroom during the hearings and the websites of NGOs contained information on the factual background of the cases. Sometimes, the parties themselves drew attention to information communicated by NGOs. In this regard, two examples may be given as an illustration. In the *Volga* case, Australia submitted as an annex to its written pleadings the transcript of a radio interview entitled 'The Toothfish Pirates',[21] in which a representative of an NGO took part. In the *Grand Prince* case (involving alleged illegal fishery activities), the representative of France in his final statement referred expressly to the fact that the decision of ITLOS was 'awaited by organizations on the international level who are trying to conserve an ecological balance and awaken world opinion against misdeeds committed by sea pirates'.[22]

---

[19] As an illustration, reference may be made to the letter sent by a Belgian official to the authorities of the Netherlands in response to their request to communicate to the ICJ the position adopted with respect to the delimitation of the continental shelf between the two countries. The letter was communicated by the Netherlands to the Court during the proceedings relating to the *North Sea Continental Shelf* cases. For the text of the letter, see ICJ, Pleadings, *North Sea Continental Shelf*, vol. I, p. 546 (see also Ph. Gautier, 'Le plateau continental de la Belgique et sa délimitation: Quelques réflexions sur la notion d'accord implicite' (1995) 28 *Rev. Bel. Dr. Int.* 110.

[20] In the *Volga* case, Australia included in its Statement in Response (see Annex 3 to the Statement) copies of *notes verbales* supporting its position against illegal fishery activities in the Antarctic Ocean, sent by New Zealand and French authorities. During the pleadings, Australia invited ITLOS to take into account 'the serious problem of continuing illegal fishing in the Southern Ocean' and the international concern this raises (judgment, para. 67).

[21] See Statement in Response of Australia, Annex 5, p. 77 *et seq.*

[22] 'Votre décision est attendue par les organisations qui, à l'échelle internationale, veillent à la préservation des équilibres écologiques et alertent presque quotidiennement l'opinion mondiale contre les méfaits commis par les pirates de la mer ', ITLOS/PV.01/4, 6 April 2001 p.m., p. 10; ['Your decision is awaited by organizations on the international level who are trying to conserve an ecological balance and awaken world opinion against misdeeds committed by sea pirates'] (transcript of interpretation from French), ITLOS/PV.01/4, 6 April 2001 p.m., p. 9.

6. CONCLUSION

Until now, NGOs have not sought to participate as *amicus curiae* or to submit unsolicited information in proceedings before ITLOS. This does not mean that information coming from NGOs which are active in the field of environment was ignored. As has been mentioned, such information was used or communicated to the Tribunal by the parties appearing before it. One should hesitate, however, to conclude from the lack of practice and the silence of the Statute and Rules that NGOs would be prevented from any form of participation in legal proceedings. ITLOS has yet to be faced with requests from NGOs concerning their participation in legal proceedings. Given the fact that the cases dealt with by the Tribunal often concerned issues relating to the protection of the marine environment, a subject matter with respect to which NGOs are particularly active, this issue is likely to arise in the future.

Chapter 18

CIEL's Experience in WTO Dispute Settlement: Challenges and Complexities from a Practical Point of View

Lise Johnson and Elisabeth Tuerk

1. INTRODUCTION

Civil society participation in state-to-state dispute settlement has proven controversial. This applies to both the participation of 'traditional' civil society groups, representing environmental, human rights or developmental interests, as well as trade or industry representatives.[1] Potentially, such participatory roles could potentially be as broad as allowing non-state actors to initiate lawsuits, or as narrow as simply permitting non-state actors to submit *amicus curiae* briefs to the tribunals.[2] WTO dispute settlement is an example of a state-to-state dispute settlement system where *amicus curiae* briefs are currently the *only* means through which non-WTO members, including businesses and civil society groups, can present their views to the tribunals (WTO Panels and the Appellate Body). However, already the mere idea that those tribunals can consider the views of non-members when resolving disputes is a controversial one, sparking much debate among WTO members and civil society.

While the issue of non-state participation in WTO dispute settlement is important to the broader debate about governance, this chapter does not aim to go down that road. Rather, the focus of this chapter is narrower, namely to provide a description and analysis of the experiences of the Center for International Environmental Law (CIEL) in submitting *amicus curiae* briefs to the WTO and to highlight some of the problems that have become apparent through those experiences. Towards this end, this chapter will first describe some of the *amicus curiae* briefs CIEL has submitted (or has tried to submit), to WTO tribunals. Next, it will discuss three main problems CIEL has faced in its role as an *amicus curiae*: these are problems related to the purpose and the function of the briefs that – from a civil society perspective – appear worth submitting; problems related to

---

[1] See, e.g., J. Atik, 'Democratizing the WTO' (2001) 33 *Geo. Wash. Int'l L. Rev.* 451; S. Charnovitz, 'Participation of Nongovernmental Organizations in the World Trade Organization' (1996) 17 *U. Pa. J. Int'l Econ. L.* 331; P.M. Nichols, 'Extension of Standing in the World Trade Organization Disputes to Nongovernmental Parties' (1996) 17 *U. Pa. J. Int'l Econ. L.* 295.
[2] Atik, n. 1 above; Charnovitz, n. 1 above; Nichols, n. 1 above.

T. Treves et al., eds., *Civil Society, International Courts and Compliance Bodies*
© 2005, T·M·C·ASSER PRESS, *The Hague, The Netherlands, and the Authors*

the criteria WTO tribunals have established for *amicus curiae* submissions; and finally, problems related to the overall political context, in which the discussion of *amicus curiae* briefs is taking place.

While this broader discussion about the pros and cons continues, it is today rather clear that WTO Panels and the Appellate Body consider themselves to have the discretionary authority to accept and consider *amicus curiae* briefs. Here, to 'accept' is used to mean receiving for the purpose of determining, at a later point, whether the arguments or evidence will actually be taken into account in resolving the dispute. To 'consider' is used to mean taking the arguments or evidence into account.

2. EXPERIENCES

2.1 United States – Import Prohibition of Certain Shrimp and Shrimp Products[3]

United States — Import Prohibition of Certain Shrimp and Shrimp Products ('*US – Shrimp (No. 1)*') involved a claim brought by Malaysia, Thailand, Pakistan and India to challenge an American import ban on certain shrimp and shrimp products that are harvested in a manner resulting in the incidental deaths of a relatively large number of sea turtles. The US defended its measure on environmental grounds and several environmental NGOs sought to submit *amicus curiae* briefs backing the USA's stance. CIEL, for example, collaborated with the Center for Marine Conservation, the Environmental Foundation, Ltd (a Sri Lankan public interest law firm), the Philippine Ecological Network and Red Nacional de Accion Ecologica (a network of 140 citizens' organizations from Chile) and submitted a brief supporting the USA's ban. The brief essentially had two main components: first it contained legal arguments supporting the Panel's authority to consider unsolicited information from NGOs; secondly, it presented technical, scientific and legal information in support of the USA's position.

The Panel concluded that it could not consider *amicus curiae* briefs independently submitted by NGOs. Specifically, it reasoned that Article 13 of the WTO Dispute Settlement Understanding (DSU) allowed a Panel only to consider information it had actually 'sought'. Because the *amicus curiae* briefs submitted were unsolicited, the Panel determined that it did not have the authority to consider them. Nevertheless, the Panel concluded that the parties could append or attach the *amicus curiae* briefs to their own submissions. The USA decided to follow this approach. Ultimately, the Panel found that the American measure violated the USA's obligations under the GATT.

---

[3] *United States – Import Prohibition of Certain Shrimp and Shrimp Products*, Report of the Panel of 15 May 1998, Doc. WT/DS58/R, adopted as modified by the Report of the Appellate Body of 12 October 1998, Doc. WT/DS58/AB/R on 6 November 1998.

As part of its appeal, the USA alleged that the Panel had erred when concluding that it did not have the authority to accept or consider unsolicited, independently submitted information from *amici curiae*. The Appellate Body agreed with the USA on that point. It declared that Panels have a broad discretionary authority to accept and consider *amicus curiae* briefs, irrespective of whether those briefs contain solicited or unsolicited information. Thus, the Appellate Body's decision overturned the *US – Shrimp (No. 1)* Panel's interpretation of Article 13, finding that interpretation to be unnecessarily formal and technical. However, the Appellate Body also took care to emphasize that the Panels' *discretionary power* to accept and consider *amicus curiae* briefs had to be distinguished from their *obligation* to consider submissions from actual participants in the case. Thus, the question of whether Panels have the *authority* to accept and consider *amicus curiae* briefs is a question entirely separate from the question whether they *will* actually accept such briefs or take them into account.[4]

Another, separate issue was whether the Appellate Body could consider the NGO briefs the USA had attached to its submission. Malaysia, Thailand, Pakistan and India argued that the Appellate Body could not take those attached briefs into account. The Appellate Body, however, disagreed and concluded that participants may attach *amicus curiae* submissions (either in whole or in part) to their own submissions, and that, when they do so, the *amicus curiae* submissions become *prima facie* an integral part of the WTO member's submission.

When attaching CIEL's and other briefs to its submission, the USA emphasized that it only agreed with those legal arguments in the attached briefs, which concurred with the arguments made by the USA in its main submission. The Appellate Body was sensitive to the USA's reservation: noting that the USA only accepted the NGO briefs in a 'tentative and qualified manner',[5] the Appellate Body stated that it would focus its analysis and discussion on the 'legal arguments in the main U.S. appellant's submission'.[6]

2.2 European Communities – Measures affecting Asbestos and Asbestos-Containing Products[7]

European Communities – Measures affecting Asbestos and Asbestos-Containing Products ('*EC – Asbestos*') dealt with a Canadian challenge to a French import ban on asbestos fibres and on products containing asbestos fibres. France defended its measure on public health grounds, asbestos being a highly carcino-

---

[4] R. Bhala and D. Gantz, 'WTO Case Review', (2003) 20 *Ariz. J. Int'l & Comp. L.* 143, at 238 (noting that the question of whether the tribunals will permit participation by *amici* is 'distinct from the question of whether the *amicus curiae* briefs, once filed, will be considered'.

[5] *US – Shrimp (No. 1)*, Report of the Panel, n. 3 above, para. 91.

[6] Ibid.

[7] *European Communities – Measures Affecting Asbestos and Asbestos-Containing Products*, Report of the Panel of 18 September 2000, Doc. WT/DS135/R, adopted as modified by the Report of the Appellate Body of 12 March 2001, Doc. WT/DS135/AB/R, on 5 April 2001.

genic substance. The Panel received five *amicus curiae* briefs − three from public interest groups and two from industry-related groups. During the proceedings, the European Communities (EC) attached one of the public interest and one of the industry briefs to its submission. The Panel concluded that it would only consider those briefs attached to the EC submission, thereby demonstrating the importance of the 'attachment' process. As regards the other three, non-attached briefs, the Panel specified it rejected one of the briefs because it was submitted late in the proceedings. However, the Panel did not provide much insight into why it rejected the other two submissions.

Ultimately, the Panel found that the French import ban for asbestos was inconsistent with France's WTO obligations and the EC appealed. It was expected that both public interest NGOs and business groups would aim to add their voices to the resolution of this appeal. Possibly motivated by the desire to regulate the procedures for such *amicus curiae* submissions, the Appellate Body drafted certain guidelines for would-be *amici* to follow. Those guidelines mandated applicants to first submit a request for leave to file an *amicus curiae* brief. This request for leave should set forth such elements as the interests, motivations, and nature of the *amicus curiae*, the purpose of the brief, and the way in which the brief could contribute to the settlement of the dispute. With respect to the actual brief itself, the guidelines stated that the document must be not longer than 20 pages and must only address those legal issues the applicant had been granted leave to address.

While it could be argued that the Appellate Body, when issuing those guidelines, only attempted to impose some order on the *ad hoc* process which had governed *amicus curiae* briefs in previous cases, the Appellate Body's move still drew much criticism from WTO members. In fact, some view the intense debate following this issue to have been sparked by the political tension between the legislative and judicial arms of the WTO.

As a response to its procedure, the Appellate Body received 17 applications for leave to file an *amicus curiae* brief, CIEL and its partners were among these 17 applications. For its request for leave CIEL collaborated with a network of environmental and other public interest groups, both in the South and in the North. Specifically, the joint request for leave was submitted by CIEL and FIELD (the Foundation for International Environmental Law) on behalf of: the World Wild Fund for Nature, Greenpeace, the Lutheran World Federation, the Ban Asbestos Network and IBAN. In their request for leave the groups stated that their brief would address the Panel's legal conclusions and other legal issues raised by the parties to the appeal. In the end, the Appellate Body denied all 17 of the applications for leave. Six of those applications were rejected for timing reasons, the other 11 were rejected without specific reasons. CIEL never received an explanation as to why its application was rejected by the Appellate Body. Some speculate that the political tension originating from guidelines and their publication on the Internet motivated the Appellate Body to refrain from granting any of the applications to file briefs. This move inspired NGOs and others to criticize the lack of transparency and predictability in WTO procedures. Together with some of its partners, CIEL issued a press release protesting the Appellate Body's actions. In relevant part, this press release reads:

> In a rare moment of clarity, the WTO issued special procedures inviting NGOs to file requests to make legal submissions in the case by 16 November. Despite misgivings about the time-frame and other restrictions imposed by the Appellate Body in its invitation, NGOs welcomed the move as one that recognized the value of their contribution to the WTO's decision-making process.
>
> However, less than twenty-four hours after it had filed its request, the group of NGOs received a standard form letter refusing the application. The WTO provided no detailed reasons for its refusal. Other applications by civil society were also refused without explanation. ...
>
> *One step forward, two steps back:* By failing to give adequate consideration to directly affected groups, the WTO runs the risk of increasing widespread distrust in its dispute settlement procedures which are already heavily criticized for giving free trade precedence over other values such health, the environment and sustainable development.
>
> The WTO's Appellate body has instructed its Members to observe principles of "basic fairness" but has proven itself incapable of honouring its own preachings. Its decision to deny the group's request was swift but, without reasoning, appears arbitrary. Failing to provide adequate reasons for its refusal demonstrates a lack of procedural fairness that is not tolerated in democratic legal systems.[8]

After this controversial experiment with procedural rules – even if applicable to that particular case only – WTO tribunals have since refrained from issuing any guidelines governing the submission of *amicus curiae* briefs.

2.3 European Communities – Measures affecting the Approval and Marketing of Biotech Products[9]

European Communities – Measures affecting the Approval and Marketing of Biotech Products ('*EC – GMOs*') involved a claim brought by the USA, Canada and Argentina against certain aspects of the European Communities' process for approving genetically modified (GM) products.[10] In essence, the USA argued that the *de facto* moratorium on GM products was harming American farmers and stopping countries from adopting the controversial technology. According to the USA, the European moratorium violates WTO rules, amongst others, by creating

---

[8] 'A Court Without Friends? One Year After Seattle, the WTO Slams the Door on NGOs', press release, available at <www.ciel.org/Announce/asbstospr.html> (last visited July 2004).

[9] The cases are numbered as WT/DS/291, 292, 293.

[10] Other American claims relate to GATT (Articles I, III, X and XI), to the Agreement on Agriculture (Article 4) and to the Agreement on Technical Barriers to Trade (Articles 2 and 5). In essence, the USA does not target the European regulatory regime, but rather its implementation. Specifically, the USA targets the suspension by the EC of consideration of application of biotech products, the failure of the EC to consider certain biotech products and certain national marketing and import bans.

a trade barrier without adequate scientific evidence that it is in the interests of either public health or the environment. The Europeans, in turn, say that approval processes will change once the new regulatory system is properly in place.[11]

Together with a group of four other USA-based organizations (Friends of the Earth United States, Defenders of Wildlife, Institute for Agriculture and Trade Policy, and the Organic Consumer Association) CIEL submitted an *amicus curiae* brief to the Panel.[12] In its motion to submit the brief the coalition of groups first very briefly set out the Panel's authority to accept and consider *amicus curiae* briefs and then, along the lines of the guidelines adopted for the Appellate Body proceedings in the *Asbestos* case, described: (1) the applicants; (2) the applicants' individual and common interests in this case; (3) the issues the applicants intended to address in their *amicus curiae* brief; (4) how the amicus *curiae* brief offered expert advice and technical information (Article 13) critical to the Panel's deliberations; (5) how the contributions would not be repetitive of party or third party submissions; and finally, (6) that the applicants were independent of parties and third parties to the dispute.

While, ultimately, many issues may or may not be relevant for deciding the case, the group's *amicus curiae* brief had one specific focus: it aimed to provide factual and technical information to assist the Panel in the interpretation of the term 'insufficient scientific evidence' under Article 5(7) of the Agreement on Sanitary and Phytosanitary Measures ('the SPS Agreement').[13] To achieve that purpose the brief provided both factual and legal information. Section II of the brief contained statements of facts, explaining that the evaluation of human, animal and plant health impacts of GMOs entails substantial scientific uncertainty; section III provided legal arguments, setting out first, that uncertainty is a critical factor in determining when scientific evidence is insufficient under Article 5(7) of the SPS Agreement, and then, that uncertainty is a critical factor in determining the application of the precautionary principle in relevant international law. Thereby, the brief aimed to 'provid[e] information that will allow the Panel to consider the full range of available scientific evidence, as well as expertise in the relevant legal regimes ... [and] seeks to constitute an instrument for a balanced and high-quality decision'.[14]

It remains to be seen how the Panel will ultimately treat this, and other *amicus curiae* briefs submitted in *EC – GMOs*.[15]

---

[11] As part of the efforts establishing a comprehensive regulatory system, the European Parliament adopted regulations authorizing and labelling genetically modified products beginning in July 2003.

[12] *EC – GMOs*, n. 9 above, *Motion to Submit* Amicus Curiae *Brief* and Amicus Curiae *Brief*, 1 June 2004, see <www.ciel.org>.

[13] Ibid., para. 3.

[14] Ibid., para. 3. It is interesting to note that the Coalition's brief does not take a clear side with the European Communities, but rather focuses on systemic questions arising in this case.

[15] Another brief, for example, was submitted by a coalition comprising GeneWatch UK; Foundation for International Environmental Law and Development (FIELD, UK); Five Year Freeze (UK);

3. POLITICAL SCENARIO

3.1 Potential roles for *amicus curiae* briefs

In theory, an *amicus curiae* brief can serve at least three different functions: (1) providing legal analysis and interpretation; (2) providing factual analysis as well as evidence;[16] and (3) placing the trade dispute into a broader political and social context. In fact, CIEL's briefs in *US – Shrimp (No. 1)* and *EC – GMOs* sought to perform these functions, by providing legal analysis on Article XX GATT and Article 5(7) of the SPS Agreement, by providing factual information regarding the sea turtles, as well as the uncertainty arising when evaluating human, animal and plant health impacts of GMOs; and ultimately, by adding the voices of environmental constituencies to the trade dispute, thereby broadening the perspectives and views directly represented in the case. Through each of these functions, *amicus curiae* can provide the crucial 'and' linking trade and the rules governing it with the myriad of social, environmental and other public interest concerns it affects. Thus more broadly, *amicus curiae* briefs can try to expand what might be a narrow conception of trade issues into a broader view of the 'trade and environment', 'trade and human rights' or 'trade and development' implications of WTO law.

More specifically, *amicus curiae* briefs which aim to serve the first goal – providing legal analysis and interpretation – can play a crucial role in shaping international law, and, in the case of WTO dispute settlement, international trade law. CIEL, for example, through its *amicus curiae* briefs intended to contribute to cutting edge legal questions, including the interpretation of Article XX GATT (in *US – Shrimp (No. 1)*), the interpretation of Article 5(7) of the SPS Agreement (in *EC – GMOs*) and, amongst others, the interpretation of 'likeness' or the application of 'non-violation' disputes in (*EC – Asbestos*). NGOs occupy an important position in that they can advance arguments WTO members fear using because they are concerned that later, in other disputes, those arguments may be used

---

Royal Society for the Protection of Birds (RSPB, UK); The Center for Food Safety (USA); Council of Canadians; Polaris Institute (Canada); Grupo de Reflexión Rural Argentina; Center for Human Rights and the Environment (CEDHA, Argentina); Gene Campaign (India); Forum for Biotechnology and Food Security (India); Fundación Sociedades Sustentales (Chile); Greenpeace International; Californians for GE-Free Agriculture; International Forum on Globalisation. See <www.greenpeace.org/international_en/press/release?item_id=484372&campaign_id=> (visited July 2004).

[16] G. Marceau and M. Stilwell, 'Practical Suggestions for Amicus Curiae Briefs Before WTO Adjudicating Bodies' (2001) 4 *J. Int'l Econ. L.* 155, at 183–185 (discussing the role of *amicus curiae* briefs before the WTO Panels and Appellate Body; noting that whereas the briefs submitted to Panels can include evidence, facts and legal arguments, briefs submitted to the Appellate Body should be limited to legal questions based on the facts already on the record); see also *Response of the United States of America to Methanex's Request to Limit* Amicus Curiae *Submissions to Legal Issues Raised by the Parties*, in the *Arbitration under Chapter 11 of the NAFTA between the United States and Methanex*, 28 April 2003 (arguing that *amicus curiae* briefs can serve two important functions: providing legal interpretation and factual analysis).

against them[17] or that may not go down well with their core, economic-oriented constituency.

Furthermore, NGOs, particularly those that work through international networks, are responding to the fact that certain issues and concerns increasingly transcend national boundaries and might consequently more thoroughly be addressed by international rather than merely national actors. International trade and its implications is one of these examples. In addition, given that WTO decisions address such fundamental (legal) issues as the extent to which trade obligations can trump a sovereign nation's ability to implement health, safety or environmental regulations, it is increasingly important that public interest organizations have a means through which to present their views of the appropriate legal analysis and interpretation relevant to that issue.[18]

Secondly, NGOs can play a crucial role in the state-to-state dispute settlement system by providing factual analysis[19] and evidence. Similarly, *amicus curiae* briefs can increase the factual record, not through analysis of a set of facts, but through independent production of evidence. Again, this can be a vitally important means through which public interest groups can use their particular expertise and perspectives to illuminate certain elements of a state-to-state dispute which are inadequately addressed or emphasized by the disputing parties.[20]

Finally, NGO briefs can set the dispute in a broader political and social context. The diverse perspectives and expertise possessed by NGOs can help tribunals to look at complex issues not only through the states parties' lenses, but from a number of different relevant viewpoints.[21] NGOs can help highlight concerns, which might be ignored or inadequately addressed by the disputing states, yet

---

[17] Charnovitz, n. 1 above, at p. 353.

[18] See ibid., pp. 353–354. Charnovitz explains that NGO participation in the dispute settlement process is important because the WTO lacks adequate concern for such issues of fundamental importance as environmental protection. He states that the WTO Agreement 'is a treaty about trade across economic borders. If there were no ocean, no atmosphere, no Antarctica, no cross-border pollution, and no biodiversity, not a single word in the WTO would need to be rewritten. The WTO is replete with constructive rules on the topic of economic interdependence, but it is vacuous on the topic of ecological interdependence'. Ibid,. p. 354; see also, D. Shelton, 'The Participation of Nongovernmental Organizations in International Judicial Proceedings' (1994) 88 *Am. J. Int'l L.* 611, at 616 (noting that, in international disputes, governments might choose 'litigation strategies that deliberately omit significant issues of broad public interest').

[19] Response of the United States of America, n. 16 above, at p. 3 (discussing the importance of factual analysis by NGOs; though the document was submitted in a dispute between an investor and a state, it drew upon cases involving disputes between states, and on domestic cases).

[20] Marceau and Stilwell, n. 16 above, at p. 180.

[21] Charnovitz, n. 1 above, at p. 351 (noting that 'NGO participation will increase the information available to the panel, thereby leading to better informed – and hopefully better quality – panel decisions'. Charnovitz also quotes David Wirth's argument that '[t]he presence of affected nongovernmental parties would widen perspectives on the underlying dispute, thereby reducing the likelihood of erroneous conclusions'. The quotation from David Wirth is taken from D.A. Wirth, 'Reexamining Decision-Making Processes in International Environmental Law' (1994) 79 *Iowa L. Rev.* 769, at 790.

which are inextricably related to the dispute.[22] As such, NGO involvement in the factual as well as legal analysis of an inter-state dispute can help prevent that dispute from being viewed in a myopic fashion,[23] providing an essential contribution to the shaping of the 'trade *and*' debate.

3.2 Limits on *amicus curiae* briefs' potential roles

In practice, however, the roles *amicus curiae* briefs can actually play in a WTO dispute may be more limited. Some of these limits are arguably mandated by the DSU, others appear to be discretionarily imposed by the WTO tribunals themselves.

An example of a limit that is mandated by the DSU is the content of an *amicus curiae* brief. According to Article 17 of the DSU, appeals must be 'limited to issues of law covered in the panel report and legal interpretations developed by the panel'.[24] Consequently, an *amicus curiae* brief to the Appellate Body would have to be similarly limited in scope, covering only those issues of law and legal interpretations the Appellate Body is authorized to consider.[25] Factual issues are outside of the scope of appellate review and would, therefore, be inappropriate in an *amicus curiae* brief to the Appellate Body.[26]

Other limits, however, appear to be more problematic. One such limit – arguably mandated by the DSU[27] – relates to the Panels' ability to rely on factual evi-

---

[22] R. Housman, 'Democratizing International Decision-Making' (1994) 27 *Cornell Int'l L. J.* 699, at 745 (explaining that *amicus curiae* briefs should be permitted, in part, because they can 'provide panels with important supplementary information that may not, for political or other reasons, be reflected in the briefs of the parties').

[23] NGO participation in WTO dispute settlement can be an important means of bringing non-trade issues, such as environmental or social concerns, into the trade sphere. In 'linking' trade issues to other important, related topics, NGOs can thereby help Panels see the broad implications of their decisions. For a discussion of 'linkage', see J.E. Alvarez and D.W. Leebron, 'The Boundaries of the WTO Linkages' (2002) 96 *Am. J. Int'l L.* 5.

[24] DSU, Article 17(6).

[25] See, e.g., *European Communities – Trade Description of Sardines*, Report of the Appellate Body of 26 September 2002, Doc. WT/DS231/AB/R, paras 160 and 169 (rejecting the part of Morocco's submission providing factual information: 'As article 17.6 of the DSU limits an appeal to issues of law and legal interpretations developed by the panel, the factual information provided in Morocco's amicus curiae brief is not pertinent in this appeal').

[26] Note however, that CIEL's brief in *US – Shrimp (No. 1)* did contain factual parts.

[27] Based upon an examination of the text of Article 13 of the DSU and Article 11(2) of the SPS Agreement, however, it is unclear from where the Appellate Body is deriving this limitation on the Panels' authority. Putting aside the somewhat ambiguous textual foundations of the Appellate Body's ruling on this issue, the rationale behind the decision appears to be sound from a broader legal perspective. Specifically, by clarifying that it is upon the disputing parties to back their claims with a certain threshold level of support, for a claim to stand a chance of succeeding, the decision acknowledges the significance of the allocation of the burden of proof. Having this initial threshold originating from an *amicus curiae* submission, in other words from a source not being any of the parties to the dispute, would discharge the relevant party from its burden to make its *prima facie* case of consistency or inconsistency.

dence supplied by non-parties.[28] According to the Appellate Body's decision in
Japan – Measures affecting Agricultural Products[29] (*'Japan – Agricultural
Products'*) a party must meet its own burden of proof; evidence provided by independent experts or non-parties cannot be relied upon by the Panel to 'make the
case' for a party. Although:

> [a] panel is entitled to seek information and advice from experts and from any other
> relevant source it chooses, pursuant to Article 13 of the DSU and, in an SPS case, Ar-
> ticle 11.2 of the SPS Agreement,[30] to help it to understand and evaluate the evidence
> submitted and the arguments made by the parties, but not to make the case for a com-
> plaining party ... [t]he Panel erred ... when it used expert information and advice as the
> basis for a finding of inconsistency with Article 5.6 [of the SPS Agreement], since the
> United States did not establish a prima facie case of inconsistency with Article 5.6.[31]

From a political and external transparency perspective, the Appellate Body's decision in *Japan – Agricultural Products* is problematic because it limits the
breadth of potential issues to be addressed in *amicus curiae* briefs and thereby
also diminishes the potential usefulness of *amicus curiae* briefs. As explained
above, *amicus curiae* briefs are useful in the sense that the perspectives and particular areas of expertise of their submitters can infuse the briefs with content that
is *different* from the one advanced by the parties to the dispute. In the procedures
established for the submission of *amicus curiae* briefs in *EC – Asbestos*, the Appellate Body seemed to acknowledge precisely this point. It stated that the value-
added of *amicus curiae* briefs truly materializes only when those briefs differ
from the parties' submissions.[32]

Nevertheless, in its decision in *Japan – Agricultural Products*, the Appellate
Body arguably places limits on the extent to which *amicus curiae* submissions
can add evidentiary value that differs from the parties' submissions Specifically,
the case addressed information from an *amicus curiae* that *is* so significant and so
different from what is advanced by the parties that a Panel would be inclined to

---

[28] Although this case addressed the extent to which Panels can rely on evidence provided by experts, its reasoning – a focus on information provided by non-parties as opposed to parties – seems
to produce the conclusion that the holding also applies to evidence provided by *amici curiae*.

[29] *Japan – Measures affecting Agricultural Products*, Report of the Appellate Body of 22 February 1999, Doc. WT/DS76/AB/R, adopted on 19 March 1999.

[30] The text of Article 11(2) of the SPS Agreement reads: 'In a dispute under this Agreement involving scientific or technical issues, a panel should seek advice from experts chosen by the panel in
consultation with the parties to the dispute. To this end, the panel may, when it deems it appropriate,
establish an advisory technical experts group, or consult the relevant international organizations, at
the request of either party to the dispute or on its own initiative'.

[31] *Japan – Agricultural Products*, Report of the Appelate Body, n. 29 above, paras. 129–130.

[32] See, European Communities – Measures affecting Asbestos and Asbestos-Containing Products – Additional Procedure adopted under Rule 16(1) of the Working Procedures for Appellate Review (*'Procedure for Submission in EC – Asbestos'*), Doc. WT/DS135/9 (8 November 2000)
(requiring applicants wishing to file an *amicus curiae* brief to 'indicate, in particular, in what way
[they] will make a contribution to the resolution of this dispute that is not likely to be repetitive of
what has already been submitted by a party or third party to this dispute'. Ibid., para. 3(f)).

exclusively rely upon it. According to *Japan – Agricultural Products* the Panel would not be able to accord such determinative weight to this information. By suggesting that a Panel cannot rely upon expert information and advice as the sole basis for finding an inconsistency – without the relevant party having established a *prima facie* case of inconsistency – the Appellate Body effectively constrains the Panel in its information-gathering and evidence-weighing functions. This begs the question whether this amounts to interfering with the mandate set forth in Article 11 of the DSU which requires a panel to 'make an objective assessment of the matter before it'.[33]

These limits on the factual evidence *amicus curiae* briefs can submit to Panels and the Appellate Body relate mainly to 'scope of review' and the 'burden of proof' and, as discussed above, they may well be mandated by the DSU. In contrast, there are other limits on the content and function of *amicus curiae* briefs which appear to have been discretionarily imposed by the WTO tribunals. One of these discretionary limits is the WTO's fairly consistent practice of only considering those briefs which are attached to a party's submission. In fact, WTO Panels and the Appellate Body rarely take into account those briefs which are *not* attached to a party or third party's submission.

In *US – Shrimp (No. 1)*, for example, the Appellate Body accepted for consideration three briefs from NGOs that the USA had attached to its appellate submission. The Appellate Body explained that, by attaching the briefs, those documents became 'at least *prima facie* an integral part of that participant's submission'.[34] In fact, however, the USA attached the *amicus curiae* briefs with the caveat that it only supported the arguments made in the briefs to the extent those arguments concurred with the ones made in the its own main submission. In light of this disclaimer, the Appellate Body clarified that it would focus its analysis merely on those arguments made in the USA's main submission.

This practice of 'attaching' *amicus curiae* briefs to government parties' submissions raises some interesting questions. For those submitting a brief, it might – at least at a first glance – seem desirable to have one's brief attached to a party's submission: this dramatically increases the chance that the tribunal will actually consider the brief or the arguments contained therein. Yet, if a party endorses or accepts the brief in its entirety, one must ask whether the brief loses value, in so far as it does not appear to provide a perspective different from the one advanced by the parties. On the other hand, the party may only endorse parts of the brief. In such cases, the tribunals appear to focus their attention on only those endorsed aspects.[35] By so focusing their attention, the tribunals might be considering only a skeletal version of the brief: a version which (similarly to the

---

[33] DSU, Article 11.

[34] Given that parties and third parties have a legal right to have their submissions considered, this characterization of attached briefs as *prima facie* integral parts of a participant's submission suggests that, at least in some cases, such attached briefs *must* also be considered.

[35] Shrimp cases (humane society).

situation above) has arguably lost precisely those features of *amicus curiae* briefs which make those submissions value-added. Specifically, the value added of an *amicus curiae* brief lies, amongst other thins, in its ability to contribute something unique to the resolution of the dispute, in so far as it provides a different perspective, and adds input free from the bounds imposed by domestic political considerations.

4.   MECHANICS OF SUBMITTING AN *AMICUS CURIAE* BRIEF

However thwarted, some NGOs might still feel it is worthwhile to keep knocking at the WTO tribunals' door, trying to get them to hear what civil society has to say about trade issues, particularly those that affect a wide range of stakeholders.[36] Although case law may be telling NGOs that they have to speak in a certain circumscribed manner, and tailor their arguments in a certain way, many NGOs are still willing to make efforts to be heard (though possibly in a muted form). But here comes the next pessimistic – or, more accurately, realistic – pronouncement: try as they might, NGOs face too many hurdles to meet the WTO tribunals' implied requirements for *amicus curiae* submissions.

A first major hurdle NGOs face is that WTO Panels and the Appellate Body have not provided adequate guidance about what – once they have *accepted* the brief – makes them *consider* it. So far, the tribunals' decisions have said little, if anything, regarding their treatment of *amicus curiae* submissions. The typical explanation for not taking a brief into account is simply that the brief was 'not of assistance' or 'not necessary' to resolving the dispute.[37]

Unfortunately, the tribunals do not provide much insight into what they mean when using the phrase 'not of assistance'. One possibility[38] is that the brief is not

---

[36] Note however, that some civil society groups may take the view that certain 'trade *and*' issues should not be addressed by trade panels at all and therefore refrain from contributing an *amicus curiae* brief. This approach may originate in the potential that such a contribution could be perceived as essentially accepting the legitimacy and appropriateness of trade tribunals deciding the case. See, e.g., <www.foeeurope.org/biteback/> (visited July 2004).

[37] The fact that the brief was 'not of assistance' or 'not relevant' was the reason given by the tribunals for rejecting the submission in US – Countervailing Measures concerning Certain Products from the European Communities ('*US – Countervailing Measures against EC*'), Report of the Appellate Body of 9 December 2002, Doc. WT/DS/212/AB/R (finding submitted brief was not of assistance); United States – Imposition of Countervailing Duties on Certain Hot-Rolled Lead and Bismuth Carbon Steel Products Originating in the United Kingdom, Report of the Appellate Body of 10 May 2000, Doc. WT/DS138/AB/R (concluding that it was not necessary to take the two submitted briefs into account); EC – Sardines, Report of the Appellate Body, n. 25 (rejecting two briefs for failing to assist in the appeal); United States – Import Prohibition of Certain Shrimp and Shrimp Products – Recourse to Article 21.5 of the DSU by Malaysia, Report of the Appellate Body of 22 October 2001, Doc. WT/DS58/AB/RW (holding that it was not necessary to take a law professor's brief into account); European Communities – Anti-Dumping Duties on Imports of Cotton-Type Bed Linen from India, Report of the Panel of 30 October 2000, Doc. WT/DS141/R (finding that it was not necessary to take the submission into account).

[38] This argument builds upon the argument advanced by some parties to disputes, urging the Panel not to consider an *amicus curiae* brief. Judging from the statements of disputing parties it

sufficiently different from a brief already submitted by a party. Briefs that merely echo the arguments presented by the party or parties whom they support might be seen by the tribunals as being of little value, and, consequently, not worthy of consideration. This interpretation of 'not of assistance' appears to be supported by the guidelines for requests for leave to submit *amicus curiae* briefs, issued by the Appellate Body in *EC – Asbestos*.[39] Those guidelines required those requesting leave to file a brief to 'indicate, in particular, in what way the applicant will make a contribution to the resolution of this dispute that is not likely to be repetitive of what has been already submitted by a party or third party to this dispute'.[40]

However, it does not follow from the above, that a brief which advances a novel or distinct argument will be found to be 'of assistance' to a tribunal. On the contrary, and as discussed above, it even appears that a tribunal might decline to accept or consider a brief precisely because the brief's arguments, facts or factual analyses are *not* the same as those advanced by the parties or third parties. For example, in the 2003 case, *United States – Final Countervailing Duty Determination with respect to Certain Softwood Lumber from Canada*, the tribunal ruled that it 'would consider any arguments raised by *amici curiae* only to the extent that those arguments were taken up in the written submissions and/or oral statements of any party or third party'.[41] Similarly, see the situation arising from *Japan – Agricultural Products* with respect to evidentiary content that differs from the parties' submissions.

Thus, it appears that *amicus curiae* briefs are caught in a type of 'Catch 22': if they advocate approaches too similar to those pressed by the parties or third parties, there is a danger the briefs will be rejected as being redundant and, hence, 'not of assistance'; yet, if they diverge too much from the points raised by the parties or third parties, there is a danger that the briefs will be rejected on that basis. Thus, the only point that can be discerned from the WTO's jurisprudence is that the tribunals have not given adequate guidance about which attributes of an *amicus curiae* submission might make it worthy of consideration. NGOs are faced with the exceedingly difficult task of tailoring their briefs so that the tribunals *will* accept and, more importantly, consider them.

A second and related hurdle is that, even if the tribunals did clearly specify whether they (a) want the briefs solely to address the same arguments raised by

---

seems possible to interpret 'not of assistance' as meaning something like 'offering nothing new' or presenting 'arguments [that] do not differ in substance from and largely repeat the arguments of the parties whom they support. See *US – Countervailing Measures against EC*, Report of the Appellate Body, n. 37 above, para 9 (giving the EC's reason why an industry association's brief, submitted in support of the USA, should be rejected).

[39] See *Procedure for Submission in EC – Asbestos*, n. 32 above (containing the 'Additional Procedure' adopted for the purposes of that appeal).

[40] Ibid., para. 3(f).

[41] United States – Final Countervailing Duty Determination with respect to Certain Softwood Lumber from Canada ('*US – Softwood Lumber*'), Report of the Panel of 29 August 2003, Doc. WT/DS257/R, at p. 130.

the parties, or (b) want the briefs to introduce new arguments, NGOs would still have a difficult time tailoring their briefs to the tribunals' standards, mainly because it is unknown what the parties' arguments are. According to Articles 14(1) and 17(10) of the DSU, Panel and Appellate Body proceedings are confidential; whether or not the content of a party's submission becomes available during the proceedings depends upon the party voluntarily disclosing its submission. Thus, even if it were clear – in abstract – what the tribunals wanted in *amicus curiae* briefs, *amici* might not be able to produce the appropriate brief. Confidentiality of the deliberations and of most of the documents creates a practical hurdle.

However, this is not yet all. Time is another issue working against *amici curiae*. So far, there is only one case, *EC – Asbestos*, where a WTO tribunal established a clear deadline and timeline for *amicus curiae* submissions. The absence of formal deadlines in all the remaining cases, however, does not mean that those deadlines did not exist. On the contrary, quite frequently tribunals have rejected or declined to consider briefs because they found the briefs untimely. Essentially, late submission appears to foreclose a brief's chances for being considered. While – from a due process point of view – the importance of timely submission is understandable, it is at the same time problematic for *amici*. Specifically, because of the confidential nature of dispute settlement proceedings, *amici* are often unaware of the timeline for the particular case. Thus, even if in theory, on time submission is a reasonable requirement, the way it is implemented in practice renders it a rather unfair requirement for would be *amici curiae*.

5.   *Amicus Curiae* Briefs in the Political Reality of Different WTO Members

In addition to the above challenges, when aiming to advance the case of *amicus curiae* briefs, *amici* face another, broader political challenge. A main argument that is frequently advanced against *amicus curiae* briefs is that developing countries are opposed to the WTO tribunals' practice of accepting and/or considering such briefs. Developing countries' resource constraints, as well as the potential of Northern *amicus curiae* submissions to advance protectionist arguments, are amongst the main reasons for developing countries resistance to more transparency in WTO dispute settlement processes. This raises concerns for those *amici* who aim to strengthen their ties with partners from the global South, and who in general aim to re-introduce balance into the multilateral trading system, including by support of the weaker members of this system.[42] For these groups, it is impor-

---

[42] This strengthening relationship between NGOs and developing countries was especially evident during the September 2003 WTO Ministerial in Cancun, Mexico. NGOs from both developed and developing countries worked to minimize the resource gap between developed and developing countries by providing developing countries with information and analysis of the various trade issues covered during the Ministerial. NGOs also threw their political clout and their ability to raise awareness behind developing country positions. Even critics of the NGO-developing country partnership recognized its depth and potential.

tant to participate as *amici curiae*, and to avoid creating tensions with developing countries. Fortunately, it seems that the NGO-developing country rift over the *amicus curiae* issue is overstated.

A major concern relates to the resource constraints developing countries face when trying to participate effectively in WTO processes. By accepting *amicus curiae* submissions from non-parties, even if ultimately deciding not to consider the submissions, WTO tribunals are arguably increasing the amount of legal and/ or factual information to which the parties must respond.[43] Developing country members argue that, especially for members with limited resources, it is exceedingly burdensome to respond to these additional, non-party submissions.[44] In light of the overall resource constraints developing country delegations are facing, this argument appears to be a valid one. While this argument has not been addressed up front in WTO case law, there is, however, an indication that the tribunals are sensitive to it.

For example, in *United States – Imposition of Countervailing Duties on Certain Hot-Rolled Lead and Bismuth Carbon Steel Products Originating in the United Kingdom* ('*US – Carbon Steel*'), the Panel held that the 'inability of the parties to present comments [on the late-submitted brief] raised due process concerns such that it would not consider the brief'.[45] The Panel also noted that if the contents of the brief warranted being addressed by the parties, it would 'have been entitled to delay its proceedings in order to provide the parties sufficient opportunity to comment on the ... brief'.[46] Another means by which the tribunals can be sensitive to due process concerns is by limiting the amount of material that can be contained in an *amicus curiae* brief. For example, in *EC – Asbestos*, the Appellate Body required any brief submitted to 'be concise and in no case longer than 20 typed pages, including any appendices'.[47]

Thus, *EC – Asbestos* and *US – Carbon Steel* both suggest that there are tools available to prevent *amicus curiae* submissions from imposing unfair burdens on developing country members. WTO tribunals can either require that the briefs conform to a specific page limit, mandate that they be submitted within a specific time frame, or adjust the timing of the dispute settlement procedure in order to allow parties an adequate opportunity to fully respond to the brief. Although it is not clear that Panels will always follow this approach, it is encouraging and noteworthy that tribunals have, in the past, been sensitive to the due process concerns raised by the consideration of *amicus curiae* briefs. This sensitivity should help

---

[43] See, e.g., Proposals on the DSU by Cuba, Honduras, India, Malaysia, Pakistan, Sri Lanka, Tanzania and Zimbabwe, Doc. TN/DS/W/18 (7 October 2002).

[44] Ibid.

[45] United States – Imposition of Countervailing Duties on Certain Hot-Rolled Lead and Bismuth Carbon Steel Products Originating in the United Kingdom, Report of the Panel of 23 December 1999, Doc. WT/DS138/R, at p. 28.

[46] Ibid.

[47] *Procedure for Submission in EC – Asbestos*, n. 32 above, para. 7(b).

to alleviate some of the challenges developing country members might face with respect to *amicus curiae* briefs.

A second concern developing country members raise with respect to the participation of NGOs in WTO dispute settlement proceedings is more political in nature. It is claimed that NGOs who participate in WTO disputes represent developed country concerns and, therefore, simply serve as another means through which developed country influences outweigh and overpower developing country interests.[48] While it is true that many developed country NGOs represent environmental, conservation or human rights issues, the traditional separation between developed and developing country interests, specifically with respect to environmental, human rights and developmental concerns, is becoming increasingly blurred. It is also true that there are many emerging NGO structures and alliances which shatter traditional notions that developed country NGOs align with developed country interests, to the detriment of developing countries. The 2003 Cancun Ministerial, which witnessed a strong alliance between developing countries and Northern NGOs, both opposed to the launching of negotiations on the so-called Singapore Round, presents an example in point.[49]

However, also past NGO participation in WTO dispute settlement helps to illustrate the fallacy of the 'developed country and NGO v developing country' paradigm. For example, when submitting the brief in *US – Shrimp (No. 1)*, CIEL collaborated with NGOs from developing countries, for example, the Philippine Ecological Network and Red Nacional de Accion Ecologia from Chile. That case represents an instance where developed and developing country NGOs collaborated to support a developed country's environmental measure from a challenge by a developing country. Another interesting scenario could have arisen in *Chile – Measures Affecting the Transit and Importation of Swordfish*.[50] Here, Northern environmental groups could have filed an *amicus curiae* brief in support of a Southern (i.e., Chilean) environmental measure. Different but related issues arose in the recent *US – Softwood Lumber* case. Here, the Interior Alliance, an NGO representing indigenous peoples in Canada, submitted a brief opposing Canada's claim against the USA. Thus, this case represents an instance where a developed country NGO supported another developed country in its defence against its own country's challenge. Together, these examples demonstrate that the dynamism of

---

[48] See quotation from India, above. While this statement raises concerns regarding industry submissions, those concerns also exist with respect to NGO submissions.

[49] For a pre-Cancun description of this growing alliance see E. Tuerk, 'Developing Countries and External Transparency at the WTO' in S. Griller, *International Economic Governance and Non-Economic Concerns, Economic Law Facing New Challenges* (Springer, Wien, New York, 2002).

[50] *Chile – Measures Affecting the Transit and Importation of Swordfish* (case WT/DS193) The European request for the establishment of a Panel addressed Chile's bans on access to its ports to foreign fishing vessels catching swordfish inside and outside its 200-mile exclusive economic zone. Eventually, the case did not proceed, with the constitution of the Panel being suspended (see *Arrangement between the European Communities and Chile – Communication from the European Communities*, Doc. WT/DS193/3 (6 April 2001).

international issues resists easy categorization into simple developed and developing country camps.

The traditional cliché that NGOs support developed country norms and values is also challenged when reviewing *amicus curiae* participation in dispute settlement processes outside the WTO. In some investor-state disputes, NGOs, including those from the North, are trying to secure substantive rights for citizens and groups in those developing countries that are challenged in the suit. The current investor-state dispute between Bechtel Corporation and the Bolivian government provides an example.[51] In that case, CIEL together with Earthjustice, an environmental law organization located in California, and the Democracy Center, an NGO in Bolivia, tried to secure the rights of citizens and public interest organizations of Cochabamba, Bolivia, to participate in the arbitration proceedings between Bechtel and Bolivia. Even if not a WTO dispute, this case demonstrates yet another way in which issues related to international trade and investment law have inspired alliances transcending traditional divisions between developed and developing countries.

In sum, while developing country concerns with the acceptance and consideration of *amicus curiae* briefs in WTO dispute settlement appear valid, most recent developments also point to ways of addressing these concerns. First, WTO tribunals have shown that they carefully consider due process issues when deciding whether to accept and consider *amicus curiae* submissions. Secondly, the increasingly borderless, collaborative nature of today's NGOs serves to shift emphasis away from a polarized developed/developing country view. Nevertheless, it remains important for NGOs who work closely with and value their partnerships with developing countries, to remain sensitive to criticisms that *amicus curiae* briefs from NGOs unfairly tip the balance against developing countries in dispute settlement.

6. CONCLUSION

The above has shown that to date, many questions about the extent and manner of civil society participation in WTO dispute settlement processes remain unsettled. Despite some progress through practice and case law, the inability of WTO members to address the issue clearly has hampered NGOs' efforts to participate effectively.

Essentially, the status quo places clear limits on what tribunals can and will accept from *amici curiae*. However, a brief tailored to comply with those limits, stands the chance of losing some, if not all, of its value as an independent source of information and/or analysis. In addition, even though WTO Panels and the Appellate Body have declared that they have the general authority to accept and con-

---

[51] Bechtel is suing Bolivia for US$25 million in lost profits after the Californian engineering giant failed in its efforts to take over Cochabamba's public water system.

sider *amicus curiae* briefs, they will rarely exercise their discretion to consider any brief independently submitted by an NGO.

Yet, the WTO tribunals' current treatment of *amicus curiae* briefs may be a political necessity. Declaring that they can accept *amicus curiae* briefs and giving the indication that civil society can play a role, even if minimal, in the state-to-state dispute settlement, can − at least in part − please civil society groups. This approach also has the potential to please those WTO members which advocate a role (even if limited) for civil society in international economic institutions. At the same time, by exercising their discretion to either not accept or not consider the briefs, the tribunals also reach out to those members who are against greater civil society involvement in WTO disputes and who were audibly irritated by the tribunals' assertion that *amicus curiae* briefs could be submitted in WTO disputes in the first case.

Thus, the tribunals have created a limited appearance of transparency and openness towards civil society, while also effectively remaining deferential to some members' position that WTO dispute settlement should maintain a strict state-to-state character. While not provoking a confrontational crisis with either members or civil society groups, from a civil society point of view the Panels' and Appellate Body's current practices, as well as members' inability truly to address the issue, still appear far from satisfactory. Currently, to achieve effective civil society participation, there still remains a long way to go.

Chapter 19

NGOs and the WTO Dispute Settlement Mechanism

Marcella Distefano

1. INTRODUCTORY REMARKS

The participation of civil society in the WTO dispute settlement system is without doubt important not only for specialized experts in WTO law and practice, but also for experts of international law in general. This issue has already been examined in detail, and I will not repeat the previous discussion here. However, a few interesting elements have arisen for consideration in the recent practice concerning the review of the Dispute Settlement Understanding (DSU) system.

The contrast on this topic between the position of legal literature and the Chairman's text of 28 May 2003, which represents the legal draft for the amendment of the DSU, is paradoxical.[1] The Report of the Special Session of the Dis-

---

[1] In fact, several authors have analysed this matter, pointing out its importance. See B. Stern, 'L'intervention des tiers dans le contentieux de l'OMC' (2003) *Rev. Gén. Dr. Int. Pub.* 257; E. Baroncini, 'L'apertura alla società civile del sistema di risoluzione delle controversie dell'OMC: gli amici curiae' (2003) 42 *Dir. Com. Sc. Int.* 115; R. Baratta, 'La legittimazione dell' "amicus curiae" dinanzi agli organi giudiziali della Organizzazione mondiale del commercio' (2002) 85 *Riv. Dir. Int.* 549; S. Charnovitz, 'Judicial Independence in the World Trade Organization' in L. Boisson de Chazournes, C. Romano and R. Mackenzie (eds.), *International Organizations and International Dispute Settlement: Trends and Prospects* (New York, 2002), pp. 219–240; J. Razzaque, 'Changing Role of Friends of the Court in the International Courts and Tribunals' (2001) 1 *Non-State Actors & Int'l L.* 169; H. Ascensio, 'L'amicus curiae devant les juridictions internationales' (2001) 105 *Rev. Gén. Dr. Int. Pub.* 897; G. Marceau and M. Stilwell, 'Practical Suggestions for Amicus Curiae Briefs Before WTO Adjudicating Bodies' (2001) 4 *J. Int'l Economic L.* 155; A. Reinisch and C. Irgel, 'The Participation of Non-Governmental Organisations (NGOs) in the WTO Dispute Settlement System' (2001) 1 *Non-State Actors & Int'l L.* 127; A.E. Appleton, 'Amicus Curiae Submissions in the Carbon Steel Case: Another Rabbit from Appellate Body's Hat?' (2000) 3 *J. Int'l Econ. L.* 697; G.A. Zonnekeyn, 'The Appellate Body's Communication on Amicus Curiae Briefs in the Asbestos Case. An Echternach Procession?' (2001) 33 *J. W. T.* 553; R. Wilkinson, 'The WTO in Crisis. Exploring the Dimensions of Institutional Inertia' (2001) 33 *J. W. T.* 397; J.H.H. Weiler, 'The Rule of Lawyers and the Ethos of Diplomats: Reflections on the Internal and External Legitimacy of WTO Dispute Settlement' (2001) 33 *J. W. T.* 191; P. Sands, 'Turtles and Torturers: The Transformation of International Law' (2001) 33 *NYU J. Int'l L. & Pol.* 527; E. Hernández-López, 'Recent Trends and Perspectives for Non-State Actor Participation in World Trade Organization Disputes' (2001) 33 *J. W. T.* 469; G.C. Umbricht, 'An "Amicus Curiae Brief" on Amicus Curiae Briefs at the WTO' (2001) 4 *J. Int'l Econ. L.* 773; P. Mavroidis, *Amicus Curiae Briefs before the WTO: Much Ado About Nothing*, (2001) Jean Monnet Working Paper 2/01 <http://www.jeanmonnetprogram.org/papers/01/

T. Treves et al., eds., Civil Society, International Courts and Compliance Bodies
© *2005, T·M·C·Asser Press, The Hague, The Netherlands, and the Authors*

pute Settlement Body (DSB) of 6 June 2003 reveals that a number of innovative proposals could not be included in the Chair's proposal due to the absence of a 'sufficiently high level of support', with special emphasis on the clarification of *amicus curiae* briefs.

2.   CASE LAW

The DSU contains no rules regarding the participation of NGOs (and of civil society in general).[2] However, Panels and the Appellate Body have examined the topic in detail, adopting different and sometimes contradictory solutions. WTO practice may be considered in three stages.

The first stage is found in the *Shrimps* case. In this case, Article 13 of the DSU, which allows the Panel to seek information from any relevant source and consult experts in order to obtain their opinion on certain aspects of the case, was initially considered the legal basis to reject by implication *amicus curiae* briefs presented by certain environmental NGOs.[3]

010201.html>; J.A Scholte, R. O'Brien and M. Williams, 'The WTO and Civil Society' (1999) 31 *J. W. T.* 107; D.C. Esty, 'Non-governmental Organisations at the World Trade Organization: Co-operation, Competition or Exclusion' (1998) 1 *J. Int'l Econ. L.* 123.

[2] The participation of civil society in the WTO Dispute Settlement mechanism reveals a general problem affecting all dispute settlement systems. This problem focuses on the need to balance confidentiality and transparency of official documents and procedures. Before considering the different issues regarding the powers of civil society in the DSU system, it is important to understand at what point the different components of civil society become aware of the topics examined by the Panels and the Appellate Body. This is preliminary to the participation of civil society in the WTO procedures. The DSU regards the confidentiality rule as a central rule of the system, and the Rules of Conduct impose confidentiality as a general rule of behaviour on all individuals who have access to the documents of the parties. This rule is mitigated by the possibility for members to make public their positions or to ask a member for a non-confidential summary of the information contained in a written statement for public disclosure. The importance of the confidentiality rule concerning, in particular, business information furnished by the members has been repeatedly expressed in the WTO jurisprudence. See *Thailand – Anti-Dumping Duties on – Angles, Shapes and Sections of Iron or Non-Alloy Steel and H-Beams from Poland*, Report of the Appellate Body (Doc. WT/DS122/AB/R). This case posed the question of the violation of the confidentiality rule and stressed the problem of public disclosure of the contents of the parties' submissions. In fact, the violation of the confidentiality rule came to light following the presentation of an *amicus curiae* brief by the Consuming Industries Trade Action Coalition (CITAC) of the United States. According to Thailand, the CITAC brief clearly indicated that this organization had had access to the appellant's communication, in violation of Articles 17(10) and 18(2) of the DSU. The Appellate Body rejected the brief of this coalition since it did not deem it appropriate to keep contact with CITAC, specifying that it did not consider the brief pertinent.

[3] *United States – Import Prohibition of Certain Shrimp and Shrimp Products*, Report of the Panel of 15 May 1998, Doc. WT/DS58/R. The facts of the case are very well known. It is interesting to note that, during the Panel proceedings, two NGOs (the Centre for Marine Conservation and the Centre for International Environmental Law) presented a joint communication. Some months after, the Panel received another brief from the World Wide Fund for Nature. Moreover, the Panel acknowledged receipt of two briefs sent by the NGOs directly to the parties.

First, it was emphasized that information submitted by NGOs had not been solicited by the Panel. This reaffirmed, on the basis of Article 13 of the DSU, the absolute and discretionary right for the Panel to seek information from the source it deemed most appropriate. Secondly, according to the Panel, the parties are free to present any type of document that they deem pertinent to the case, including from NGOs. In fact, the United States took advantage of this possibility, annexing the document presented by the Centre for Marine Conservation and the Centre for International Environmental Law to its second submission.

The Panel followed Article 13 of the DSU to the letter, interpreting the acceptance of non-requested information as incompatible with the provisions of the DSU. The United States lodged an appeal against the decision of the Panel on this issue and they added three *amicus curiae* briefs presented by three groups of NGOs to their submission.[4]

The Appellate Body modified the ruling of the Panel that the request for intervention by the NGOs was incompatible with Article 13 of the DSU. It pointed out that this provision should not be interpreted literally. The Panel has, according to the Appellate Body, the discretionary power to accept, consider or reject any information and opinions offered.[5]

Notwithstanding the acceptance of the NGOs' briefs as an integral part of the American submission,[6] the Appellate Body posed a very precise question to the US government: 'to what extent do you agree with or adopt any one or more of the legal arguments set out in the three briefs prepared by the non-governmental organizations and appended as exhibits to your appellant's submission? In particular, do you adopt the legal arguments stated therein relating to paragraphs (b) and (g) and the chapeau of Article XX of the GATT 1994?'.[7]

---

[4] The US government emphasised, moreover, that 'three groups of these organizations – each with specialized expertise in conservation of sea turtles and other endangered species – have prepared submissions reflecting their respective independent views with respect to the use of TEDs and other issues. The United States is submitting these materials to the Appellate Body for its information'.

[5] *United States – Import Prohibition of Certain Shrimp and Shrimp Products*, Report of the Appellate Body of 12 October 1998, Doc. WT/DS58/AB/R, especially paras. 102-110. The Appellate Body, however, specified that 'this practical disposition of the matter by the Panel in this dispute may be detached from the legal interpretation adopted by the Panel of the word "seek" in Article 13.1 of the DSU' (ibid., para. 109). In particular, the Appellate Body concluded that 'the Panel erred in its legal interpretation that accepting non-requested information from non-governmental sources is incompatible with the provisions of the DSU. At the same time, we consider that the Panel acted within the scope of its authority under Articles 12 and 13 of the DSU in allowing any party to the dispute to attach the briefs by non-governmental organizations, or any portion thereof, to its own submissions' (ibid., para. 110).

[6] 'We have decided to accept for consideration, insofar as they may be pertinent, the legal arguments made by the various non-governmental organizations in the three briefs attached as exhibits to the appellant's submission of the United States, as well as the revised version of the brief by the Centre for International Environmental et al., which was submitted to us on 3 August 1998' (ibid., para. 83).

[7] Ibid., para. 84.

The American government suggested that the Appellate Body should take the NGOs' briefs into consideration as representing an independent point of view. The role of the NGOs, as suggested by the United States, was to give a specialized opinion on the question of conservation of sea turtles and other endangered species. However, the US government approved only those legal arguments contained in the NGOs' briefs that concurred with their opinions.

Two evolutionary aspects are to be emphasized in the WTO jurisprudence. First, on the basis of the provisions of the DSU, of the rights of the parties to the dispute and of the discretionary powers of the Panel to seek information, the issue of the admission of the NGOs' briefs was resolved with the acceptance of the NGOs' briefs as an integral part of the American submission.

The second issue pertains to the relevance to be attributed by the Appellate Body to the legal arguments proposed by NGOs. Although in principle the Appellate Body intended to confer legal relevance on the arguments submitted by NGOs,[8] explicit reference to the points made by NGOs never appeared in the final report.

Some perplexity therefore arises from the Appellate Body's decision, as these briefs put forward legal arguments and not new allegations of violations of the WTO agreements. The Appellate Body itself noted this distinction in the *Hormones* case.[9] In order to develop its legal reasoning, the Panel could adopt the legal arguments made by NGOs, as long as these do not exceed the scope of the original claim.

The second stage in our analysis is to be found in the *British Steel Products* case. The first difference from the *Shrimps* case is that the communications were presented in the appeal phase and not in the Panel proceedings. Secondly, the Appellate Body received two documents (described as '*amicus curiae* briefs' in their accompanying letters) directly from the American Iron and Steel Institute and from the Speciality Steel Industry of North America, which are two private associations of steel producers.

The reaction of the member states was immediate. The European Communities sent a letter indicating that these briefs were not suitable for acceptance at the appeal phase. Article 13 of the DSU only allows receipt of *amicus curiae* briefs at the Panel proceedings stage. It was stressed that this article could not be ap-

---

[8] The CIEL communication affirms the desire to furnish not only scientific information but also 'legal arguments supporting interpretation of WTO rules in light of international environmental law principles for sustainable development'. The same holds true for the WWF brief that 'ensures that the WTO Dispute Settlement System has before it both the scientific and other technical facts relevant to the conservation of sea turtles; and the relevant international, regional and national law and policy governing the conservation of sea turtles'.

[9] *EC – Measures Concerning Meat and Meat Products (Hormones)*, Report of the Appellate Body of 16 January 1998. 'Panels are inhibited from addressing legal claims falling outside their terms of reference. However, nothing in the DSU limits the faculty of a panel freely to use arguments submitted by any of the parties – or to develop its own legal reasoning – to support its own findings and conclusions on the matter under its consideration' (ibid. para. 156).

plied in appeal proceedings and concerns the facts and the opinions of experts and not legal arguments or legal interpretations from non-state actors.

The Appellate Body pointed out that neither the DSU nor the Working Procedures expressly prevent the examination of briefs during the appeal stage. Article 17(9) clearly indicates that the Appellate Body enjoys great discretion regarding any procedures which are not in conflict with the rules of procedure set out in the DSU or in the multilateral agreements. The Appellate Body felt that it should be free to decide whether or not to accept and examine the information that could be considered pertinent and useful in each given dispute. At the same time, the Appellate Body stressed that:

> Individuals and organizations, which are not Members of the WTO, have no legal right to make submissions to or to be heard by the Appellate Body. The Appellate Body has no legal duty to accept or consider unsolicited *amicus curiae* briefs submitted by individuals or organizations, not Members of the WTO. The Appellate Body has a legal duty to accept and consider only submissions from WTO Members which are parties or third parties in a particular dispute.[10]

The most important aspects of the appellate procedure appear to be the assessment of the rights of the parties and the determination of the powers of the Appellate Body. The latter ensures a regular procedure by asking the participants to express their opinions on the question in issue. Most importantly, in the light of its regulatory powers, the Appellate Body affirmed the possibility of considering *amicus curiae* briefs from civil society. This decision could result in real progress, through the introduction of an evaluation of the pertinence and usefulness of the information received. If the communications are pertinent it is possible to take them into consideration whether they are from NGOs, industry associations or other non-state actors.

The third stage coincides with the *Asbestos* case.[11] For the first time, the Appellate Body decided to adopt an *ad hoc* rule on the issue of NGOs' participation

---

[10] The *amicus curiae* participation of NGOs was also taken into consideration in the same way by an arbitral tribunal established under Chapter XI of the North American Free Trade Agreement (NAFTA). The parties argued for the confidentiality of the documents, the jurisdiction of the tribunal and the equitable development of the procedure, which constituted three sensitive aspects. The tribunal stressed that to accept 'written submissions from a person other than the Disputing Parties is not equivalent to adding that person as a party to the arbitration'. In order to demonstrate the legal reasoning, the tribunal quoted the Appellate Body's decision in the *Steel* case: 'This WTO practice demonstrates that the scope of a procedural power can extend to the receipt of written submissions from non-party third persons, even in a judicial procedure affecting the rights and obligations of state parties; and further it also demonstrates that the receipt of such submissions confers no rights, procedural or substantive, on such persons'. see *In the Matter of an Arbitration under Chapter 11 of the North American Free Trade Agreement and the UNCITRAL Arbitration Rules, Methanex Corporation v United States of America*, Decision of the Tribunal on Petitions from Third Persons to Intervene as 'Amicus Curiae' of 15 January 2001, para. 30.

[11] See *European Communities – Measures Affecting Asbestos and Asbestos-Containing Products*, Report of the Appellate Body of 12 March 2001, Doc. WT/DS135/AB/R.

in the proceedings.[12] This prompted a strong reaction from member states.

According to the additional procedure to deal with written communications received from non-members, adopted by the Appellate Body, the request for authorization to deposit a written brief must contain a description of the applicant, its aims, nature of activity, financial sources, interest in the dispute, and the legal issues and interpretations of the Panel to which objection is made. Finally, the applicant must make a contribution to the solution of the dispute and declare if it has any direct or indirect ties with any party or third party or if assistance, either financial or otherwise, has been or will be received from a disputing party (in order to prepare the authorization or written brief).

According to the Appellate Body, in order to implement a supplementary rule on the participation of civil society, it is necessary to guarantee the rights of the disputing parties. In the presence of non-requested communications, any states participating in the procedure must have the possibility to express their views and to prepare written or oral comments. If, at any stage in the proceedings, a third party could present a brief and request the Appellate Body to consider it, the regular administration of justice and the basic procedural right of the disputing parties would be compromised.

This decision of the Appellate Body provoked negative reactions among the member states even though its aim was to enhance the principle of due process. This reaction mainly arose because the position of the Appellate Body was seen as affecting the rights and obligations of the WTO members and modified the relationships among the organs of the system. Egypt,[13] representing the informal group of developing countries, requested an immediate meeting of the General Council. According to Uruguay, any decision by an organ of the Organization that affects the functioning of the system must be explicitly based on the existing rules of the WTO agreements.[14]

Member states were concerned about the possibility that individuals and NGOs could be afforded a right which they themselves did not possess. In brief, according to member states, the Appellate Body had exceeded its powers. This raised the issue of the relationships among the different WTO organs.

The situation was paradoxical. On one hand, the Appellate Body decided to adopt an additional procedure in order to further the principle of due process. On the other, the majority of member states objected to this decision, reaffirming the exclusive powers of the General Council and the prerogatives of members in this matter. The participation of civil society in the dispute settlement procedures be-

---

[12] See the procedure in *European Communities – Measures Affecting Asbestos and Asbestos-Containing Products*, Communication of the Appellate Body of 8 November 2000, Doc. WT/DS135/9.

[13] See *Minutes of Meeting of General Council of 22 November 2000*, Doc. WT/GC/M/60 (23 January 2001).

[14] See *Decision by the Appellate Body Concerning Amicus Curiae Briefs – Statement by Uruguay at the General Council on 22 November 2000*, Doc. WT/GC/38 (4 December 2000).

came a factor of institutional instability among the political and legal organs of the Organization.

This fear that a procedural privilege was being afforded to NGOs over the procedural rights of member states was dispelled by a further decision of the Appellate Body. In the *Sardines* case the Appellate Body extended the possibility to submit an *amicus curiae* brief to a member, Morocco, which decided to waive its right of intervention as a third party.[15] The Appellate Body stated that:

> It is true that, unlike private individuals or organizations, WTO Members are given an explicit right, under Articles 10.2 and 17.4 of the DSU, to participate in dispute settlement proceedings as third parties. Thus, the question arises whether the existence of this explicit right, which is not accorded to non-Members, justifies treating WTO Members differently from non-WTO Members in the exercise of our authority to receive *amicus curiae* briefs. We do not believe that it does. We have been urged by the parties to this dispute not to treat Members less favourably than non-Members with regard to participation as *amicus curiae*. We agree. We have not. And we will not. As we have already determined that we have the authority to receive an *amicus curiae* brief from a private individual or an organization, *a fortiori* we are entitled to accept such a brief from a WTO Member, provided there is no prohibition on doing so in the DSU. We find no such prohibition. None of the participants in this appeal has pointed to any provision of the DSU that can be understood as prohibiting WTO Members from participating in panel or appellate proceedings as an *amicus curiae*. Nor has any participant in this appeal demonstrated how such participation would contravene the DSU.[16]

3.   REVIEW OF THE DISPUTE SETTLEMENT UNDERSTANDING

The Ministerial Conference of Doha in November 2001 initiated the DSU review. This investigated the issue of civil society participation in the meetings of political organs and, especially, the presentation by civil society organizations of *amicus curiae* briefs to judicial organs. Among the proposals considered is that of the European Communities. The European Communities communication focuses on three aspects: the admission of *amicus curiae* briefs, the procedures and the

---

[15] The decision of the Appellate Body in September 2002 to modify the Working Procedures ensures the member states a broader participation in the procedure. This modification was applied provisionally from 27 September 2002, and was still in force in May 2003. See the consolidated, revision version of the Working Procedures for Appellate Review, 1 May 2003, Doc. WT/AB/WP/7. The document prepared by the Appellate Body, which considers the observations of the members, underlines the necessity to adopt a flexible approach regarding the intervention of a third party. The most important modification concerns the definition of 'third participant'. The new formulation considers the 'third participant' any third party that has filed written submission or any third party that appears at the oral hearing. Accordingly, the rule requiring third parties to file a written communication in order to participate at the hearing was revoked. The Appellate Body can accept a third participant as long as due process is respected.

[16] See *European Communities – Trade Description of Sardines*, Report of the Appellate Body of 26 September 2002, Doc. WT/DS231/AB/R.

relationship between *amicus curiae* briefs and the disputing parties, particularly developing countries.

The European Communities emphasized the need to avoid slowing down the work of the Panel and the Appellate Body. The European Communities suggested two steps: first, the request for authorization to submit briefs and second, the actual presentation of the briefs. The Panel and the Appellate Body should be responsible for deciding if the briefs refer to factual or legal findings of the dispute. The European Communities suggested leaving the organs to evaluate the ties between those requesting intervention and the parties and third parties. If the Panel or the Appellate Body accept the briefs they must give their reasons for this decision. Most importantly, it was proposed that 'The Appellate Body/Panel would be free to address ... arguments included in *amicus* briefs that have been admitted' and not allegations of violations of the agreements.[17]

As far as the parties are concerned, the European Communities repeated the need to guarantee their right to reply to the arguments contained in the briefs.[18]

As to third parties, the negotiations for the DSU review show that this represents a fundamental issue. Numerous communications stress the need to guarantee such participation in all proceedings. For example, Costa Rica underlines that the DSU must be modified to allow third parties access to any submissions and general information sent to the Panel or Appellate Body.[19] The Kenyan government, on behalf of the African Group, presented a communication entitled 'The Diminutive Participation of the Developing Members to the DS Procedures'.[20] In order to clarify the rights of third parties the African Group proposed that developing-country members should not be required to demonstrate a trade or economic interest in the dispute as a precondition for admission and should always be admitted as third parties at any stage of the proceedings.

Finally, the European Communities paid attention to the rights of the developing countries, emphasizing that 'the acceptance of *amicus curiae* should not create substantial additional burdens for the developing Members'. On this point the negotiations regarding Article 13 of the DSU are particularly interesting. The communication of India[21] proposes the introduction of a footnote to Article 13 of

---

[17] See *Dispute Settlement Body – Special Session – Negotiations on the Dispute Settlement Understanding – Communication from the European Communities*, Doc. TN/DS/W/1 (13 March 2002).

[18] The most sensitive aspect of this participation is the consideration given by the Panel to communications from these entities. In order to influence the legal conclusion of the Panel, the members have used various arguments, such as the nature of the WTO agreements, which through inheriting the characteristics of the GATT 1947, are similar to contractual obligations; the previously mentioned confidentiality of business information; respect for state sovereignty; and the danger of modifying the negotiated agreements in the Uruguay Round. The members are unwilling to grant any more power to the Panels and the Appellate Body than that outlined in the DSU.

[19] See *Dispute Settlement Body – Special Session – Proposal by Costa Rica – Third Party Rights – Communication from Costa Rica – Revision*, Doc. TN/DS/W/12/Rev. 1 (6 March 2003).

[20] See *Dispute Settlement Body – Special Session – Negotiations on the Dispute Settlement Understanding – Proposal by the African Group*, Doc. TN/DS/W/15 (25 September 2002).

[21] See *Dispute Settlement Body – Special Session – Dispute Settlement Understanding Proposals: Legal Text – Communication from India on behalf of Cuba, Dominican Republic, Egypt, Honduras, Jamaica and Malaysia*, Doc. TN/DS/W/47 (11 February 2003).

the DSU according to which the term '"Seek" shall mean any information and technical advice that is sought or asked for, or demanded or requested by a panel. A panel shall not accept unsolicited information'. The proposal by the African Group is even clearer. Regarding the right of the Panels to seek information the communication proposes that 'un-requested information may be directed to the parties and shall not be directed to the panels. The Appellate Body shall not receive information that is inconsistent with its exclusive function of examining questions of law and legal interpretations raised on appeal'.[22]

The US government simply indicated that 'it would be helpful to propose guideline procedures for handling *amicus curiae* submissions to address those procedural concerns that have been raised by Members, Panels and the Appellate Body'. The US government does not believe that an amendment to the Dispute Settlement Understanding is necessary for this purpose.

The Chair's text of 28 May 2003, which proposes amendments to the DSU, addresses many issues, including, *inter alia*, the enhancement of third party rights, both at the Panel and appellate stage, the introduction of an interim review stage and remand at the appellate stage, and clarification and improvement of the sequence and details of procedure at the implementation stage.[23] However, the Chair's proposal, as mentioned above, does not contain any specific provision on the participation of NGOs as *amici curiae*. This absence adds to the tensions between the legal and political dimensions in the WTO process.

4. FUTURE DEVELOPMENTS

In the author's opinion, the jurisprudence of the Appellate Body influences both WTO practice and the evolution of the principles regulating international judicial procedures.

In the specialized area of international trade, this evolution leads to the affirmation of the need to adopt clear formulas on the participation of civil society in WTO dispute settlement procedures.[24] This opens up three possibilities: First, revision of the WTO Dispute Settlement Understanding, but, as we have seen, there is not sufficient political support for this among member states; secondly, modification of the Appellate Body's Working Procedures by the Appellate Body itself;

---

[22] See *Proposal by the African Group*, n. 20 above.

[23] See *Dispute Settlement Body – Special Session – Report by the Chairman, Ambassador Péter Balás, to the Trade Negotiations Committee*, Doc. TN/DS/9 (6 June 2003). The proposals include: the enhancement of compensation; the strengthening of the notification requirements for mutually agreed solutions; and the strengthening of special and differential treatment for developing countries at various stages of the proceedings.

[24] Recently (27 May 2004), an international coalition of 15 public interest groups filed an *amicus curiae* brief to the Panel charged to settle the dispute *European Communities – Measures Affecting the Approval and Marketing of Biotech Products* (Docs WT/DS291, WT/DS292, WT/DS293). The decision is expected at the end of 2004. The full brief and background information is available at <www.genewatch.org/WTO.htm>.

thirdly, leaving things as they are, namely, to leave the Panels and the Appellate Body the discretion to find a jurisprudential solution to the issue on a case by case basis. In practice, if the states are late in coming to a solution acceptable to all members, the adoption of ad hoc rules on the basis of the Working Procedures will be the only alternative.

The practice of the WTO finally raises the question of the future evolution of the participation of NGOs, private associations or individuals in the international mechanisms for the settlement of disputes. Other international tribunals cannot ignore this evolution, as the *Methanex* case[25] demonstrated. These indications are also fundamental in the light of the characteristics of international tribunals. The autonomy of these tribunals allows them to adopt independent solutions in each case. This autonomy appears necessary to ensure an appropriate level of legal protection. The Appellate Body's cautious approach to establishing rules on the nature and functions of NGOs underlines this.

---

[25] See n. 10 above.

Chapter 20

The Accessibility of European Integration Courts from an NGO Perspective

Jessica Maria Almqvist

1. INTRODUCTION

The international community of states increasingly relies upon the activities of non-governmental organizations (NGOs) in the development and implementation of international law.[1] In this regard, NGOs perform an invaluable function as providers of information, expertise and evidence about international law and fact to international public (judicial and quasi-judicial) bodies. They also serve as defenders of unrepresented persons and public interests. These functions are critical components of the effective delivery of international justice. Still, it is precisely in the international judicial context where NGOs often experience obstacles. Their ability to play a role in the international judicial process, whether it is to institute proceedings, intervene or act as *amicus curiae* ('friend of the court'), can be very limited. This is especially true for NGOs in relation to the regional integration courts in Europe: the European Court of Justice (ECJ), the Court of First Instance (CFI) and the European Free Trade Agreement (EFTA) Court.

2. ROLE OF THE EUROPEAN INTEGRATION COURTS

The regional courts are critical institutional players in the European integration process. The ECJ, to begin with, is the judicial body created by the Treaties establishing the Coal and Steel Community,[2] the European Economic Community[3] and the Atomic Energy Community.[4] Economic integration, free and fair trade among the members, access to resources and mobility of goods and labour formed the bedrock of the initial undertakings of the interlocking Community Treaties. Since 1951, however, there have been several amendments to the found-

---

[1] Dinah Shelton, 'The Participation of Nongovernmental Organizations in International Judicial Proceedings' (1994) 88 *Am. J. Int'l L.* 611, at 616.

[2] Treaty instituting the European Coal and Steel Community 1951, Article 7.

[3] Treaty establishing the European Economic Community 1957, Article 7 (ex 4).

[4] Treaty establishing the European Atomic Energy Community 1957, Article 3.

T. Treves et al., eds., Civil Society, International Courts and Compliance Bodies
© 2005, T·M·C·ASSER PRESS, *The Hague, The Netherlands, and the Authors*

ing Treaties extending the competences of the various Community institutions. In broad terms, the task of the ECJ is to ensure that 'in the interpretation and application of this Treaty [Treaty establishing the European Community] the law is observed'.[5] To this end, the ECJ has competence to review omissions by member states[6] as well as acts[7] and omissions[8] by the Community institutions. It also gives preliminary rulings,[9] settles compensation claims in relation to the Community institutions,[10] and staff cases.[11]

The Single European Act provided for the creation of a Court of First Instance.[12] The CFI was then established in 1988.[13] The CFI is attached to the ECJ. It has jurisdiction to hear and determine, at first instance, subject to a right of appeal to the ECJ on points of law and in accordance with the conditions laid down by the Statute.[14] The CFI has been created to improve the judicial protection of individual interests and to respond to the growing caseload of the ECJ so as to enable the ECJ to focus on its main task of ensuring a uniform interpretation of Community law.[15] Through successive decisions in 1988, 1993 and 1994, the Council has conferred to the CFI jurisdiction to hear actions brought by natural and legal persons concerning acts and omissions by Community institutions as well as fines, staff regulations and contractual obligations.[16] The EC Treaty now reserves to the ECJ only the jurisdiction to deliver 'preliminary rulings'.[17]

The Agreement on the European Economic Area ('EEA Agreement') established the EFTA Court in 1992.[18] Similarly to the EC Treaty, the EEA Agree-

---

[5] EC Treaty, Article 220.

[6] EC Treaty, Article 226 (the Commission may bring such an action) and Article 227 (a member state may bring such an action).

[7] EC Treaty, Article 230(1). It reads: 'The Court of Justice shall review the legality of acts adopted jointly by the European Parliament and the Council, of acts of the Council, of the Commission and of the ECB, other than recommendations and opinions, and of acts of the European Parliament intended to produce legal effects vis-à-vis third parties'.

[8] EC Treaty, Article 232.

[9] EC Treaty, Article 234.

[10] EC Treaty, Articles 235 and 288.

[11] EC Treaty, Article 236. The list is not exhaustive. See also EC Treaty, Articles 237, 238 and 239.

[12] Single European Act 1986, Articles 4, 11 and 26.

[13] Council Decision of 24 October 1988 establishing a Court of First Instance of the European Communities [1988] OJ L319/1.

[14] EC Treaty, Article 225(1).

[15] The CFI was initially envisaged by the Single European Act (entered into effect on 1 July 1987). Through successive decisions in 1988, 1993 and 1994, the Council of the EU has conferred upon the CFI jurisdiction in matters concerning Community institutions and individuals.

[16] See Council Decision 93/350 Euratom, ECSC, EEC of 8 June 1993 amending Council Decision 88/591/ECSC, EEC, Euratom establishing a Court of First Instance of the European Communities [1993] OJ L144/21; Council Decision of 7 March 1994 amending Decision 93/350/Euratom, ECSC, EEC amending Decision 88/591/ECSC, EEC, Euratom establishing a Court of First Instance of the European Communities [1994] OJ L66/29.

[17] EC Treaty, Article 177.

[18] Agreement on the European Economic Area ('EEA Agreement') (2 May 1992), Article 108(2).

ment promotes economic integration, free and fair trade among the members, access to resources and mobility of goods, service, people and capital. The EFTA Court has been set up to hear and deliver rulings in cases involving (a) the surveillance procedure regarding the EFTA states; (b) decisions in the field of competition taken by the EFTA Surveillance Authority; and (c) disputes between two or more EFTA states.[19] More specifically, it has jurisdiction in disputes between two or more EFTA states over the interpretation or application of EFTA law (the EEA Agreement, the Agreement on a Standing Committee of the EFTA States or 'the present Agreement')[20] as well as actions[21] and omissions[22] by the EFTA Surveillance Authority, and claims related to compensation for damages caused by the Authority.[23] Finally, it gives advisory opinions on the interpretation of the EEA Agreement on request from the national courts of the EFTA states.[24]

The CFI and ECJ form a two-tier court system. The CFI is not created as a special jurisdiction separate and independent from the ECJ. Instead, the operation of the CFI has been framed around the idea that a single institution, the ECJ, houses two separate bodies: the ECJ itself and the CFI.[25] A hierarchy exists since the ECJ is the final arbiter on points of Community law. The EFTA Court, in contrast, is independent from the ECJ and CFI. Even so, many provisions of the EEA Agreement and the EC Treaty overlap or are identical with one another. The EEA Agreement stipulates that it is a fundamental objective to arrive at as 'uniform an interpretation as possible of the provisions of the Agreement and those provisions of Community legislation which are substantially reproduced in the Agreement'.[26] To this end, the EEA Agreement sets up a 'system of exchange of information' concerning judgments of the EFTA Court, the ECJ and the CFI.[27] Moreover, the EFTA Court is required to follow the relevant rulings of the ECJ with respect to provisions of EFTA law which are identical in substance with Community law given prior to the date of signature of the EEA Agreement.[28] After that date, the EFTA Court is not required to follow the reasoning of the ECJ; instead, it should 'pay due account to the principles laid down by the relevant rulings by the Court of Justice of the European Communities' with respect to provi-

---

[19] EEA Agreement, Article 108(2).

[20] Agreement between the EFTA States on the Establishment of a Surveillance Authority and a Court of Justice, signed in Porto on 2 May 1992 ('ESA/Court Agreement'), Article 32.

[21] ESA/Court Agreement, Article 36(1).

[22] ESA/Court Agreement, Article 37(1).

[23] ESA/Court Agreement, Articles 39 and 46(2).

[24] ESA/Court Agreement, Article 34; Rules of Procedure of the EFTA Court, Articles 96 and 97.

[25] P. Mengozzi, 'The Protection of Individual Rights and the Court of First Instance of the European Communities' (2000) 23 *Fordham Int'l L. J.* 707, at 712.

[26] EEA Agreement, Article 105(1). For an analysis of the relationship between the EFTA Court and the ECJ, see T. Ingadottir, 'The EEA Agreement and Homogenous Jurisprudence: The Two-Pillar Role Given to the EFTA Court and the Court of Justice of the European Communities' (2003) *The Global Community* 193.

[27] EEA Agreement, Article 106.

[28] ESA/Court Agreement, Article 3(1).

sions that are 'identical in substance'.[29] In practice, the EFTA Court tends to follow the reasoning of the ECJ on expressions in Community law when those expressions are identical in substance to those that fall to be interpreted by the EFTA Court.[30] However, a commitment to ensure homogeneity has led also the ECJ to consider, at least occasionally, the reasoning of the EFTA Court.[31]

3.   CIVIL SOCIETY AND NGOs

There is no generally accepted definition of 'non-governmental organization' (NGO) in international law. Instead, each international organization adopts its own definition. So accordingly has the European Union. According to the European Commission, the term 'NGO' refers to a range of organizations that normally share the following characteristics:

(a) NGOs are non-profit: although they may have paid employees and engage in revenue-generating activities, NGOs do not distribute profits or surpluses to members or management;

(b) NGOs are voluntary: NGOs are formed voluntarily and there is usually an element of voluntary participation in the organization;

(c) NGOs have a formal or institutionalized existence: NGOs are distinguished from informal or *ad hoc* groups by having some degree of formal or institutional existence. Usually, NGOs have formal statutes or another governing document setting out their mission, objectives and scope. They are accountable to their members and donors;

(d) NGOs are independent: in particular of government and other public authorities and of political parties or commercial organizations;

(e) NGOs have no self-serving aims and related values: their aim is to act in the public arena at large, on concerns and issues related to the wellbeing of people, specific groups of people or society as a whole. They are not pursuing the commercial or professional interests of their members.[32]

The Commission recognizes that, in the wider usage of the term, trade unions and business or professional organizations might also qualify as NGOs, but then en-

---

[29] ESA/Court Agreement, Article 3(2).

[30] E-1/94 *Restamark* [1994–95] EFTA Court Report 15, at paras. 24, 33 and 34; E-2/94 *Scottish Salmon Growers Association v EFTA Surveillance Authority* [1995] EFTA Court Report 59, at paras. 11-13; E-2/02 *Technologien Bau- und Wirtshaftsberatung GmbH and Bellona Foundation v EFTA Surveillance Authority* [2003], at para. 39.

[31] See, e.g., C-192/01 *Commission v Denmark* [2003] in which the ECJ overruled its older case law with reference to the EFTA Court's judgment in E-3/00 *EFTA Surveillance Authority v Norway* [2000–01] EFTA Court Report 73.

[32] Commission Discussion Paper, *The Commission and Non-Governmental Organizations: Building a Stronger Partnership* (approved by the Commission on 18 January 2000 and presented by President Prodi and Vice-President Kinnock), pp. 3–4.

dorses a narrower definition.[33] Thus, it makes a clear distinction between NGOs (on the one hand) and organizations, such as trade unions and agricultural and professional associations or federations (on the other). The latter are defined as 'special interest groups' as they exclusively represent the interests of their members. Their representative function distinguishes them from NGOs whose objective is to defend interests of common concern, such as consumer protection, human rights and the environment.[34]

The Economic and Social Committee also employs a narrow definition of NGOs. It understands civil society as comprising a range of organizations that mediates between the public and private sector, including:[35]

- labour-market players, i.e., trade unions and employers federations ('social partners');
- organizations representing social and economic players (not 'social partners' in the strict sense of the term);
- NGOs which bring people together in a common cause, such as environmental organizations, human rights organizations, consumer associations, charitable organizations, educational and training organizations, etc.;
- community-based organizations (CBOs), i.e., organizations set up within society at a grass roots level which pursue member-oriented objectives, e.g., youth organizations, family associations and all organizations through which citizens participate in local and municipal life; and
- religious communities.

In sum, both Community institutions want to reserve the term to organizations seeking to protect a public interest, i.e., an interest (believed to be) of common concern for society as a whole.

The present chapter adopts a broader definition of NGO. While the Community institutions essentially reserve the term 'NGO' to public interest groups, in the wider usage of that term, a variety of civil organizations are included, in particular special interest groups, such as trade unions and professional associations. In other words, it embraces all sorts of associations that make up civil society.

---

[33] Ibid.

[34] See Commission's Approach to Special Interest Groups: A General Overview, available at <http://europa.eu.int/comm/secretariat_general/sgc/lobbies/approche/apercu_en.htm> (last visited 6 October 2003). 'Special interest groups' can be further divided into two categories: non-profit organizations, e.g., European, international or national associations/federations, and profit-making organizations, e.g., legal advisers, public relations firms and consultants. The former are mainly professional organizations.

[35] The definition of 'civil society' is available at <www.ces.eu.int/pages/en/acs/ SCO/SCO_accueil_en.htm>.

4. AVENUES FOR PARTICIPATION IN THE EUROPEAN JUDICIAL PROCESS

Civil society and its many associations are believed to be critical vehicles in the European integration process and especially in the context of the European governance project. Above all, they play an active role as consultants, i.e., providers of information and expertise, and representatives of vulnerable groups, such as disabled persons or ethnic minorities, or of specific issues, such as the environment, animal welfare and world trade, in relation to the Commission of the European Union, the European Parliament, the Economic and Social Committee, the Committee of the Regions and the Council.[36] However, NGOs are not merely interested in influencing the legislative and administrative branches of the European Union; a variety of NGOs, in particular special interest groups, but also public interest groups, have demonstrated an interest in having recourse to the European judicial process to demand review of decisions made by these institutions.

In light of the increasing importance given to civil society organizations, one might expect a relative openness toward the claims and concerns voiced by them from the standpoint of the judicial branches of European integration. This is by no means the case. As the present section seeks to demonstrate, the avenues that in principle are available for associations are essentially open only to special interest groups and exclude public interest groups.

4.1 *Amicus curiae* briefs

None of the courts confers an explicit right to submit *amicus curiae* briefs. The rules governing the ECJ and the CFI, i.e., the Statute of the European Court of Justice, the Rules of Procedure of the European Court of Justice, and the Rules of the Court of First Instance, do not mention *amicus curiae* briefs. This omission may depend on the role given to Advocates-General before the ECJ. It is a unique system to represent the public interest. According to Article 222(1):

> It is the duty of the Advocate-General, acting with complete impartiality and independence, to make, in open court, reasoned submissions on cases brought before the Court of Justice, in order to assist the Court in the performance of the task assigned to it in Article 220.

Still, the Advocates-General do not assist the CFI. A judge designated for the purpose of reasoned submissions may only perform the role of Advocate-General in a limited number of cases. Nevertheless, there is no right for a public interest group or any other NGO for that matter to provide information and expertise to the CFI.

The Statute of the EFTA Court, in contrast, includes a provision allowing that Court to consider *amicus curiae* briefs. Article 22 of the Statute stipulates that it

---

[36] Commission Discussion Paper, n. 32 above, at p. 5.

may 'at any time entrust any individual, body, authority, committee or other organization it chooses with the task of giving an expert opinion'.[37] While this provision does not confer a right to provide information and expertise about facts and law, it indicates a potential openness toward such submissions.

4.2 Third party interventions

NGOs have a limited possibility to make *amicus curiae* submissions as interveners in proceedings before the ECJ, the CFI and the EFTA Court provided they have a specific, direct and concrete interest in the case. According to Article 37 of the ECJ Statute, member states and institutions of the Community may intervene in cases before the ECJ and the CFI.[38] Any other person must establish:

> an interest in the result of any case submitted to the Court, save in cases between Member States, between institutions of the Community or between Member States and institutions of the Community.[39]

The expression 'result' refers to the operative part of the final judgment that the parties ask the court to deliver.[40] In other words, a mere interest in the pleas in law put forward is not sufficient.[41] For example, it is not enough that the prospective intervener is only interested in the success of certain of the applicant's arguments.[42] The interest must not relate merely to abstract legal arguments but to the actual form of order sought by a party to the main action.[43] Neither is it sufficient that the situation of a prospective intervener is similar to that of one of the parties.[44]

This said, however, both the ECJ and the CFI have adopted a broad interpretation of the expression 'an interest in the result of the case' in order to allow intervention by certain special interest groups (representative associations) whose purpose it is to protect their members in cases raising questions of principle liable

---

[37] Statute of the EFTA Court, Article 22.

[38] According to Article 47 of the ECJ Statute, Title III on Procedure shall apply to the CFI, with the exception of Articles 20 and 21.

[39] Protocol on the Statute of the Court of Justice, signed at Brussels on 17 April 1957, as last amended by Article 6III(3)(c) of the Treaty of Amsterdam: submissions made in an application to intervene shall be limited to supporting the submissions of one of the parties; see, e.g., T-191/96 *CAS Succhi di Frutta SpA v Commission*, Order of the Court of First Instance, 20 March 1998.

[40] C-157/97 P(I) *National Power and PowerGen* [1997] ECR I-3491, para. 57.

[41] CFI: T-18/97 *Atlantic Container Line AB and 15 other Liner Shipping Companies v Commission*, Order of the Fifth Chamber of the CFI on 23 March 1998, para. 10. ECJ: 116/77, 124/77 and 143/77 *Amylum and others v Council and Commission* [1978] ECR 893; and C-151/97 P(I) and C-157/97 P(I) *National Power and PowerGen* [1997] ECR I-3491, para. 66.

[42] 111/63 *Lemmerz-Werke v High Authority* [1965] ECR 677, at 717–718.

[43] *Consten and Grundig v Commission*, No. 56 and 58/64 [1966] ECR 382, at 383.

[44] C-76/93 P *Scaramuzza v Commission* [1993] ECR I-5715 and I-5722, para. 11; see also the orders of the Court of First Instance in T-97/92 and T-111/92 *Rijnoudt and Hocken v Commission* [1993] ECR II-587, para. 22, and T-87/92 *Kruidvat v Commission* [1993] ECR II-1375, para. 10.

to affect those members.[45] Even if such a group has not taken part in the preliminary administrative procedure, it may intervene if:

(a)   it represents an appreciable number of undertakings active in the sector concerned;
(b)   its objects include that of protecting its members' interests;
(c)   the case may raise questions of principle affecting the functioning of the sector concerned; and
(d)   the interests of its members may therefore be affected to an appreciable extent by the forthcoming judgment.[46]

According to the CFI, the purpose of a broad interpretation is to enable it to assess more fully the context of such cases while avoiding multiple individual interventions, which would compromise the effectiveness of the procedure.[47]

Thus, in *Confédération Nationale des Producteurs de Fruits et Légumes and others v Council*, the ECJ granted leave for intervention to an association of producers on the basis of the mere fact that the regulation at issue was capable of affecting the interests of national producers of certain goods. The producers and, thus, their representative had a 'direct, existing and undeniable interest in the continuation or annulment of the regulation at issue'.[48] Moreover, in *Telefis Eireann v Commission*, the ECJ granted leave to intervene to a non-profit making association whose interest was no more than an interest in establishing a general principle with which the original applicants hoped to persuade the Court.[49]

A similar openness toward interventions is exhibited in *Société anonyme Générale Sucrière and others v Commission* in which the prospective intervener was an Italian consumer organization (Unione Nazionale Consumatori) with an interest in representing and protecting consumers in a series of cases concerning the protection of the Italian market. The ECJ considered its interest as sufficient to justify intervention. As stated by the ECJ:

> Since it is the particular objective of the union to represent and protect consumers, it can show an interest in the correct application of community provisions in the field of competition, which not only ensure that the common market operates normally but which also tend to favour consumers. ... Accordingly, the intervention must be permit-

---

[45] Orders of 8 December 1993 in T-87/92 *Kruidvat v Commission* [1993] ECR II-1375, para. 14; and *National Power and PowerGen* [1997] ECR I-3491, para. 66.

[46] Orders of 8 December 1993 in T-87/92 *Kruidvat v Commission* [1993] ECR II-1375, para. 14; T-18/97 *Atlantic Container Line AB and 15 other Liner Shipping Companies v Commission*, Order of the Fifth Chamber of the CFI on 23 March 1998, para. 18.

[47] Orders of 8 December 1993 in T-87/92 *Kruidvat v Commission* [1993] ECR II-1375, para. 14.

[48] Order in 16/62 and 17/62 *Confédération Nationale des Producteurs de Fruits et Légumes and others v Council* [1962] ECR 487.

[49] C-241/91 *Radio Telefis Eireann v Commission* (unpublished), referred to in *National Power and PowerGen* [1997] ECR I-3491, paras. 33 and 67. The reason for this permission is the specific nature of the case and the composition and object of that association.

ted insofar as it supports submissions of the Commission with regard to its finding as to the protection of the Italian market.[50]

In another case, however, the ECJ denied a trade union leave for intervention in spite of its status as an organization representing workers employed in the industrial sector in which the applicant's undertakings were engaged. The original applicants sought to obtain compensation for the loss that the applicants claimed to have suffered when the Community had fixed an appropriate price for durum wheat. In support of its application for leave to intervene, the trade union argued that many skilled workers employed by the applicants stood to lose their employment because of the fixing of the price of the wheat. Nevertheless, the ECJ found that, since the trade union only sought to protect the economic wellbeing of persons employed in the sector, its interest in the result of the case (payment of compensation) was too remote to justify intervention in the proceedings.[51]

NGOs may also intervene in preliminary rulings proceedings before the ECJ.[52] However, only third parties who are also involved in the action before the national court making the request for a preliminary ruling have the right to submit statements or written observations to these kinds of proceedings.[53]

The Statute of the EFTA Court entails a provision on intervention that is identical in substance to that of the Statute of the ECJ. According to Article 36 of the Statute of the EFTA Court:[54]

> Any EFTA State, the EFTA Surveillance Authority, the Community and the EC Commission may intervene in cases before the Court.
> The same right shall be open to any person establishing an interest in the result of any case submitted to the Court, save in cases between EFTA States or between EFTA States and the EFTA Surveillance Authority.
> An application to intervene shall be limited to supporting the form of order sought by one of the parties.

In practice, interventions are rare in the context of the EFTA Court. During its nine years of operation, there have only been three interventions by member states in contentious proceedings of the Court.[55] However, there have been inter-

---

[50] 41/73, 43-48/73, 50/73, 111/73, 113/73, 114/73 *Société anonyme Générale Sucrière and others v Commission*, Order of the Court, 11 December 1973, para. 8.

[51] 197-200/80, 243, 245 and 247/80 *Ludwigshafener Walzmuhle Erling KG v European Economic Community*, Order of the Court, 8 April 1981.

[52] See, e.g., C-182/02, judgment of the ECJ on 6 October 2003 (intervener: union of federations: intervener in national proceedings and submission of written and oral observations in ECJ proceedings); C-140/02, judgment of the ECJ on 30 September 2003 (intervener: a company: intervener in national proceedings and submission of written and oral observations in ECJ proceedings).

[53] 6/64, Order of the Court of 3 June 1964 [1964] ECR 614.

[54] Protocol 5 to the ESA/Court Agreement on the Statute of the EFTA Court ('EFTA Statute').

[55] Judgment of the EFTA Court in E-2/02, 19 June 2003 (Norway intervened); judgment of the EFTA Court in E-3/00, 5 April 2001 (Denmark intervened); and judgment of the EFTA Court in E-4/97, 3 March 1999 (Norway intervened).

ventions (submission of written and hearing of oral observations) by natural and legal persons in advisory opinion proceedings.[56] Until now, no natural or legal person has sought leave to intervene in a contentious case before the Court. Given the careful consideration of the case law produced by the Community as regards the provision on *locus standi*, it is logical to expect an identical interpretation of the expression 'interest in the result of any case' under Article 36(2) of the Statute of the EFTA Court.

4.3 *Locus standi*

A variety of NGOs has a possibility to bring actions before the Community courts. Natural or legal persons may challenge the legality of acts[57] or omissions[58] by the Community institutions as well as make compensation claims for damage arising out of the non-contractual liability of the Commission.[59] Still, the issue of standing for associations is subject to heated debate as reflected in the Community courts, such as in the Opinion of Advocate-General Jacobs in *Unión de Pequeños Agricultores*.[60] It is also acknowledged by the EFTA Court.[61] It is the implications of the procedural requirements for standing for associations with a more general interest in judicial review of decisions by the Community institutions or the EFTA Surveillance Authority that constitute the upshot of this debate.

The prevailing interpretation of the procedural requirements laid down in Article 230(4) EC (former Article 173.2) is the root of the problem. It stipulates that:

> Any natural or legal person ... may institute proceedings against a decision ... which, although in the form of ... a decision addressed to another person, is of direct and individual concern to the former.

Persons who wish to bring proceedings against a decision that is not addressed to them are defined as 'non-privileged applicants'. Their ability to challenge such a decision depends on whether that decision nevertheless is of 'direct and individual concern' to them.

The meaning of the notion of direct concern is straightforward. In order to produce effects *vis-à-vis* the applicant, the contested measures must not require

---

[56] E-1/98, Advisory Opinion of the Court of 24 November 1988 (intervener: a company: intervener in national proceedings and submission of written and oral observations in EFTA proceedings); E-8/00, judgment (Advisory Opinion) of the Court of 22 March 2002 (intervener: the Norwegian Confederation of Municipal Employees: intervener in national proceedings and submission of written observations in EFTA proceedings).

[57] EC Treaty, Article 230(4).

[58] EC Treaty, Article 232(4)

[59] EC Treaty, Articles 230(5) and 288.

[60] C-50/00 P *Unión de Pequeños Agricultores v Council*, 21 March 2002.

[61] E-2/02 *Technologien Bau- und Wirtschaftsberatung GmbH and Bellona Foundation v EFTA Surveillance Authority*, 19 June 2003.

the adoption of any additional measures, at either Community or national level. In other words, the contested measures are of direct concern to the applicant if 'they constitute a complete set of rules which are sufficient in themselves and which require no implementing provisions'.[62] The measures in question must directly affect the legal situation of the individual and leave no discretion to the addressee of those measures who is entrusted with the task of implementing them. Such implementation must be purely automatic and result from Community rules without the application of intermediate rules.[63]

The meaning of 'individual concern' is more complex. The question was raised for the first time in 1963 in *Plaumann v Commission*.[64] The ECJ declared Plaumann's action inadmissible. In support of its decision, the Court held that:

> Persons other than those to whom a decision is addressed may only claim to be individually concerned if that decision affects them by reason of certain attributes which are peculiar to them or by reason of circumstances in which they are differentiated from all other persons and by virtue of these factors distinguishes them individually just as in the case of the person addressed.[65]

The disputed decision affected Plaumann as an importer of clementines. The ECJ concluded that since any person at any time may practise this commercial activity, his status as an importer of clementines did not distinguish him in relation to the contested decision in the same way as an addressee.

The Community courts and, as we shall see, the EFTA Court, have upheld the '*Plaumann* test' in the vast majority of cases where the issue of standing for natural and legal persons has been raised.[66] This has led to a considerable number of dismissals of cases involving NGOs, occasionally special interest groups and consistently public interest groups.

In *Union Syndicale – Service public européen and others v Council*,[67] the ECJ dismissed an action brought by trade unions due to their lack of individual concern with the contested measures. The Court held that:

---

[62] 294/83, *Parti écologiste 'Les Verts' v European Parliament* [1986] ECR1339, para. 31.

[63] C-354/87 *Weddel v Commission* [1990] ECR I-3847, para. 19; 4-4/96 P *Glencore Grain v Commission* [1998] ECR I-2435, para. 41 and C-386/96 P *Dreyfus v Commission* [1998] ECR I-2309, para. 43; and T-177/01 *Jégo-Quéré et Cie SA v Commission* [2002] ECR II-2365, para. 26.

[64] Case No. 25-62 *Plaumann v Commission* [1963] ECR 95.

[65] Ibid. See also C-309/89 *Codorníu SA v Council* [1994] ECR I-1853, para. 20; T-435/93 *Association of Sorbitol Producers within the EC (ASPEC), Ceresar Holding BV, Roquette Frères SA and Merck oHG v Commission* [1995] ECR II-1281, para. 62

[66] The *Plaumann* test is reaffirmed in, e.g., the following cases: 231/82 *Spijker v Commission* [1983] ECR 2559, 97/85 *Deutsche Lebensmittelwerke and others v Commission* [1987] ECR 2265, C-198/91 *Cook v Commission* [1993] ECR I-2487, C-225/91 *Matra v Commission* [1993] ECR I-3203, T-2/93 *Air France v Commission* [1994] ECR II-323 and T-465/93 *Consorzio Gruppo di Azione Locale 'Murgia Messapica' v Commission* [1994] ECR II-361.

[67] 72-74 *Union syndicale — Service public européen and others v Council* [1975] ECR 401.

An organization formed for the protection of the collective interests of a category of persons cannot be considered as being directly and individually concerned by a measure affecting the general interests of that category.[68]

It continued by noting that the mere fact that the trade unions took part in the discussions preceding the disputed measure is not sufficient for individual concern. The ECJ also referred to the possibility of intervention (Article 37 of the Statute of the ECJ) for trade unions representing Community staff, in particular in the context of proceedings referred to in Article 179 EC Treaty (now Article 236 EC).[69]

In *Parti écologiste 'Les Verts' v European Parliament*, in contrast, the ECJ admitted an action for annulment by an association that, at the time, aspired to gain seats in the European Parliament. Les Verts contested a decision by the Bureau of the European Parliament concerning the allocation of public funds among the parties with seats in the European Parliament in order to prepare for elections. The ECJ held that it cannot be considered that only groups that were represented and therefore identifiable at the date the contested decision was adopted are individually concerned. It continued by noting that:

Such an interpretation would give rise to inequality of protection afforded by the Court to the various groupings competing in the same elections. Groupings not represented could not prevent the allocation of the appropriateness at issue before the beginning of the election campaign because they would be unable to plead the illegality of the basic decision except in support of an action against the individual decisions refusing to reimburse sums greater than those provided for. It would therefore be impossible for them to bring an action for annulment before the Court prior to the elections or to obtain an order from the Court under Article 185 [now Article 242] of the Treaty suspending application of the contested basic decision.[70]

In the *Stichting Greenpeace Council* case, in contrast, a number of individuals and environmental organizations sought to challenge the validity of a decision granting Community funding to Spain for the construction of two power plants in the Canary Islands. The applicants argued that the CFI should set aside the *Plaumann* test and instead focus on the fact that third party applicants had suffered or would potentially suffer loss or detriment from the harmful environmental effects resulting from the funding decision. The CFI nevertheless dismissed the action due to a lack of individual concern.[71] The Court held that the proposed criterion for standing was unsatisfactory. The nature of the harm in question is such that it might affect, in a general and abstract manner, a large number of people who could not be determined in the same way as an addressee.[72]

---

[68] Ibid., para. 17.
[69] Ibid., para. 18.
[70] Ibid., para. 36.
[71] T-585/93 *Greenpeace and others v Commission* [1995] ECR II-2205, para. 48.
[72] Ibid., para. 51.

The applicants appealed to the ECJ against the order of the CFI, but without success.[73] In their appeal, they took issue with the fact that the notion of individual concern favours economic issues and economic rights inasmuch as an individual must belong to a 'closed class' in order to be individually concerned. Nonetheless, it is necessary to take account of the nature and specific character of environmental interests, which, by their very nature, are common and shared.[74] In response to this argument, the ECJ held that:

> Where, as in the present case, the specific situation of the applicant was not taken into consideration in the adoption of the act, which concerns him in a general and abstract fashion and, in fact, like any other person in the same situation, the applicant is not individually concerned by the act .... The same applies to associations which claim to have *locus standi* on the basis of the fact that the persons whom they represent are individually concerned by the contested decision.[75]

In addition, the ECJ held that the decision concerning Community financing of the two power stations affected environmental rights under Directive 85/337 only indirectly. The decision of the Spanish government to build the plants must be challenged in national courts.[76]

The issue of *locus standi* for public interest groups resurfaced in *Unión de Pequeños Agricultores v Council*. This time, the trade association Unión de Pequeños Agricultores (UPA), a representative of small Spanish agricultural businesses, brought an action against Regulation No. 1638/98, which amended substantially the common organization of the olive oil market. The CFI dismissed their action due to a lack of individual concern.[77] The Court noted that these kinds of actions are admissible when:

(a) trade associations are expressly granted a series of procedural powers;[78]
(b) the association represents the interests of undertakings which would, themselves, be entitled to bring proceedings; or
(c) the association is distinguished individually because its own interests as an association are affected, in particular because its negotiating position has been affected by the measure whose annulment is being sought.[79]

---

[73] C-321 *Stichting Greenpeace Council (Greenpeace International) and others v Commission* [1998] ECR I-1651.

[74] Ibid., paras. 18 and 19.

[75] Ibid., paras. 28 and 29.

[76] Ibid., paras. 30 and 31.

[77] T-173/98 *Unión de Pequeños Agricultores v Council* [1999] ECR I-3357.

[78] See, e.g., 19/62–22/62 *Fédération Nationale de la Boucherie en Gros du Commerce en Gros des Viandes and others v Council* [1975] ECR 401; 60/79 *Fédération Nationale des Producteurs de Vins de Table et Vins de Pays v Commission* [1979] ECR 2429; 117/86 *UFADE v Council and Commission* [1986] ECR 3255, para. 12; and T-447/93, T-448/93 and T-449/93 *AITEC and others v Commission* [1995] ECR II-1971, paras. 58–59.

[79] 67, 38 and 70/85 *Van der Kooy and others v Commission* [1988] ECR 219, paras. 21–23; C-313/90 *CIRFS and others v Commission* [1993] ECR I-1125, paras. 29 and 30.

The CFI concluded that none of these circumstances applied to UPA.[80] It also refuted two further arguments put forward by the applicants, namely, that a review of the contested Regulation is a matter of Community public interest, and that there is a risk that the applicant (and its members) will not receive effective judicial protection.

In its appeal to the ECJ, UPA argued that the order of the CFI amounts to a denial of its fundamental right to effective judicial protection. If a preliminary ruling by the ECJ through national proceedings is the only alternative it must be effectively guaranteed for everybody. Advocate-General Jacobs issued an opinion ('the Opinion') in response to this concern.[81] According to Jacobs, the issue of standing must be determined without any consideration of judicial protection at the national level. However, the ECJ should reconsider its restrictive interpretation of individual concern.[82] The fact that a measure affects a large number of people, causing widespread rather than limited harm, makes it all the more important to accept a direct challenge by one or more of those individuals.[83] Thus, instead:

> A person is to be regarded as individually concerned by a Community measure where, by reason of his particular circumstances, the measure has, or is liable to have, a substantial adverse effect on his interests.[84]

Prior to the final judgment in the case of UPA, the CFI had to decide on the admissibility of another case.[85] It followed the Opinion and declared the action brought by a Spanish fishing company, Jégo-Quéré et Cie SA (Jégo), against a Commission Regulation establishing measures for the recovery of the stock of hake as admissible.[86] Jégo explained that fishing whiting formed a key element of its activities and that its ability to do so would be seriously affected by the new Regulation as to the mesh size of the nets. It was the only operator fishing for whiting in the waters in question and the contested provisions had greatly reduced its catches. The CFI held that:

> A natural or legal person is to be regarded as individually concerned by a Community measure of general application that concerns him directly if the measure in question affects his legal position, in a manner which is both definite and immediate, by restricting his rights or imposing obligations on him. The number and position of other persons who are likewise affected by the measure, or who may be so, are of no relevance in that regard.[87]

---

[80] T-173/98 *Unión de Pequeños Agricultores v Council* [1999] ECR I-3357, paras. 40–50, 52–57.

[81] Ibid., para. 3.

[82] Ibid., para. 4.

[83] C-50/00 P *Unión de Pequeños Agricultores*, Opinion of Advocate-General Jacobs, 21 March 2002, para. 59.

[84] Ibid., para. 60.

[85] T-177/01, *Jégo-Quéré et Cie SA v Commission* 2002.

[86] Ibid., para. 49.

[87] Ibid., para. 51.

Thereafter, the ECJ ruled in the case of UPA.[88] Unlike the CFI, however, it did not follow the Opinion, refuted the argument about the lack of alternative effective judicial protection as irrelevant, but reaffirmed its restrictive approach.[89] According to the ECJ, individuals are given such protection against Community measures through national proceedings since national courts may request a preliminary ruling.[90] Whether national courts in fact provide such protection in each case was irrelevant. The ECJ would exceed its competence if it gave any weight to this consideration. It is simply not part of the procedural requirements laid down under Article 230(4) EC Treaty.

Article 36 of the Statute of the EFTA Court regulates the issue of standing in actions against decisions by the EFTA Surveillance Authority. The provision is identical in substance to that of the ECJ/CFI. According to Article 36(1):

> The EFTA Court shall have jurisdiction in actions brought by an EFTA State against a decision on the EFTA Surveillance Authority on grounds of lack of competence, infringement of an essential procedural requirement, or infringement of this Agreement, of the EEA Agreement or of any rule of law relating to their application, or misuse of power.

Just as in the case of ECJ/CFI, not only member states but also natural or legal persons may bring such actions before the EFTA Court provided they meet the procedural requirement of 'direct and individual concern'. Thus, according to Article 36(2):

> Any natural or legal person may ... institute proceedings before the EFTA Court against a decision of the EFTA Surveillance Authority ... if it is of direct and individual concern to the former.

The issue of standing for associations before the EFTA Court came up for the first time in *Scottish Salmon Growers Association v EFTA Surveillance Authority*.[91] In that case, an association of Scottish salmon growers brought an action against a decision by the EFTA Surveillance Authority that it lacked jurisdiction to assess whether the Norwegian salmon industry had been granted state aid contrary to the EEA Agreement. The EFTA Court examined the preliminary objection about the lack of individual concern in light of the prevailing approach in Community law.[92] To this end, the Court considered that the applicant association represents the overwhelming majority of, if not all, Scottish salmon growers. As such, it promotes the profitable sales of Scottish salmon and the carrying on of any trade, industry or business which will further its objectives. Furthermore,

---

[88] C-50/00 P *Union de Pequenos Agricultores v Council* [2002] ECR I-6677, paras. 32 and 33.
[89] C-209/94 P *Buralux v Council* [1996] ECR I-615, paras. 35 and 36.
[90] 294/83 *Les Verts* [1986] ECR 1339, para. 23.
[91] E-2/94 *Scottish Salmon Growers Association Ltd v EFTA Surveillance Authority*, 21 March 1995.
[92] Ibid., para. 39.

it negotiates with the UK government and with the EC Commission in respect of those objectives. In addition, the applicant association had already lodged complaints on behalf of Scottish salmon growers with both the EC Commission and the EFTA Surveillance Authority prior to the decision of the latter. Finally, if the EFTA Surveillance Authority had decided to open a procedure under Article 1(2) of Protocol 3, the applicant association would have had the opportunity of taking an active part in that procedure. For these reasons, the EFTA Court concluded that the interests represented by the applicant association are centrally concerned by the outcome of the case and the action brought by it against the decision must be considered as admissible.[93]

The admissibility of claims involving environmental interests was examined in *Technologien Bau- und Wirtschaftsberatung GmbH and Bellona Foundation v EFTA Surveillance Authority*.[94] The two applicants, Technologien Bau- und Wirtschaftsberatung GmbH (TBW) and the Bellona Foundation, jointly brought an action before the EFTA Court against a decision by the EFTA Surveillance Authority. The decision involved a refusal to assess a proposal by the Norwegian government to amend its Petroleum Taxation Act (1975) designed to permit a natural gas project (Snøvit) to go forward even if it could be harmful to the environment. The applicants complained that the amendments were state aid under Article 61(1) of the EEA Agreement and incompatible with it. The EFTA Surveillance Authority argued that its decision was of no individual concern to the applicants.

TBW is a limited liability company established under the laws of Germany and engaged in environmental consulting and organizational development.[95] The Bellona Foundation, on the other hand, is a foundation established as a legal entity under the laws of Norway, whose main objective is to combat problems of environmental degradation, pollution-induced dangers to human health and the ecological impact of development strategies.[96] Bellona argued that it had brought the original complaint that led to an investigation by the EFTA Surveillance Authority. In addition, it had been a prominent player in relation to the Snøvit project, both at the national and the EEA level, and had had a decisive impact not only on the procedure of the case, but also on its outcome.[97] It also argued that the contested decision would harm its activities because it had shares and options dealing with sustainable energy production. Furthermore, TBW's commercial activities, the production of sustainable energy, would be adversely affected by the contested decision since the electricity produced by TBW competes with electric-

---

[93] E-2/94 *Scottish Salmon Growers Association Ltd v EFTA Surveillance Authority*, 21 March 1995, para. 22.

[94] E-2/02 *Technologien Bau- und Wirtschaftsberatung GmbH and Bellona Foundation v EFTA Surveillance Authority*, 19 June 2003.

[95] Ibid., para. 7.

[96] Ibid., para. 2.

[97] Ibid., para. 25.

ity produced by gas or liquid fossil fuels.[98] Finally, TBW argued that the EFTA Court should reconsider the approach developed by the Community courts in order to conform to the provisions on standing for environmental associations laid down in the Aarhus Convention 1998.

In response to this argument, the EFTA Court held that:

> 'Access to justice' is an essential element of the EEA legal framework and the Court was set up precisely to protect the value of the judicial defence of rights conferred by the Agreement on individuals and intended for their benefit .... The Court is aware of the ongoing debate with regard to the issue of the standing of natural and legal persons in actions against Community institutions. This discussion is important at a time when the significance of the judicial function appears to be on the increase, both on the national and international level. The idea of human rights inspires this development, and reinforces calls for widening the avenues of access to justice. The Court finds nevertheless that caution is warranted, not least in view of the uncertainties inherent in the current refashioning of fundamental Community law.[99]

Thus, the EFTA Court remained faithful to the prevailing approach developed by the Community courts.[100]

The EFTA Court then concluded that the decision was of no individual concern to the Bellona Foundation as its competitive position has not been affected by the state aid decision. Bellona is a non-profit environmental foundation whose main objectives are non-commercial: to combat problems of environmental degradation, pollution-induced dangers to human health and the ecological influence of economic development strategies.[101] The decision concerned Bellona merely by virtue of its objective capacity in the same manner as any other person who is, or might in the future be, in the same situation. The state aid decision had general application, covering situations that are determined objectively and entailed legal effects on categories of persons envisaged in a general and abstract manner. Hence, Bellona was not individually concerned.[102]

The EFTA Court thereafter examined whether Bellona could challenge the contested decision before the Court as a representative and defender of the economic interests of its partners and supporters. In this respect, the Court noted that it had given standing to representative bodies in order to challenge a decision of the EFTA Surveillance Authority in relation to matters of aid in respect of associations representing the interests of its members.[103] However, Bellona was not a

---

[98] Ibid., paras. 26–27.

[99] Ibid., paras. 36 and 37.

[100] Ibid., paras. 39 and 40.

[101] Ibid., para. 59.

[102] Ibid., para. 61.

[103] Ibid., para. 66; E-2/94 *Scottish Salmon Growers Association v EFTA Surveillance Authority* [1995] EFTA Court Report 59, para. 22; E-4/97 *Norwegian Bankers' Association v EFTA Surveillance Authority* [1999] EFTA Court Report 3, para. 33. See also C-321 *Stichting Greenpeace Council (Greenpeace International) and others v Commission* [1998] ECR I-1651, para. 59.

representative: a foundation is a legal entity representing itself, its officers or trustees, without any defined membership.[104]

Finally, the EFTA Court responded to the argument about the role of Bellona in the administrative proceedings that led to the decision taken by the Authority on the matter. According to Community case law, 'individual concern' can be demonstrated by a person's participation in the administrative procedure that led to the contested decision.[105] The Court recognized that an association's involvement in the proceedings before the EFTA Surveillance Authority might in certain circumstances warrant standing for that association to bring action for annulment before the Court. This was particularly so where the association was a representative of its members, at the origin of a complaint to the Authority and where its views were heard during the procedure and information was gathered from the state in question regarding the complaint from the association.[106] However, in general an association formed for the protection of the collective interests of a category of persons was not individually concerned by a Community measure affecting the general interests of that category.[107] Only in very special circumstances could the role played by an association in a procedure that led to the adoption of a decision justify standing for an association even if its members were not directly or individually concerned.[108]

The EFTA Court concluded that it did not overlook the role Bellona plays in the national and international environmental discourse. It then contended that the purpose of the state aid provisions was to protect competition in the EEA. Although environmental protection was a significant area of cooperation between the EFTA states (Article 78 EEA Agreement), the EFTA Surveillance Authority was not at liberty to consider environmental factors when assessing the compatibility of state aid with the EEA Agreement. That power could only flow from a specific legal basis.[109]

5.   PARTIAL EXCLUSION: THE CASE OF PUBLIC INTEREST NGOs

It is evident that the procedural requirement of individual concern is especially hard to pass for environmental NGOs. However, the same difficulties would be encountered by any NGO whose objectives are defined in non-economic and non-individualistic terms, such as NGOs seeking to defend human rights, animal rights or, say, the cultural heritage.

---

[104] Ibid., paras. 65 and 66.

[105] Ibid., para. 68.

[106] Ibid., para. 69; Case No 169/84, *Cofaz and Others v Commission*, [1986] ECR 391.

[107] E-2/02 *Technologien Bau- und Wirtschaftsberatung GmbH and Bellona Foundation v EFTA Surveillance Authority*, para. 71.

[108] *Stichting Greenpeace*, citing 67, 38 and 70/85 *Van der Kooy and others v Commission* [1988] ECR 219, at paras. 21–23; and C-313/90 *CIFRS and others v Commission* [1993] ECR I-1125.

[109] E-2/02 *Technologien Bau- und Wirtschaftsberatung GmbH and Bellona Foundation v EFTA Surveillance Authority*, 19 June 2003, para. 75.

Nevertheless, access to justice, at least for environmental NGOs, is one of the rights guaranteed in the Convention on Access to Information, Public Participation in Decision-Making and Access to Justice in Environmental Matters ('the Aarhus Convention').[110] It recognizes that environmental NGOs have a legitimate interests in bringing review proceedings before the Community courts in spite of their collective nature.[111] According to Article 9(2) of the Convention:

Each Party shall, within the framework of its national legislation, ensure that members of the public concerned:
(a) having a sufficient interest or, alternatively,
(b) maintaining impairment of a right, where the administrative procedural law of a Party requires this as a precondition,
have access to a review procedure before a court of law and/or another independent and impartial body established by law, to challenge the substantive and procedural legality of any decision, act or omission subject to the provisions of article 6 and, where so provided for under national law and without prejudice to paragraph 3 below, of other relevant provisions of this Convention.
What constitutes a sufficient interest and impairment of a right shall be determined in accordance with the requirements of national law and consistently with the objective of giving the public concerned wide access to justice within the scope of this Convention. To this end, the interest of any non-governmental organization meeting the requirements referred to in article 2, paragraph 5, shall be deemed sufficient for the purpose of subparagraph (a) above. Such organizations shall also be deemed to have rights capable of being impaired for the purpose of subparagraph (b) above.

The European Community has only signed the Aarhus Convention. Prior to ratification, it must bring the laws and practices of its own institutions in conformity with the obligations of the Convention.[112] In order to do so, it will be necessary to relax the prevailing understanding of the procedural requirements for standing.

Against the background of the reaffirmation of its restrictive approach to standing in 2002, the ECJ has made it clear that it is not its task to revise that approach in spite of a growing dissatisfaction. The ECJ would exceed its powers if it reinterpreted Article 230(4) in order to give standing to NGOs that seek to defend interests of common concern for society as a whole. Instead, only member

---

[110] UNECE Convention on Access to Information, Public Participation in Decision-making and Access to Justice in Environmental Matters (Aarhus, Denmark, 25 June 1998), available at <www.unece.org/env/pp/treatytext.htm>.

[111] According to Article 2(5): '"the public concerned" means the public affected or likely to be affected by, or having an interest in, the environmental decision-making; for the purposes of this definition, non-governmental organizations promoting environmental protection and meeting any requirements under national law shall be deemed to have an interest'. See also Article 9 of the Aarhus Convention.

[112] Information about the work undertaken to realize this objective is available at <www.europea.eu.int/environment/aarhus>. Two relevant working documents have been produced: Second Working Document on Access to Justice in Environmental Matters and Complaint Procedures and Access to Justice for Citizens and NGOs in the field of the Environment within the European Union.

states could revise the EC Treaty in such a way that environmental NGOs have standing before the Community courts. Their intention to give such standing is manifested in the Draft Treaty Establishing a Constitution for Europe. According to Article III-270(4) of the Draft Treaty:

> Any natural or legal person may ... institute proceedings against an act addressed to that person or which is of direct and individual concern to him or her, and against a regulatory act which is of direct concern to him or her and does not entail implementing measures.

In the Report on the Draft Treaty by the European Parliament,[113] the Committee on the Environment, Public Health and Consumer Policy calls on the Committee of Constitutional Affairs to respond to 'the need for access to the European courts for citizens and their organizations, especially in the environmental field in line with the Aarhus UN-ECE Convention'.[114] If the amendments are adopted, they open up the Community courts to a broad range of NGOs that currently remains excluded from the European judicial process.

The proposed amendments indicate that, as the Community seeks to transform itself from being an essentially economic organization seeking to protect the economic interests of its citizens and members into a more complex and complete community, the Community courts will have wider competence on environmental and other matters of common concern for society as a whole (including human rights). If successful, such a transformation will inevitably change the status and role of European public interest NGOs in the development and implementation of international and European law before the Community courts. However, unless the EFTA states follow this development and amend the foundational laws of their organization, the jurisprudence of the EFTA Court is likely to remain the same.

6. CONCLUSION

This chapter has analyzed the state of affairs as regards the limited role and influence of NGOs and, in particular, public interest groups in proceedings before the European integration courts. It concludes that while a broad range of NGOs has possibilities to bring proceedings against decisions by Community institutions, the ECJ/CFI rarely, if ever, give standing or allow third party intervention for public interest groups. The same conclusion applies to the EFTA Court.

---

[113] Report on the Draft Treaty establishing a Constitution for Europe and the European Parliament's Opinion on the Convening of the Intergovernmental Conference (IGC) (11047/2003-C5-0340/2003-2003/0902(CNS), Committee on Constitutional Affairs, 10 September 2003, FINAL A5-0299/2003, available at <www.europa.eu.int/futurum/documents/other/oth100903_en.pdf>.

[114] Ibid., p. 51.

It is clear that the ECJ believes that it would exceed its competence to reinterpret the notion of individual concern in order to conform to the developments in international law regarding individual access to international justice, especially in the field of human rights. This may be an unnecessarily cautious stance of a court otherwise known for its progressive interpretations of Community law in the name of European integration. Nevertheless, a change in the fundamental laws by the member states is deemed necessary. The proposed amendments to the provision on standing for NGOs reflect an awareness of an unjustified and *de facto* exclusion of NGOs whose substantive interests in judicial review of decisions by European institutions of integration cannot be defined in economic and individualistic terms, but instead relate to interests that are common and shared. Nevertheless, it remains uncertain whether the proposed amendments will be successful in terms of actually enabling public interest NGOs to nullify decisions by European institutions of integration held to be in violation of Community and international law. There may still be no specific legal basis for them to rely upon in the pursuit of their substantive objectives.

Part V

Concluding Remarks

Chapter 21

The *Amicus Curiae* in International Courts: Towards Common Procedural Approaches?

*Ruth Mackenzie**

1. INTRODUCTION

The question of *amicus curiae* intervention in international courts touches upon two key aspects of the agenda of the Project on International Courts and Tribunals (PICT):[1] first, the specific issue of access of non-state actors to international courts and tribunals; and secondly, understanding common challenges facing the growing number of international courts and tribunals and identifying areas where there might be scope for common approaches in rules and practices.

This chapter focuses on one particular kind of civil society participation in international courts and tribunals: participation of non-governmental organizations (NGOs) as non-party *amici curiae*.[2] It does not address the opportunities that exist in some courts and tribunals for non-state actors to initiate proceedings directly or the possibility of intervention as a third party. In addition, the focus is on situations in which NGOs seek to furnish information to courts or tribunals on their own initiative. These can be distinguished from situations where a court itself invites *amicus curiae* submissions, for example, from academics, from counsel, or from others to address novel or complex issues of law,[3] or to present

---

* This chapter is based on research undertaken by the Project on International Courts and Tribunals with the support of the Volkswagen Foundation and the William and Flora Hewlett Foundation.

[1] The Project was established in 1997 to address the legal, institutional and financial issues arising from the multiplication of international courts and tribunals and the growing number of cases which these bodies are called upon to settle. See <www.pict-pcti.org>.

[2] The term '*amicus curiae* brief' is used throughout this chapter to describe, in general, submissions from non-party non-state actors in international dispute settlement proceedings. The term is not always used by international courts and tribunals to describe such participation. See, e.g., European Convention on the Protection of Human Rights and Fundamental Freedoms (European Convention, Article 36(2)). The NAFTA Free Trade Commission has used the term 'non-disputing party participation', see further below.

[3] See C. Chinkin and R. Mackenzie, 'Intergovernmental Organizations as "Friends of the Court"' in L. Boisson de Chazournes, C. Romano and R. Mackenzie (eds.), *International Organizations and International Dispute Settlement: Trends and Prospects* (Transnational, 2002), pp. 135–162, at pp. 148–149.

T. Treves et al., eds., Civil Society, International Courts and Compliance Bodies
© 2005, T·M·C·ASSER PRESS, *The Hague, The Netherlands, and the Authors*

arguments that might not otherwise be made before the court but that might assist it to reach a proper determination of the case before it.[4]

Other chapters have addressed international courts and tribunals in which NGO participation has been controversial and which have, for one reason or another, remained rather impermeable to non-state actors.[5] Other international tribunals, however, particularly in the fields of human rights and international criminal law, have been much more receptive to the possibility of receiving submissions from non-state actors that are not parties to the proceedings. Over the course of this conference, speakers have addressed a diversity of procedures and practice in international courts and procedures regarding treatment of *amicus curiae* submissions. How far does this diversity allow for a discussion of common procedural approaches? Clearly, across such a diverse range of courts and tribunals, one could not expect to find a single procedural approach to *amicus curiae* submissions that would fit all circumstances. However, the question of *amicus curiae* participation in international courts and tribunals does raise some common challenges. In this chapter, the basic procedural approaches to *amicus curiae* intervention are addressed briefly; the objections that have been raised in relation to such intervention in certain international courts and tribunals; as well as more practical problems that might be posed by *amicus curiae* briefs. The chapter then addresses, in a general manner, the kinds of procedural approaches that might be used to address some of these objections and problems; and, finally, considers the extent to which there has been, or might in the future be, a move towards common procedural approaches to *amicus curiae* submissions.

2.   BASIC PROCEDURAL APPROACHES TO *AMICUS CURIAE* BRIEFS

There are various ways in which *amicus curiae* briefs can come before international tribunals. The governing instruments of some courts incorporate a procedural bar to the submission of *amicus curiae* briefs by non-state actors. For example, the Statute and Rules of the International Court of Justice (ICJ) have generally been interpreted to the effect that *amicus*-type submissions can only be made by intergovernmental organizations in both contentious and advisory proceedings.[6] NGOs have been excluded. The International Tribunal for the Law of the Sea (ITLOS) contains similar provisions to those of the ICJ, although these have yet to be tested in practice.[7]

---

[4] See, e.g., the appointment of *amici curiae* in the *Milosevic* proceedings before the International Criminal Tribunal for the Former Yugoslavia (ICTY); and, at the national level, the appointment of an *amicus curiae* in the Supreme Court proceedings in Canada over the question of Quebec.

[5] See, e.g., the International Court of Justice, the International Tribunal for the Law of the Sea and the dispute settlement procedures of the World Trade Organisation.

[6] See E. Valencia-Ospina, Chapter 16 above. On the participation of intergovernmental organizations as *amici curiae* before the ICJ, see Chinkin and Mackenzie, n. 3 above.

[7] See P. Gautier, Chapter 17 above. In addition, the UN Convention on the Law of the Sea and the ITLOS Statute makes specific provision for the participation of non-state actors as parties to certain categories of disputes before ITLOS.

By contrast, the governing instruments of some courts and tribunals expressly allow for the submission of *amicus curiae* briefs, albeit upon leave of the tribunal, generally by way of a specific provision in the rules. The most prominent examples are the international criminal tribunals,[8] and the European Court of Human Rights (ECHR).[9]

Other courts and tribunals neither expressly bar nor provide for *amicus curiae* submissions. However, they may provide in more general terms for the tribunal to seek or receive information relevant to the dispute before it.[10] In other cases, tribunals have used or implied a general power to fill gaps in procedures in order to allow the submission of *amicus curiae* briefs.[11] The latter constitute the most difficult and controversial cases, where the approach of the court or tribunal concerned to *amicus curiae* submissions has not always been in full accord with the wishes or expectations of the states parties that established it.

Whatever the nature of *amicus curiae* participation and the procedural route through which it occurs, it seems possible to discern a number of common factors. First, the *amicus curiae* brief represents a type of 'non-party' participation, that is the *amicus curiae* does not have the same interests as the parties to the proceedings and does not acquire their rights and obligations; and second, *amicus curiae* participation depends upon the discretion of the court or tribunal concerned in that the tribunal retains a right to determine the form and extent of *amicus curiae* participation. A third common factor may be that the *amicus curiae*

---

[8] See Rule 74 of the Rules of Procedure and Evidence of both the International Criminal Tribunal for Rwanda (ICTR) and the International Criminal Tribunal for the Former Yugoslavia (ICTY); Rule 103 of the Rules of Evidence and Procedure of the International Criminal Court; and Rule 74 of the Rules of Procedure and Evidence of the Special Court for Sierra Leone.

[9] European Convention, Article 36(2).

[10] Article 13 of the WTO Dispute Settlement Understanding; see *United States – Importation of Certain Shrimp and Shrimp Products*, Report of the Appellate Body of 12 October 1998, Doc. WT/DS58/AB/R, paras. 101–108.

[11] See, e.g., in relation to the WTO, Article 17.9 of the WTO Dispute Settlement Understanding and Rule 16(1) of the Working Procedures for Appellate Review; see *US-Imposition of Countervailing Duties on Certain Hot-Rolled Lead and Bismouth Carbon Steel Products Originating in the United Kingdom*, Report of the Appellate Body of 10 May 2000, Doc. WT/DS/138/AB/R, paras. 39–42; see also *European Communities – Measures affecting Asbestos and Asbestos-Containing Products* – Communication from the Appellate Body – Additional Procedure adopted under Rule 16(1) of the Working Procedures for Appellate Review (hereinafter 'Additional Procedure'), Doc. WT/DS135/9 (8 November 2000). In relation to investment arbitration under Chapter 11 of the North American Free Trade Agreement (NAFTA) see, *Methanex Corporation and USA*, Decision of the Tribunal on Petitions from Third Persons to Intervene as '*Amici Curiae*', 15 January 2001, in which it was held that Article 15(1) of the UNCITRAL Arbitration Rules conferred on the tribunal the power to accept *amicus curiae* submissions. Article 15 provides that subject to the UNCITRAL Arbitration Rules, the arbitral tribunal may conduct the arbitration in such manner as it considers appropriate, provided that the parties are treated with equality and that at any stage in the proceedings each party is given a full opportunity of presenting its case: *Methanex*, para. 26. See also *UPS v Canada*, Decision of the Tribunal on Petitions for Intervention and Participation as *Amici Curiae*, 17 October 2001, para. 61.

should always in some way assist the tribunal in the disposition of the case. In some tribunals, this role is made explicit in the rules.[12]

3.   OBJECTIONS TO *AMICUS CURIAE* SUBMISSIONS

In international courts and tribunals where they have not been accepted widely or at all, *amicus curiae* submissions from non-state actors have been the subject of objections both in principle and on the basis of the potential practical difficulties that they may pose. The main objection in principle is that questions of *amicus curiae* participation are not procedural questions at all, but rather raise a substantive issue, insofar as such participation grants significant rights to a non-party to the proceedings, thereby somehow diminishing the rights of parties.[13] Such an objection rests on the assumption that allowing non-party participation changes the nature of the judicial process, extending it beyond the narrow function of resolving the dispute between the parties. Such objections have been prominent in dispute settlement bodies that have been designed specifically to resolve disputes between sovereign states, such as the ICJ and the WTO, particularly where some explicit procedural bar exists in the governing instrument of the court or tribunal concerned, or where the possibility of *amicus curiae* intervention has been proposed, but rejected, during the negotiation of the governing instruments of the court or tribunal concerned.[14] In the WTO, the question of *amicus curiae* participation has been characterized by many states as a systemic and institutional issue, rather than a mere question of procedure.

In addition to these challenging issues of principle, a variety of other objections and practical problems have been raised in relation to *amicus curiae* submissions. These relate to a number of issues including (i) the 'added value' of *amicus curiae* submissions; (ii) the additional burden imposed on the parties and on the tribunal by *amicus curiae* submissions; (iii) the identity, interests and affiliations of potential *amici curiae*; and (iv) issues related to confidentiality and transparency. These categories of concerns are addressed briefly below.

---

[12] Chinkin and Mackenzie, n. 3 above, at p. 138. See further below.

[13] See, e.g., Statement of India, Doc. WT/DSB/M/83, 7 July 2000, para. 18; Statement of Thailand, ibid. para. 27; Statement of Egypt on behalf of the Informal Group of Developing Countries, Doc. WT/GC/M/60, 23 January 2001, para. 12.

[14] See, e.g., Doc. WT/GC/M/60, WTO General Council, Minutes of Meeting, 22 November 2000, paras. 16 and 38. The representative of India recalled that '[i]n November 1993, one major participant had made a negotiating proposal to the effect that the panel may invite interested persons, other than parties or third parties to the dispute, to present their view in writing. This proposal had not been accepted because of overwhelming opposition. What the Appellate Body had done through its communication [in the *Asbestos* case] was to introduce into the dispute settlement system of the WTO an element which had been considered and rejected by members during the negotiations'. In the same meeting, the representative of India recalled that a large number of delegations had pointed out in the Dispute Settlement Body that the acceptance of *amicus curiae* briefs by the Appellate Body had changed the intergovernmental nature of the organization, as well as members' rights and obligations: ibid., para. 32.

3.1   Added value of *amicus curiae* submissions

While proponents of *amicus curiae* briefs emphasize the potential role of the *amicus* in bringing before the tribunal concerned the broader public interest ramifications of the dispute before it, and enhancing the legitimacy and transparency of international tribunals, opponents have questioned the extent to which unsolicited *amicus curiae* submissions add anything of value to the materials that are put before the tribunal by the parties. This argument rest on the assumption that tribunals are not in need of the assistance of *amici curiae*, insofar as the parties can adequately marshal relevant evidence and legal arguments and the judges assess them; and, if the tribunal needs additional assistance on factual issues, it can use its powers to appoint experts. A related objection is that *amici curiae* may often simply duplicate the submissions of the parties, supporting the position of one or the other. Alternatively, *amici curiae* may align themselves on opposite sides of the dispute, resulting to all intents and purposes in a debate between interest groups,[15] again raising the question whether the submissions really assist the tribunal.

3.2   Additional burden imposed by *amicus curiae* submissions

Concerns are often raised about the additional burden imposed on parties and on the tribunal by *amicus curiae* submissions, both in terms of time and resources.[16] Such concerns relate to the scope of submissions – what issues might they address – as well as more practical questions such as the length and language of submissions. These kinds of questions have caused most concern where *amicus curiae* interventions have been made predominantly in support of the position of one of the parties to the dispute, raising the possibility that the sheer volume of submissions in favour of one position may adversely affect the position of the other party.[17] Again, this has been a matter of particular focus for developing countries in the WTO. If *amicus curiae* submissions are allowed, parties will want to know how they will be dealt with by the tribunal and how their contents will be taken into account. Will they form part of the formal record of the case or not? What time and resources do parties need to devote to reading them and responding to the factual and legal material contained in them? How can the parties expect the submissions to be treated – will they be read by the judges, and what influence, if any, might they have on the judgment?

---

[15] Examples of such cases might include the *Hatton* case in the ECHR, concerning night flights, in which *amicus curiae* submissions were made both by British Airways and by Friends of the Earth, see *Hatton v United Kingdom* [GC], No. 36022/97, judgment of 8 July 2003, para. 9, (2003-VIII) ECHR Reports; or the *Pretty* case in the ECHR, which gave rise to *amicus curiae* submissions from the Voluntary Euthanasia Society and the Catholic Bishops' Conference of England and Wales, see *Pretty v United Kingdom*, No. 2346/02, judgment of 29 April 2002, (2002-III) ECHR Reports.

[16] See, e.g., Statement of Hong Kong/China, Doc. WT/GC/M/60, 23 January 2001, para. 27.

[17] See, e.g., *Methanex*, n. 11 above, at para. 50.

In relation to the burden on the tribunal, the most common objection has been that tribunals would be overwhelmed by an unmanageable tide of *amicus curiae* briefs if they are allowed. In relation to the WTO, it has been argued, the dispute settlement system would be deprived of its central attributes of speed and efficiency.[18]

3.3   Identity of the potential *amicus curiae*

Another set of concerns centres around what kind of individuals or institutions might constitute 'appropriate' (or 'inappropriate') *amici curiae* in the different international courts and tribunals. As has been illustrated in other chapters of this book, while the 'typical' non-state *amicus curiae* may be an NGO or interest group, in practice a wide range of entities seek to become involved in international dispute settlement proceedings: NGOs, research institutions, private companies, law firms, industry associations, other interest groups such as trade unions or professional associations, individuals, academics, and law school clinics.

The source of the *amicus curiae* submission raises issues related to the resources of the *amicus* – particularly concerns among developing countries in the context of the WTO that *amicus curiae* submissions would emanate principally from relatively well-resourced 'Northern' NGOs, espousing interests related to the environment, labour standards and the like,[19] or from powerful business associations.[20] Such concerns relate primarily to the resources that might be required by parties to respond to *amicus curiae* submissions and the risk of excessive influence on the part of one or a limited set of interests in dispute settlement proceedings. In the WTO, some countries have also linked these issues to concerns about potential politicization of the dispute settlement process.[21]

Other issues around the identity of the *amicus curiae* relate more specifically to interests being represented by the *amicus*, and questions of the accountability and representativeness of NGOs. Among concerns here are the campaigning or lobbying nature of some *amicus curiae* submissions which appear to be aimed principally at promoting specific interests. Other more specific questions have been raised about potential overlaps, interrelationships and conflicts of interest

---

[18] See, e.g., Statement of Mexico, Doc. WT/GC/M/60, 23 January 2001, para. 5.1.

[19] See, e.g., Statement of Egypt on behalf of the Informal Group of Developing Countries, Doc. WT/GC/M/60, 23 January 2001, para. 21; Statement of India, ibid., para. 59.

[20] See Statement of India, Doc. WT/DSB/M/83, 7 July 2000, para. 18.

[21] For example, in a special meeting of the WTO Governing Council convened to discuss the *amicus curiae* brief issue, Brazil stated that: 'Apart from the reality that the number of applications to file briefs would multiply exponentially, Brazil was also concerned with the notion that the panels and the Appellate Body would be deciding who had a right to file written briefs on the basis of the applicant's membership, legal status, objectives, interests, nature of activities, sources of financing, or relationship with parties or third parties to the dispute. If jurisprudence advanced in this direction, the dispute settlement mechanism could soon be contaminated by political issues that did not belong to the WTO, much less to its dispute settlement mechanism': Doc. WT/GC/M/60, 23 January 2001, para. 46.

between *amici curiae* and parties, witnesses, counsel or even judges,[22] and the appearance of law firms as *amici curiae*.

3.4   **Confidentiality and transparency issues**

Provision for *amicus curiae* briefs also raises issues about what access the *amicus* (or potential *amicus*) should have to pleadings and other information about the proceedings. As they deal with disputes that touch closely on matters of public and private interest, international courts face often competing demands to operate in a transparent manner and to protect the confidentiality of commercially or other sensitive information that comes before them in the course of proceedings. Where *amici curiae*, or the wider public, are given access to pleadings of the parties, concern has been expressed about the protection of commercial information, particularly in the context of investment arbitration.

In courts and tribunals where pleadings are not made generally available to the public (or are made public only at a certain stage of the proceedings, or with the consent of the parties) should a non-party granted leave to file an *amicus curiae* brief have access to the pleadings of the parties?[23] In *Methanex v USA*, the claimant argued that the requirement in Article 25(4) of the UNCITRAL Arbitration Rules to the effect that hearings are to be held *in camera* carried with it the requirement that documents prepared for the arbitration be confidential. Methanex argued that the confidentiality agreement between the parties in the Consent Order regarding Disclosure and Confidentiality required that transcripts, written submissions, witness statements, reports, etc., were to be kept confidential and did not allow for disclosure of material to NGOs or public interest groups. In *UPS v Canada*, the petitioners seeking leave to file an *amicus curiae* brief argued that they were prejudiced in being able to describe the full nature of their interests and potential contribution by not knowing the investor's particular claims and the arguments it had brought forward.[24]

4.   CAN PROCEDURAL APPROACHES MEET CONCERNS ABOUT *AMICUS CURIAE* INTERVENTION?

International courts and tribunals that have allowed for *amicus curiae* participation have utilized a range of procedural guidance and rules to address the kinds of objections and challenges surveyed above.[25] Proposals have also been put for-

---

[22] In *Furundzija*, the ICTY Appeals Chamber rejected an appeal based, *inter alia*, on the allegation that a former association between a Trial Chamber judge and an *amicus curiae* created an apprehension of bias, IT-95-17/1-A, *Prosecutor v Furundzija*, Appeals Chamber Judgment, 21 July 2000, paras. 213–215.

[23] See the submissions of the claimant Methanex in *Methanex*, n. 11 above, at para. 12.

[24] *UPS v Canada*, n. 11 above, at para. 47.

[25] As noted earlier, some international courts and tribunals contain special provision allowing *amicus curiae* submissions in their constitutive instruments or rules of procedure. Examples of the

ward in relation to specific tribunals by commentators,[26] and by WTO members in the context of the review of the WTO Dispute Settlement Understanding.[27] Rules and procedures of national courts which make provision for *amicus curiae* submissions may also provide instructive examples, although, of course, it would be inappropriate to seek to transpose the approach of specific national courts directly into the international arena.[28]

4.1 Filtering mechanisms: procedures for applications for leave to file an *amicus curiae* brief

In general terms, courts and tribunals that allow for *amicus curiae* submissions are granted a power, but not a duty, to receive them. It is in the court's discretion whether a particular *amicus curiae* brief should be admitted. A filtering process is normally applied whereby a potential *amicus curiae* submits an application to file a submission with the court. The application is required to address a number of issues, including the matters which the *amicus curiae* brief would deal with, the interests and expertise of the potential *amicus*, and the potential value of the submission to the court. Filtering mechanisms may also require the *amicus curiae* to identify the public interest element of the case.[29]

The filtering test applied by the court generally requires that there be some benefit to the court in receiving the submission: thus, in the ECHR, the President of the Court may, 'in the interest of the proper administration of justice', invite any contracting party which is not a party to the proceedings or any person concerned who is not the applicant to submit written comments or take part in hearings.[30] In the International Criminal Courts for the former Yugoslavia and Rwanda (the ICTY and ICTR), a Chamber may, 'if it considers it desirable for the proper determination of the case', invite or grant leave to a state, organization or person to appear before it and make submissions on any issue specified by the Chamber.[31] The *Asbestos* Additional Procedure issued by the WTO Appellate

provisions of additional guidance include ICTY's Information concerning the Submission of Amicus Curiae Briefs, IT/122, 27 March 1997; the WTO Appellate Body Additional Procedure, n. 11 above; and most recently, the Statement of the NAFTA Free Trade Commission on non-disputing party participation, available at <www.dfait-maeci.gc.ca/nafta-alena/Non-disputing-en.pdf>.

[26] See, e.g., in relation to the WTO, G. Marceau and M. Stilwell, 'Practical Suggestions for *Amicus Curiae* Briefs before WTO Adjudicating Bodies' (2001) 4 *J. Int'l Econ. Law* 155.

[27] See, e.g., Contribution of the EC and its Member States to the Improvement of the WTO Dispute Settlement Understanding, TN/DS/W/1, 13 March 2002; Jordan's Contribution towards the Improvement and Clarification of the WTO Dispute Settlement Understanding, TN/WS/W/43, 28 January 2003.

[28] See *Methanex*, n. 11 above, Submission of Mexico in response to Application for *Amicus* Standing, 10 November 2000, para. 9, and *UPS v Canada*, n. 11 above, at para. 56.

[29] See, e.g., Statement of the Free Trade Commission, para. 6(d); *Methanex*, n. 11 above, at para. 49.

[30] European Convention, Article 36(2).

[31] Guidance issued by the ICTY in 1997 required an applicant for leave to file an *amicus curiae* brief to state its reasons for believing that its submissions would so aid the proper determination of the case or issue, ICTY 1997, IT/122, 27 March 1997, para. 3(e).

Body required an application for leave to file an *amicus curiae* brief to state 'why it would be desirable, in the interests of achieving a satisfactory settlement of the matter at issue' for the applicant to be granted leave.

The filtering procedure may also require an applicant to demonstrate that its submission will not simply replicate evidence or arguments adduced by the parties themselves. Thus, in the *UPS v Canada* case, the NAFTA Chapter 11 tribunal found that one governing consideration would be whether the petitioners were likely to be able to provide assistance beyond that provided by the disputing parties.[32] This standard has been taken up in the Statement of the NAFTA Free Trade Commission on non-disputing party participation which requires the tribunal to consider, in deciding whether to grant leave to file an *amicus curiae* submission, whether the submissions would assist the tribunal in the determination of a factual or legal issue related to the arbitration by bringing a perspective, particular knowledge or insight that is different from that of the disputing parties.[33] Similarly, the *Asbestos* Additional Procedure required applicants to indicate in what way it would make a contribution to the resolution to the dispute that was not likely to be repetitive of what had already been submitted by a party or third party to the dispute.[34] While avoidance of duplication is clearly desirable, it is evident that this may be a difficult hurdle for a potential *amicus curiae* to overcome where it does not have access to pleadings submitted by the parties, and thus cannot fully determine in advance whether or not the information or arguments it would submit to the court might duplicate those of one or more of the parties.

Where filtering mechanisms exist, a related question that arises is whether the parties to the proceedings should be given an opportunity to comment upon, or object to, applications to submit *amicus curiae* briefs. In the ECHR, acceptance of such briefs is at the discretion of the President of the Court. In NAFTA Chapter 11 investment arbitration, parties have been given the opportunity to make submissions on the petition to file an *amicus curiae* brief.[35] The Statement of the Free Trade Commission in relation to non-disputing party participation would now require the tribunal to set a deadline by which disputing parties may comment on any application for leave to file a submission.[36] In the ICTR, the Prosecutor and defence have been given an opportunity to respond to applications made under Rule 74. By contrast, the Additional Procedure adopted by the WTO Appellate Body in *Asbestos* contained no explicit requirement to this effect and provided that the Appellate Body would review and consider each application for

---

[32] *UPS v Canada*, n. 11 above, Decision of the Tribunal on Petitions for Intervention and Participation as *Amici Curiae,* 17 October 2001, para. 70.

[33] Statement of the Free Trade Commission, para. 6(a).

[34] WTO Appellate Body Additional Procedure, n. 11 above, at para. 3(f).

[35] See, e.g., the proceedings relating to petitions for leave to file *amicus curiae* submissions in the *Methanex* and *UPS v Canada* cases, n. 11 above, available at <www.naftalaw.org>.

[36] Statement of the Free Trade Commission, para. 5.

leave to file a written brief and, without delay, render a decision whether to grant or deny such leave.[37]

Where such filtering mechanisms are put in place, it is important that applications receive a response, whether admitting or rejecting the applications, and, in case of rejection, an indication of the ways in which the applicant failed to meet the required criteria. Failure to respond in this manner prompted criticism of the WTO Appellate Body by non-governmental organizations in the *Asbestos* proceedings.[38]

Filtering mechanisms of the types described above do, of course, impose an additional procedural step in the proceedings which could be considered an additional burden on the court or tribunal which has to deal with them. However, they also provide a way of balancing the need to keep the workload of the court to manageable proportions on the one hand, and going some way to meet public interest concerns, on the other. Through the use of such filtering mechanisms the court can manage the source, nature and volume of *amicus curiae* submissions, and seek to ensure that *amicus curiae* briefs that it does receive assist it in some way. Procedures for filtering *amicus curiae* submissions may also encourage potential *amici* to form coalitions to meet any criteria established by the court as to interest in the case and/or relevant expertise.

4.2   Procedural rules to clarify the role of the *amicus curiae* brief

Procedural rules for the admission of *amicus curiae* briefs can also clarify the role of the *amicus* – for example, to what extent will parties have the right or be required to respond to factual information or legal arguments in the *amicus curiae* brief; how will the *amicus curiae* brief be considered by the court; and should the court specify any reliance on the *amicus curiae* brief in its judgment? In the Additional Procedure issued by the WTO Appellate Body in the *Asbestos* proceedings, it was made clear that the grant of leave to file a submission would not necessarily imply that the Appellate Body would address legal arguments made in the *amicus curiae* brief.[39] Practice in the WTO has sometimes been to

---

[37] WTO Appellate Body Additional Procedure, n. 11 above, at para. 4. The Additional Procedure did, however, provide for parties and third parties to the dispute to be given full and adequate opportunity to comment on and respond to any written brief filed under the procedure, see further below.

[38] *European Communities – Measures affecting Asbestos and Asbestos-Containing Products*, Report of the Appellate Body, Doc. WT/DS135/AB/R, 12 March 2001, para. 56. See M. Distefano, Chapter 19 above and L. Johnson and E. Tuerk, Chapter 18 above.

[39] WTO Appellate Body Additional Procedure, n. 11 above, at para. 5; see also TN/DS/W/5, India's Questions to the European Communities and its Member States on their Proposal relating to Improvements of the DSU, Communication from India, 7 May 2002, para. 38: India asked whether the Panel/Appellate Body would be required to give a reasoned explanation of why certain submissions or parts thereof were addressed in its report, to the exclusion of other submissions or parts thereof. It further asked if the EC would agree that in the absence of such reasoned explanation, arbitrariness in consideration of *amicus curiae* briefs cannot be ruled out, while on the other hand this would be a time-consuming exercise.

recognize that *amicus curiae* briefs have been submitted but to specify that the Appellate Body did not find it necessary or helpful to take them into account in deciding the dispute.[40] In other cases, *amicus curiae* briefs received have not been mentioned at all. Such approaches, however, are not particularly helpful in giving guidance either to potential *amici curiae*, or to parties to disputes, as to what kinds of information or argument the panels or Appellate Body might find it necessary or helpful to consider in any future case. By contrast, some human rights courts have referred specifically to *amicus curiae* submissions, often summarizing the information and arguments made therein in judgments.[41]

4.3   Identity of the *amicus curiae*: disclosure of interests and affiliations

As noted above, filtering mechanisms may go, *inter alia*, to the identity of the potential *amicus curiae* in terms of relevant qualifications, expertise and interests. Other concerns about the identity and affiliations of any *amicus curiae* might, in large part, be met by disclosure requirements. By way of example, in domestic legal systems which provide for *amicus curiae* participation, an *amicus* may be required to disclose its authorship and funding, and in particular whether any party to the proceedings has solicited or contributed to financing the submission.[42] This approach was utilized in the Additional Procedure adopted by the WTO Appellate Body in *Asbestos*, paragraph 3(g) of which required that an application for leave to file a brief contain a statement disclosing whether the applicant has any relationship, direct or indirect, with any party or third party to the dispute, as well as whether it has or will receive any assistance, financial or otherwise, from a party or a third party to the dispute in the preparation of its application for leave or its written brief.[43]

Similarly, the ICTY information note on *amicus curiae* submissions issued in 1997 required applications for leave to file *amicus curiae* briefs under Rule 74 to contain a statement identifying and explaining any contact or relationship the ap-

---

[40] See, e.g., *US – Imposition of Countervailing Duties on Certain Hot-Rolled Lead and Bismouth Carbon Steel Products Originating in the United Kingdom*, Doc. WT/DS/138/AB/R, Report of the Appellate Body, 10 May 2000, para. 42.

[41] See J. Razzaque, 'Changing Role of Friends of the Court in International Courts and Tribunals' (2001) 1 *Non-State Actors & Int'l L.* 169. It now appears to be common practice in the ECHR to summarize pertinent elements of *amicus curiae* briefs in the judgment. See also in the Inter-American Court of Human Rights, e.g., Advisory Opinion OC-17/2002, Legal Status and Human Rights of the Child, para. 15, in which the court summarizes relevant parts of written submissions of, among others, NGOs.

[42] Rule 37, Rules of the Supreme Court of the United States, requires that a brief filed under Rule 37 shall indicate whether counsel for a party authored the brief in whole or in part and shall identify every person or entity, other than the *amicus curiae*, its members or its counsel, who made a monetary contribution to the preparation or submission of the brief. The disclosure must be made in the first footnote on the first page of text of the submission.

[43] More generally, the Additional Procedure required, in relation to information about the applicant, a description of sources of financing of the applicant, n. 11 above, at para. 3(c).

plicant had, or has, with any party to the case. The Statement of the Free Trade Commission requires applications to disclose whether or not the applicant has any direct or indirect affiliation with any disputing party, and to identify any government, person or organization that has provided any financial or other assistance in preparing the submission.[44]

4.4   Other procedural rules to manage any additional burden on the court and on the parties

While filtering mechanisms are intended to limit the number and nature of *amicus curiae* briefs coming before a court or tribunal, other procedural rules can also assist in managing any additional burden that might be imposed by such submissions.

(a) Time limits on applications to file and on filing

Time limits on applications to file *amicus curiae* briefs, and on the actual filing of such briefs where leave is granted have been used, for example, in the ECHR,[45] in the ICTY,[46] and were foreseen in the WTO Appellate Body Additional Procedure in *Asbestos*.[47] Such requirements can also specify the phase of the proceedings at which such applications can be made, so as to avoid or minimize any delay in the proceedings and to avoid according any right to a non-party that is not available to a potential third party to the dispute.[48] It might be noted here, however, that there may be some tension between imposing short time limits for the filing of submissions in order not to unduly prolong proceedings (for the benefit of the court and the parties) and the desire to provide equality of opportunity for all potentially interested and qualified *amici curiae* to make submissions.

(b) Limits on the scope and nature of *amicus curiae* submissions

In granting leave to file an *amicus curiae* brief, courts and tribunals can limit the potential subject matter of the submission. Procedural guidelines in place in vari-

---

[44] Statement of the Free Trade Commission, para. 3(d) and (e).

[45] See, e.g., *Ashingdane v United Kingdom*, No. 8225/78, judgment of 28 May 1985, para. 6, ECHR A93; *Observer and Guardian v United Kingdom*, No. 13585/88, judgment of 26 November 1991, para. 6, ECHR A216.

[46] ICTY 1997, IT/122, para. 5(d).

[47] WTO Appellate Body Additional Procedure, n. 11 above, at para. 6. Such time limits were also included in the EC's submissions to the review of the WTO Dispute Settlement Understanding, TN/DS/W/1, Article 13*bis*, para. 5.

[48] One of the objections to the filing of *amicus curiae* briefs in the WTO Appellate Body has been that the granting of leave to make submissions gave non-members greater rights than members of the WTO in the sense that a member could only intervene in the appellate phase if it had reserved its third party rights at the Panel stage of proceedings. In the *Goddi* case in the ECHR, a request for leave to make a submission was rejected as it was made at too late a stage in the proceedings, see *Goddi v Italy*, No. 8966/80, judgment of 9 April 1984, para. 7, ECHR A76.

ous tribunals require that an application for leave to file an *amicus curiae* brief specify the issues that the applicant intends to address in its submission.[49] Leave to file a submission may be granted on narrower terms than sought, where the court concerned deems it appropriate.[50]

Limiting the scope of submissions might be done on a general basis, depending upon the competence of the tribunal concerned, for example, limiting submissions to legal argument only in the case of the WTO Appellate Body; or more specifically by requiring a potential *amicus curiae*, in its application to file, to specify matters within its competence and expertise which would be covered by its submissions (this also ensuring the 'added value' of the *amicus curiae*). Procedural rules on *amicus curiae* submissions might also limit the scope of submissions by providing that no new claims or issues should be introduced by the *amicus*, so as to ensure that it is the parties that frame the dispute that is before the tribunal. However, it is important to bear in mind here that often the very function of an *amicus curiae* submission will be to bring to the attention of the tribunal broader issues raised by the case that have not been raised by the parties themselves.

Some courts and tribunals have restricted *amicus curiae* participation to the filing of written submissions only. Others, however, have made provision for participation in oral argument. The ICTY 1997 guidance, for example, provides for written submissions indicating that *amici curiae* may be invited to participate in oral argument at the Chamber's sole discretion. In the Inter-American Court of Human Rights, *amici curiae* have been permitted to participate in public hearings, particularly in advisory proceedings.[51] In other cases, however, human rights courts have limited participation to written proceedings.[52] Where participation in oral hearings is permitted, *amici curiae* will not generally be allowed the rights of parties, for example to call or cross-examine witnesses.[53]

(c) Limits on length of submissions

Where *amicus curiae* briefs are allowed, their length is generally limited by the

---

[49] See, e.g., ICTY 1997, IT/122, para. 3(b); WTO Appellate Body Additional Procedure, n. 11 above, at para. 3(e); Statement of the NAFTA Free Trade Commission, para. 2(g).

[50] See, e.g., in the ECHR, *Ashingdane v United Kingdom*, n. 45 above, at para. 6; *Malone v United Kingdom*, No. 8691/79, judgment of 2 August 1984, para. 8, ECHR A82, in which permission to file written submission was granted but on narrower terms than originally sought by the applicant.

[51] See, e.g., Advisory Opinion OC-14/94, International Responsibility for the Promulgation and Enforcement of Laws in Violation of the Convention, para. 10; Advisory Opinion OC-16/99 of 1 October 1999, The Right to Information on Consular Assistance in the Framework of the Guarantees of the Due Process of Law, paras. 14–16 and 22.

[52] See, e.g., in *Open Door and Dublin Well Woman v Ireland*, Nos. 14234/88 and 14235/88, judgment of 29 October 1992, paras. 5 and 7, ECHR A246-A. The ECHR granted leave to the Society for the Protection of Unborn Children to submit written comments but refused the same organization leave to address the court.

[53] See, e.g., ICTY 1997, Information Note, para. 5(e).

court. Typically guidelines have provided that submissions should not exceed 20 pages in length.[54]

(d) Costs

In practice, costs considerations are likely to limit the volume of *amicus curiae* interventions in international proceedings, at least from NGOs. The ICTY specified that the *amicus curiae* should meet its own costs.[55] Another possibility may be to provide for allocation of costs associated with *amicus curiae* submissions. In the context of the review of the WTO Dispute Settlement Understanding, Jordan proposed establishing a fund to assist developing countries or least developed country members in reviewing, analyzing or responding to issues raised in unsolicited *amicus curiae* briefs should they be permitted in WTO proceedings.[56] Some national courts go further, with the South African Constitutional Court Rules, for example, allowing that an order of the court may make provision for payment of costs incurred by or as a result of intervention by an *amicus curiae*. Such provisions should not be adopted lightly, however, since they may operate so as to make *amicus curiae* intervention by some non-state actors impossible in practice. The avoidance of excessive costs related to addressing *amicus curiae* submissions might better be dealt with by adopting some of the limitations on the number, length and timing of submissions in accordance with the kinds of procedural rules considered above.

4.5 Right to respond

Concerns about the potential influence of *amicus curiae* submissions on the outcome of a case could in part be met by providing a full opportunity for parties to respond to any submissions filed. Such an opportunity has commonly been accorded to parties in courts which allow *amicus curiae* submissions, such as the European Court of Human Rights[57] and the ICTY.[58] A similar provision was contained in the *Asbestos* Additional Procedure issued by the WTO Appellate Body.[59]

---

[54] WTO Appellate Body Additional Procedure, n. 11 above, at para. 7(b) (20 typed pages including appendices); Statement of the Free Trade Commission, para. 3(b) (20 typed pages including appendices); ICTY 1997, para. 5(d) (the Chamber may set page limits on the length of submissions).

[55] ICTY 1997, para. 5(f). The ICTY information note states that in general *amici curiae* bear their own expenses but that the Chamber may authorize the Registry to reimburse reasonable expenses incurred in connection with participation in the ICTY's proceedings if the *amicus* has been specifically invited to apply or to appear by the Chamber.

[56] TN/DS/W/53, Jordan's Further Contribution towards the Improvement and Clarification of the Dispute Settlement Understanding, 21 March 2003, p. 2.

[57] See, e.g., *Pretty v United Kingdom*, n. 15 above, para. 5; *Pellegrini v Italy*, No. 30882/96, judgment of 20 July 2001, (2001-VII) ECHR Reports, para. 10; *Nikula v Finland*, No. 31611/96, judgment of 21 March 2002, (2002-II) ECHR Reports, para. 4.

[58] ICTY 1997, IT/122, para. 5(e).

[59] WTO Appellate Body Additional Procedure, n. 11 above, at para. 9.

4.6   Addressing issues of confidentiality and transparency

Confidentiality and transparency concerns clearly raise issues for international courts and tribunals that extend beyond questions of *amicus curiae* submissions. The manner in which these are addressed in relation to *amici curiae* will depend in large part upon how written and oral pleadings, hearings and judgments or awards are dealt with generally by the tribunal concerned. In *Methanex*, the tribunal found that as *amici curiae* had no rights under Chapter 11 NAFTA to receive any materials generated within the arbitration, they were to be treated by the tribunal as any other members of the public, so that materials could only be disclosed as allowed in the Consent Order on Disclosure and Confidentiality between the parties. It noted, however, that under that Order either party was at liberty to disclose the major pleadings, orders and awards of the tribunal into the public domain (subject to the redaction of Trade Secrets Information).[60] Similarly the *UPS* tribunal noted that under Chapter 11 and UNCITRAL Rules, provision was made for communication of pleadings, documents and evidence to the other disputing party, other NAFTA parties, the tribunal and the Secretariat, and to no one else. The tribunal found that while principles of transparency might support the release of some documentation, it was not a matter that could be the subject of a general ruling.[61]

5.   Conclusion

While measures to manage any additional burden that might be imposed on a court or on the parties resulting from *amicus curiae* submissions are desirable, some caution is needed in accepting without question the proposition that allowing such submissions would open the floodgates to an overwhelming number of submissions from NGOs. The chapters in this volume do not seem to bear out this assumption. In the *ad hoc* international criminal tribunals, despite permissive rules on *amicus curiae* briefs, there has, in fact, been relatively little NGO involvement as *amici curiae*. On the other hand, significant *amicus curiae* briefs in cases before the *ad hoc* tribunals have been submitted by academics, and these have in several instances been encouraged or even solicited by the tribunals themselves in order to garner input in relation to complex and novel issues of international criminal law.[62] The most extensive *amicus curiae* practice to date appears to be within the Inter-American Court of Human Rights,[63] which so far seems to have shown no real sign of closing down procedural routes for *amicus*

---

[60] *Methanex*, n. 11 above, at para. 46.

[61] *UPS v Canada*, n. 11 above, at para. 68. It should be noted that in relation to NAFTA Chapter 11 arbitrations, some documentation may be available by an agreement of the parties or an order relating to confidentiality, or through the operation of freedom of information legislation.

[62] See Chinkin and Mackenzie, n. 3 above.

[63] See M. Pinto, Chapter 3 above.

curiae briefs. A survey of *amicus curiae* submissions in Inter-American Court proceedings suggests that they come from a wide range of sources – from NGOs, certainly, but also from academics, law school clinics and others. The ECHR has also seen extensive *amicus curiae* practice,[64] but while the ECHR may be over-whelmed by its sheer caseload,[65] it does not really seem to have been over-whelmed by *amicus curiae* briefs. NGOs, as has been emphasized in some of the previous chapters, have to make difficult choices about where and how to apply their limited resources, and they are unlikely to 'flood' international courts and tribunal with *amicus curiae* briefs. Instead, they are more likely to select and seek to intervene in the most important cases involving issues of principle – precisely those cases where, like the *ad hoc* criminal tribunals, the court or tribunal con-cerned is most likely to benefit from a wide range of inputs.[66]

There is already significant evidence of elements of common approaches in the procedures of international courts and tribunals relating to *amicus curiae* sub-missions. They have borrowed from each other, and from national courts. For ex-ample, there are significant similarities in the procedural rules of the ICTY, ICTR, ICC and the Special Court for Sierra Leone. Some similar approaches have emerged in the Inter-American Court and the ECHR, and in the correspond-ing procedural provisions of the Human Rights Chamber for Bosnia established under Annex 6 of the Dayton Peace Agreement.[67] Moreover, procedural develop-ments in NAFTA regarding *amicus curiae* submissions owe much to the evolu-tion of practice (if not of rules) in the WTO. Numerous international courts and tribunals have now promulgated specific rules and guidelines on dealing with *am-icus curiae* submissions. Reliance on general procedural powers of arbitral tribu-nals in NAFTA investment arbitration suggests that potential *amici curiae* in other international arbitral proceedings in future might also seek to rely on Ar-ticle 15 of the UNCITRAL Rules – for example, the Arbitration Rules of the Per-manent Court of Arbitration are also based on the UNCITRAL model.[68] And if arbitral tribunals dealing with foreign investment disputes between an investor and host state under NAFTA have begun, as a matter of principle, to allow for *amicus curiae* submissions, similar pressures are likely to be brought to bear on tribunals established through the International Centre for Settlement of Invest-ment Disputes (ICSID).[69] Finally, it is notable that organizations petitioning for

---

[64] See N. Vajic, Chapter 6 above.

[65] For example, in 2001 alone the ECHR received 13,858 applications.

[66] This observation might apply, e.g., to the decision of a number of NGOs to form an '*Amicus* Coalition' to make a submission to the Panel in the case between the USA and the European Com-munities concerning biotech products in 2004.

[67] Rule 32*ter* of the Rules of Procedure of the Human Rights Chamber, available at <www.hrc.ba/ENGLISH/rules/r.3.htm>.

[68] See, e.g., Article 15(1) of the PCA Optional Rules for Arbitrating Disputes between Two States; Article 15(1) of the Optional Rules for Arbitrating Disputes between Two Parties Only One of which is a State. PCA Arbitration Rules may be varied by consent of the parties.

[69] Provisions for *amicus curiae* intervention in foreign investment arbitrations (including under ICSID) are now being incorporated into the USA's bilateral investment treaties, see USA-Singapore

amicus curiae status in the hitherto more impermeable courts and tribunals have tended to support their petition in part by reference to the rules and practice of other tribunals.

Given these developments, some further exchange of information might usefully be promoted among international courts and tribunals about how *amicus curiae* participation is functioning in practice: to what extent have *amici curiae* helped or hindered the work of the various tribunals; what procedural approaches have proved most useful; and what outstanding problems need to be resolved?

Any move towards common procedural approaches to *amicus curiae* intervention obviously cannot ignore the important differences among international courts and tribunals. This diversity suggests that it would be neither desirable nor feasible to seek to establish a set of hard and fast rules applicable to tribunals across the board, and that the precise criteria and conditions applicable to *amicus curiae* submissions, and how they are applied, will vary depending upon the tribunal involved and its procedures. Nonetheless, as this survey has sought to show, in courts and tribunals where *amicus curiae* submissions have been accepted, one can discern some broad commonalities in approaches taken to ensure the manageability, relevance and utility of submissions. The key criterion has been the extent to which the court or tribunal is of the view that the submission in question assists it in properly disposing of the case before it.

Any systemic changes and procedural approaches to *amicus curiae* participation need to balance the interests of civil society as potential *amici*, with the interests of those who are intended to be the primary users of the court or tribunal in question, be they states, investors or individuals,[70] as well as the interest in the proper administration of the court or tribunal concerned. At present, in most international courts and tribunals at least, this balance appears to be shifting towards provision of at least some level of participation by non-party non-state actors. The states that established these courts and tribunals seem to have accepted that non-state non-party participation is acceptable, at least in tribunals dealing with matters of human rights and international criminal law. It remains to be seen whether the kinds of existing procedural approaches and safeguards outlined in this brief survey will be sufficient to persuade them that courts and tribunals that are available exclusively or primarily to states – ICJ, ITLOS and WTO – can accommodate *amicus curiae* participation without being fundamentally altered in nature.

---

and USA-Chile bilateral investment treaties, and Article 28(3) of the Draft Updated US Model Bilateral Investment Treaty, 5 February 2004, available at <www.state.gov/e/eb/rls/psrl/2004/28923.htm> (site last visited 8 June 2004).

[70] See D.B. Hollis, 'Private Actors in Public International Law: *Amicus Curiae* and the Case for the Retention of State Sovereignty' (2002) 25 *Boston College Int'l & Comp. L. Rev.* 235. Hollis concludes that, '[i]t may be true that the international legal order will have to address questions regarding its legitimacy raised by NGOs and other private actors. At the same time, however, in addressing those concerns, in admitting or expanding roles for private actors in public international law, one cannot lose sight of the need to ensure that the system maintains its legitimacy with respect to its existing actors–states': ibid., at p. 255.

Index